—— THE INDEPENDENT REPUBLIC OF AREQUIPA ——

Joe R. and Teresa Lozano Long Series
in Latin American and Latino Art and Culture

THE INDEPENDENT REPUBLIC OF AREQUIPA

Making Regional Culture in the Andes

THOMAS F. LOVE

UNIVERSITY OF TEXAS PRESS
Austin

Requests for permission to reproduce material
from this work should be sent to:
Permissions
University of Texas Press
P.O. Box 7819
Austin, TX 78713-7819
http://utpress.utexas.edu/rp-form

♾ The paper used in this book meets the minimum requirements of
ANSI/NISO Z39.48-1992 (R1997) (Permanence of Paper).

LIBRARY OF CONGRESS CATALOGING-IN-PUBLICATION DATA
Names: Love, Thomas F., author.
Title: The Independent Republic of Arequipa : making regional
culture in the Andes / Thomas F. Love.
Other titles: Joe R. and Teresa Lozano Long series in Latin American
and Latino art and culture.
Description: First edition. | Austin : University of Texas Press, 2017. |
Series: Joe R. and Teresa Lozano Long series in Latin American and
Latino art and culture | Includes bibliographical references and index.
Identifiers: LCCN 2017003986
ISBN 978-1-4773-1392-3 (cloth : alk. paper)
ISBN 978-1-4773-1459-3 (pbk. : alk. paper)
ISBN 978-1-4773-1460-9 (library e-book)
ISBN 978-1-4773-1461-6 (non-library e-book)
Subjects: LCSH: Arequipa (Peru)—History. | Regionalism—Peru—
Arequipa. | Arequipa (Peru)—Politics and government. | Ethnicity—
Political aspects—Peru—Arequipa.
Classification: LCC F3611.A7 L68 2017 | DDC 985/.32—dc23
LC record available at https://lccn.loc.gov/2017003986

doi:10.7560/313923

To everyday Peruvians, past, present, and future, in honor of the resilience they have shown in the face of so much change.

CONTENTS

MAPS, TABLES,
AND ILLUSTRATIONS

PREFACE

Modern Arequipa—the "Independent Republic of Arequipa," has one of the strongest senses of regional identity anywhere in the central Andes. This regionalist sentiment is symbolically marked by populist, rural, largely secular elements anchored in the purported character and practices of urban plebeians and rural smallholder farmers. The central question animating this monograph is the oddity that these symbols should have come to represent the very identity of such an urban commercial place as Arequipa—Peru's second city, widely known as the "white city" not just for the now-UNESCO-recognized colonial architecture of its urban core, as is widely assumed, but also for being the most Spanish and nonindigenous of Peruvian cities. The entire representation of the region, including the burgeoning tourism of recent decades, centers on the rural culture in surrounding villages (e.g., the colonial mill in Sabandía, bull-on-bull fighting) as well as on the colonial Spanish elements in the city. Visitors desiring to experience "indigenous" culture are directed to the Colca or Cotahuasi valleys—not the "mestizo" Arequipa basin countryside (*campiña*).

To uncover the origin, purpose, and meaning of this extolling of rural life, in particular what was meant by the claim of mestizo identity, I began a long journey analyzing the history and makeup of regional society and culture. Utilizing tools largely from practice theory, I zero in on discovering how and when such claims came about, who was behind describing regional society in these ways, and how and why it became a hegemonic structure of feeling in regional social space.

This monograph is the result of trying to solve this complex puzzle. Having lived and worked for almost two years (with repeated subsequent visits) among the campiña smallholders who were the purported bearers of this vital, if disappearing, "traditional" local culture, I found bare traces of the local speech, music, food, and even dress they were said to possess and practice. While pilgrimage to the desert shrine of the Virgen de Chapi and bullfighting were pretty big during my several fieldwork periods, as I describe below, they were not central to the ways people wrote or talked about the heart of the organically generated traditional folk culture characterized as anchoring regional identity, which instead emphasized muleteers, *chicha* (maize beer), spicy food, sad music, a legacy of popular uprisings, and a rich vernacular Spanish heavy with Quechuaized localisms (see fig. 4.3).

Given how prominent for regional identity a vibrant folk culture was said to be, how could I miss it? Was it somehow hidden in plain sight? I was earlier focused on different issues—the determinants of Arequipa's highly fragmented *minifundio* land-tenure system analyzed in a macropolitical economic theoretical frame (Love 1983, 1989)—but was I, despite my best planning, somehow away on certain key feast days or other ritual events when the last, hidden vestiges of this "disappearing tradition" were symbolically revealed in their full essence? I fretted about the apparently poor decisions I had made about both method and theory during dissertation fieldwork that must have led me astray. About method, several connected decisions spread me thin: focusing on the region, via three separate villages that spanned altitudinal zones in the valley, rather than on a single community; utilizing a semistructured survey instrument with a stratified random sample of 117 local farmers instead of depending on a more conventional deep sojourn in one community. Perhaps having had to deal with so many small farmers led me to miss key actors?

Along with difficulties of method were apparent problems of theory: the structural Marxist articulation of modes of production theoretical framework I had utilized in my dissertation to make sense of smallholder persistence in local agriculture—already nearing exhaustion, I soon learned—blinded me to agency and subjectivity even as it provided a simplified but comprehensive framework for making sense of Arequipa's rich, complex political-economic history (Love 1989; Roseberry 1989). Also, in large part because of the risks associated with violence in rural Peru from the mid-1980s to the mid-1990s, like many foreign and Peruvian ethnographers I chose to invest research time in other areas and on other topics, and I veered away from further systematic examination of Arequipa's complex political-economic history.[1]

My renewed interest in these matters was fired by encountering Raymond Williams's *The Country and the City* (1973), which helped launch this project with two crucial insights. First, Williams experienced a curious disconnect between the workaday lives of relatives and people he remembered from growing up in a small village in southern Wales, with all their varied interests and multiple social connections, and the literary depiction of rural England as much less complex and less connected with the city. This led me to similarly begin more critically investigating who was depicting whom in the Arequipeño literary tradition. Peeling away layers, I came to understand, particularly in relation to my own direct experience in both rural and urban Arequipa (albeit much later than the main period of this cultural production, I learned), that all this writing and painting about country life was very selective—an arm's-length urban imagining of the countryside, quite far from people's lived reality. While this was perhaps most so with the poetry of Percy Gibson and least so in the murals of Teodoro Núñez, as we will see, nevertheless it became clear that the bulk of this cultural production was urban and destined as much for national as for local audiences.

Second, Williams discerned a literary theme in the depiction of this settled, ordered "traditional" countryside as "passing away"; as he dug back into the history of British literature, from the works of the nineteenth-century romantics all the way back to *Beowulf* (albeit in different genres and with different tones and emphases), he learned that the countryside was often portrayed as already passing away, that "merrie Olde England" and the "traditional" countryside had been constructed largely by literary hands, and that construction constituted a way these generally urban, bourgeois intellectuals (in the nineteenth century) fretted about the worrisome social changes underway in an always-changing England. As we find in many of the nation-building episodes around the world in the period from the late nineteenth through the early twentieth centuries (e.g., the European fringe, from Norway to Romania), the countryside and the folk who inhabited it became a sort of lodestone, anchoring an imagined nonbureaucratic (or perhaps antibureaucratic) world in time and space (Graeber 2015, 173).

These twin insights led me to realize that talk in Arequipa about the "traditional" rural culture as "already disappearing" pointed to larger, continuing debates about national identity (*peruanidad*), the "Indian question," and personalist authoritarian rule from Lima with which Peruvians grappled during the long century after independence. The construction of this imaginary also pointed to how acute was the huge cultural (if less material) impact that the War of the Pacific had had on the south. All these were key factors for the urban intellectuals writing about this "disappearing" tradition in the early twentieth century.

While the evocation of rural life and characters in modern national cultures is common enough, the Arequipa case is of particular interest because central to the widely held sense of regional exceptionalism is the additional claim made by some that Arequipeños are fundamentally mestizo. Given enduring colonial racialist attitudes in all the central Andean countries, my analysis of this remarkable, early twentieth-century project to *brown* regional identity forms the core and perhaps main contribution of this monograph.

Things started to come into focus as I looked afresh on regional culture with new conceptual tools during many, almost annual postdissertation visits and fieldwork periods (1997, 2005, 2012, and 2014)—especially after the state and guerrilla violence of 1980–1995 (the "Sendero" period, after Sendero Luminoso, the main, Maoist guerrilla group), when fieldwork again became practicable. It slowly became clear that the folk culture presented to me as rural and vibrant was at heart much more about an evolving, urban-based, largely middle-class, and increasingly nostalgic way of talking about Arequipa and Arequipeños vis-à-vis Limeños as well as indigenous in Puno (and Cuzco).

Even as it became clear that despite appearances, Arequipeño traditionalism wasn't fundamentally a cultural project of the rural smallholders among whom I had lived and worked, this discourse had affected them, not least because of their close social ties with the city. Early twentieth-century cultural entrepreneurs behind the invention of this regional culture hardly mentioned pilgrimage to various Marian sites and most surprisingly, I found, never mentioned locals' bullfighting—now the spectacular, central part of regional identity and seemingly a most "traditional" sort of performance. If something now so prominent was not part of the main traditionalist project, then where had it come from?

Questions kept emerging. What had motivated urban Arequipeños to imagine a community so centrally symbolized by rural smallholders? Who among them was chiefly responsible for this effort, and why? In inventing this tradition, what was really at stake? What was the nature of this many-layered tradition, and what was to be made of its nostalgic tone—that a simpler, rural life was already disappearing? What were the key periods in which this regional identity crystallized? How was—or is—this subnational identity reproduced or transmitted? How did this urban tradition intersect with what rural smallholders and urban plebes themselves were actually doing and thinking, and how does it play out now? You can see why Williams was so seminal.

Shortly after arriving in Lima on my first exploratory journey to Peru in 1976, as I was buying my ticket for Arequipa in the Lima Ormeño bus station, the agent asked me, only half jokingly, if I had my Arequipa passport. Though my antennae went up, I had little context and next to no experience, and I was already overwhelmed by the complexity of central Andean nature and culture. Given the prominence of the military's agrarian reform project, I had already charted out (and been funded for) dissertation research on the determinants of Arequipa's noted *minifundio* land-tenure system, which came during an economic downturn at the end of the 1968–1980 military era, when the regime of Francisco Morales Bermúdez was trying to dismantle the reforms instituted by the predecessor regime of Juan Velasco Alvarado while saving face for the military. This was a crisis of deindustrialization and government disinvestment due to policies focusing on various sectoral reforms in mining, fishing, but above all agriculture (Wilson and Wise 1986). State and private withdrawal of investment had left Arequipeños frustrated and resentful toward the military regime—and poorer. I soon learned that Arequipeño opposition to the military's agrarian-reform project resurrected perennial grievances about Lima's inappropriate, even at times illegitimate, domination of the nation.

Continuing in this prefatory vein, I also went through personal tragedy, including the accidental death of my sister back home in the States, about nine months into my fieldwork period. My recovery came with the courage and encouragement of my parents and my academic mentors, but also of various friends in Arequipa—mostly young professionals my age in town. Spending time with them pulled me away from direct fieldwork with local farmers for a while and opened up an emotionally new space in which I caught, for almost the first time, this urban view of the countryside. Shades of Rosaldo. It was the beginning of my understanding of the urban origins of the purported rural folk culture, said to be already disappearing. Such are the vagaries of fieldwork!

Setting out to make sense of the seemingly phantom basis of this intense regionalist sentiment has taken me on a journey far more historical and certainly far longer than I had imagined. Given the central set of questions, it has also meant that the book hovers at a somewhat higher height than I had expected. Though I provide ethnographic traction in several chapters and scattered throughout, much of the book—especially the first four chapters—lies more distant from cultural anthropology's traditional grounding in ethnographic detail. And though I draw inspiration from the sort of approach exemplified in the collection edited by John Murra, Nathan Wachtel, and Jacques Revel (1986), a big, sweeping, *longue durée* monograph of this sort is not only rather out of fashion these days, but also vulnerable to charges from historians and others of inadequate engagement with relevant, especially archival, literature—what my mentor Arnold Bauer once coyly termed "drive-by scholarship," or what Frank Salomon once derisively called anthropologists' "sprayed-on history."

With this sort of ambition and scope, I am acutely aware that the monograph has any number of holes, some of historical detail and some created by the very method of trying to stitch together fragments and elements of the entirety that my interpretive efforts link but cannot comprehensively or seamlessly "explain." There are many areas for further scholarship in the pages ahead. I am also well aware that my understanding and representation of the evolution of regional culture is hobbled by having to rely on literary representations (with little ethnography) during the formative 1890–1970 period, but on ethnographic data (without much about literary representations) during the more recent period, since the regionalist literary boom had by the time of my fieldwork largely subsided. Short of detailed archival work for the first decades of the twentieth century, like that undertaken by Sarah Chambers (1999) for developments a century earlier, or an extensive foray into recent touristic representations of the region, I find no tractable way around this methodological dilemma. And the book is already long.

As a further disclaimer, my revelation in this monograph of the complexities surrounding the much more populist strain in Arequipeño regional culture is not to deny the strength of alternative visions of regional identity—ones that are either much whiter, more overtly anti-indigenist, and more patrician or, on the other hand, much more proletarian and class conscious. My effort here is certainly not some impossible effort to describe the entirety of the Arequipeño social formation.

I therefore hope that "the vision of a complex, problematic, partial ethnography lead[s] . . . to more subtle, concrete ways of writing and reading, to new conceptions of culture as interactive and historical" (Clifford 1986, 25). It is now routine in ethnographic writing to fret about all this and to acknowledge such fretting. But fretting is not just worry; one also frets to produce music, which finally sets down or freezes in some form—here textual—the distilled experience I have had in almost annual interaction with a diverse array of people in rural and urban

Arequipa since the late 1970s and in my wide reading since in literature by and about Arequipa and Arequipeños.

With appropriate apologies, I might have titled this book *One Overly Long Interpretive Essay on Arequipeño Reality*. Whatever charges may be made about intellectual poaching, insensitivity to disciplinary boundaries or methods, or lack of awareness of the inherently interpretive nature of a historical anthropology like this, I trust readers will appreciate a robust, interdisciplinary, ethnographically grounded and historically informed examination of regional culture and agree that the gains for cultural description and analysis from a grounded yet panoramic view of social, political, and economic history are worth whatever omissions or blind spots may exist.

Apart from the specific ethnographic, cultural, and historical contributions of a case study on a fascinating and well-known, though surprisingly little-examined, region of Peru, then, in writing this monograph I had three principal goals in mind:

• To help understand subnational identity formation, discerning general processes at work in the specificities of a regionalist movement, particularly how such sentiments get reproduced in the absence of the sort of institutionalized political machinery available to state actors.

• To insert Arequipa into the central Andean anthropological scene, inviting more sustained work by anthropologists, historians, and other social scientists on a host of issues the region presents (particularly now immigration and assimilation, e.g., Ødegaard 2010).

• To contribute to a largely Bourdieuian set of concepts from practice and related theory of imagined community, field, capitals, and symbolic power, specifically in relation to the social space and changing fields within which regionalist discourse developed.

ACKNOWLEDGMENTS

I am acutely aware of the interpretive nature of this enterprise. My intention has been to draw on the inspiration of various people and all they invested in me to develop insights that Andeanists as well as Arequipeños and those who love the region may in turn use to make sense of this rich reality and make it better than what they found. My biggest hope is that this book might encourage others to fill the many gaps and correct whatever mistakes of fact or interpretation I have made, since so much more can be done.

Fortunately for my effort to tell the story of Arequipeño traditionalism, an extraordinary and sustained literary tradition itself lies at the heart of traditionalist sentiment. Indeed, it is these intellectual entrepreneurs who drew upon a reservoir of symbols and sentiments in their social milieu to contribute centrally to creating the tradition we now know. A series of "test digs" led me to undertake an archaeology of this regionalist discourse and particularly to discover its major florescence in the first half of the twentieth century.

"As with any interpretive synthesis, this book builds largely on the fine-grained archival work of many scholars" (Larson 2004). How true. I have been saved an impossible amount of primary research by the work of many local historians, sociologists, and anthropologists, many of them Arequipeño, on whose shoulders I stand. I have tried to acknowledge my intellectual debts here and throughout the text as I cite relevant materials.

The list is long. I am grateful for a small predissertation grant from the University of California, Davis, for travel to Peru in 1976, as well as support from the Social Science Research Council that enabled me to conduct dissertation research and live in Arequipa for almost two years in 1978–1979. My good fortune in landing an academic post right out of graduate school, during the recession of the early 1980s (until 2008 the worst since the 1930s), wound up committing me professionally to a teaching career at Linfield College—a marvelous experience but with less time and support for scholarship than I had hoped. I am nevertheless grateful for support from several small faculty development grants for travel to Peru in 1983, 2005, 2012, and 2014. Coupled with the Sendero period, as noted, as well as our decision to start a family and my own natural tendencies to be interested in too many things ("*dispersión de fuerzas*," my mentor Ben Orlove would lament), I found myself with never enough time to bring this project to completion. But as a result of incredibly valuable sabbatical and release time and a recent faculty writing award, you finally have in your hands a monograph that has languished for far too long.

Where do my ideas begin and others' end? While what I write here is sufficiently original, I humbly think, to warrant my self-designation as sole author, I am much indebted to a great many people for contributions to this project at various points along the way. Some particularly broad shoulders on which I stand belong to friend and stimulating colleague Hector Ballón Lozada (Universidad Nacional de San Agustín [UNSA] Sociology) as well as to the late Guillermo Galdos Rodríguez (director of the Archivo Regional de Historia and self-proclaimed, latter-day Extirpador de Idolatrías) for stimulating conversations, archivally informed insights, and several field trips to the lower valley and his natal Tiabaya. For useful insights and critical assessment of various of these ideas over the years: Ben Orlove (who originally suggested Arequipa as a dissertation fieldsite), Arnold Bauer, and Bill Davis, mentors and friends; Carlos Aguirre, Andy Boeger, Julio Bustinza, Alfred Darnell, César Delgado, Blenda Femenías, Paul Gelles, Nils Jacobsen, the late Catherine Julien, Alan Knight, Lisa Markowitz, Joel Marrant, Felix Palacios, Brad Stoner, and Paul Trawick, for various insights large and small; Linfield students in several domestic and travel courses and seminars too numerous to single out; Juan Carpio T. and Isabel Valdivia S. who helped me with dissertation interviewing; Alberto Salinas, Felipe Urday, and Jorge Díaz, who helped me track down documents in Arequipa. A fortuitous encounter with poet José Ruiz Rosas in 2005 was delightful; I thank him for providing me with copies of the rare *El Aquelarre* poetry journal from 1916–1917. I am grateful to Patricio Ricketts Rey de Castro for stimulating encounters in Lima and again in Arequipa; to Enrique Zileri Gibson (editor of *Caretas*) for help in locating several people; to ingenieros Jorge Tejada and Luis Montalván for assistance with cadastral records at the Ministry of Agriculture and a memorable journey to the Arequipa highlands to investigate a community boundary dispute; to Roberto Damiani (Banco Agrario, retired) for sharing his love of the *yaraví* (a song form at the center of the regionalist tradition) and for several delightful excursions to his beloved Quequeña; to Juan Manuel Guillén Benavides, ex-mayor as well as ex–regional president of Arequipa and UNSA rector, for a 2005 interview; to Alejandro Málaga and Angel Taypicahuana for stimulating conversation and opportunities to engage students at the Universidad Nacional de San Agustín; to Ray Bromley, for an unanticipated encounter at a fruitful moment at the Quinta Bates in Arequipa; to historian Eusebio Quiróz Paz Soldán, ever enthusiastic, generous, and articulate; to Federico and Juan López Apolo, and their families, my dear friends and knowledgeable informants in Sabandía; to Juan Gómez Rodríguez, anthropologist formerly with UNSA; and to knowledgeable, affable artist Leo Ugarte and his son Mauricio of Vallecito. I am indebted to the work of Juan Carpio Múñoz, latter-day folklorist and prolific, insightful author who has blazed important trails in the social history of Arequipa. I owe special thanks to my friends Arnaldo Ihl, Miguel Angel Calderón, Isabel Borja, ingeniero Juan Borja, as well as students in my UNSA seminars, for stimulating conversation and for helping me through that life crisis in the midst of fieldwork.

I am very appreciative of Theresa May's initial encouragement and patience, and since her retirement it has been a delight to work with Casey Kittrell, Amanda Frost, and Angelica Lopez-Torres at the University of Texas Press and copyeditor Kathy Delfosse. They and three anonymous reviewers made very constructive criticisms that helped me refine and tighten the argument. I bear sole responsibility for the views and ideas expressed, of course. It has been a long road; I presented elements of this book in papers at the 1983 Eleventh International Congress of Anthropological and Ethnological Sciences; the 1985, 1986, and 1987 meetings of the Society for Economic Anthropology; the 1997 and 1998 meetings of the Latin American Studies Association; the 1999 and 2012 meetings of the American Anthropological Association; and the 2006 first meeting of the International Society for the Study of Religion, Nature, and Culture; as well as in two Linfield faculty lectures, a 2005 article in *Yuyayninchis* (with translation help from Felix Palacios), and a lecture at the Universidad Nacional de San Agustín in June 2012.

Finally, my wife Penny has been incredibly supportive over the more than a decade that this book has been in the making. She and our sons

Nathan and Benjamin have been more than forgiving of my periodic absences and office clutter.

Note: To reduce stilted writing I have chosen to sparingly use English conventions regarding possessives, such as "Arequipa's" or "Peru's." Translations and graphics throughout are mine unless otherwise noted.

ONE

INTRODUCTION

Nation, State, Culture, and Region in Arequipa

> *El orgullo de sus hijos no conoce límites.*
> *[The pride of her children knows no limits.]*
>
> CHARLES WIENER, AREQUIPA, (1880) 1996

The spectacular natural features of the Andes lead to striking relationships between geography and culture. With race and place so closely intertwined in mountainous western South America (Orlove 1993), at 2,300 meters Arequipa straddles modern Peru's great geographic and cultural divide between coast and sierra. As locals say, the sierra ascends from the *tuturutu* (the statue of San Miguel on the fountain at the center of the Plaza de Armas, blowing his long horn), and the coast starts there and goes down to the ocean—an echo of the *hanan/hurin*, upper/lower, highland/lowland binary that is a key element of pre-Hispanic Andean culture.[1]

Whether in Ecuador, Peru, Bolivia, northern Chile, or northern Argentina, no other major city in this vast central Andean *Tawantinsuyu*-inscribed geographic space conceives of itself quite so clearly as lying "in between." A quick comparison with other cities in the central Andes suggests that Arequipa's situation is rather unusual. Trujillo—Peru's "other" second city—is obviously geographically, historically, and culturally of the coast. Both Cuzco and Cajamarca, with their altitude and strong historical connections with the Inka state, are clearly linked to the sierra. Huánuco is both east slope and too far from the coast to participate in this highland/coastal divide. Jauja, Huancayo, Huancavelica, and Ayacucho are highland centers, and Puno and Juliaca epitomize the Altiplano for Peruvians and foreigners alike.

In Ecuador, the Quito/Guayaquil polarity shows the same highland/coastal pattern, but in the national culture of Ecuador there is no major "in-between" city or region like Arequipa, and Quito as national capital muddies the comparison. Maybe Cuenca? In emphasizing its *cholo* (mixed-race) nature, Cuenca shares certain cultural affinities with Arequipa, but again, as for Cajamarca, the geographic setting and strong historical ties to imperial Spain and the Inka state link that beautiful city to the sierra in the modern mind. Bolivians, on the other hand, lacking a coastline, conceive of themselves quite differently: only Cochabamba lies between major elevation zones, with a spatially inverted but politically similar relationship to La Paz and Santa Cruz that invites comparison (see Larson 1998).

No major population center of any significance emerged on the long, lonely Arequipa coast, with its narrow continental shelf and especially rugged coastline—the longest of any department or region in the country, and before the territorial losses to Chile a full quarter of Peru's coastline.

> A map of Peru explains Peruvian regionalism better than any complicated, abstract theory. . . . The south is basically of the sierra. Here, where the coast shrinks to a slender strip of land, coastal and mestizo Peru has not been able to establish itself. The Andes advance to the sea, converging the coast into a narrow cornice dotted with ports and coves and forcing the cities into the sierra. The south has been able to maintain its sierra, if not its Indian, character in spite of the conquest, the viceroyalty, and the republic. (Mariátegui [1928] 1971, 165)

The *puna* really begins to dry out in southern Peru and on down the Andean spine to northern Argentina, and few valleys are large enough for a truly highland population center to have emerged. Consequently, because the highland/lowland duality works only in paired situations, there was no coastal city in the south with which Arequipa could be the highland pairing. From an Altiplano perspective, however, Arequipa was the "coastal" twin, as we shall see.

Arequipeños are to the rest of Peru what Catalonians are to Spain, Texans are to the United States, or Luxembourgians are to the Low Countries—members of commercially important regions with distinctive subnational identities and self-proclaimed wisdom (Fernandez 2000), both disliked and admired by others. While some primate cities, such as Moscow, Paris, Tokyo, or Buenos Aires, may have no rivals in their respective nations, most larger countries have competing urban centers. Citizens

2

in second cities such as Barcelona, Guadalajara, and Medellín struggle for distinction in their respective national and even global fields against their better-known primate-city rivals. When they are close in size and political or economic activity—such as Shanghai and Beijing, Toronto and Montreal, Quito and Guayaquil, or São Paulo and Rio de Janeiro—the struggle for distinction can be even more intense.[2]

Yet given that Arequipa is the second city of Peru, and given how very well known is Arequipeños' inflated, exceptionalist sense of themselves, why has this tradition so far escaped serious historical and especially anthropological attention? To put it bluntly: with heightened attention to regional differences and the unevenness of nation building in Latin America, why with but a few notable exceptions (e.g., Flores Galindo 1977) has regional culture in modern Arequipa so far essentially been written off by most historians, anthropologists, and other social scientists?

My ability to grasp Arequipeño traditionalist writing around regional identity as being fundamentally about debates over citizenship, indigeneity, and national identity was stimulated by changing emphases in Andean anthropology and historiography. Until at least the 1970s, it seemed that social science work in Peru was altitudinally split: historians had worked on the coast and anthropologists in the highlands. (Mallon 1995, 324–325)

My own development coincided with growing literature on central Andeans' long and troubled experience with nation building (e.g., Flores Galindo 1977; Gootenberg 1991a; Jacobsen 1993; Jacobsen and Alvojín de Losada 2005; Mallon 1995; Chambers 1999; de la Cadena 2000; Larson 2004; Thurner 1997), which increasingly and consciously bridged coast/highlands, Indian/white, rural/urban, and other misleading binaries. Anthropologists were becoming more conscious of how much we had fallen into constructing the objects of our study (e.g., Painter 1991; Starn 1994)—an idealized Andean cultural essence that had skewed generations of anthropological work in the Andes. Working within this paradigm, ethnographers were driven to focus on traces of pre-Hispanic cultural elements and to search out and salvage examples of continuities in Andean culture still remembered, if not practiced, in remote valleys and isolated areas—cultural elements that had somehow miraculously survived conquest and nearly three long centuries of Spanish imperial rule, labor recruitment for haciendas and mines, disease, political and other forms of economic exploitation, and wars around independence

3

and afterward, let alone the long-term, complex impacts of an increasingly globalized market system.[3]

Historians, for their part, built on Hobsbawm's work on the construction of tradition (Hobsbawm and Ranger 1983) and nationalism (Hobsbawm 1992), as well as on Anderson's ([1983] 1991) concept of imagined community, by engaging in traditional anthropological concerns with identity in time and space (e.g., Centeno and López-Alves 2001). Historians were moving from the study of political, diplomatic, and administrative history toward new approaches to economic and social history (e.g., R. Miller 1987 and many authors I cite in the text), examining a broad range of agents entailed and involved in nation building.

The historiography of Arequipa has also grown significantly since the early 1980s (e.g., Neira Avendaño et al. 1990; Rivera Martínez 1996; Ballón Lozada 1987), particularly work dealing with transitions from the colonial experience (e.g., Chambers 1999; Fisher 1979, 1987) and with the early twentieth century (e.g., Flores Galindo 1977; Flores Galindo, Plaza, and Oré 1978; Burga and Reátegui 1981; Deustua and Rénique 1984; and especially Ballón Lozada 1992, 1999, and 2000). Until now, though, nobody has built on these crucial developments and insights to construct a coherent overall picture of the making of Arequipa's oft-noted extreme regionalist culture.

In their splendid mountain desert isolation, then, Arequipeños have been irritated at being under the thumb of distant Lima, suffering from a particularly acute case of "second-city syndrome," and have long chafed at their second-class status within the modern Peruvian nation. This feeling among Arequipeños is more than mere love of *patria chica* (love of one's childhood place); Arequipeños feel themselves members of an imagined community whose identity pivots on a deeply rooted sense of having been held back, wronged—shortchanged in their ability to control their own destiny and denied the opportunity to create wealth in a geographic space they consider rightfully theirs.

While Arequipeños' inordinate pride of region must therefore be understood fundamentally as a response to Limeño centralism in both space and time, their regionalism occurs in a field of regional identities. Regionalism makes sense only in relation to a system of regions, which in turn presupposes a state-organized attempt to dominate other fields. Deploying a suite of place-specific symbols is therefore politically decentralist as well as a struggle for distinction against provincial rivals, so Arequipeños always seem determined that their regionalist sentiment be understood as more than "mere provincialism" (see Zevallos 1965, 13–

4

15). Thus the seriousness with which memoirs are written and conferences are held about the "uniqueness" of Arequipeños (e.g., Ballón Landa [1908] 1958; Rivera Martínez 1996), for what is at stake is maintaining position in a highly regionalized space by forcing recognition in a field of provinces against a center.

Unlike the mestizo north or center of the Peruvian highlands, the southern Peruvian highlands are home to "indigenous" Peru—"deep" Peru, the *mancha indígena*. Southern Peru and adjacent Bolivia—the greater Altiplano—constitute the indigenous heartland of the Andes, where roughly 80 percent are mono- or bilingual speakers of Quechua or Aymara. Arequipa (primarily the urban-dominated valley) stands in sharp contrast, and in many ways Arequipeños had long thought of themselves in colonialist terms as a Spanish island in an Indian sea, a bulwark of Spanish control in southern highland Peru and Alto Perú (Bolivia) throughout the colonial period. With its firmly entrenched Spanish Catholic culture, it was also, despite republican developments, the "Rome" of the Andes.

In their intense regionalism, then, Arequipeños have had to deal with both coast and sierra not only politically and economically but also culturally and linguistically. Several phrases widely used in Arequipa—especially *ni chicha ni limonada*[4] or *ni grande ni pequeño* (both mean "neither one nor the other," or "six of one/half-dozen of the other")—capture the deep ambivalence and hybridity stamped on Arequipeño identity by these cultural, geographic, and political binaries. Symbols of regional identity and the traditionalist discourse about it are therefore situated between the two main poles of modern Peruvian national identity—traditional, highland, and indigenous (*chicha, pequeño*) on the one hand, and modern, coastal, and Hispanic (*limonada, grande*) on the other—creating a cultural space in which the powerful metaphors of mixed-race heritage made some sense, as we will see.

This leads us to imagine and understand Arequipa as so many historians and poets have understood it: as some unfolding essence, as an actor held back by twin sets of forces, still waiting to play a role on the stage of modern history. The cultural entrepreneurs of the 1890–1970 period, on whom I principally focus, experimented with mestizaje as a way of arguing that Arequipeños are not just some mix of races but rather one hybrid people, fit for the huge task of nation building—a model for all Peruvians. Inspired by recent social historians' work on nation building (e.g., Hobsbawm 1992) and by literary analyses of mestizaje (e.g., Martínez-Echazábal 1998), my task in this book is to tackle the formation of Arequipeño regional subjectivity from this "in-between" vantage point, as a set of cultural possibilities—a reservoir of symbols constructed and available for use by actors in the ongoing play of regional society in a state-dominated national field (see Thurner 2008). By placing these cultural movements in the context of important political and economic processes under way in Peru and the central Andes, I show how regional identity here developed so strongly, and why in Republican and modern Peru Arequipeño regionalist identity moved from political to cultural terrain.

While Arequipeño regionalist sentiment has deep colonial and even pre-Hispanic roots, as we will see, it understandably came to life as larger political, economic, and cultural contexts shifted profoundly with late-colonial imperial reforms and then independence from Spain, which thrust problems of national identity to the foreground. Though possibilities for mostly impoverished indigenous at the bottom of the social ladder remained precarious, creoles and others began to move into new social spaces formally freed of Spanish legal and cultural distinctions, including local and interregional commerce and ownership of agricultural land, factories, and shops.

Much of this regional pride got established in the nineteenth-century struggle for nationhood, when Arequipa came to symbolize Republican Peru. For Jorge Basadre, the middle third of the nineteenth century defined Arequipeño identity, when tensions with Lima were running highest; "until 1867, [Arequipa was] a pistol pointed at the heart of Lima" (Basadre [1931, 1978] 1992; quoted in Ballón Lozada 1987, epigraph). Critical of the increasing concentration in Lima of an extralegal, personalistic style of governing the national political, cultural, and especially economic life of the country, Arequipeño (or backed by Arequipeño interests) legal caudillos such as Agustín Gamarra Messia, Felipe Santiago de Salaverry, and Manuel Ignacio de Vivanco Iturralde launched rebellions against the center in an effort to restore and build constitutional and institutional order. Other regional caudillos later inclined toward the center, such as Nicolás de Piérola, who championed the landed aristocracy and led economic (less political) modernization under the Civilista Party, and Andrés Avelino Cáceres, who became president after having fought bitterly against a regime widely regarded as having betrayed the national interest.

In the mid-twentieth century, José Luis Bustamante y Rivero rose to the presidency defending a more federal, more decentralized, and less autocratic vision of the Peruvian state. On into our own time, from neoliberal economist Hernando de Soto Polar and Nobel-laureate writer Mario Vargas Llosa to Vladimiro Montesinos (Rasputin to disgraced ex-president Alberto Fujimori) and even Abimael Guzmán (charismatic founder of the 1980s Shining Path guerrilla movement), Arequipeños have figured prominently in the national life of Peru, challenging the center even as they gravitate toward it.

Arequipeños at all versed in their own history are quick to point all this out—especially to people from Lima. As I noted in the preface, Peruvians are always advising one to be sure to have one's passport in order when traveling to Arequipa, as if it really were the "Independent Republic of Arequipa." Drawing on something put together by the Peruvian company Leche Gloria for a convention years earlier, an enterprising local journalist recently created a remarkably realistic Arequipeño "passport" (fig. 1.1); showing my Arequipa "passport" to harried immigration officials at the Lima airport is sure to draw a wry smile or laugh. Paper "currency" and "gold coinage" has been issued by the "Banco Central de Reservas de Arequipa," valued at "one *characato*'s worth of gold" (see chapter 6 on "*characato*," a mildly derisive term used by outsiders to describe Arequipeños as "country bumpkins.")

Seemingly obsessed with defining the exceptional nature of their cultural essence and historic mission, and in the face of criticism (if not derision) from other Peruvians, Arequipeños are quick to rush to the defense of their regionalism:

> Other Peruvians are always upset with us Arequipeños for our insufferable regionalism and our pretense at viewing the world from our provincial window. But to our countrymen we would respond that the first ethical obligation of man is to know himself . . . and if we, a hybrid society like Arequipa, are to arrive at the heart of Peru, and even to the universal spirit, we must reach into the hidden depths of our being to discover its full potential and then to nourish the broad horizon of Peruvian identity. This is the historical significance of the Arequipeño people. . . . [After having visited Cuzco, Puno, and Bolivia] I then grasped that Arequipa also has its message of a vigorous and humane mestizo tradition. . . . Arequipa's is a dignified platform, noble and of high pedigree. (Zevallos 1965, 13–15)

Arequipeños' marked political and cultural regionalism has deeply popular roots. Nowhere else in Peru, indeed arguably in any central Andean country, did urban plebeians and rural smallholders so effec-

FIGURE 1.1

Arequipa "passport." Reproduced with permission of Willy Galdos Frias,
Colegio de Periodistas del Peru, Consejo Regional Arequipa.

tively gain political or cultural voice. Because their goals largely coincided with those of regional elites and urban middle sectors, pivoting on
their insistence on being included as full citizens in the regional community, many observers have misunderstood the cross-class nature of
regional sentiment. The regional identity emerging from these struggles was fundamentally conservative, focused on preserving presumed
rights in the regional community much more than on staking claims on
the postcolonial state as classed (or racialized) national citizens. I begin
to trace ways this sentiment from below continued to inform and nour-
ish middle- and upper-class Arequipeños' political efforts, though such
a project is longer and more involved than I can accomplish here (see

Ballón Lozada 1987, 1992). Since this regional identity was founded not only on what it was (recognized and invented local traditions in music, dress, cuisine, etc.) but also on what it wasn't (Indian/*serrano* ["highlander"] *or* Limeño), Arequipeños across classes—especially in the early decades of the twentieth century—were deeply uneasy about both growing Limeño power and the inclusion of the nation's indigenous majority as full modern citizens, and they closed ranks around regional identity to forestall both. Hence plebeians' insistence on being dealt with as full citizens of regional society and on not being mistaken for being "Indian" (and thereby excluded from customary privileges)—a matter to which I particularly turn in chapter 5.

From its founding in 1540, Arequipa was fundamentally an urban, Spanish, Catholic society firmly tied to mercantilist, global commercial circuits and the colonial political structure. Plebeians and valley smallholders were largely confined by race or class to particular occupations and narrower social spaces. By at least the middle of the colonial period, when Arequipa's nodal position in trade circuits had been established, particularly its relationship with Altiplano mining, Arequipeño political and economic leaders came to think of themselves as quite distinct sorts of citizens from Limeños, Cuzqueños, or those in Charcas (later Upper Peru) (Wibel 1975; Fisher 1987; Romero 1929). Though linked tightly with colonial administrative agents and policies, a localized Hispanicized culture developed in the valley, propelled by isolation and its trade position but resting on the rich but environmentally circumscribed agriculture of the Arequipa valley and several nearby coastal valleys, especially of the Vítor, lower Majes, and lower Tambo rivers (Davies 1984; Brown 1986).

Following independence from Spain, this especially Spanish city came to think of itself as occupying not only a geographically intermediate space between lowlands and highlands, but more importantly a hybrid cultural space between modern and traditional ways of being Peruvian. This worldview intensified after the War of the Pacific as the national question became paramount. Some Arequipeño intellectuals began to argue that Arequipeños, more than other Peruvians, were fundamentally entrepreneurial and literate, a harmonious blending of both Spanish and Indian races, and were thus a model for a new Peruvian identity. I argue that with its shift from an overwhelmingly conservative, Catholic, Spanish identity to one emphasizing mestizo traits, Arequipa of the early twentieth century constitutes an unusual, if quite particular, case of an effort to *brown* (rather than "whiten") identity (see Applebaum 1999, 2003).

9

Connected with this process of cultural regionalization, Arequipa provides an early example in Latin America of the beginnings of inclusion of the popular classes in nation building. While popular political participation (or clamors for it) grew throughout Latin America from the early 1900s on, Arequipa provided a prototype of this broader participatory nationalism (see Domingues 2006, 544). Surprisingly, popular and elite interests more often than not coincided, especially in a long series of mid-nineteenth-century, cross-class uprisings but also well into the twentieth century (Caravedo 1978). We will examine how this egalitarian theme was rooted in the region's unusual *minifundio* land-tenure system and grew both in postindependence struggles over nation building, with elite and cross-class struggles against the central government, and in the political space opened in the wake of the War of the Pacific. It is in this context, then, that the proud, mestizo, local smallholder, often portrayed as a rustic country-bumpkin figure, came to be the condensed, multivocal symbol representing the essence of *lo Arequipeño* (see fig. 4.3). (The recognition sat rather uneasily on their shoulders, however, as we will see.)

So this is an anthropological history of the origins, contexts, and consequences of a deeply regionalist cultural identity—the roughly century-long career of Arequipeño traditionalism, from its formulation in the middle third of the nineteenth century to its peak in the early decades of the twentieth century and then its slow decline in the last third of that century.[5] It is about the indigenous foundations of regional identity, the legacies of colonial jurisdictions and policies, the political attempts at statehood just after independence, and the reasons and ways Arequipa's fundamentally Spanish colonial identity was so dramatically transformed into a purported "mestizo" essence even as Arequipa's commercial vocation continued.

It is not that such processes were not at work in other areas of Peru or elsewhere in the central Andes as postindependence power arrangements and identities developed, for example in Ica (Hammel 1969), Huancayo (Long and Roberts 1979), Chachapoyas (Nugent 1997), or even Cuzco (de la Cadena 2000). It is rather that in no others did the urban plebeians and small farmers so deeply insert themselves into the development of a regional culture as transpired in Arequipa—an urban culture itself centrally linked not only with the broadest and oldest political and economic currents of the colonial and Republican eras, but also with the tristate (among Peru, Chile, and Bolivia) warring over the Ata-

FIGURE 1.2
Campiña farmers welcoming visitors to Arequipa airport. Photograph by Juan Borja.

cama Desert, the most intense, longest-running border conflict in modern South American history (Skuban 2007).

In tracing the lineages of the several strands of Arequipeño regional culture, my central assertion is that while regional identity currently flies under the flag of rural and even plebeian symbols, the development of those symbols was fundamentally an urban-based, largely middle-class invention of tradition addressing the national question as this developed in relation to growing authoritarianism in Lima, especially in the half century after the war with Chile. Drawing from independence struggles (e.g., as represented in the work of Mariano Melgar), in its classic iteration (by Juan Gualberto Valdivia) regional identity centered on cross-class resistance to real and perceived abuses by the political center, with some aspiration for real political autonomy. Reminiscent of the exaggerated place of the cowboy in US national identity or of the gaucho in Argentinian national identity, by the early twentieth century, in the hands of intellectuals such as Jorge Polar, Francisco Mostajo, and Jorge Vinatea (see fig. 4.3), regional identity had long since lost its overtly secessionist strand and shifted to center on symbols associated with a prosperous, hard-working mestizo peasantry—valley smallholders working pre-Inka terraces to produce staple crops for a distinctive cuisine of *rocotos rellenos* and *chicha de jora*, talking about it all in a rich Spanish full of Quechua-influenced localisms *"como aúntes"* (see figs. 1.2 and 4.3). By the latter part of the twentieth century, regional identity had morphed to center on spectacular performances of bull-on-bull fighting (*peleas de toros*).

Now, again centering on nostalgia for this "disappearing" idyllic village way of life punctuated by uprisings in defense of justice and liberty, Arequipeños at home and abroad extol and re-create this cultural identity through poetry, novels, histories, music CDs, DVDs of bullfights, movies on YouTube, Facebook, blogs, and other means. Its doxic, taken-for-grantedness has become part and parcel of the fabric of Arequipeño culture; everyone "just knows" that this is how Arequipeños "are." But how did this consensus of subjectivities, such widely shared sentiments as that of Zevallos, quoted just above, get constructed, interpreted, reproduced, and periodically politicized?

While "Arequipa" names not only former political (*corregimiento, intendencia*) and ecclesiastical (*doctrina, obispado*) units but now also a formal region, a department, a province, and a city, it is also a state of mind. The entanglement of these formal names and spaces, and what they stand for, with the subjective experience of being part of the imagined community of Arequipa, within the social space of "Arequipa," is central to my project. As we will see, the symbols defining this strongly felt regional identity steadily narrowed after the early Republican period to center on Arequipa city and the rural dwellers of its surrounding countryside—a key clue to the urban, literary basis of the traditionalist narrative. Its repertoire of symbols is also markedly secular, again pointing to the central role of urban intellectuals with their generally anti-clerical, positivist modernism.

The central organizing symbol in this narrative is the campiña, the rural countryside surrounding the city. While the term can be found as a place-name in many parts of coastal Peru—in Moquegua, Ica, Lima (where it is the name of a former countryside now an urbanization in the Chorrillos District south of the city center), as well as in Trujillo, Chimbote, Santiago de Cao, and Lambayeque on the north coast (Collin Delavaud 1968, 132)—in the Peruvian mind the term is most closely associated with Arequipa, where "campiña" is not just a place or a symbol but a powerful metaphor anchoring and territorializing regional identity (see

Kaiser 2002). Arequipeños love their campiña (even as they expand the urban footprint onto it)—they write poetry and sing about it, they hike in it and post videos to YouTube about it, they flock on weekends to rural *picanterías* (traditional taverns; see chapter 5) for some fresh air and to go swimming or horseback riding. They name shops and restaurants after it elsewhere in Peru and even abroad.

In Arequipa "campiña" evokes a sense of a harmonious human-natural landscape—a social product, a "worked," lived-in landscape. The campiña is not just a *vega* (fertile plain or valley; meadow), a *campo* (field), or a *cuenca* (basin, watershed) but a geography of the mind, a cognitive landscape of memory and accreted stories. What looks like a messy cluster of irregular fields in Yumina or Chiguata is in reality an organized social landscape replete with familial and cultural memory (see Basso 1996).

Though campiña smallholders are now at the symbolic center of regional tradition, there are several other layers and strands, various symbols and practices of this imagined community, that have diverse origins of varying time depth. Threaded together, they form a traditionalist discourse involving such elements as *peleas de toros* (bull-on-bull contests) rather than *corridas de toros* (human-versus-bull contests replete with capes and swords), the proud rural campiña smallholder at the center of those to be sure, but also religious pilgrimage, fiery orators leading cross-class popular uprisings in defense of liberty, and pride in a virtual pantheon of diverse *héroes y próceres* (heroes and illustrious men) (Oviedo 1992) (which for some is even coming to include, oddly enough, Abimael Guzmán, though not Vladimiro Montesinos). While, to be sure, its main focus is resentment toward growing Lima centralism in postindependence nation building, it is also about not being "Indian"—despite resting on layers of earlier Altiplano-centric colonial and pre-Hispanic political, economic, and cultural circuitry.

Importantly, traditionalist discourse was developed over the course of this long century through several changing literary and musical forms. Earlier narrative "histories" of Arequipa by local clerics and intellectuals established the tradition, recounting and retelling the story of Arequipeño uniqueness—its heroic spirit, its position as the "cradle of revolutions," and so on. In the main florescence of this tradition at the turn of and in the first several decades of the twentieth century—the center of my analysis below—writing about Arequipa shifted: it began to include not only history but also studies of local dialect and folklore; it began to be expressed in various lyrical genres such as poetry, short stories, some painting, and the occasional novel; and it extolled the virtues of the rural peasantry and closely tied urban plebeian and included some social commentary. Finally, in its decline by the 1950s–1970s, traditionalist writing had shifted to the memoir—an uncommon genre in Peruvian letters (Pacheco Vélez 1967, xii), mostly written by Arequipeños residing in Lima or abroad. The memoir intensified the nostalgic tone so prominent in more recent traditionalist discourse.

In the last few decades, Arequipeños have found themselves in the midst of a huge social experiment, with explosive urban growth due to massive immigration from Puno, Cuzco, and elsewhere. Though there is a scarcely concealed racialist undertone in some older Arequipeños' resentment of these massive changes and "*serrano*" influx, the mix of these immigrants' descendants into the more traditional society imagined by Arequipeños of generations ago (see Ødegaard 2010) is re-creating Arequipa into the highland-linked region it turns out to have always been.

ORGANIZATION OF THE BOOK

In 2001 a devastating earthquake shook Arequipa, the latest in a long series of earthquakes that have periodically leveled the city over the centuries. In 2002 Arequipeños successfully moved to stop the regime of Alejandro Toledo from privatizing the regional electricity company. Since 2010 Arequipeños have again taken to the streets opposing development of the proposed Tia Maria mine south of the city over concerns about contamination of water for irrigating the fertile Tambo valley.

Earthquakes, popular uprisings, mountains, desert, Lima, Indian highlanders from Puno and Cuzco—these are perennial elements of the story of Arequipa. Its people have periodically drawn upon local symbols to both accommodate and resist dominant influences originating from outside and, in turn, to dominate peoples and regions of the highland interior. Such resistance/accommodation/domination, expressed in both material and symbolic terms, is predicated on complex relations both within the region and without—with the national capital, with neighboring regions of Cuzco and Puno, and even with Bolivia and Chile.

The traditionalist narrative that fuels and informs such movements is heterogeneous; its many threads point to different social origins, but woven together, they make up this cultural project, always "under construction" and malleable with the bricolage of cultural entrepreneurs interpreting and reinterpreting dominant symbols and metaphors for a surprisingly literate public. Print media have played a central role in reproducing the imagined community of Arequipa. Since the package became understood as "regional," we will need to understand how and why the narrative structure persists over time and in this social-political space, and why, though "cultural" it began on, and periodically gets dragged back onto, political terrain. It will be important to unpack two of its most striking features—its nostalgic mood, and its claim of cross-class unity.

Both the linear format of written text and the need to trace cause-and-effect relationships over time among a variety of rather disparate data and trends suggested the largely narrative organization of this book. While there is a rough chronology to the emergence of the various themes, the book's task is more like examining different layers of an onion, digging in from the outer skin to start from the oldest at the center and work back out to the most recent layers. Cultural entrepreneurs have combined and recombined these layers or threads (to confuse the metaphor somewhat), each with intertwined but somewhat separate histories and places in the social space of Arequipa.

As the book peels back these many layers, many readers will be surprised at the revelation of fundamentally Andean, indeed Altiplano, contours in Arequipeño regional culture. Because the deeply populist nature of regional culture that I analyze in chapters 4 and 5—the heart of the monograph—rests on important pre-Hispanic and colonial foundations, I devote chapter 2 to understanding the social origins of these underlying sedimented layers. These include regional effects of the highland-centered periods of broad political-economic (if not social) unification—the Altiplano-based Tiyawanaku "state" and the Ayacucho-based Wari state in the Middle Horizon (400–1100 CE), as well as the domination by the Cuzco-based Inka state during the regionally brief Late Horizon (1470–1534). Spanish imperial interests largely incorporated Inka boundaries and many state practices (e.g., *mita* labor—mandatory labor for state projects) in their focus on highland mining, with Arequipa emerging as a royal entrepôt in the quickly established, Altiplano-oriented trade circuitry. Though I rely heavily on generally available secondary sources to do so, I synthesize this background both because it is important for the shape taken by regional culture in the twentieth century and because such an overview is nowhere else collected in one place.

Syncretism and hybridity abound, cultural legacies of long experience with ethnic and linguistic difference as well as with having to deal with various episodes of control by distant states. After the brief recap of central Andean prehistory and colonial history, I move to the main task of examining how various elements of preconquest society and culture became bound up in Spanish institutions, particularly the most primordial fount and enduring site of regional identity—the regional, folk Catholic, pilgrimage-based cults around various representations of the Virgen de la Candelaria.

In chapter 3 I describe the postindependence emergence of a regionalism somewhat more recognizable today. I move directly to examine the Peru-Bolivia Confederation—a brief attempt to maintain the unity of colonial and pre-Hispanic political-economic linkages with the Altiplano. The confederation's early collapse dashed whatever non- or anti-Lima and pro–southern highlands nationalist hopes some local elites had and fueled midcentury regionalist sentiment. Lima's primacy in the political space of "Peru" remained firm, even as "Peruvian" national identity lagged. Two men—Juan Gualberto Valdivia, populist cleric, teacher, lawyer, and advocate of regional autonomy, and poet and independence martyr Mariano Melgar—frame and were used by later writers to found the major outlines of regionalist discourse. I argue that this regionalist sentiment took hold not just among regional elites jockeying for position in the emerging national field, but also (following Chambers 1999) among second-class citizens, mostly urban but with strong social ties to the adjoining countryside, striving for position in a postindependence regional field marked by the legacy of very exclusionary Spanish concerns with respect (*dignidad*) and authority. Anxious about social exclusion, perhaps even abandonment, and under continuing de facto Spanish social codes that privileged Spanish descent and customs, progressive intellectuals reproduced a certain egalitarian challenge throughout the nineteenth century at important local educational institutions, chiefly the Colegio de la Independencia and the closely affiliated Universidad Nacional de San Agustín. I argue that what turned this sentiment *regionalist* was urban intellectuals' close social ties with urban plebeians in Arequipa—unusual for Peru at the time (Deustua and Rénique 1984, 24)—projecting their shared insistence on inclusion as social equals into wider discussions in the consolidating national field about the chronic inability to construct a convincing postcolonial model of national identity, of *peruanidad*, around which most Peruvians could rally.

While in the previous chapter I dwelled on the development of this sentiment as *regionalist*, in chapter 4 I move to the heart of the monograph to explore why and how a series of writers and politicians at the turn and in the first half of the twentieth century reconfigured this regionalist sentiment as fundamentally *mestizo, secular,* and *rural.* In the wake of the Chilean debacle (the 1879–1883 War of the Pacific) and in the context of ongoing political centralism and colonial white/Indian racial categories, Arequipeño writers, artists, and musicians as diverse as Jorge Polar, Francisco Mostajo, Víctor Andrés Belaúnde, and Teodoro Núñez Ureta essentialized Arequipeño mestizaje and projected it as an implicit model for developing an authentic national spirit between the extreme poles of national identity then framing debates about the character of the nation. Though mestizaje is typically understood as fundamentally a sort of camouflage, however ambiguous or malleable, that privileges "whiteness" (e.g., Telles and Flores 2013), I argue that in Arequipa this discourse of mestizaje was not just this, that it was also much more inclusive than exclusive in nature *within the urban social space,* largely because it was driven by that popular desire for inclusion as citizens in the imagined community of Arequipa. Its inclusiveness as a cognitively salient region—lived and understood as such—was predicated on a contrast with what it wasn't: Indian or Limeño. As I explore in the final chapter, traditionalist discourse, centering on attributes of the local mestizo everyman in Arequipa, thus became *both* a discourse of inclusion that key Arequipeños thought necessary for constructing an overdue sense of and commitment to decentralized, truly national *peruanidad, and* an ideology of dominance over indigenous highlanders and of distinction from corrupt Limeños.

In chapter 5 I examine how and why this coherent regional identity began to fragment and evolve from the 1950s on. In particular I focus on *gender,* for the imagery undergoes a profound masculinizing shift. Whereas the early twentieth-century image of the prototypical traditional Arequipeño centrally evoked matronly *picanteras* (the women who ran *picanterías*) and women as milkmaids, by midcentury the imagery had been repositioned around the male owners of fighting bulls (bullfighting was discursively absent in the earlier formulations). This shift occurred as smallholders and plebeians themselves rather than urban intellectuals began to control the ongoing construction of rural tradition. Urban intellectuals had been evoking elements of a "disappearing" rural tradition; by contrast, in this chapter I detail the paradoxical synergy between the pervasive presence of multinational capital and the ongoing vitality of the traditionalist narrative, now much more in the hands of farmers themselves. The persistence of smallholder agriculture in the valley has been due to the relatively seamless transition of campiña peasants into commercial farmers in the post–World War II growth of commercial agriculture in the region—a process that oddly enough did not alter the *minifundio* land-tenure system of the valley on which Arequipeño traditionalism fundamentally rests (Love 1989). Along with increasing cattle buying, facilitated by the development of highways and trucking, increased regular cash flow from dairying enabled some enterprising dairymen to amass expensive bulls (and fancy horses) and compete for honor in the *canchas* (arenas) of the *peleas de toros* for which Arequipa is now so well known. Traditionalist imagery was masculinized in the process. I deploy an ethnography of the particular to ground these processes in the life of one emblematic individual and his family. This most recent iteration of regional identity intersects the legacy of urban nostalgia around earlier failed attempts to create alternatives to Limeño centralism.

Finally, in chapter 6 I conclude by delving into two interrelated theoretical questions: First, how and why did regional efforts to counteract growing political economic centralism in Peru shift (albeit unevenly) from political to cultural terrain? And, second, how was regionalist identity reproduced without the main levers and institutions of state making that are available to central state actors? After a relatively succinct review of relevant concepts, including imagined community, field, social space, forms of capital, and symbolic power—largely drawn from practice theory—I reprise the overall argument by looking through these conceptual lenses at three key episodes in the long evolution of regional identity:

1. Early-colonial Marian apparitions, when popular resistance to elite encroachment on lands and practices was early established and encysted in popular regional pilgrimage.

2. The 1890–1970 apogee of modern regional identity, during which an urban-based discourse of mestizaje was attempted.

3. The post–World War II rise of wildly popular, rural-centered bull-on-bull fighting now at the core of regional identity. The surprising recency of this "traditional" practice is paradoxically tied to the entry of multinational capital into the Arequipa countryside, giving some rural smallholders an income stream they converted into cultural capital symbolic of their self-perceived status as full members of regional society.

TWO

PRE-HISPANIC AND
COLONIAL AREQUIPA

Altiplano Ties and Religious Pilgrimage as
the Popular Foundations of Regional Identity

On my first visit to Arequipa (and to Peru)—a scouting trip for dissertation fieldwork—I made the journey out to the shrine of the Virgen de Chapi. It was 8 September (1976)—the traditional date when Catholics celebrate Mary's birth. We had left the central market area the evening before, a procession of pilgrims in buses loosely caravanning to arrive in the middle of the night. The rickety Bluebird bus, pressed into night service by its owners from its normal daily run, bounced along in the cold desert blackness, the mood quiet, as much sleepy as solemn. I was too excited to nap yet had little idea what to expect. We passed a number of small groups making the pilgrimage on foot—a testimony to one's devotion to the Virgin, my seatmate averred. The most faithful, I learned, walk all the way from Arequipa, or from some intermediate point like Characato, a few even traveling on their knees, it's said. We stopped at three *apachetas* (traditional devotional rock cairns) on the way: Tres Cruces; then over Alto del Hornillo to the second *apacheta*, the cross at Pampa de Tumbambay; and finally by Siete Toldos to the third *apacheta* at Salto de la Escalarilla (Málaga Núñez-Zeballos 2011). Siete Toldos ("seven awnings") was a traditional site where vendors set up shop to provide food, drink, and other supplies to pilgrims. Though the route down La Escalerilla into the rather narrow dry valley is now paved and accessible to vehicular traffic, when I was there it was customary to walk the remaining kilometer or so to the sanctuary (at 2,447 meters elevation).

While the journey there was expectant, if long and tiring, our time at the shrine that night and in the valley the next day was numinous. Our makeshift group, some families and couples but mostly people who clearly did not know each other, began that final leg of the trip on foot, clambering down the rutted road into the valley in the dry, biting cold. There was indeed a feeling of discovering each other as part of a larger community, of being bound together in our determination to be with "La Mamita."

Arriving at the already crowded temple, people crammed in for midnight Mass and confessions to priests there (fig. 2.1). (For the May pilgrimage, apparently the Virgin is brought out briefly at 3:00 p.m. on the eve of the main festival day to greet weary pilgrims.) Groggy from the late hour and tired from the two-hour journey, people worked their way through ranks of vendors into the throng inside the church, joining the other worshipers in a liminal space to fill the nave and sway in unison, singing and praying, gazing for long periods at the Virgin above the altar. The utter ineffability of their experience was very moving as people sought the Virgin's intervention in their this-worldly affairs. While perhaps two thousand people in all were there that night and the following morning, I had no idea how this pilgrimage compared to others in the year or in previous years. That year, 8 September fell on a Wednesday, so perhaps the midweek date suppressed participation. Participation has certainly grown in succeeding years as now tens of thousands of worshipers visit many times during the year.

Vendors were there with fruit, *panes de Omate*, and *chicharrones*, street foods traditionally sold at the shrine. Blazing *castillos* (wood towers) of fireworks were set off at midnight. After at least an hour of Mass, with many people lighting small candles and praying in front of the main altar, I joined some others for a few hours of fitful sleep off to one side of the plaza. It was surprisingly cold, though I should have expected that in September. Not long after dawn, people exited the temple for a warm-up procession around the square fronting the church. After that emotional pandemonium, an older woman in the group where I had slept motioned me over to join her and some others to walk down the valley to a miraculous spring. We walked down the barren rocky desert gorge, its sparse patches of mesquite and other desert shrubs indicating some water underneath the parched riverbed. After several kilometers—longer than I had expected—we arrived at the little spring. After washing her hands and running them through her hair, my friend and the others took out several small glass bottles and a Coke can and filled them with water from the spring. This act in and of itself has strong Andean (Julien 2002, 11) as well as Catholic roots. She urged me to do so as well—*agua milagrosa* (miraculous water) she said, famed for its curative properties, which would cure whatever illnesses or relationship problems I might have. I was deeply thankful that she gave me one of her little bottles, as I obviously had not come prepared. It is considered miraculous

FIGURE 2.1
Chapi worshipers at midnight Mass. Photograph by the author.

that even in this hostile, arid environment, the spring never seems to dry up or overflow.

After returning up the valley to the sanctuary, we watched as the Virgin was brought out in the main procession in the morning, a bed of flowers strewn in her path. Emotional as this was, it seemed rather anticlimactic; perhaps because we were tired from having been up all night, once the intense emotion of the experience had passed, the liminality of the experience seemed to quickly evaporate. We trudged back up the slope we had descended just hours earlier, found the same bus, and headed home; most of us dozed off, and we had little further interaction. My Chapi experience had drawn to a quick close.[1]

My own experiences of those two days at Chapi and of Arequipa more generally throughout my almost two years of fieldwork and since all testify to the almost-complete infusion by Catholicism of time and space in valley society. It is not just the Chapi pilgrimage; one encounters nuns and monks scurrying along cobblestone streets in the old colonial center of town, churches seemingly on every corner, figures of speech ("Dios guarde a usted" [God keep you] or "Vaya con Dios" [Go with God]), bells ringing, feast days, decorations on local buses and long-haul trucks, Holy Week processions, tourists visiting the Santa Catalina Convent (only recently opened after almost four hundred years of strict cloistering)—all constituting a vast reservoir of Catholic practices, doxic understandings, and cultural memory. It is certainly on display and performed during the three periods of official pilgrimage to Chapi—2 February, 1 May, and 8 September. Now, though, there is regular transportation on a paved road and people can get to Chapi any day of the year.

This folk pilgrimage system and intense popular Catholic devotion in Arequipa anchor regional identity, and tracing its origins takes us into the deep foundations of this regional society. We learn that populations in the valley and scattered along the southern flanks of Pichu Pichu, the rugged mid–Tambo River watershed in what is now Moquegua, and south into Tacna were tightly linked politically, economically, and culturally with populations in the Altiplano from at least the Middle Horizon—the archaeological period in the Andes roughly corresponding to the European Middle Ages. Though whatever existing political and economic unity in the Arequipa basin was decisively reconfigured by the Spanish in the decades after their arrival in 1537, the Spanish state nevertheless built on long-standing regional trade, political, and cultural ties that people in the Arequipa region had with Altiplano societies.

Despite the disruptions of Spanish conquest and Inka collapse, within a century of conquest enduring ties to the Altiplano remained vibrant for valley residents, reorganized within the framework of a regional religious system centering on Cayma, Characato, and several other places with shrines to the Virgen de la Candelaria—whose shrine at Copacabana on the southern shores of Lake Titicaca was emerging by 1600 as the most popular among indigenous Andeans throughout what is now southern Peru and highland Bolivia. The rapidly emerging mining-based colonial political and economic circuitry surprisingly mirrored this folk cultural geography. Marian worship quickly spread throughout this central Andean space; by the early twentieth century Marian devotion in Arequipa had become centered on pilgrimage to the Virgen de Characato and to the desert shrine of the Virgen de Chapi—now la Mamita de Arequipa.

In this chapter I examine these pre-Hispanic and colonial economic, political, and especially cultural foundations of Arequipeño regional identity. I explore how syncretized folk Catholic sentiment developed and how ongoing pilgrimage encysts earlier Andean cultural understandings of space (though not time). For the broad mass of rural and urban Arequipeños, participation in pilgrimage and identification with this devotional system came to define citizenship in the imagined community of Arequipa (see Thurner 2004), serving as a fertile substrate for regional intellectuals' later development of more secular and urban-based understandings of regional identity.

I. PREHISPANIC AREQUIPA

Three majestic peaks stand like sentinels guarding the northern and eastern edges of the valley of Arequipa, separating the basin from the vast central Andean highlands and Altiplano (well captured in the first thirty seconds of the YouTube video *Montonero Arequipeño* (https://www.youtube.com/watch?v=Bo1sHrddJ5I). To the north, at 6,057 meters, sits the highest peak—Chachani, dry and snow-capped. El Misti (5,822 meters), the central, Mt. Fuji–like cone, breathes wisps of steam from fumaroles high on its nearly dry summit. Many-peaked Pichu Pichu (5,664 meters), a long ridge of peaks toward the south (fig. 2.2), is the lowest and, at first glance, least impressive of the three.

These three volcanoes looming over the Arequipa basin stand as barely muted testimony to the power of the telluric forces at work in southwestern Peru, one of the most tectonically active regions in the world. With the exception of a small volcano near Tinta in southern Cuzco, volcanoes in Peru are confined to greater Arequipa—the arid southwest toward the Chilean border (though as fig. 2.2 shows, it does rain here seasonally, sometimes heavily). This chain is the northern part of the Andean Central Volcanic Zone, which forms the western boundary of the Altiplano. Coropuna, the highest and largest volcano and third-highest peak complex in Peru (6,425 meters), lies just 150 kilometers northwest of Arequipa city and crowns the Peruvian volcanic chain.

Volcanic eruptions and earthquakes serve as defining events for residents of the city, the surrounding valley, and the region (Barriga 1951)—telluric anchors to the regional identity practiced in Candelaria pil-

FIGURE 2.2

Pichu Pichu volcano from Yanahuara lookout (4 July 2015). Photograph by the author.

grimages and general identification with mountains, particularly Misti. The eruption of Misti (also known as Putina) in "1454" (sometime between 1438 and 1471) constitutes the first historically documented volcanic eruption in South America (Siebert, Simkin, and Kimberly 2010, 181; Chávez Chávez 1993, 91). The earthquake of 23 January 1582 was the first major earthquake experienced by Spanish residents of Arequipa; among weeks of daily processions and prayer, the only image officially venerated outside the small grid of the city proper was the Virgen de la Candelaria de Cayma (Málaga Núñez-Zeballos 2002). But the explosion of Huaynaputina ("young" Putina) in February 1600 (see below) stands as the defining natural event of the early-colonial period—the greatest eruption in the recorded history of South America (Verosub and Lippman 2008; Siebert, Simkin, and Kimberly 2010, 180–195; Chávez Chávez 1993).

Succeeding tectonic events have also elicited responses from the populace.[2] The severe earthquake of 13 May 1784, for example, prompted not only massive reconstruction of the city utilizing *sillar*, the white volcanic tuff that now characterizes the colonial architectural heart of the city, but also an expedition to the top of Misti under orders of the recently arrived imperial administrator (*intendente*) Antonio Alvarez y Jiménez (Marchena F. 2005). From his military background, Alvarez y Jiménez took a personal interest in putting the regional affairs of state in order by conducting a thorough *visita* (census), including carefully describing the natural features of his domain (presaging Polar 1891), particularly in regard to the mountain that had so recently terrorized the citizens (apparently there was some volcanic activity in relation to the 1784 earthquake), by mounting an official ascent of Misti and the planting of a cross carried by Indians from the Santa Teresa monastery. Bishop Fray Miguel de Pamplona granted eighty days of indulgence to those who prayed the three creeds on the slopes of Misti, and forty days for those who did the same looking at the mountain from the city (Motta Zamalloa 1985, 81). A decade later another cross was placed on the summit, and that night a fire was lit on top of the mountain simultaneously with one in the city. A hundred years later, to celebrate the incoming twentieth century, Archbishop Manuel Segundo Ballón trekked with a retinue of notables to place an iron cross on the summit of Misti (the cross is still there) and to celebrate Mass there on 21 October 1900.

All three peaks were and are important in both sacred and secular regional landscapes. Chachani, the highest of the three peaks, was the tutelary *apu* (lord) of Cayma. On the eve of village feast days, *ccaperos* trek up the slopes of all three, especially Chachani and Pichu Pichu, to harvest resinous *ccapo* (*tola* brush, presumably *Baccharis tola*, and another *Baccharis* species) and ceremoniously bring it back on burros in procession through village squares. Flags and musicians accompany their dusk entrance, signifying the start of celebrations. The municipal government of Cayma has fostered this in recent decades, and the practice continues in Socabaya, Yumina, and Characato.

Misti is the central volcano in this trio and is the most symmetrical, conical (as well as canonical, as we shall see), and obviously volcanic—conferring on the mountain a singular awesomeness and power that is palpable even to today's casual observer. The name "Misti" is a mystery, however; until the late-colonial period the volcano was referred to by the Spanish simply as El Cerro o Volcán de Arequipa (Miró Quesada Sosa 1998).[3] Though José Antonio Chávez Chávez (1993) repeats the idea that the Spanish didn't learn the local name, in fact the Spanish had indeed known the name Putina, even though they didn't go on to use it (Julien 2002).[4] In the 1780s the name "El Misti" started being applied to this central, dominating peak by Bishop Ventura Travada y Córdoba (Julio A. Bustinza Menéndez, pers. comm., 4 July 2015)—right about the time of the 1784 earthquake and the official summiting of the crater. "Misti" was slow to gain popular acceptance, and what name or understandings locals actually had in mind then remains unclear (Julien 2002, 32n1); Flora Tristán noted the mountain had no name when she visited in 1834 (Tristán [1838] 1971).

At least during the modern period, Misti has virtually defined the spirit of the city at its base. "No en vano se nace a pie de un volcán" (One is not born at the foot of a volcano in vain), wrote Jorge Polar ([1891] 1958, 151), referring to Arequipeños' legendary volcanic political temperament. While roaming the campiña I would often offer my binoculars to children. For example, I shared them with a teenaged herder on one bitterly cold August morning in Mosopuquio, upslope from Characato at the upper boundary of agriculture in the valley. Though Mosopuquio lies high on the slopes of Pichu Pichu, like most people he instantly looked for the cross on the summit of Misti, metaphorically echoing locals' worship of Putina.

Though Pichu Pichu is lowest and is often relegated to third place, even now it seems that just about every Arequipeño can refer to the Ixtaccihuatl-like *indio* (or Inka) *dormido* (sleeping Inka) outline on the left/north end (as viewed from the valley) of Pichu Pichu's jagged ridge (fig. 2.2)—toward the east where the sun rises, the "eastern altar [where] the Sun officiates," an "enormous sepulcher" (Mostajo [1924] 1956, vii). One of the first Inka-era summit *adoratorios* (shrines) in the central Andes was found on the highest (central) point of Pichu Pichu in the 1950s, a large platform with a two-hundred-meter paved path leading to the highest point, where another platform with retaining walls was found (Chávez Chávez 1993, 100). (Six Inka-era mummies were found on the crater rim of Misti in 1998.)

The bare flanks of Chachani and Misti indicate more recent eruptions and relative geological youth compared to Pichu Pichu. Their ash slopes are too porous to hold much moisture, and so they are starkly dry, devoid of terraced agriculture and stripped during the colonial period of their little vegetation. While Chachani and Misti dominate the city skyline, these days Pichu Pichu is often almost obscured by the valley's increasing dust and haze. Yet both orography (these slopes receive the most direct force of afternoon winds ascending from the coast) and hydrology combine to make the slopes of Pichu Pichu the naturally wettest (nonriparian) part of this bone-dry, midelevation Andean valley. Pichu Pichu features the valley's best developed *queñuales* (visible as a dark band between the nearer brown ridge and the snowline in fig. 2.2): high-elevation stands of hardy, ochre-trunked, flaky-barked *Polylepis rugulosa* trees, which support both a unique avifauna and (now illegal) charcoal makers supplying fuel to local bakeries in campiña villages. Central Andean *Polylepis* groves like these constitute earth's highest-elevation woodlands.

These somewhat stark facts about volcanoes, climate, orography, botany, and hydrology set the stage for understanding why people dependent on agriculture in this arid basin primarily settled where they did. The valley's spectacular terracing is the main archaeological legacy of pre-Hispanic Arequipeños. Skirting the flanks of the Rio Chili valley, especially the western and southern flanks of Pichu Pichu, are extensive agricultural terraces, some abandoned, which constitute the major part of the terraced agricultural area of the valley—the largest area of pre-Hispanic terracing still in use in the New World (Donkin 1979, 101). Though it was cool and showering when I visited Churajón on 6 January 1979, for example, the area is obviously very dry; in such a rugged and dry environment, building and maintaining these extensive terraces—from Paucarpata through Sabandía to Characato and on through Churajón (see below), Puquina, and valleys at this elevation south through Tacna into northernmost Chile—seems clearly to have been worth someone's effort.

But who built all this terracing, and when? If the Arequipa basin is so agriculturally rich now, its terracing so central to the green campiña and the life of this desert oasis city, why is there so little evidence of other pre-Hispanic construction pointing to the centralized polities that must have been responsible for it all? While this topic warrants extended treatment, I devote some space here only to sketch out the environmental and political basis for a key regional pre-Hispanic polity on the southern slopes of Pichu Pichu—Churajón. I will then argue that this pre-Hispanic, indeed pre-Inka, sacred site forms the basis for more recent beliefs and pilgrimage practices centered on Chapi, which is very close by. All this is to demonstrate the antiquity of Arequipa's strong Altiplano ties, now sedimented in the regional pilgrimage system.

Dating terraces is extremely difficult, given movements of soil and water and the long, continued use and maintenance of terraces throughout the region.[5] In Yumina, locals have modified terraces over the years—for example, widening a couple of terraces from 1.5 to 5 meters to accommodate small tractors. As one farmer there told me, "The Inkas had the concept of terracing, but we've been transforming them over all these years."

Where there is adequate water, the midelevation *quechua* climate zone on the western slope presents an optimal combination of temperature and sunshine for cultivation of maize and a wide assortment of temperate crops ("Characato" probably derives from Quechua *zara-q'atu*, "place where maize is traded"). Unlike in many other parts of highland Peru, though, eucalyptus trees and shrubs are surprisingly (and fortunately) uncommon in the campiña, for reasons I never quite ascertained, though it is rather common and is increasingly planted at higher elevations on the flanks of Pichu Pichu. Lower valleys are warmer and present excellent conditions for growing sugar, cotton, and some fruits, but limited cultivable land and meandering rivers there combine to limit large-scale cultivation on the coast. A narrow *chaupi-yunga* zone allowed cultivation of some eastside crops, such as coca in the lower Tambo River valley at "Cocachacra." Barter exchange by locals among these westside ecological zones continues (Love 1988).

While precipitation increases dramatically with elevation, temperatures drop (Winterhalder 1994). Given lower and even less reliable precipitation in the Arequipa basin, terracing appears to be even more reliant on springs than in the nearby but rather different, better understood Colca Valley. With the Inka state's emphasis on maize, this dependence on springs may be especially true of their Late Horizon settlements, since maize cultivation requires reliable moisture over a longer growing season (Denevan 2001, 201). The magnificent Inka-era faced-bench terracing in Yumina (fig. 2.3), Paucarpata, and elsewhere in the southern valley—the finest-quality terracing not only in the campiña but in all of southwestern Peru—is tied to the most reliable, prodigious springs in the Arequipa basin. These spectacular terraces were probably intensified from preexisting terracing, both benched and broad-field benched types, so much in evidence elsewhere in the valley.

The bulk of the valley of Arequipa lies at lower elevations than the prime maize-growing zone on the western escarpment.[6] Lands of this elevation are located in the upper basin of Arequipa, in the villages (and subvalley) of Chiguata and its outlying *anexos* (hamlets) such as Mosopuquio, where rainfall is a third greater than it is in the main basin floor (400 versus 300 mm/year) (Winterhalder 1994, 39). Limited lands at the prime maize elevation and overall aridity may be the reason direct Inka settlement in the Arequipa basin proper seems so light—apparently focused on Yumina, a high knoll near Characato, and adjacent Paucarpata (and perhaps Quequeña) in the areas with springs in the southeastern, better-watered part of the basin.[7]

28

FIGURE 2.3
Yumina terracing. Photograph by the author.

Water use in such an arid region is of great interest. Most canals in use
in the Arequipa basin away from the Chili River are short, the longest
being those identified by Guillermo Galdos Rodríguez on the left/south-
eastern bank of the Rio Chili, where the Spanish settled. (There may be
longer, abandoned canals on Pichu Pichu.) During my fieldwork in Sabandía, where the water supply was very good, it quickly became apparent that farmers were more focused on the timing of water flow than on
the total amount of water to which they had access, so apart from threats
to total water supply, there was little organized behavior around irrigation. The infrequent canal maintenance was easily handled by hired
workers, as seems to be the general case in the Colca. As peripheral urban expansion continues almost unchecked onto barren hillsides north,
east, and south of the city, however, previously rare tension over water is
rapidly accelerating, with urban uses starting to preempt traditional irrigation uses. For example, there is now tension over misappropriation of
water for new hillside settlements from the main spring in Yumina.

A. Dealing with State-Organized Polities

The slightly less arid, better-watered southern part of the Arequipa basin, then, held the densest human population in the Province of Arequipa before Spanish conquest. For at least 1,500 years, from at least Middle Horizon times forward, the valley on the left/south bank of the Rio Chili was well populated by peasant farmers growing a variety of typical midelevation Andean crops (Cardona Rosas 2002).

A rethinking of pre-Hispanic central Andean political boundaries and cultural linkages is now underway at all scales in space and time (Isbell and Silverman 2006; Heggarty and Beresford-Jones 2010). Ethnohistorical, archaeological, linguistic, and cultural data are being integrated in ways that are revealing a more complex and yet clearer and in some ways radically different picture of state making, population movement, long-distance trade, and cultural processes in the central Andes (Hornborg 2014). Both Middle (roughly 400–1100 CE) and Late (1470–1534 CE) Horizon periods of widespread unification stem from the highlands and seem to involve some sort of political integration among altitudinal, cross-Andean production zones, though perhaps not as in John Murra's (1975) now-classic archipelago models. In between these episodes of widespread political economic unification is a period of fragmentation and relocalization—the Late Intermediate Horizon (1100–1470 CE).

Though our story in southwestern Peru really begins with the Middle Horizon, when this general region seems to have first been incorporated in larger state-level processes, it is important to briefly review some antecedent developments. Recent discoveries in the historical linguistics of the central Andes are particularly relevant, since part of regionalist discourse has been establishing the meaning of key words like "Arequipa" as well as the uniqueness of vernacular campiña speech patterns, said (problematically) to be fundamentally Quechua admixtures into Spanish emblematic of Arequipa's mestizo identity (Carpio Muñoz 1999). At stake, in part, is whether "Arequipa" was fundamentally more tied (later) to the Inka state or (earlier) to Altiplano-based polities and their predecessors, refracted through modern associations of the former with magnificent (if failed) statecraft and the latter to long-forgotten statecraft and seemingly unremarkable Indian backwardness.

Though it has long been presumed that Aymara was the language of the Tiyawanaku state/confederation, given Aymara's current distribution, there is growing linguistic and archaeological evidence favoring

Pukina as the Tiyawanaku state language, suggesting that Aymara instead radiated during the Early Horizon period (900–200 BCE) from a Chavín heartland in north-central highland Peru southward toward southern Peru (Cerrón-Palomino 2010). The widespread radiation of Chavín art styles was thus presumably accompanied by proto-Aymara as a trade language, though how far south of Cuzco this stretched remains unknown (Heggarty and Beresford-Jones 2010).

The overall picture in Peru seems to be that trade ties were periodically established between the north and central coasts with the north, central, and southern highlands, including the Altiplano. The rugged, drier, more sparsely populated south coast seems to have been integrated with but peripheral to these main highland developments, leaving the arid southwest connected more directly and locally with neighboring parts of the Altiplano.

After many decades of etymological confusion, it is now clear that "Arequipa" is Aymara for "the other side of the mountain(s)" (Bustinza Menéndez and Huamán Asillo 2002; Bustinza Menéndez, pers. comm., 4 July 2015), meaning the west slope and entire long coastline from Acarí to the Atacama Desert. Cristóbal de Albórnoz had noted in his 1582 *relato* (report) that all the volcanoes in this region "looked to the sea" (cited in Julien 2002, 37). Like "Putina," the Pukina term for the volcano Misti, along with a host of Pukina and Aymara toponyms throughout the region, the very name "Arequipa" thus points to this long-standing Altiplano domination of the volcanic, west-slope south coast.[8]

The Middle Horizon—the next phase of widespread political, economic, and cultural integration in the central Andes, was characterized primarily by interaction between the Wari and Tiyawanaku polities. Quechua was probably the language of the Wari state (Isbell 2010), which they spread during their expansion phase southeast down the spine of the Andes as they connected trade across the central Andes from the Pacific to the Amazon. Pukina was probably the language of the Tiyawanaku confederation, as noted above, which connected west and east slopes through their highland center on the south shore of Lake Titicaca.

Though Wari-Tiyawanaku boundary dynamics in the Arequipa basin during the Middle Horizon remain unclear, refracted as they have been through later Lupaqa, Colla, Inka, and Spanish polities, it is certain that the longer occupation of Tiyawanaku and Wari left a far greater imprint on the region than did the relatively brief Inka presence, as we will see. In any case, the Spanish found a largely trilingual (Quechua, Aymara, and Pukina) population inhabiting an area roughly corresponding to "greater Arequipa"—the present-day regions of Arequipa, Moquegua, and Tacna (Cerrón-Palomino 2010, 273; Bouysse-Cassagne 2010).

Regional identity, cultural frontiers, and political-economic autonomy have thus been issues for a very long time in the Arequipa basin. To consolidate power, Wari and Tiyawanaku, like the later Inka state, were compelled to deal with local leaders, people, and identities here and throughout the central Andean region through forced or voluntary relocation as well as through acculturation. Recent archaeology is constructing a more nuanced picture of state making in the central Andes, creatively revealing the many ways state dominance seems to have played out on the ground.

Legacies of demographic erasure, migration, and mixing are still felt centuries later, not least in the area's complex toponymy, which provides important clues to the still-murky linguistic and cultural convergences and divergences here. Because Altiplano ties are so crucial to understanding the evolution of Arequipeño regional identity, particularly in regard to Marian apparitions, and because this material has not been accessibly pulled together elsewhere, we need to pause for a further moment to understand what is known about the late prehistory of the Arequipa region.

B. Middle Horizon (400–1100 CE)

Rival highland Wari (550–950) and Tiyawanaku (400–ca. 1050) polities dominated the central Andes during the Middle Horizon (Isbell and Silverman 2006). Both Wari and Tiyawanaku state policies seem to have focused on major rivers with reliable irrigation and direct trade access to the highlands—such as the Cotahuasi/Ocoña, Majes/Colca, and Tambo—and to have had less concern for direct control of smaller, more dispersed, and probably less threatening or exploitable local polities like those that probably existed in the Arequipa basin. The valley of Arequipa was located between their spheres of influence (Neira Avendaño 1990; Cardona Rosas 2002, 66–91), though just what was going on politically, culturally, and linguistically in frontiers like Arequipa is not yet well understood (Jennings 2010; Malpass, n.d.). Forward settlements and administrative centers reflect Wari policy, but direct political control and settlement of the Moquegua valley seem unusual for Tiyawanaku (Isbell and Silverman 2006, 510; cf. Bauer and Stanish 2001, 39), suggesting that Tiyawanaku may not have fully constituted a state formation, at least as conventionally understood (Goldstein 2009).

Tiyawanaku influence seems to have been tied both to trade and to herding, extending north and west from the Tambo drainage into the

Arequipa basin. Apart from Moquegua, the main focus of Tiyawanaku in the general Arequipa area seems to have been the obsidian mines near Chivay. "Tiwanaku created a network of strategically located, surplus-producing colonies that furnished the state with the goods that maintained its complex political economy" (Stanish 2003, 42). At least six Tiyawanaku-style hilltop sites have been found in the Arequipa basin itself, mostly on the slopes of Pichu Pichu (Cardona Rosas 2002, 78). Ceramic analysis reveals local variations on basic Altiplano and Moquegua styles (ibid., 84), suggesting that the well-settled southern campiña was relatively autonomous politically but engaged in trade or tribute relationships with Tiyawanaku (directly or via their Tambo colonies) or even Wari lower-elevation settlements (in Majes and via their outpost in the Tambo). The site of Sonqonata, near Quequeña (and not far from Churajón), appears to have been the most important of these Middle Horizon sites in the valley. (*Sonqo* is Quechua for "heart" or "center," suggesting later Inka recognition of its ritual importance; cf. Bastien 1978 on Kaatan's role as the beating heart of the mountain in maintaining *ayllu* [kin-based village] integrity.)

Pukina, the putative language of the Tiyawanaku polity, seems to have been dominant from the Ocoña River and southern Cuzco Department south throughout the Altiplano during this period (Cerrón-Palomino 2010, 263). The prevalence of Pukina place-names ending in -*baya*, such as "Tiabaya," "Polobaya," and "Mollebaya," or -*laque*, such as "Matalaque" and "Coalaque," among others, throughout the Arequipa basin and south into and beyond the Tambo drainage strongly suggests trade and cultural, though perhaps not political, ties of these people with the Altiplano. Whether they predate a Tiyawanaku polity is unclear, though it seems probable. And, of course, there is the village of Puquina itself near the Moquegua-Arequipa departmental boundary— very close to Chapi. While it therefore seems that the Arequipa basin was near the center of a blurry political, economic, and especially cultural and perhaps linguistic frontier between Tiyawanaku and Wari spheres of influence, the important point is that ties with the Altiplano were strong, Wari intrusions notwithstanding.

C. Late Intermediate (1100–1470 CE)

The waning of Tiyawanaku and Wari power ushered in the politically fragmented Late Intermediate, or Altiplano, period, when two chiefdoms—Lupaqa and Colla—emerged in the west and north ends of the

Altiplano, respectively. The more northern chiefdom, the Colla, was Pukina and/or Aymara speaking (Bouysse-Cassagne 2010; Sillar 2012, 314) and heir to the Pukara polity. It seems to have maintained trade ties via the Colca—the nearest major river valley—though the Collaguas of the upper Colca drainage were Aymara speakers, tied to camelid herding.[9]

The Lupaqa maintained or reestablished a Tiyawanaku-like relationship with colonies in the Tambo valley and valleys further south, elaborated by Murra (1975) into a classic example of the Andean verticality model on the basis of a 1560s *visita* there. Colonists were undoubtedly sent, as revealed by Tiyawanakoid influences in architecture and local pottery from this period. Chucuito, the Lupaqa capital, seems to have been the primary, if not the sole, origin of these colonists.

Tiyawanaku-era trade and ritual circuits continued and perhaps intensified as they were reorganized under these Late Intermediate lacustrine kingdoms. Yet the degree of Colla or Lupaqa influence in the Arequipa basin remains unclear. One or the other, or both, could have maintained ties with valley cultivators and/or sent colonists. Existing evidence suggests that the Arequipa basin was most probably under the control of several local, relatively autonomous chiefdoms based on vertical control of the entire west slope, from Laguna Salinas (at 4,320 meters) to Punta de Bombón (at the mouth of the Tambo River), and lying between the Lupaqa colony in the Tambo valley and the Colla focus on the upper Colca valley; perhaps they played the two against each other.

Between Tiyawanaku/Wari and Inka horizons, then, we see in Arequipa a continuation of the pattern of Altiplano-linked altitudinal colonies in west-slope river valleys, mixed with local agriculturists. Hilltop settlement patterns in ruins all along the lower slopes of Pichu Pichu, among which I often walked before or after interviewing farmers in Chiguata, point to a need for defensive preparation, perhaps linked to endemic, drought-impelled warfare among lakeside chiefdoms in the Titicaca basin that was characteristic of this period (Stanish 2003).

Emerging archaeological data indicate the existence of several power centers in the Arequipa basin during the Late Intermediate period, including Cerro Gordo (aka Colorado) near Characato, Sonqonata (continuing from Middle Horizon) near Quequeña, and Churajón near Polobaya (Cardona Rosas 2002). After briefly examining the Late Horizon site of Yumina, near Characato, I will discuss Churajón and its crucial ties to the shrine and increasing adoration of the Virgen de Chapi as a symbol of the Arequipa region, demonstrating the deep pre-Hispanic roots of regional identity—our principal topic in this chapter.

D. Late Horizon (1470–1534):
La Chimba, Characato, Inka Yumina

Economic and perhaps ritual and political ties with the Altiplano were strong when the Inka arrived in the Arequipa basin about 1470. The Inka state was much more focused on maintaining its control of trade ties to the coast along routes farther north through Chincha (hence "Chinchay-suyu," from Quechua *suyu*, "region" or "province") and Pachacamac, and especially south to the Altiplano "Collasuyu"—hence their relatively late and light presence in the Arequipa basin. Inka interest in the greater Arequipa region was strongest in the much better watered Colca valley to the north and in Cotahuasi near the Coropuna snow peak—the highest mountain, and therefore most sacred *apu*, in the Kuntisuyu quarter of their empire (see Guaman Poma de Ayala [1615/1616] 1987, 274; Cardona Rosas 2002). Kuntisuyu seems to have been a much less important administrative division in the Inka imperial scheme and may well reflect as much a sediment of Wari control of this area from nearby Ayacucho as a way of cosmologically ordering an empire of four quarters (pairing Kuntisuyu with Antisuyu) onto the wider central Andean political, linguistic, and ethnic patterns that the Inka encountered.

There is growing recognition that by the Late Horizon period, and perhaps even in the Late Intermediate period, the population of the Arequipa region was ethnically diverse and much more polyglot than has been conventionally supposed (Galdos Rodríguez 1990b, 2000; Cardona Rosas 2002; Cardona Rosas and Wise, n.d.; Julien 2002; Cerrón-Palomino 2010). Various highland groups—Quechua-speaking Yanaguaras and Chumbivilcas of highland Arequipa toward Cuzco, Aymara-speaking Collaguas of the Colca valley, and their down-valley, now-Quechua-speaking congeners the Cavanas (hence, "Cabana-Kunti," now "Cabana-conde," with uncertain ties to the major southern Titicaca site of "Copa-cabana"; see the discussion of Marian networks below)—maintained altitudinal colonies not only in the valleys of the Siguas, the Chili, and others, but also in the coastal *lomas* (episodically fog-nourished vegetated coastal bluffs) to collect and dry fish, shellfish, seaweed, and eggs, such as at Islay (Galdos Rodríguez 1990b, 194), and to collect guano (Julien 1985). Other groups with apparently even stronger ties to Altiplano lacustrine communities—perhaps Pukina speaking—lived along the southern flanks of Pichu Pichu, including Pocsi and Churajón and in the mid–Tambo drainage, as well as the narrow Sama, Locumba, and other valleys farther south.

During their brief tenure, the Inka resettled various *mitmaq* populations from the Altiplano and Cuzco areas. The nature of the mix of these resettled with preexisting colonists and local people in the Arequipa valley remains unclear, though *mitmaq* were settled on both sides of the Chili River (Julien 2002). Catherine Julien (2002, 31) argued that the Rio Chili was probably the boundary between the Inka jurisdictions of Conde(Kunti)suyu and Collasuyu.[10] In any case, Inkan Kuntisuyu maps awkwardly onto the trilingual region of "Arequipa," and Inka boundaries probably represent their attempt to incorporate an earlier cultural and political geography stemming from the outlines of Wari and Tiyawanaku political influence (cf. Cerrón-Palomino 2010, 273).

No Inka structures remain (if there were many to begin with from their short tenure), and it is hard to determine what infrastructural improvements the Inka may have made (or intended) in the Arequipa valley other than the spectacular terracing in the Paucarpata and Sabandía Districts (fig. 2.3)—almost certainly substantial modification of existing terracing. The Inka had built a suspension bridge over the Chili to communicate between the smaller northern and the more populated southern parts of the valley. This bridge, which survived into the first decade of Spanish occupation, was replaced by a Spanish arched bridge in the latter 1540s; that bridge, the Puente Viejo (now Puente Bolognesi), remained the only bridge spanning the Chili River and was therefore the main trade route linking the two sectors of the valley for the next three centuries.

Evidence from chroniclers, including from Felipe Guaman Poma de Ayala, describes a local population still recovering from the 1454 eruption of Putina (Misti), but the great concentration of colonists in the Arequipa basin may be as much due to the Chili River being the *suyu* boundary as to a state repopulation effort in the wake of volcanic disaster. Since archaeological evidence describes a well-populated valley in the Late Intermediate, conventional lore stemming from the chronicler Garcilaso de la Vega about the Inka Mayta Cápac (or Inka Pachacutec [1438–1471]) saying, "Ari-quepay" ("Yes, we'll stay here," that is, in this fine valley)—often retold by writers during the early twentieth century—both repeats self-serving Inka mythology about their great civilizing role as they expanded into the area and links Arequipa with Inka greatness (versus Altiplano backwardness). Collasuyu—the Altiplano—was the primary focus of Inka state expansion south of Cuzco, and incorporation of these scattered, Altiplano-linked valley populations all along the western slope on "the other side of the mountains" probably came along with Inka conquest of Altiplano polities.

In any case, extant and resettled groups were made tributary to the Inka state, which engaged in the time-honored practice of control by incorporating worship of local deities. In the immediate area of the Arequipa basin, the Inka appear to have been principally focused on Putina. And in centering the cult to this volcano in Yumina, Paucarpata, and Characato, the Inka capitalized on the best water sources in the valley and what was apparently the largest extant population. Every volcano was staffed with priests (*canónigos*) by the Inka, and Guaman Poma ([1615/1616] 1987, 277) seems to suggest that Putina was second only to Coropuna in the Kuntisuyu region, indicating that the Inka state retained a special interest in Putina and its staff of worshipers and priests at Yumina.[11]

Yumina (at 2,545 meters), with its spectacular terracing (fig. 2.3), was apparently the principal Inka site in the valley and was centrally located in the belt of settlements from Yura in the north to beyond Puquina in the south (that is, between the deep, well-watered Majes and Tambo canyons). It appears to have been a royal Inka *panaqa* (estate) devoted to maize cultivation and water ritual propitiating Apu Putina/Anuqara (that is, Misti). There was probably co-optation of local elites at the nearby Late Intermediate site of Cerro Gordo (Characato), perhaps similar to the imperial strategy deployed in the Cotahuasi valley (Jennings and Yépez Alvarez 2008). The very high quality faced-step terracing in Yumina and nearby Paucarpata, with which it was linked in Spain's earliest organization of *encomienda* (labor grants) (Julien 2002), as well as in nearby Characato and even in Quequeña, indicates intense state interest in supplying crops and animals to the volcano cult. Early-colonial documents reveal that Yumina was staffed by three *mitmaq* populations,[12] including kin of Inka nobility ("Orejones") (Galdos Rodríguez 1990b, 209–210; Julien 2002, 30).[13] That Guaman Poma does not mention Yumina by name suggests it was a rather artificial foreign enclave in the valley that quickly disappeared when the central state collapsed in the 1530s.

In sum, Inka conquest of the Arequipa valley was late and their reign short. Though some conquest into what is now "Arequipa" toward the Cotahuasi valley had already taken place, perhaps in relation to the most direct Inka route from Cuzco to the coast, because of their cultural, economic, and political focus on the Altiplano, Inka conquest of the valley of Arequipa came later, perhaps about 1470 or even later, with Pachacutec's southward march after the defeat of the Chancas—and after the eruption of Putina (1454). The Late Horizon in the Arequipa basin therefore runs a scant seven decades, roughly 1470–1534.[14]

Altiplano ties continued, therefore, and the Spanish picked them up and reorganized them into the "Arequipa" region of the Viceroyalty of Peru with its strong ties to the Altiplano ("Charcas," the original Spanish name for this Altiplano-centered administrative unit of Peru). Tahuantinsuyu divisions of Kuntisuyu and Collasuyu briefly imposed on the region appear to have had consequences that were less substantive than formal, since the Spanish continued Arequipa's Altiplano orientation even as they carried forward some of these Inka administrative divisions (Julien 1983, 1991).

E. Churajón, or "La Huaca"

Churajón, or La Huaca (sacred place) for locals and the early-colonial Spanish priests who evangelized the area, seems to have been a major area of ritual focus and perhaps even a locus of political power in the Arequipa basin during the Late Intermediate—that four-hundred-year period framed by the collapse of Tiyawanaku influence in the region about 1050 (sometime between 900 and 1100) and the arrival of the Inka about 1470 (Cardona Rosas 2002).

All modern observers are impressed by the truly spectacular terracing all along the flanks of Pichu Pichu, from Chiguata through and south of Puquina but especially at Churajón (Donkin 1979). As we learned, it is still not clear, though, whether this extensive terracing and irrigation infrastructure so readily apparent in the southern campiña dates primarily from the Middle Horizon (or even earlier), the Late Intermediate, or even the Late Horizon. There appear to be no big springs in Churajón, meaning that the water supply for agriculture was probably precarious, reliant on meager seasonal precipitation and surface and ground water from snow or glacier melt.

Recent archaeological work at the Late Intermediate *señorío* (local polity, perhaps a chiefdom) of Churajón has greatly expanded our understanding of this site (Szykulski et al. 2000; Galdos Rodríguez 2000, 200) and helps clarify its relationship with Chapi (which I discuss below). There are indications of a much longer occupation here than had previously been thought, perhaps dating to the Early Horizon (or Formative) period (900–200 BCE) (Galdos Rodríguez 2000, 205). Whether directly or only indirectly tied to the Lupaqa or Colla kingdoms during this Altiplano period, Altiplano influences are particularly evident in ceramics and in architecture at Churajón. Three *chullpas* (round burial towers like those at Sillustani near Puno and elsewhere in the western Titicaca basin) dominate the skyline at the central complex, suggesting ritual, political, and/or economic ties.[15] Churajón lacks evidence of elite segregation and correspondingly impressive administrative buildings, however (Szykulski et al. 2000).[16]

The degree to which the population inhabiting this area was ethnically or linguistically distinct from that of its neighbors, as well as from people in valleys farther north or south, also remains unclear. Following the groundbreaking work of Leonidas Bernedo Málaga (1949), strongly seconded by Thérèse Bouysse-Cassagne (e.g., 2010), key regional scholars have come to argue for the existence of an autonomous, Pukina-speaking polity in this area after the collapse of Tiyawanaku (J. Kimmich, "Arquología arequipeña" [1921], cited in Galdos Rodríguez 2000, 198–200; Neira Avendaño 1990; Galdos Rodríguez 2000). Drawing from passing references in some documents, Galdos Rodríguez (1990b) argued for a Copoata ethnic group, perhaps Pukina speaking, populating the entire Paucarpata-Sabandía-Chiguata stretch.

Regardless of the political status of these societies, there is evidence for Pukina language ties with the Altiplano, which in turn points to a legacy of linkages with the Tiyawanaku state or confederation (Cerrón-Palomino 2010). These sources cite not only the profusion of local toponyms ending with Pukina suffixes, as noted above, but also scattered ecclesiastical documents referring to the need to translate the Christian gospel into Pukina (Galdos Rodríguez 2000).

> It's been noted, in addition, that on such a late date as the first half of the seventeenth century (1638), the constitutions of the bishop of Arequipa's first synod ordered that "the priests of the villages of Arumas (Carumas), Ilabaya and Locumba who are those that best know the language shall translate a catechism and diverse prayers in that language." In other words, in those dates, the basic texts of evangelizing remained untranslated into puquina. (Barriga 1952, 142, as translated in Bouysse-Cassagne 2010, 285)

Below we will examine the importance of these ties for the emergence of Chapi worship, now central to folk practice of regional identity.

II. THE SPANISH COLONIAL PERIOD

Relocating from the insalubrious conditions on the coast at Camaná, so the conventional story goes, Francisco Pizarro and the first Spaniards founded the city of Arequipa on 15 August 1540. In the valley of Arequipa they encountered an ethnically mixed population of about ten thousand people (Málaga Medina 1975), apparently still recovering from the "1454" eruption of Putina. Despite the official narrative, transfer from the coast up to the Arequipa basin in the late 1530s was more probably predicated on a desire for better access to the adjacent highlands, whose geography and demography were quickly coming into focus for the Spanish, and for control of the larger labor force they found, which Pizarro and his men divided among themselves into *encomiendas*.

With its Pacific access, abundant local resources, and delightful climate, Arequipa soon emerged as a key Spanish administrative, commercial, and transportation hub in the developing colonial political and economic circuits that centered on mining in the highlands, both nearby (e.g., in Cailloma) and in more distant parts of Cuzco, Puno, and Charcas/Upper Peru (that is, in Potosí, in present-day Bolivia). The fertile valley oasis of Arequipa quickly came to feature private holdings of urban Spaniards as well as subsistence-focused households, some still organized into indigenous communities, supplying both urban households and local markets. But importantly, the wealth of the Spanish city throughout the colonial period came mainly from commerce, administrative posts, and the export of wine and brandy from estates in lower, hotter coastal valleys like Siguas, Majes, and especially Vítor, Tambo, and Moquegua (Davies 1984). Their small campiña properties were managed by relatives or poorer Spanish *mayordomos*, rented out for small but secure incomes, or still held by descendants of Indians.

Consequently, the Arequipa basin was somewhat cocooned from the direct force of Spanish colonial land-tenure institutions. The peasant population of the valley thus experienced neither wholesale displacement nor much development of indigenous community organization tied to labor on adjacent haciendas—the familiar hacienda-community complex broadly characteristic of the central Andes and highland tropical America generally. While the Spanish appropriated the best lands in the valley, the concentration of lands in fewer larger holdings was hindered by partible inheritance, urban jobs, and shortage of labor from Indian demographic collapse that was exacerbated by the exodus of many

Indians, especially after the 1582 earthquake (as well as the subsequent 1600 eruption of Huaynaputina volcano), when "many colonists were leaving for their home communities" (Galdos Rodríguez 1990a, 252). With *mitmaq* populations apparently largely gone, by 1587 indigenous communal lands were already scarce in the campiña away from Characato, at least near the city (Galdos Rodríguez 2000).

Within a century of conquest, cultivation in much of the campiña had shifted from the characteristic suite of midelevation Andean grains, tubers, and other cultivars to wheat as well as maize and many nonindigenous vegetables and fruits. Wheat was primarily confined to the campiña proper; unlike Lima, Arequipa was by and large self-sufficient in grains (Wibel 1975, 64) throughout the colonial period. Locals continued cultivating maize in the mostly narrow valleys of the arid west slope at midelevations throughout the bishopric (later intendancy), and given these cultural continuities it is not surprising that most of the maize seems to have gone into the production of *chicha* (Galdos Rodríguez 1990a, 254), which became a staple of rural life; there were three thousand *chicherías* in the region by the latter eighteenth century (Travada y Córdoba [1752] 1996; Galdos Rodríguez 1990a, 255).

As in northern Argentina and Cochabamba, alfalfa was raised to feed the vast numbers of mules for the caravans that plied the mountain vastness of the central Andes supplying the towns and mines in highland Arequipa, such as Cailloma and Orqopampa, and in Charcas/Upper Peru, especially Potosí. Since Potosí, Huancavelica, and other mines were the main motor of the colonial economy, with the hacienda-community system its lateral support system (Wolf 1983, 141–149), most food had to be imported to such high-elevation mining centers for political, economic, and ecological reasons. Muleteers emerged as key actors linking disparate nodes in this circuitry; below I examine their part in Candelaria devotion and their early construction of and continuing role in the stitching together of an imagined community of Arequipa.

From earliest postconquest times, then, local developments in the central Andes have been linked to wider developments in north Atlantic civilization. Politically, the 1570s *visitas* of Viceroy Francisco de Toledo tightened imperial control and restructured Kuntisuyu (Galdos Rodríguez 1985, 1990a, 240), both reinforcing and extending the Audiencia of Arequipa far south toward the Atacama in order to control ports for the export of bullion north along the Pacific coast to Panama.

"Arequipa," we learned above, meant the west slope and entire long coastline from Acarí to the Atacama Desert—the "other side of the mountain(s)," pointing to a surprisingly stable political and economic geography recognized administratively by successive Tiyawanaku, Colla, Lupaqa, Inka, and Spanish polities. Up to the latter nineteenth century this was the space Arequipeños rightfully considered theirs; as we will learn, Moquegua, Tacna, Arica, and Tarapacá were administratively separated or lost later, in the run up to, during, or in the wake of the early 1880s War of the Pacific.

From an imperial point of view, then, the Arequipa region (intendancy, finally) and the city itself were basically about administrative control of port-related mining traffic. Toledo had early on shifted the official port for Upper Peru from Quilca south to Arica (both part of "Arequipa"), since technological developments had led Potosí mining to really pick up in the 1570s and Arica was a much more direct route from there to the sea lanes. The Audiencia of Charcas (Upper Peru) was basically Inka Collasuyo plus much of unexplored tribal southeastern Peru, with its capital in La Plata (now Sucre).

Though local jurisdictions were nested within this overall imperial framework, itself drawing from Inka administrative units as we have begun to see, closer examination reveals important contours that frame our understanding of local cultural continuities linked to veneration of the Virgen de la Candelaria (including Chapi), explored next.

Viceroy Toledo had created seven corregimientos—administrative units that included thirty-five *repartimientos* (labor grants revised from the earlier *encomienda* system) and seventy-three *reducciones* or *pueblos de indios*) (resettled, concentrated Indian settlements)—in the 1560s–1570s under the jurisdiction of the city of Arequipa, extending across a vast stretch of Pacific South America from Acarí south to the Atacama:

1. Arequipa, capital Arequipa, with its repartimientos of Tiabaya, La Chimba, and Paucarpata

2. Characato y Vítor, capital Characato, with its *repartimientos* of Chiriguata (Chiguata) and Characato

3. Camaná (carved out from Characato y Vítor in 1565), capital Camaná, with Majes, Quilca, Ocoña, Caravelí y Atico, Molleguaca, Acarí, and Atiquipa

4. Condesuyos ("Aruni," perhaps divided into upper and lower halves), capital Chuquibamba, with Achamarca, Chilpacas, Arones,

Chachas y Ucuchachas, Pampacolca, Chuquibamba, Andagua, Machaguay, Viraco, and Achanguillo Yayanque

5. Collaguas, with upper (Yanque-Collaguas) and lower halves (Laricollaguas [Recollaguas] and Cabanaconde)

6. Ubinas (Colesuyo/Moquegua), capital Ubinas, with Ubinas, Carumas, Puquina, Cochuna, and Pocsi (see below)

7. Arica y Tarapacá, capital Arica, with Ilo e Ite, Hilabaya, Tacna, Lluta y Arica, Pica y Loa, and Tarapacá. (Málaga Medina 1975)

Several of these early corregimiento (later *partido*) boundaries in this vast "greater Arequipa" are of particular relevance to our interests, as they inform the broadly popular devotion to the Virgen de la Candelaria that virtually defines membership in regional society. While the Corregimiento of Characato y Vítor was officially created on 5 September 1565 to administer the native population of the Arequipa basin and adjacent valleys—the campiña and nearby midelevation valleys including Chiguata, Yumina, Paucarpata, Socabaya, and the Siguas, Vítor, and lower Tambo valleys (Málaga Medina 1990)—Characato had been established in 1541 as the capital of this space and was the nodal point in a commercial circuit linking coastal valleys with the highlands.

In chapter 6 I analyze the close association of the Virgen de la Candelaria with Characato—central to the coalescing of regional identity around local Marian pilgrimage. Here I describe the relationship between the early-colonial political developments in the Moquegua area with the eruption of Huaynaputina volcano—key developments leading to the establishment of the regionally significant pilgrimage site of Chapi.

The Corregimiento of Ubinas, established on 2 August 1565, comprised the *repartimientos* of Pocsi, Puquina, Omate, Quinistacas, Carumas, and Ubinas; the creation of this corregimiento began the sundering of west-slope political unity with the Altiplano. In 1575 Ubinas was extended to include the *encomienda* of Cochuna (which included Escapalaque, Samegua, and Tumilaca) in the valley of Moquegua, and Torata was transferred from Chucuito to Moquegua (Colesuyo).

Ubinas was renamed the Corregimiento of Ubinas and Moquegua in 1590, Ubinas having been extended to include Moquegua, as noted above. A curious overlapping ecclesiastical jurisdiction (Chucuito and

Arequipa) had persisted for several decades (Espinoza de la Borda 2003, 186–188), since for three decades Torata had been under the control of Chucuito, itself part of the Bishopric of La Paz, as well as the Corregimiento of Arica. This signals a certain Spanish imperial recognition of west-slope cultural ties stemming from former Lupaqa control of the area; Galdos Rodríguez (1990a, 242) speculated that Spanish authorities had by this early point become aware of a Puquina ethnic group which may also have included villagers in Locumba, Hilabaya, Ite, and Ilo wrongly assigned to the Corregimiento of Arica.

Regardless of the historical linguistic status of Pukina, the Ubinas Corregimiento encapsulated much of the heart of the district of Colesuyu. "Colesuyo" appears to refer to a Lupaqa-era or perhaps some earlier administrative district, in the process of being incorporated by the Inka into Collasuyu (Cañedo-Argüelles 1993; Galdos Rodríguez 1987, 202–211) but surviving as a distinct cultural community, roughly coincident with modern Moquegua and Tacna. Colesuyu may originally have included just the mid-Tambo region of Esquilache, Carumas, and Ubinas, or the name may derive from "Khurisuyu"—the other side (from La Chimba) in the valley of Arequipa—since the Spanish described their founding settlement of 1540 as lying in "Colesuyo" (Mostajo [1925] 1958, 64–68). Following Mostajo, Julien (2002) argues that the Inka had understood the distinction, so they assigned Colesuyu to highland Collasuyu, terminating Kuntisuyu in the valley of Arequipa (at least at this midelevation). Colesuyo, then, may have included territory farther north than the current Moquegua border, well into the valley of Arequipa, perhaps even to Camaná, as well as farther south into Arica and the Atacama (Rostworowski de Diez Canseco 1988).

Reflecting preconquest material and cultural altitudinal linkages, Indian leaders in Chucuito continued to press for jurisdiction over Colesuyu despite imperial efforts from Toledo forward to separate all the coastal areas from highland control to the jurisdiction of the city of Arequipa. Next we will learn that the Huaynaputina eruption of 1600, occurring in the very midst of these dismembering jurisdictional disputes between the *corregidores* (leaders of corregimientos) of Chucuito and Arequipa (Málaga Medina 1975), was tied in the popular mind with this imperial severing of Colesuyu unity. Devotion to the Candelaria at Churajón and later at Chapi may well derive more centrally than imagined from this underlying Lupaqa-centered, if not Colesuyu, ethnic unity between highland and coast.[17]

III. VIRGENES DE LA CANDELARIA:
CAYMA, COPACABANA, AND CHARACATO

Far from a detour, the thrust of this brief summary of preconquest and colonial society, polity, and culture in the Arequipa region has been to reveal the surprisingly deep, fundamentally Altiplano orientation of Arequipeño indigenous communities and to highlight the enduring legacy of cultural, jurisdictional, and perhaps linguistic ties and boundaries from these earlier periods that point to the unity of the southern Arequipa basin with the adjacent Altiplano and coast.[18] I now return to discuss how this Altiplano orientation became encysted in popular, emotional pilgrimage to the Virgin of Chapi—La Mamita—who has become the central symbol of Arequipeño identity.

By the time the Spanish arrived, waning trade and perhaps political ties with Lupaqa and/or Colla kingdoms, set in motion centuries earlier with the collapse of Tiyawanaku, had apparently rendered Churajón a Pukina-speaking enclave in the region. In any case, whatever west-slope, Altiplano-centered political unity existed in southwestern Peru was successively severed in the century after Spanish conquest. As we just learned, there was a certain Spanish imperial recognition of old Lupaqa claims to this area, especially in the roughly five decades from the 1540s to 1590, reflected in various jurisdictional disputes and adjustments described by Álvaro Espinoza de la Borda (2003, 185).

One of the very earliest colonial institutions imposed by the Spanish was of course the Catholic faith and its various practices and symbols, major elements of which were quite quickly adopted by locals, who unevenly merged new practices and beliefs with their own in a highly syncretic process. Early-colonial reorganization of the southwestern Peruvian space both entailed and relied on a unified discourse and practice centering on Mary. The galaxy of Marian apparitions and shrines that developed in the decades after conquest both reflected and cemented the region's Altiplano ties and perpetuated a space and a discourse of both accommodation and resistance.[19]

Arequipa has long been a center of Marian devotion in South America. As mother of Jesus, the "light of the world" (Matthew 5:14), Mary is sometimes represented as "La Candelaria"—the candleholder. Mary's presentation of the infant Jesus at the temple, by Jewish custom forty days after his birth, completed her ritual of postpartum purification (so she can also be named the Virgen de la Purificación). Because, as we Chris-

45

tians believe, she had brought the Light into the world, this act is symbolized by candles.[20] As the church calendar had solidified by about 300 CE, 2 February—forty days after 25 December—became the traditional date for Candlemas and for celebrating and worshiping La Candelaria.[21]

The Canary Islands were the last jumping-off point for Spaniards sailing to the New World; they wisely sought protection there from the Virgen de la Candelaria for the hazardous transatlantic journey ahead.[22] She came to the Andes with the conquerors (much as St. Patrick was carried to the United States and elsewhere by Irish immigrants). "Reverence for the Virgen . . . began to spread, particularly in the latter half of the sixteenth century. Churches were dedicated to her in native sacred spaces and she began to be substituted for, blended with, and understood as formerly Andean representatives of the powerful and the holy" (Hall 2004, 137–138).

Mary's close association with the Spanish was quickly recognized by Andeans generally and by the Anansaya at Copacabana in particular (Maccormack 1991; Hall 2004, 167). The best-known site of central Andean Candelaria worship—Copacabana—was dedicated to the Virgen de la Candelaria on 2 February 1583 (Vargas Ugarte 1956, 56–57). The Virgen de la Candelaria is now the patron saint of Bolivia; her shrine has deep roots in the Inka and especially Tiyawanaku pasts (Bauer and Stanish 2001; Salles-Reese 1997). A statue had been brought from Spain via Buenos Aires to the shores of Lake Titicaca; she was invoked to help villagers of Santa Ana de Copacabana deal with a series of devastating frosts in the early 1580s. Francisco Titu Yupanqui, the grandson of Huayna Cápac, carved an image of the virgin "which was almost instantly credited with several miracles" (Bauer and Stanish 2001, 59).

Though the Virgin of Copacabana is now the most famous of Marian images in the central Andes, she actually came to Arequipa before going to the Altiplano. Legend has it that just five years after the founding of Arequipa, about 1545, a group of Spaniards and Indians were moving cargo to Cuzco from Arequipa, including three statues of saints and La Candelaria. The first night they camped at a place called Lari in La Chimba, now the District of Cayma. The next morning, as they were loading the cargo, one of the trunks was so heavy they couldn't lift it. The Virgen de la Candelaria appeared to the Indians, who heard her say, "C'aiman, c'aiman" (Quechua imperative for "here," "in this place"). So they built a small chapel, and there she stayed as an object of local veneration (Málaga Núñez-Zeballos 2011, 35–36). By 1556 a friar was charged with evangelizing local Indians, and the district became known as "Cayma"; by the early 1600s the original site had become a local cemetery.[23]

Cayma seems therefore to be the first site of veneration of the Virgen de la Candelaria in the central Andes (only a few short years after her first South American veneration in Huanchaco, Trujillo, in early February 1537), predating Copacabana by several decades. The apparition of the Virgin in Cayma, unlike in Characato or Churajón, as we will see, was in association with a cemetery, not water. Given this very early date it is hard, therefore, not to suspect a linkage between Mary's appearance and locals' association of "Arequipa" with highland beliefs about death (see the analysis in chapter 6).[24]

La Candelaria de Cayma was venerated during the 1582 earthquake and has since been credited with many miracles (Málaga Núñez-Zeballos 1997)—especially when she stopped a plague (probably smallpox) in the city on 28 August 1604, St. Augustine's feast day. A chapel was built on the site of the current church, and the Universidad Nacional de San Agustín dates its founding from this act. She had been carried in procession, perhaps for the first time, down to the Chili River on the La Chimba side of the old bridge. The Virgen de la Concepción from San Francisco Church and the Virgen del Consuelo from La Merced Church were waiting for her across the river in the main plaza; as soon as she arrived at the bridge, the plague ended. The *ccalas* (white, Spanish, and/or wealthy; literally *desnudos*, "naked") (Basadre 1962, 2638; but see below) wanted to take her for their own, but she refused to cross the bridge.

Such stories of the Virgen de Cayma being brought out to intercede to stop disease, earthquakes, and volcanoes early established her authority. Similar stories, old and new, come from other parts of the Arequipa region. For example, "sometime" in the colonial period the Virgin appeared in Quilca in a cave, with documented recognition by the late 1700s. In 1760 an old resident who cared for the image in a small grotto told a visiting Arequipeño, who was staying on the coast for health reasons, that sometime earlier a bishop had been sailing and had sought protection from her, which she had provided. He built a small shrine for her on an altar stone of the Inka there. She continues to provide safety for area fishermen and sailors to this day (Málaga Núñez-Zeballos 2011, 41–42). She is taken out in procession to the local *lomas* to help it rain, but she is never to leave her sanctuary for fear of damage to the local people and the port.

The development of an entire galaxy of Marian (Candelaria) shrines in southwestern Peru thus points both to long-standing connections of

Arequipa with the Altiplano and to the cultural unity of this regional space. "The southern Titicaca zone, through the pilgrimage traffic that its Marian shrines acquired and generated, through the replication of the Copacabana icon elsewhere and through the determinate itineraries of its legendary founder and that of Cocharcas [Apurimac], its most famous scion—in these ways the zone became once again the religious fulcrum of the central Andes, the source and origin of an extensive sacred geography that consolidated the spatial structure of the colonial political economy" (Sallnow 1987, 72–73).

Both Cayma and Characato, emblematic districts for Arequipeño regionalist sentiment past and present, were central nodes in the network of Marian worship throughout the vast region of the Altiplano-tied coastal central Andes (greater "Arequipa"). Cayma itself was largely populated by Collaguas, to whom were added Indians from Chucuito in the 1565 Toledan reforms (Gutierrez 1997, 39). All images of the Virgin were produced by native artisans (Sallnow 1987, 71).

Like Cayma, Characato was also populated by Indians of Chucuito. Unlike Cayma, however, Characato lay on the Khurisuyu/Colesuyo side of the basin, with seemingly deeper ties to the Altiplano. Given the Altiplano connections, the friars charged with conversion eagerly introduced veneration of La Candelaria. Characato was the very early (1541) site of Spanish administrative control of the indigenous peoples in the region, the capital of the Corregimiento de Characato y Vítor. Characato was also a *curacazgo* (seat of imperially sanctioned indigenous leadership) and parish, made up of the current districts of Sabandía, Characato, Mollebaya, Socabaya, and Chiguata but originally the entire province outside the city. As we have seen, Characato, like Cayma, had strong pre- and postconquest Altiplano connections as well as strong preconquest ties with the Inka site of Yumina.

The Virgin appeared in Characato under somewhat different circumstances than in Cayma, however. One version relates that an image of the Virgin, also carved by Titu Yupanqui, was commissioned by Mercedarian monks and was brought to Arequipa in 1590 to be installed in the church at Characato. When it arrived, however, they considered it so poorly made and disfigured that they decided to store it away, and it stayed out of sight for a half century. In the early 1640s a monk went to check on the image, and when he opened the door a strong fragrance and light shown out. Drawing from Rubén Vargas Ugarte (1956), Sallnow continues with another version: "The image of this Virgin was apparently brought from Copacabana by an Indian pilgrim in 1590. On ar-

48

rival it was put to one side because of a defect. The priest commissioned a sculptor to correct it, but when it was brought out the blemish had miraculously disappeared" (Sallnow 1987, 69). Either version of this story almost exactly mirrors the story of the Virgen de Copacabana (Hall 2004). In any case, from Characato, very near the old pre-Hispanic cult center of Cerro Gordo and the Inka royal estate of Yumina, veneration of the Virgen de la Candelaria spread.[25] (I will analyze the circumstances of the Virgin's appearance in Characato in chapter 6.)

Thus, as early as 1590 a regional system of Marian worship came to define the greater Arequipeño social space—a space that was inhabited primarily by ordinary plebeian and rural Arequipeños and that was much bigger and more deeply anchored in indigenous culture than that imagined by modern Arequipeños or by the urban intellectuals of the 1890–1970 period discussed in chapter 4. Well into the twentieth century, Characato was the primary destination for pilgrims among these three centers, until the back-to-back earthquakes of 1958 and 1960 severely damaged the temple there, after which regional Candelaria pilgrimage shifted centrally to Chapi. Even before then, however, popular devotion to Chapi had been growing, and from about 1900 it became a key focus of church officials. These factors, along with improved transportation, have made Chapi central to the current Arequipeño pilgrimage system.

Before closing this chapter by returning to Chapi with a description and analysis of Mary's apparition and local veneration there, I briefly pause to examine the crucial role of muleteers in binding together a much larger, Altiplano-centered "Arequipa" region—one surprisingly coincident with the highland mining–centered economic space that urban merchants and political officials also imagined as their rightful hinterland.

IV. TRANSPORTATION CIRCUITS, PORTS, AND THE GALAXY OF MARIAN (CANDELARIA) WORSHIP

The whole syncretized system of pilgrimage, discourse, and belief centering on Candelaria worship spread rapidly, encouraged by priests of several orders but especially carried by *arrieros* (muleteers; fig. 2.4) along well-worn trade routes throughout the region (see Sallnow 1987). *Arrieros*, both Indians and mestizos, were the hard-working entrepreneurs who, by traveling across these spaces and frontiers, stitched together a vast central Andean region from Tucumán, Salta, and Jujuy to Arequipa

Los Arrieros y Chachani , Arequipa 1920

FIGURE 2.4

Arrieros near Chachani, 1920. Enlarged photo-poster on the wall of a traditional
picantería in Characato, July 2014. Used with permission of the owner.

and her ports, and from Huancavelica to Cuzco, eastern Puno, and Potosí, even Madre de Dios during the rubber era. *Arrieraje* could be relatively lucrative (Stern 1993, 161).

Arrieros were anchored in the peasant economy, generally livestock
communities raising either alpaca, as in Tarucani (Love 1988), or cattle,
as in Sabandía, working part-time in *arrieraje*. Many, such as my key
informants' father (see chapter 5), had amassed enough wealth as muleteers to move into the cattle business, roaming far and wide among
west-slope and Altiplano communities to buy up cattle for fattening and
sale. Many—for example, Juan Cuadros, in whose Sabandía house I lived
for over a year—converted wealth from the cattle business into campiña
landholdings.

While defending free trade has been a key, well-known element of
Arequipeño regionalism (Flores Galindo 1977), few appreciate how anchored it is in the culture of *arrieros* (and therefore how cross-class a
sentiment this is). Muleteers and drovers sought the Virgin's protection

as they transported goods across the vast, lonely landscapes of the central Andes from the earliest colonial times. The apogee of *arrieraje* came in the mid to late nineteenth century, when goods from Europe and all parts of the central Andes, and thousands of mules from Tucumán, were traded during the Feast of Pentecost (varying from early May to early June) at the annual fair in Vilque, in northern Puno (Basadre 1962, 585–586).

Arequipeños are still represented as *arrieros* in traditional highland dances, such as in the *lanlaco* dance of the Colca valley (Manrique 1986, 182), and in many Cuzco folk dances (Mendoza 2000), such as those at the feast of the Virgen del Carmen in Pisac (fig. 2.5).[26] Dancers there dress as Arequipeño muleteers, in very Spanish-looking makeup and dress (pink skin, long nose, horsehair moustache, and leather jacket and boots) and portray them as haughty and prideful.

Muleteers, the very sinews of colonial commerce, were among the

FIGURE 2.5

Dancers in Pisac impersonating Arequipeño muleteers at the feast of the Virgen del Carmen. From "Peru Festivals Calendar 2014/2015," The Only Peru Guide, http://theonlyperuguide.com/wp-content/uploads/2012/10/virgen-del-carmen -pisac-peru.jpg. Accessed 20 February 2017.

earliest and most faithful of Candelaria devotees and pilgrims. The circulatory lifeblood of the Arequipa region has been commercial transportation, and La Candelaria is closely associated with these transportation routes and nodes (Jorge Bedregal La Vera, pers. comm., 15 July 2014). With their fundamentally commercial orientation, Arequipeños—whether landowners exporting their wine and brandy from coastal valleys or the *arrieros* actually transporting such goods to the mining districts of Alto Peru—came to see themselves as a distinctive sort as they traveled across a broader, coherent central Andean cultural space variably marked by more recently created frontiers and imposed ecclesiastical and state boundaries.[27]

By the latter 1500s veneration of La Candelaria in the Arequipa basin was prominent at Cayma and Characato and had been introduced at Churajón (Chapi); thanks to both *arrieros* and priests intent on conversion, devotion spread to Yura and throughout greater Arequipa to virtually every settlement of the Altiplano and the coast, from the early-colonial port of Quilca through the Arequipa basin to the Colca and Tambo drainages (e.g., Torata), as well as further south through Moquegua, Tacna, Puno, Arica, and Tarapacá.[28]

Arequipa's strong trade ties with the Altiplano are also being revealed by recent archaeological research indicating that before the Spanish conquest there were four main roads connecting the Arequipa basin with the wider world beyond (Málaga Medina 1975; Cardona Rosas n.d.).[29] Seeking Mary's protection for the journeys ahead, *arrieros* helped develop veneration of Candelarias along all four routes in and out of the valley.

One road left the valley to the north via Cayma over the pass either at Cabrerías on the south side of Chachani (to the right behind the muleteers in fig. 2.4) or at Pampa de Arrieros on the north side (to the left of the muleteers), then across the Pampa de Cañaguas for Collaguas (the Colca valley). From there it continued on through La Pulpera and the mine at Cailloma toward Cuzco. The Cabrerías route was also the road to the slopes of Chachani for firewood and *ccapo*; we have examined above the history and importance of the Virgen de Cayma.

A second road left the valley to the east/northeast to Lake Titicaca and the Altiplano, via La Pampa de Miraflores, up the Río Socabaya/Andamayo to Chiguata and the Laguna Salinas, and on to western Puno (the Vilque trade fair was on this road), then turned south through Chucuito, La Paz, Potosí, and Chuquisaca and on to Humahuaca and points south. As the rubber trade grew at the turn of the twentieth century, *arrieros* trekked around the north of the lake through Huancané and on to Madre de Dios. "On their route they would encounter small piles of stones known as apachetas, as well as various rest stops among which the hot pepper and salt tambos stand out, two very important products in the Andean diet" (Galdos Rodríguez 1987).

The importance of Chiguata as a rest stop for both preconquest llama caravans and colonial-era muleteers carrying brandy, wine, oils, and other valley products en route to the Altiplano is also being revealed by recent archaeological work. It seems that the church in Chiguata was graced with a Candelaria Virgin, but since the eighteenth century she has been relegated to a side chapel; the main patron saint is an image of the Lord of the Holy Spirit.[30] Almost on par with the churches in the Colca valley, Chiguata's is one of the finest examples of colonial architecture remaining in the Arequipa valley proper outside the city itself. Salinas (now the District of San Juan de Tarucani) remains a center of both borax and salt collection as well as continued llama caravanning both down into the campiña itself and to the adjacent Tambo drainage (Love 1988).

A third route left the valley to the west, over the Puente Viejo (the site of the Inka suspension bridge) to Antiquilla, Challapampa, and Uchumayo toward the coastal valleys of Vítor, Siguas, Majes, and Ocoña. Congata, a hamlet in Uchumayo District, was populated by Collaguas and Yanahuaras in the sixteenth century, and the church at Uchumayo has a Candelaria (though it was merely a "simple replica," the chaplain at Characato told me in 2014). This was a principal route throughout the colonial period, given the importance of valley haciendas in the economic life of colonial Arequipa and of access to the port at Quilca, at the mouth of the Siguas River, and subsequently the port at Islay.

The fourth road, leading south out of Arequipa, left the city near Santa Marta (La Ranchería o La Palma), what is now Siglo Veinte Street—the old "Camino al Mar" to the Tambo valley via Characato from the sixteenth century. The nineteenth-century railroad line generally followed this route, in that the coast was reached via the lower Tambo valley (though the rail line left the valley via the lower Rio Chili at Uchumayo and then swung south across the La Joya and Clemesí pampas). The main road even today retraces part of that old mule-trade route, passing through Paucarpata, Sabandía, Characato, Mollebaya, and Yarabamba, then splitting into a route through Pocsi and Puquina to Omate on the rugged upper Tambo River, and another down the Chapi valley to the Quebrada de Linga on the lower Tambo River and the lower Moquegua valley. The spring at Chapi was a most welcome stop in the arid stony hills of the region. This road, out the most populated, southern end of the valley, passed not far from the central citadel of Churajón. The three *apachetas* along the pilgrimage route to Chapi that I noted earlier reflect ongoing Andean practice: "Along the way one encounters dispersed petroglyphs, and rest stops from different eras. During the Republic [i.e., the nineteenth century] merchants in shrimp and liquors frequently used this road" (Galdos Rodríguez 1987, 32–33).

Despite its inland location, then, Arequipa—a port (or ports) for highland centers on "the other side of the mountain(s)"—is perhaps better understood as a key coastal node in west-slope trade circuitry. Arequipa's long Pacific frontage has been and continues to be a primary factor in its economic orientation.

V. THE VIRGEN DE CHAPI

Devotion to La Virgen de (la Candelaria de) Chapi has steadily grown since her apparition to muleteers and local farmers in the colonial period. While Characato defined the community for most rural valley residents as noted, Chapi joined Cayma, Chiguata, and Quilca as key points for muleteers on the periphery of the valley.

What are the origins and nature of Chapi pilgrimage? Chapi may have been a hamlet as early as the 1570s, for it is named as an *anexo* of the *reducción* of Pocsi by Málaga Medina (1975, 78), though it is unclear whether the author is relying on documentary sources rather than merely supposing that the now-important site of Chapi was then in existence. While Chapi was clearly not important enough to attract much imperial notice until well into the seventeenth century, it was apparently part of the general system of villages and people under the control of the cacique of Puquina, who by 1570 had authority over Indian settlements from Yumina through Puquina to Omate and to Chule on the coast (see note 18 in this chapter).

The close proximity of Chapi to Churajón, to the Huaynaputina volcano, to Lupaqa colonies in the Tambo drainage, and to the southern road to the coast draws our attention to this otherwise-nondescript dry coastal valley. Two important early *curacazgos*—Pocsi and Puquina—lie very near Churajón. The ruins of Churajón, the largest Late Intermediate settlement in the Arequipa basin, as discussed above, lie on the edge of the Arequipa basin, not far from Huaynaputina, in the better-watered and more populated southern end of the Arequipa valley and what is now northern Moquegua.

Recent archaeological work is renewing interest in Churajón. We have already learned about the strong Altiplano orientation of Churajón, to which we can now add the strong ties of presumed Pukina speakers there and in the neighboring north side of the Tambo valley to island and lakeshore shrines managed by Pukina speakers in Capachica and Copacabana. Lupaqa lords in Chucuito had conspired with their Inka conquerors to take over these old, very sacred, and therefore extremely desirable lakeside shrines (Bouysse-Cassagne 2010). Thus Inka and Lupaqa agents added to already-extant Pukina ties among Churajón, Capachica (in Puno), and Copacabana—all of which quickly became interconnected points of intense Candelaria worship.

Though archival records indicate Candelaria worship at Churajón by 1609 (Málaga Núñez-Zeballos 1997, 62), earlier Spanish influence is evident in the reworked Late Horizon chapel at La Huaca, or Sahuaca, which dates from the last quarter of the 1500s (Szykulski et al. 2000; Galdos Rodríguez 2000, 202)—*beneath* the ashfall from Huaynaputina's 1600 eruption. As part of the Pocsi *doctrina*, Churajón pertained to the Corregimiento of Ubinas and Moquegua, which had been part of the Corregimiento of Chucuito. Borrowing the idea of La Candelaria from Characato, Cayma, and Copacabana, Jesuit priests from Moquegua had built a small shrine on top of the Inka structure, which in turn was built on top of an earlier structure—three layers of pre-Huaynaputina occupation of the principal administrative and religious portion of Churajón, corresponding to Bernedo Málaga's "Templo del Sol." Local pottery was found here and in all the *chullpa* burial sites, suggesting that local control continued throughout these different political phases.

The site appears to have been largely abandoned sometime before the explosion of the nearby Huaynaputina volcano in 1600, reflected in the relative scarcity of *encomienda* tribute records. But what caused people to abandon Churajón? There appears to be no single cause for this depopulation, but we can speculate that a number of factors combined before the eruption pushed an already-stressed population over the edge. While Spanish political reorganization of regional economic ties was important, Churajones could conceivably have responded as did other indigenous in the area (see Saignes 1985). General depopulation from the shock of conquest and diseases in the 1500s certainly also contributed to the abandonment, but, again, these were general processes. Perhaps the ethnic enclave idea has some additional merit; with the devastation from the eruption, Colla (Pukina) refugees returned to Altiplano home villages. (Perhaps there is some trace in lakeside church archival records?)

Lack of reliable water must also have played a role, since similar areas along the flanks of Pichu Pichu did not suffer such complete and permanent abandonment. Perhaps recurring drought simply undermined agriculture in such a marginal area. Perhaps seismic activity changed the hydrology, leading to widespread terrace abandonment. Perhaps labor conscription for the mines led to canal abandonment (Angel Taypicahuana, pers. comm., 15 July 2015). Borrowing from the Colca irrigation studies (Denevan 2001), we would surmise that people would have chosen to apply labor to nearer terraces, so terraced fields on higher, steeper slopes would be the first to be abandoned under these stresses. This appears to be what happened, at least in part, as Churajón farmers moved to better-watered valleys, from Polobaya to Puquina.

On 19 February 1600, Huaynaputina ("young Putina," that is, young Misti) erupted violently, spreading up to a meter of white ash over much of the adjacent area of southwestern Peru, northern Chile, and western Bolivia, severely damaging crops and livestock. Much of that massive ashfall can be seen in white plumes still draping barren hills in the region—for example, south from the city itself toward Cerro Verde or along the road past Puquina to Omate. Greater than Krakatoa, the eruption seems to have affected global weather the following year, contributing to, for example, bitter cold in Europe and famine in Russia in 1601 (Siebert, Simkin, and Kimberly 2010).

The eruption of Huaynaputina generated understandable terror and panic in the valley of Arequipa and throughout the region, including Copacabana itself on the shores of Lake Titicaca. Indians were ordered to come from the Colca valley, southern Cuzco, and elsewhere to help aid and rebuild, and various taxes were suspended for several years (Málaga Núñez-Zeballos 2002, 910). Indians still living in Paucarpata were transferred to Characato (Málaga Medina 1975, 60). Martín de Murúa visited a decade later and noted the terrible destruction wreaked by the eruption on Arequipa city, though he also noted the rapid recovery in the ensuing years because of the rich soils left by the ash. Guaman Poma, writing shortly after the eruption, depicted the city of Arequipa under a cloud of volcanic ash (fig. 2.6) and portrayed the damage as punishment from God.

Huaynaputina seems to have finished off whatever was left of the *señorío* of Churajón, since the site (or at least the central area) appears to have been abandoned by 1600 when eighty centimeters of ash fell on it

FIGURE 2.6
Guaman Poma, drawing of early 1600s Arequipa.
From Guaman Poma de Ayala [1615/1616] 1987, 1061.

(Szykulski et al. 2000). Again, though, Churajón seems to have fallen into the relative obscurity of a local *huaca* even before the Spanish arrived, since it escaped Guaman Poma's account of idols in Kuntisuyu;[31] though he prominently mentions Putina, he makes no reference to this local *huaca* in his descriptions of different aspects of the Arequipa region (Guaman Poma de Ayala [1615/1616] 1987, 264). Colonial documents do not give it much notice, whether earlier (the Toledo *visita* does not mention Churajón) or later (the site—perhaps already largely abandoned—receives only passing notice in the 1780s *visita* of Alvarez y Jiménez).

By their shared Pukina names, it is clear that locals connected Huaynaputina's eruption with Putina (Misti) and presumably with cultural memory of its eruption 150 years earlier. Since the mountain began rumbling soon after 2 February, their practice of Candelaria devotion would

57

almost certainly have been part of that connection. There had been Candelaria devotion not only at Churajón but also in the upper Tambo drainage itself as early as the 1560s, when La Candelaria de Yalagua was named as an *anexo* of the Repartimiento of Ubinas, the principal town in the region (Málaga Medina 1975, 75).

Parallel to these events in the city, the campiña, and Majes estates, with the volcano's tremendous explosion, nativist sentiment flared up in the Tambo valley of Moquegua. Various shamans urged locals to return to their roots and make traditional sacrifices to Pichinique (that is, Coa; see below) so that the volcano would cease its eruption (Motta Zamalloa 1985, 89–90; Málaga Núñez-Zeballos 2002, 908). The local farming population scattered to nearby areas such as Polobaya, Pocsi, Quequeña, and elsewhere in the basin and lower in the Tambo drainage, including the valley of Chapi.

> It was a punishment by God how the volcano erupted and fire, evil spirits and flame came out and a cloud of ash and covered the entire city and its region where many people died and all the vineyards, wells and plantings were lost. (Guaman Poma de Ayala [1615/1616] 1987, 1061)

The Virgen de Chapi story unfolds in this context. Multiple, overlapping narratives point to a deeply folk origin of Marian worship near and at Chapi, for there has been no officialized narrative reflecting control by a central authority. Along with early corregimiento divisions that built on preconquest jurisdictional boundaries, such narratives also point strongly to ethnic unity among locals in the broad stretch from the southern slopes of Pichu Pichu around south into the Tambo drainage.

The story I was told on my 1976 visit, similar to the version recounted by Eusebio Quiroz Paz Soldán and Alejandro Málaga Medina (1985, 15), is that some travelers, apparently muleteers, were resting one day in this dry valley when they looked up and saw an image of the Virgin on a nearby hill. They went to the spot, took the image, and decided to take her to Arequipa so as not to leave her in such a desolate place. But they were astonished when the image shouted, "Ch'aypi, ch'aypi" (Quechua imperative for "there," "in that place"; see the relation between "Cayma" and *"c'aiman"* mentioned above; Bustinza Menéndez, pers. comm., 4 July 2015). One of the travelers spoke Quechua and translated, but the others didn't pay attention to this and decided to continue. They looked to one side and found that a spring of water had suddenly appeared. The sky darkened and it began to rain volcanic ash, lasting for eight days (Quiroz and Málaga speculate that this might have happened in February 1600, with Huaynaputina's eruption). Whether or not the story points to some actual date(s), the significance is that the association with ash and the spring ties the apparition to volcanoes and water in general and to Huaynaputina in particular. Given the ashfall, the travelers decided to stay and enthrone the Virgin on the spot.

A syncretic belief system emerged, centering on locals' ongoing anxiety about the prominent natural hazards of this most volcanic of regions, particularly in finding sufficient water in an arid region to irrigate their crops. In a singularly original essay, Edmundo Motta Zamalloa (1985) argues for continuities among pre-Hispanic religious belief and the valley's prominent set of Candelaria sanctuaries, not only in Churajón/Chapi but also in Cayma and Characato. Whenever natural disaster threatened, farmers appealed to supernatural forces, whether Pichinique (Pukina), Pachamama (Aymara), or La Candelaria (Catholic).

> Thanks to Calancha, it's known that the inhabitants of Tiahuanaco adored a coiled snake. . . . I postulated that the god Titicaca, in snake form, had been the *coa* [god] of Pukina speakers on the basis of these references and the information from Calancha, who signaled "in Cuzco they call this evil serpent by the name of Chanco-Chaba, in Collao by the name Titicaca, and in the Andes by Antiviracocha (Calancha)," and that the "puquina colla" and the "uro colla" of Umasuyu adored the same lake god. (Bouysse-Cassagne 2010, 297)

It is hard not to think that many locals connected their ancestral Pukina (perhaps Aymara) cultural beliefs with such an unprecedented eruption, merging their mountain worship directly with Candelaria devotion in an area beginning to be evangelized by the Jesuit fathers from Moquegua. In particular, Motta argues for the existence of a pre-Inka cult centering on the god Con (that is, Coa), whose local name was Pichinique (suggesting some Pukina admixture with a local language and/or ethnic group). Con was represented by the serpent and was strongly associated with natural disasters, especially from water (including flash floods) and fire (especially volcanic fire). Earthquakes were said to be produced by the failure to properly propitiate this irritable god (Motta Zamalloa 1985, 14–15). The close association of snakes with water is apparent in the rock art of the Arequipa region (see Tacca Quispe 2010). Such village place-names as "Coalaque" and "Calacoa" in the mid–Tambo valley, very near Huaynaputina, as well as the name of the main pre-Hispanic irrigation canal in the city of Arequipa (Coa), point to locals' connection of Coa with water in this region and to their use of snakes in ritual (see Guaman Poma de Ayala [1615/1616] 1987, 277, 280).

The eruption of Huaynaputina, then, was seen by Guaman Poma, locals, and Catholic priests alike as the Virgin's (Coa's/Pichinique's) rebuke of Spaniards' sinful excesses. Father Bernardo de Torres wrote in 1657 about the number of shamans (*hechiceros y magos*) in the area of Huaynaputina (cited in Málaga Núñez-Zeballos 2002, 908). Paraphrasing Torres, Galdos Rodríguez (2000, 100) relates that

> Beelzebub entered the river and what a horrible serpent with an ugly human face spewed out a whole discourse emulating an apostle and urging them to pursue worship of that aborted figure that the natives call Pichinique, who reacted to the volcanic eruption "with barbarous ceremonies and with the sound of tambourines and flutes they gave themselves to drunkenness and all kinds of unseemliness and when they walked wrapped up in these abominations, the volcano stopped erupting."

The lack of priests who could speak Pukina meant that evangelization in this area occurred relatively late, so it is not hard to imagine that even by the time of the eruption in 1600, the inhabitants along the whole swath from Pichu Pichu through the town of Puquina into the upper Tambo drainage, and probably further south into present-day Tacna, persisted in speaking Pukina (or Aymara/Pukina). Some appear to have continued defending their ties to Pukina beliefs, and perhaps even directly their ties with Pukina-speaking communities like Capachica and Coata, on the shores of Titicaca very near modern Puno, and Copacabana (see Bouysse-Cassagne 2010, 288–289).

The close ethnic and linguistic ties between these peoples and the cult centers of Lake Titicaca correspond closely with the geography of the Candelaria cult—from Cobacabana to Cayma, Characato, and Chapi. Virgen de Chapi pilgrimages are thus a key legacy of this pan-regional, Pukina- and Lake Titicaca–tied pre-Hispanic cultural space (see the discussion of Colesuyu above), tied to worship of Coa, or Pichinique, the serpent—an indigenous appropriation of Mary. Locals noted Spaniards' invocation of Mary in regard to placating the volcanoes, and they presumably would have associated her with Coa/Pichinique. Coa was in turn associated not only with volcanoes but, as a fish or serpent, also with water.

Sallnow, following Deborah Poole (1982), notes the close association with water of the three principal Marian shrines in Arequipa (also true of Charcani; see below). While apparitions of the Virgin were closely associated with water both in Chapi and in Characato, this does not seem to be the case with Cayma, as I described above and analyze in chapter 6. "Mary was the natural successor to the emasculated pagan gods of the Andean landscape, in the eyes both of the natives and of the missionaries who cannily exploited their religious sensibilities" (Sallnow 1987, 71).

La Candelaria's central association with water is contained not only in such stories about Chapi but also in stories of her miraculous deeds at many sites throughout this cultural region. In Characato, for example, I was told that during a severe drought the Virgin was implored for help; apparently the main spring had stopped flowing because of some seismic shift. The Virgin was taken in procession to the spring, several kilometers up-valley out of town, and at the very moment in the Mass where the host was lifted in offering, the spring resumed flowing. That spring, the Ojo del Milagro, continues to flow to this day (and is very near the sacred hilltop spot of Cancahuani, scene of an annual procession during the Feast of the Cross). This story is repeated by Galdos Rodríguez (2000, 184), though he discounts an 1804 claim by Archdeacon Francisco Javier Echeverría that the large "Agua del Milagro" spring had newly appeared in 1690 as a miracle of the Virgen de la Candelaria (Galdos Rodríguez 1990b, 209).

Of course such local faith and practice, past and present, play out in larger fields. Bourbon reforms starting in the 1740s realigned the relationship between church and state and fostered a certain modernizing notion of the self as subject of the state. Gone was the old two-republic model of earlier colonial rule, with caste markers; *doctrinas de indios* run by regular clergy (that is, members of a religious order) came to be seen as sixteenth-century anachronisms. From an imperial vantage point, members of religious orders were instead better deployed along the periphery of empire (e.g., Amazonia or Central America) for missionizing, out of the way of the effective administration of colonies by direct agents of the state. Jesuit missions in Paraguay, launched originally from Arequipa, later became problematic in these shifting bureaucratic fields. Parishioners resisted the takeover of spiritual property by the state, and there was probably support if not involvement by friars in their resistance (for example, in Characato; see chapter 6). The fusion of religious and community identities strengthened as a result, and in resistance became tied to place and the polyvalence of Christian symbols—a locus of community memory, reinforced through pilgrimage.

In this context, in 1743 most remaining Churajones were forced to move down to the valley of Chapi, just a few kilometers away, carrying with them the image of the Virgin. There they built a little chapel to house her (this was about four kilometers down-valley from the current shrine). This suggests not only that Candelaria worship continued at Churajón for more than a century after the Huaynaputina eruption, but, again, that there was a direct tie between Churajón and Chapi.[32] People moved because the Spanish government had ordered the shifting of remaining irrigation waters from the extensive terracing of Churajón to the villages of Quequeña and Yarabamba, though it is not clear what motivated this decision: Was it a response to general depopulation and the presumed consequent abandonment of the higher-altitude terracing there? Was it to put down some resistance at Churajón? Was it in response to a disruption by an earthquake of the water flow for irrigation in the zone? Given the preceding discussion, the first situation seems most likely, as the others would have left some trace in the documentary record, which has been relatively well searched. In 1785 management of the tiny Chapi chapel was transferred to the Franciscans, since the Moquegua Jesuits who had originally evangelized there had been expelled in 1767.

Spreading devotion to the Virgen de Chapi eventually led to the development of other sites of Chapi veneration in the region. Chapi Chico, located in the district of Miraflores just south of central Arequipa city, was built in the twentieth century with popular support for those who could not travel all the way to the main site out in the desert valley in Chapi proper. Recall that Miraflores, the old Indian quarter tied to the parish of Santa Marta, was the "Indian parish" just outside the colonial urban core. Indian merchants and travelers congregated and stayed in *tambos* (way stations) there, as it lay on the sierra side of the city. During the conquest local Yarabaya had been pushed there from their homes in the area where Arequipa was founded (including San Lázaro). In La Ranchería, as it was called, a rich indigenous heritage developed, from cuisine to the informing of the Chapi Chico story itself (see Mostajo's 1904 story "Quimsa-Mocco," cited in Ballón Lozada 1999, 40–45). This area was originally called "Pampa de Perros"—Anuqara Pampa, which links to the original Aymara name for Misti (Anuqara, as discussed above and in note 4 in this chapter). The "official" history put out by the Hermandad (Brotherhood) of Chapi at the Chapi Chico church in Miraflores district of the city (*El Santuario de Chapi Chico*, n.d.) asserts that ordinary people of the region were the first to "venerate the sacred image of Mary, via advocation of the Virgin of the Purification or Virgin of Candlemas."

As exemplified by the Hermandad of Chapi, it was popular sentiment that led to the prominence of Candelaria Virgins throughout greater Arequipa. Popular devotion to La Candelaria contrasts with devotion to officially designated saints. Though by tradition patron saints were officially decided upon according to the date of founding of a village or entity, they were by no means fixed or static. For example, though the Virgen de la Asunción was promoted by Pizarro as the patron saint of Arequipa, given the city's official founding in 1540 on her day of 15 August, colonial Arequipa at one point had as many as three patron saints simultaneously (Motta Zamalloa 1985, 65). The *cabildo* (city council) had named Santa Marta their patron in 1555, later adding San Sebastián (1589), San Genaro (1600, in the wake of the Huaynaputina eruption), and even another in 1632. But by a papal bull of 1693, cities were allowed only one patron, so the *cabildo* selected Santa Marta as patron saint of Arequipa. Believed to have powers against earthquakes, Santa Marta had become the primary focus of devotion following the eruption of Huaynaputina in February 1600 and after other earthquakes throughout the seventeenth century.

Pilgrimage to Chapi by other than locals spread and appears to have begun not long after she moved down-valley. In 1798 some Chapi residents went to the parish in Pocsi (whose jurisdiction covered Quequeña, Yarabamba, Sogay, and Polobaya, among others), "soliciting that the festivities to the Virgen de la Candelaria be suspended; as pretext, they alluded that the visitors were committing many excesses and disorder, and not showing the fervor that the celebration warranted" (Galdos Rodríguez 2000). This was apparently in response to complaints from local farmers that the numerous pilgrims were turning the event into a drunken, quite pagan celebration, as well as damaging their crops with their animals. What makes this case notable is that the appeal came from local residents, not higher church officials who had long campaigned against profane dancing and dress in various religious processions and celebrations, both in the city and in outlying villages (e.g., Chambers 1999, 129).

It is hard to know how to interpret this 1798 event. There are suggestive connections between this situation of drunken disorder and the intentions of the Virgin herself, on the one hand, and the shamanic activity reported by Father Torres (1657) around the 1600 eruption of Huaynaputina and the Virgin's intentions then, on the other. Alternatively, a renewed claim of Marian connection to this place erupted (with symbolic ties to the original apparition), suggesting that, like the Characatos in 1640 (see chapter 6), locals sensed a new threat to their livelihoods and appealed to the (symbolic) power of the Virgin. In response to the petition from the local Chapi farmers, the parish priest of Pocsi, Juan de Diós Tamayo, decided to transfer the image of the Virgin to Sogay, whose people wanted her to calm things down. But again, the party got as far as one *legua* (4–5.5 kilometers), up to the base of a steep ascent (La Escalarilla, as described earlier), where they rested. As they were preparing to resume the journey, they were hit with "a rain of sand or a strong wind that blew a fine, white sand with such force that it hit people painfully, especially in the face" (*El Santuario de Chapi Chico* n.d., 4)— again evoking the Huaynaputina eruption. They decided to make a go for it, but as they tried to lift the Virgin, they found her stuck fast to the ground. Quiroz and Málaga (1985, 16) mention another version, that, according to Bernedo Málaga, the image of the Virgin "weighed 'as much as a mountain' being impossible to lift." They built a similar small chapel here, and this has become the location of the shrine we know today, up-river a few kilometers from the original spring location I had walked to with my fellow pilgrims.

Clearly, local people interpreted this as the Virgin expressing her wish to remain with them in this place, which is where the Chapi sanctuary has been located ever since. Pilgrimages "by simple peasants" to Chapi and devotion to the Virgin there increased in the early 1800s as word of this new Chapi miracle spread widely among rural campiña smallholders and the urban lower class.[33]

The ecclesiastical establishment in Arequipa was somewhat slow to recognize Chapi worship and bring it under its jurisdiction, pointing to the peripheral, rural social origins of Chapi devotion; until the beginning of the twentieth century, church authorities generally ignored popular Chapi worship, focusing instead on other saints, including Santa Marta. Despite the "official" status of the Virgen de la Asunción and her location in the main cathedral at the center of Arequipa city, the focus of pilgrimage in Arequipa for popular classes has always been the Virgen de la Candelaria—first in Cayma and Characato, more recently in Chapi and Charcani (see below)—a situation that church leaders finally recognized.

That said, the Altiplano links dormant in this galaxy of Marian shrines from the sixteenth and seventeenth centuries, embodying a sense of a much vaster Arequipa, were by the twentieth century largely forgotten, overtaken by wider events explored below and mixed with an accretion

FIGURE 2.7
La Virgen de la Candelaria de Chapi—La Mamita de Arequipa. From
http://rafaelescobarperu.blogspot.com/2014/04/la-virgen-de-chapi-arequipa.html,
accessed 27 March 2017.

of other images of the Virgen (del Rosario, del Carmen, etc.), other saints, and of course Jesus Christ himself. Signs honoring the Virgen de Copacabana are increasingly common in urban Arequipa, presumably among Puno immigrants but also among locals (e.g., one displayed by a Characato woman I met at the Cancahuani Feast of the Cross on 5 July 2015).

Lying as it does on the periphery of the valley—a geographic space now conventionally (as well as politically) defined as Arequipa—the pilgrimage to Chapi is of considerable importance in having helped define a regional identity. Each year upwards of two hundred thousand pilgrims make the journey from center to periphery and back. While earlier Candelarias had represented plebeian and rural Arequipa, as we have seen, by the middle of the twentieth century the Virgin of Chapi had, with ecclesiastical promotion, come to symbolize all Arequipa—"La Mamita de Arequipa" (fig. 2.7).

The Virgen de Chapi is distinguished from other Candelaria Virgins, such as those of Cayma, Characato, Puno, or, most notably, Copacabana, by carrying a basket in her right hand and wearing a hat typical of valley farmers. These iconic elements aside, she can always be dressed differently according to the occasion (for example, in Colca valley dress). That said, the belief that the Virgins of Cayma, Characato, Chapi, and Charcani are all "sisters" is of course not doctrinal and is popular, not ecclesiastical, in origin.

The overarching unity resulting from general Catholic appropriation of such sacred sites as Churajón was augmented by the unity derived both from specific religious orders and from early-colonial jurisdictions that often mirrored native political and ethnic boundaries. We have seen, for example, that it was the Jesuits from Moquegua who established a chapel at Churajón. Augustinians, as noted, controlled the most important shrine of Copacabana (Bauer and Stanish 2001, 14) and had brought the Señorita de la Candelaria, or de la Purificación, to Titicaca in the 1580s. In Arequipa, the Dominicans had evangelizing responsibility in Cayma, Yanahuara, Paucarpata, and Chiguata, while the Mercedarians had Characato, Omate, Moquegua, Pocsi, and Polobaya (which included Chapi).

At Chapi several chapels have been built over the years, each one larger than the last, to accommodate the growing numbers of pilgrims. Miracles continued to spread, again in association with water; for example, a spring miraculously appeared in 1897 at the building site, due to the faithful prayer of one of the sillar workers, tradition says, which aided the workers building the new temple (Quiroz Paz Soldán and Málaga Medina 1985, 11). Another of the workers was cured of eye problems when he washed his eyes in the water from the spring. This temple—now known as the "old church"—was completed in 1898. A fire in 1922 severely damaged this structure, and local committees dedicated themselves to raising funds to build a new one.

With Mary's immense popularity and symbolic value among the people established, growing recognition of the power of the Chapi Virgin by the official church hierarchy in Arequipa finally followed. Manuel Segundo Ballón, archbishop of Arequipa, made a pastoral visit to Chapi about 1900—the first visit to Chapi by an archbishop. (Chapi lay in the parish of Quequeña, which had been transferred from Pocsi in 1901.) The September pilgrimage date (when I first visited) had been established in 1907 by the parish priest of Pocsi. Growing popular devotion further attracted the attention of ecclesiastical authorities; again in 1910 Chapi was visited by a high church official, Monseigneur Mariano Holguín (the new availability of automobiles certainly made these visits more feasible). During these visits authorities also visited the Chapi sanctuary down-valley, "issuing precise instructions to promote devotion to the Virgin." In 1906 a large group of high school and university students was organized by elder (*presbítero*) Antero Gutiérrez Ballón to make the pilgrimage.

Popular devotion continued to grow, though exactly when the primary locus of control of Chapi worship sites passed from local *cofradías* (brotherhoods) to official purview is both variable and hard to determine. On 20 October 1952 the archbishop of Arequipa, José Leonardo Rodríguez Ballón, elevated the Chapi sanctuary to the category of *capellanía* (chaplaincy), officially separating Chapi from the surrounding villages and parishes to which it had been attached since its founding and bringing Chapi devotion firmly within the church's institutional jurisdiction.

Other pilgrimage dates have been officially added in the twentieth century—1 May, 8 September (as in Cocharcas in the Apurimac region), and 8 December. More than simply signaling the association between Chapi pilgrimages and official Catholic calendric ritual, the addition of these days as permissible for pilgrimage represented a jurisdictional extension by the central church ecclesiastical bureaucracy over deep and widespread popular devotion, which had for centuries been at the margins of official purview.[34]

Despite locals' opposition to taking the Virgin from her chapel, for fear of negative consequences—a common sentiment throughout the Andes—she has been removed with increasing frequency in recent decades, indicative of yet another important jurisdictional extension by the ecclesiastical bureaucracy. (The Virgen de Cayma has also traveled, but without apparent local opposition. For example, she was taken to the main cathedral in 1997 on the fiftieth anniversary of her coronation by President Bustamante y Rivero.) In 1985 La Mamita was flown by air force helicopter to Arequipa to meet Pope John Paul II on 2 February; she stayed nine days in the main cathedral. On this occasion La Mamita de Chapi was proclaimed "Reyna y Señora de Arequipa." Each of nine parishes in the region (though not Chapi Chico, curiously) cared for her on one of these days.

In the last two decades, especially since Pope John Paul II's more general public embrace of Marian worship and, on his 1985 visit to Arequipa, specifically of devotion to and his coronation of the Virgen de Chapi (see the YouTube video at https://www.youtube.com/watch?v=JpYpPeeJoy4, at 1:14), devotees have been increasingly willing to allow her to be taken from her shrine to various areas within the valley, including to other villages as well as the central cathedral. Though many sources claim that the Virgen de Chapi has been to Arequipa only once—in 1985—in fact she has made several visits. Indeed, many years ago (in 1890) the Virgin was also in Arequipa, apparently for some time, perhaps to raise funds during the 1887–1893 building campaign (Carpio Muñoz 1981–1983, 10).

She was present in the main cathedral for seven days in late 1983, carried in a police pickup truck in solemn procession from Chapi, visiting each village en route and staying some hours in each church. Some people along the route, especially in Polobaya, resisted her leaving and being carried to Arequipa. She entered Arequipa at the boundary of the Cercado District itself (at the corner of Castilla and Independencia Avenues), wearing a typical rural hat (*sombrero huachano*, which she is typically shown wearing in pictures; see, for example, fig. 2.7) rather than her crown. A great multitude accompanied her to the Plaza de Armas, where the mayor placed a Medal of the City on her. Afterward she was ferried by helicopter back to Pocsi, then carried back to Chapi in a special pickup truck accompanied by a caravan of devotees.[35]

The Virgen (de la Candelaria) de Chapi appeared yet again to local farmers in Cayma at Charcani Chico, where the Chili River first emerges from a narrow canyon in a rushing torrent at the head of cultivation in Chilina. Here, I was told by the local caretaker, "about seventy years ago" (in about 1940?) a couple of local Cayma farmers were trying to open a hole in the wall to get some water (the river was much higher then) when suddenly an image of the Virgen de Chapi appeared to them in a little cave, where they then built a little chapel. As devotion to her grew, improvements were made by the *hermandad* at the church in Carmen Alto (Cayma). Charcani Chico now draws over a hundred thousand people every 1 May; a hundred police officers are needed to maintain order. The rock wall at the site is covered with black smudges from all the candles left burning in niches on the wall (fig. 2.8; see also the YouTube video *Virgen de Chapi Charcani: Arequipa* at http://www.youtube.com /watch?v=sTYPYt8Y4FU).

Veneration of the Virgen de Chapi continues to intensify, and pilgrimage numbers continue to grow. In 1984 a group of devotees traveled to Chapi from Irrigación San Isidro, one of the new irrigation projects on the desert pampas north of the city, pleading to her for rain. (San Isidro, after whom the irrigation project was named, is the patron saint of *agricultores* [farmers].) This was near the height of the 1983–1984 drought related to the extreme Niño event of that period. In April 1997 an Arequipeña friend who works as a tour guide told me a story about the 1985 papal visit, which had come during that prolonged dry spell. People prayed for rain, and as soon as the air force helicopter lifted her off to return to Chapi it began to rain, continuing for much of the period from March through May, filling the region's reservoirs. "That virgin is very miraculous," she said.

68

FIGURE 2.8
Virgen de la Candelaria de Chapi de Charcani Chico. Photograph by the author.

Chapi Chico is central among these alternate sites, built in Miraflores for those who weren't able, for whatever reason, to travel to Chapi itself. I asked César Fuentes, head of the Chapi Chico Hermandad, how it was that the Virgen de Chapi came to symbolize Arequipa, when the Virgin of the Assumption—whose image rests in the main cathedral—is the "official" Virgin of Arequipa, Santa Marta notwithstanding. He said that it was because of the many miracles the Virgen de Chapi has performed over the years: expressing her wish to stay in Chapi when they tried to move her in 1798; not being damaged when the temple was demolished in the 1868 earthquake; causing it to rain in Arequipa on multiple occasions; and many smaller, personal healings and other miracles. The official Virgin "hasn't done anything like these" (pers. comm., 14 July 1997).

In sum, Candelaria worship in Arequipa is not merely a preconquest or colonial vestige but an ongoing folk Catholic, ecclesiastically encouraged practice anchored in regular pilgrimage to key sites where the Virgin has appeared to ordinary people in the valley. Such apparitions and practices have created a landscape of memory and shared community in the valley, symbolized by shared devotion to the same version of the Virgin, thereby anchoring the imagined community of Arequipa. The elevation of the Virgen de Chapi to regional prominence emerged first from popular devotion and then from its confluence with ecclesiastical interest in consolidating and strengthening the church and Catholic faith. She is a Candelaria who represents the broad mass of everyday Arequipeños, distinguished by carrying a basket in her right hand and, starting in 1983, by wearing the typical campiña sombrero, coincident with church leaders' stepped-up interest in Chapi adoration. That bureaucratic incorporation of Chapi was complete by the late twentieth century is symbolized by the fact that the first act of Javier del Río Alba, upon his installation as the current archbishop of Arequipa in 2006, was to make a pilgrimage to Chapi. In addition, on 2 May 2013 the celebration of the Virgen de Chapi was declared a Patrimonio Cultural de la Nacion, "for her tradition and contribution to the cultural identity of the Arequipeños" (Ticona and Palomino 2013).

This folk Catholic sentiment has long constituted a fertile substrate nourishing regionalist identity among a general public, particularly the popular classes in the city and the campiña. As we explore next, a more recent, progressive, anticlerical, politicized, and mestizo version of regional identity was invented out of these cultural materials, proffered by urban intellectuals at the turn of and into the early twentieth century during a period of profound economic and political strain. How the symbolic power of this regional community identity intersected and contested nineteenth- and twentieth-century literary representations of rural smallholders is the subject of our next two chapters. Starting in late colonial times, but primarily after independence, as we will see, average people, in the city and in the countryside, came to regard themselves as cultural citizens of an imagined regional community of Arequipa, the foundation on which twentieth-century cultural entrepreneurs constructed the "Independent Republic of Arequipa."

THREE

FROM COLONY TO
THE WAR OF THE PACIFIC

*Crises, Nation Building, and the
Development of Arequipeño Identity as Regional*

If devotion to the Virgen de la Candelaria already embedded participants in a large, Altiplano-linked imagined community of "Arequipa," then becoming a citizen in a post-independence collective subjectivity required a re- or co-embedding of people increasingly dislocated from local communities of place and politically severed into three states in an accelerating modernization process (see Domingues 2006). It is to these re-embedding and centralizing processes in postcolonial, postindependence Peru that we now turn.

My central concern in this chapter is with the cultural effects in Arequipa of the political and economic shifts emerging out of the late colonial period and independence from Spain, with how and why Arequipa's intensely regionalist culture has been so closely linked to the long, difficult process of nation building in postindependence Peru. While during the fifteen to twenty years after independence there was a real chance for regional political autonomy, built on preexisting Altiplano unity, larger and subsequent postindependence developments revealed many old as well as new political, economic, and cultural fracture lines and fields in the central Andes that overwhelmed ideas about some integrated southern highland–Altiplano autonomy.

Altiplano ties had long been faltering with the inability of Altiplano peoples to continue making political claims on former lower-elevation colonies after Inka, and especially during Spanish control. From a Lupaqa perspective, the first century of Spanish rule was a failing attempt to reassert shared cultural ties over colonists in the Tambo watershed. As we have learned, Colesuyu was left abandoned to fight on cultural rather than political grounds for an Altiplano-oriented region. Though this trajectory intersects my interests here, in the form of Candelaria worship at Chapi, the history of the idea of Colesuyu is a story still to be fully told, as noted above.

Arequipa's more overtly political regionalist tradition was, rather, set in motion by late-colonial imperial policies that brought about seemingly relentless shrinkage of the political and economic space that Arequipeños imagined was theirs to control. With independence and the failure of the Peru-Bolivia Confederation, once-optimistic regional sentiment turned increasingly anxious about continuing political instability and became largely hostile toward Lima-based political and economic centralization. Peru's national borders hardened, threatening free trade with the Altiplano. Matters sharpened four decades later with the 1879–1884 Chilean war and occupation, coming to a head in the several decades after that in recriminations, unresolved questions of constitutionality, and elusive national identity still burdened by colonial racial categories.

In this chapter my principal focus is on the legacy of colonial jurisdictions and policies in relation to established and emerging cultural frontiers in both defining the Arequipa region and informing ongoing debates about citizenship. (I take up the race, class, and gender aspects of these debates in chapters 4 and 5.) These debates informed struggles around the Peru-Bolivia Confederation as well as among regional caudillos and everyday Arequipeños alike in the volatile period leading up to the War of the Pacific and then in the several decades after it.

Though Arequipeño regionalism during the middle of the nineteenth century was most evident as a project of a liberal "white" elite in relation to nation building, it was founded on popular unity embodied and reproduced in pilgrimage, *arrieraje*, and local practices in the city and the valley. As I demonstrated in chapter 2, popular sectors strongly influenced the cultural content of regional identity in Arequipa—perhaps more than in any other part of Peru. Chambers (1999) has argued persuasively that with independence, regional identity fundamentally pivoted on a cultural shift from status (one's position in an institutionally determined field) to honor (personal habits of virtue recognized by one's peers), driven by elites' racialized and gendered concerns with crime and indecency and joined by plebeians' emphasis on their rightful citizenship in regional society based on honor from virtuous behavior.

Common interests emerged from the joint need to reestablish norms and control disorder in the chaos of the immediate post-Spanish period, not only in towns but also the countryside (e.g., banditry against muleteers; Flores Galindo 1977, 46). This cross-class effort became entwined with growing anticentralist fervor, as Limeño elites increasingly asserted and usurped control over the direction of the new state. Growing popular participation by urban middle and lower classes is evident in the long series of rebellions against central authority from 1780, especially in the caudillo period between independence and the war with Chile. Popular claims of cultural citizenship in the region drew on this experience and forced a symbolic and discursive shift in the latter nineteenth and early twentieth centuries—an unusual "browning" of regional identity, to which I will turn in chapter 4.

With the collapse of the Spanish order and in the midst of and resulting from the political tumult of the early-Republican period in Arequipa came diverse understandings of what the region and the country did and should consist of (see Knight 2005, 36). Since the Peru-Bolivia Confederation and the war with Chile constituted the most serious challenges to the nascent Peruvian state, debates over what "Peru" or "Arequipa" meant pivoted on these episodes in this area of the most prolonged border dispute in modern South America.

In the period from independence to the end of the nineteenth century, we see contrasting economic trends between northern and southern Peru. In the north, economic activity quickly became centered on the emergence of an *exportador* (export-dependent) class based on coastal guano extraction (Bonilla 1974) and on plantation enclave agriculture—first cotton, then sugar. Market and labor ties with the interior were weak, so the bulk of the population there remained dependent on trade with Chile for access to basic foodstuffs (e.g., wheat). Highland production of basic foodstuffs and labor emigration to coastal plantations came after these external trade ties weakened in the 1880s.

The situation in the south was almost the opposite—its legacy of a different colonial political economy led to strong ties to mining in the highlands and other extraction in the interior and to international capital. As Mariátegui had noted (see chapter 1), the narrow coastal plain in southern Peru, sparsely populated to this day, did not permit the establishment of an extensive system of plantations like the one that emerged on the central and northern Peruvian coast, more or less continuous from Ica to Piura.[1]

The Arequipeño commercial elites came to focus not only on continued cotton-, grape-, and sugar-plantation agriculture in the Tambo, Vítor, and Majes (as well as Moquegua) valleys, but also on stepping up the export of primary materials from the interior—in succession quinine bark, hides, and, increasingly, sheep and alpaca wool—and the import of luxury goods from western Europe. The majority of Peru's commercial export and import traffic from independence through the nineteenth century was with Great Britain (Bonilla 1980), with a generally positive balance of trade for Peru, and there was strong British influence in Arequipa.

Cultural frontiers and political boundaries continued their dialectical relationship, each affecting the other, proxies for and outcomes of agents' interested jockeying for position in the newly reconfigured and intersecting fields emerging with independence. Just as the underlying Altiplano orientation of the colonial political economy was embodied in ongoing practices and predicated on pre-Hispanic cultural patterns predating even Tawantinsuyu, so the new postindependence states struggled to consolidate control over these territories, responding to and influencing people's loyalties and identities. Puno and Bolivia (the Altiplano), along with Cuzco, remained the primary focus of Arequipeño cultural, economic, and political interest, a geopolitical shatterbelt in which Arequipeños continued to see themselves as the primary brokers of trade in and out of this central Andean highland hinterland. For example, the superior court established in Arequipa in 1825 had jurisdiction not only over the provinces of the old elongated coastal intendancy, now the Department of Arequipa, but also over Puno (Chambers 1999, 146).

Arequipa's ties to its three southern coastal provinces—sparsely populated and of little economic value—were always much weaker than its ties to its highland interior. Therefore, while Arequipeños later certainly resented the loss of the Bolivian littoral and Peruvian Tarapacá to Chile after 1883, it was more for political and national than economic reasons. Tarapacá was distant and economically unimportant until the mid-nineteenth-century mining boom (see Núñez 1986), while Arica remained a competitor for Altiplano-coast commerce, especially to the new state of Bolivia. The later nineteenth- and twentieth-century wool trade renewed Arequipeño focus on its Altiplano hinterland, even as Arequipeños joined Peruvians elsewhere in fighting to retain Tacna and Arica as part of Peru, right through to 1929 and beyond.

Independence intensified the late-colonial political break between the northern and southern Altiplano—Puno and highland Bolivia having been split into separate viceroyalties. Competing claims on the Altiplano, with its adjacent littoral, fueled political and economic instability for much of the nineteenth century, along with continuing irredentist movements toward reuniting the northern and southern Altiplano. While such claims on this entire Altiplano space remain alive today, they are and were generally distant from Arequipeño interests, which were always fundamentally commercial, sometimes political, but, as we will see, never ethnic and certainly not "racial."[2]

Within these broader contexts, the Arequipa basin itself constitutes an early, rather isolated example in the south of the development of a local economy—a more or less valley-wide market in foodstuffs, indirectly tied to these wider commercial developments. Popular engagement with regionalist sentiment was therefore largely congruent with elite interest in continuing commercial development in southern Peru, since trade benefited just about everyone in the city and valley directly or indirectly, and elite wealth did not depend on campiña agricultural production. These broader forces conditioned the early erosion of racialized distinctions within regional society, since productive land was scarce and "Indian" legal claims on it were continually threatened. Campiña smallholding continued, since, given the vicissitudes of commercial prosperity in Arequipa, urban families across social classes had long since become predisposed to keeping one foot in their rural smallholdings, even as their members ventured to town and far and wide outside the valley in search of other livelihoods.

The earliest and still-central figures in regionalist discourse are Mariano Melgar, poet and independence martyr at a young age, and Juan Gualberto Valdivia—"el Deán" (the Dean)—long-lived critic of rigid, Lima-based authoritarian colonial institutions. Together they frame the major outlines birthing regionalist discourse: Melgar embodying its tragic-romantic passion and nostalgia; Valdivia, its anticentralist, populist, and iconoclastic, revolutionary tenor.

I. LATE-COLONIAL DEVELOPMENTS

Since the shrinkage of "Arequipa" as an imagined community is entangled in the seemingly unrelenting contraction of greater political and economic Arequipa, we must examine the complex political history and geography of the central Andes from the late-colonial period through the Confederation and its aftermath up through and after the war with Chile.

Though my streamlined review here of this evolving political geography adds little new knowledge of the era, it does accomplish three things: it synthesizes historical and geographic knowledge about this crucial transitional era in the central Andes in one place (versus Skuban 2007 and many other works on nineteenth-century Atacama border issues), it reveals important social contexts for the jockeying of Arequipeño with national and other regional elites, and it begins to help us understand how elite claims on this shifting space intersected both the emerging national bureaucratic field and popular understandings of the region and their demands for social inclusion. Most important, it sets the stage for my central purpose—examining how regional identity developed on political ground but then shifted to cultural terrain.

In an attempt to reassert royal control over the silver trade, plugging the hemorrhage of contraband silver south toward Buenos Aires, Bourbon King Charles III of Spain in 1776 elevated the Audiencia de Charcas, with its capital in La Plata (now Sucre), to the Viceroyalty of La Plata, with its capital at Buenos Aires. There was also significant contraband and official corruption in the various ports (e.g., Quilca) along the long Arequipa coast (Quiróz 2008, 75–76). In 1796 the Intendancy of Puno, formed from several partidos (Chucuito, Paucarcolla [Guancané or Puno], Lampa, Azángaro, and Carabaya) carved out of Cuzco and assigned to the Viceroyalty of La Plata in 1784, was reincorporated under pressure from the Cuzco Archbishopric back into the Viceroyalty of Peru by Viceroy Francisco Gil de Taboada.

Though the assignment was soon reversed, in initially assigning Puno to the new Upper Peru–based viceroyalty, elements of the royal administration seem to have recognized an outline of the cultural and linguistic unity of the entire Altiplano. These initial Bourbon reforms had threatened to sever Arequipa from official, if not de facto, control over its perceived highland hinterland, even as relaxation of central administrative control over trade opened up some commercial opportunities for Arequipeños. Fig. 3.1 illustrates the political-geographic situation, which was pretty much the map of Peru upon independence.

Though the mines of Upper Peru (as Charcas was increasingly called in the late-colonial period) had been the centerpieces of Spanish colonial economic interest in the central Andes, silver output was declining by the eighteenth century, which had pernicious effects on commercial interests in Arequipa (Wibel 1975, 60). Production had initially been high, but mining in Arequipa itself was always hampered by lack of labor and capital, and it became less worthwhile as the grade of ore declined. Both the Huantajaya silver mine in Tarapacá and the silver mine at Caylloma were in decline by the latter 1700s, ironically for the latter just as the name of the new partido changed from the old corregimiento's ethnic name "Collaguas" to "Caylloma"—the name of that mine itself (Manrique 1986, 168). Nevertheless, valuable actual and potential resources remained in Upper Peru, including copper, zinc, and tin as well as gold

FIGURE 3.1
Viceroyalty of Peru in 1810, showing the Intendancy of Arequipa.
From Pons Muzzo 1961, 47.

and silver (even lithium—who knew?), and a tug of war ensued over the littoral needed to gain access to shipping and world markets.

The main maritime route to Europe from western South America had been north along the coast to the Isthmus of Panama; it took at least three or four days to sail from Islay just to Lima. By the middle of the eighteenth century, technological developments in oceangoing sailing ships favored the faster, if more hazardous, route south around Cape Horn over the shorter but slower northward route. For example, Juan Pío de Tristán y Moscoso, the last viceroy before independence, had sailed around the cape when he left Arequipa in the early 1780s as a boy for education in Spain. His niece Flora Tristán likewise sailed from France around the cape in 1833–1834 on her brief visit to Arequipa. At the same time, Bourbon reforms had effectively demoted Arica as the main port of Charcas in favor of Buenos Aires—a not unfavorable development for Arequipeño merchants. Independence finally opened up Andean ports and markets to foreign, especially British, commercial interests (Bonilla 1980, 13).

By the 1780s, then, there was growing tectonic strain in this overall political and economic space. Intensification of imperial authority had provoked understandably mixed political (Fisher 2003, 43) and economic responses, including viceregal resentment in Lima and the Túpac Amaru rebellions in the Cuzco and La Paz highlands. In the midst of the Bourbon reforms, Arequipeños temporarily weighed the idea of incorporating themselves with Cuzco—a harbinger of growing yearnings for southern Peruvian autonomy (Mostajo's 1923 essay "Una Manifestación Regionalista de Arequipa y Centralistas de Lima, Dentro del Coloniaje," in Ballón Lozada 2000, 288–307). Despite such highland leanings, stronger Limeño and Spanish interests kept Arequipa administratively and customarily dependent on Lima (Galdos Rodríguez 2000, 267).[3]

Though there had been periods of tension throughout, Arequipeño opposition to Lima-based centralism was effectively birthed in 1780, though not on an ethnic basis like the almost simultaneous Cuzco and La Paz uprisings. Landholders' opposition to the tightening of imperial taxation, which had been increased with the Bourbon reforms, led that year to the "rebelión de los pasquines" (rebellion of the posters) (Galdos Rodríguez 1990a, 383–394; Wibel 1975, 16), a cross-class movement opposing the imposition of new taxes on agriculture. Shortly before the new taxes were set to be implemented, threatening but anonymous posters started showing up mysteriously each morning on the doors of churches and government buildings.[4]

The rebellion of Túpac Amaru in Cuzco later that very year catalyzed these growing fault lines (Walker 1999; Stavig 1999), adding to royalist fears of a general Indian uprising. Tupacamaristas reached the Colca valley, where the caudillo was warmly received (Manrique 1986, 165). Royal officials mistakenly conflated the poster rebellion in Arequipa with the Túpac Amaru movement in the highlands, since Indian participation in Arequipa's rioting suggested to them that a broader mass movement was developing. Both tellingly revealed the disconnect between Lima and the provinces, the relatively smaller social gap between the Spanish and the broad mixed-race and indigenous underclass in Arequipa, and a deep, cross-class, widespread resistance there to imperial authority and local ambivalence toward, even hatred of, peninsular officials.

Nevertheless, in the early 1790s, "there were more Spaniards in Arequipa than in Lima in both absolute numbers (39,587 to 24,557 inhabitants) and proportionally (twenty-nine vs. sixteen percent)" (Wibel 1975, 55). A 1794 census of Arequipa city showed continuing predominance of Spanish in the regional population even after more than 250 years of contact; of 23,900 people in the city proper, there were 15,700 Hispanos (66 percent), 1,500 Indios (6 percent), and 6,700 mestizos (28 percent) (Bustamante y Rivero [1947] 1996, 617). Spanish hegemony extended even to the countryside; in a total of 37,241 people in the province (the city and the surrounding campiña and valley villages to the coast) in 1796, there were 22,207 Españoles (60 percent), 5,929 Indios (16 percent), 4,908 mestizos (13 percent), 2,487 *castas libres* (free castes) (7 percent), 1,225 esclavos (slaves) (3 percent), 387 *religiosos* (people in religious orders, both men and women), and 5 *beatas* (uncloistered religious laywomen) (Zegarra Meneses 1973, 13).

Though we might note the clustering of "mestizos" in the city, on the ground "mestizo" meant an acculturated Indian (what we might now term *cholo*)—someone who claimed Spanish ancestry in order to be "white enough" to avoid a head tax. There was no shared mestizo identity at this time, even though this had already become an official colonial census category. Local Spanish officials and priests in Arequipa were reluctant to apply earlier colonial racial categories to the increasingly mixed-race population, for fear of stirring up trouble given the tax implications of being categorized as "Indian" (Chambers 2003).

Even though these census categories are somewhat porous and population estimates from the late-colonial and early-Republican periods are notoriously unreliable (Gootenberg 1991b), the strongly Spanish identity of Arequipa city is nevertheless clear. These data also probably undercount the underclasses, who would have had a strong interest in avoiding census authorities. (We will pick up the themes of status and honor in the next chapter.) In addition, we should note how small the population of the province (city and campiña) was, at least to our eyes—only some 37,000 people! Arequipa from independence to the War of the Pacific was by all accounts not much larger than it was in the 1790s—still a relatively small city and province of some 50,000–60,000 people (Gootenberg 1991b, 114, 126).

Agricultural land in the region, particularly the campiña, was generally fragmented into smallholdings, with very few large haciendas. Various religious orders owned some land, typically acquired when someone willed it or died intestate, but apart from the lands owned by the Jesuits (who were expelled in 1767), these did not amount to much. "There were

few large estates in any part of the Arequipa region. . . . Large estates occupied only a small part of the region's cultivated lands and represented
only a minor share of total agricultural production" (Wibel 1975, 92–93).
With but a handful of exceptions (e.g., the aristocratic Goyeneche family), partible inheritance among typically large families continually undermined the concentration of landholdings and therefore wealth, leading to Belaúnde's (1987, 13) later wry observation that Arequipeños were
"todos hidalgos como el Rey, dineros menos" (all gentlemen like the
king, except for money)—a largely Spanish population with aristocratic
pretensions but relatively lacking in wealth or formal titles (Wibel 1975,
14). This attitude stamped developing Arequipeño regional identity, particularly for elites.

A late-colonial upsurge in immigration, mostly by young men from
northern Spain and the Basque country, injected new life into commercial Arequipa (and into Chile). Many elite as well as common Arequipeños of our day have Basque and other northern-Spanish origins, reflected in such surnames as Belaúnde, López de Romaña, Goyeneche,
and Múñoz-Nájar, many dating from this period. Landowning families were eager to marry their daughters to successful Spanish immigrants; after independence, British as well as German and French immigrant mercantile agents and interests continued the pattern, replacing
something of a vacuum caused by the departure of some royalist Spanish
merchants (Basadre 1962, 185).

Intermarriage between creoles and *peninsulares* (Spaniards born
in Spain) and movement among professional careers all led to a quite
tightly integrated regional elite by the time of independence. "Perhaps
the most eloquent testimony of the complex integration of the leaders
of the Arequipa community is the repetition of the same family names
among those local notables who belonged to the most prestigious *cofradías*, owned large estates, were most active in commerce, became leading
priests and lawyers, or who served as *alcaldes* [mayors and councilmen]
and royal officials" (Wibel 1975, 196).

Such mixing was the case not only among elite families but also among
the middle and plebeian ranks, since although "illegitimate birth and a
mixed racial heritage were stigmas in colonial Arequipa, [they were] not
impossible obstacles to social and economic success" (Wibel 1975, 141).
Caste categories were more fluid in Arequipa than in most other Andean
cities (Chambers 1999), though colonial racial divisions lingered after independence: 11.7 percent of the population of the Cercado (Arequipa city
center) in 1827 was classified as "Indian" (Gootenberg 1991b, 138), little

changed from the 1790s, though this declined precipitously shortly thereafter as people of largely native ancestry confronted a situation of little
access to communal land and therefore chose to pass as "white" to avoid
the head tax (Chambers 2003).

In such a confined social space Spanish status distinctions were strong,
reflected in the importance of family names and honor and of contract-
ing appropriate marriages for children, especially daughters (Chambers
1999, 2003). The repeated intermarriage of Arequipa's landed elite reinforced their tight-knit community; Arequipeños took on multiple roles
as "hacendado, merchant, or official almost as desired" (Wibel 1975, 85),
evidencing an entrepreneurial, generalist survival strategy that continues
to mark regional culture.

The size of the field within which both elites and commoners moved
in the late-colonial and early-Republican periods must be kept in mind
as we drill down into local matters here and elsewhere. Many prominent
priests (e.g., Pedro Chávez de la Rosa) or scions of prominent Arequipeño families were born in Spain and/or had family ties and direct experience throughout the Spanish American colonies. The Moscoso family
is a better known but typical example: family members from Arequipa
pursued careers that led them to hold religious, civil, and military posts
in Spain as well as in what are now Chile, Argentina, and Bolivia (Wibel
1975, 103). But *arrieros* too traveled far and wide, so more than most Peruvians, Arequipeños across social strata thought of themselves as occupying a larger social space (fig. 2.5).

Some Arequipa landowners held sheep and cattle *estancias* (small
farms) in Puno, but these did not generate much wealth and were not
the major focus of their economic activity (Wibel 1975, 105–106) until (for
some) the rise of the wool trade in the late nineteenth and early twentieth centuries. With their focus primarily on commerce with Puno,
Cuzco, and the highland interior or on the exercise of bureaucratic positions, many elite families with land, such as the Goyeneche, preferred
to rent out their campiña parcels. Whether large (few) or small (many),
landholdings in the Arequipa valley were typically managed by agents
(*mayordomos*), often a son or other close relative, who in turn may have
rented these lands out to local residents. "Most mayordomos were described as Spaniards, but many were probably mestizos and might even
be slaves" (Wibel 1975, 106).

Market ties of campiña smallholders and muleteers strengthened according to the pace of commerce through, and therefore economic activity in, the city—which was somewhat improved in the last decades of

the colonial period but then drastically decreased during the decade before and in the decades after independence. The emergence of Arequipa
as the main commercial entrepôt of the south began with Cuzco's post-
indpendence decline (Flores Galindo 1977, 51) but did not consolidate
until the construction of the railroad and the growth of the wool trade
by the 1870s (explored below).

In sum, despite the relative unity and prosperity of the Arequipa regional elite, the mixed effects of the Bourbon reforms generally reinforced their constant fear of economic ruin, anxious as they were
about taxes and other state policies that threatened to undermine the
scarce profits to be made in this hostile terrain. Such anxiety reverberated among other social sectors, tied socially and economically to the
pace of commercial activity. Arequipa was one of the principal gateways
to the highlands; in consequence, the relatively small society of Arequipeños, backed by state policy, imagined themselves in control of a very
large space—the western littoral of the central Andes—with commercial
dominance of southern Peru (Cuzco and Puno) and most or all of Upper
Peru (now Bolivia, roughly). Threats to that control, real and perceived,
were looming.

II. POLITICAL BOUNDARIES
AND CULTURAL FRONTIERS

With scattered precursors in Arequipa, such as in Pampacolca, in northern Arequipa (priest Juan Pablo Vizcardo's 1792 "Letter to Spanish
Americans," urging rebellion, written while in he was exile in London),
or even protonationalist stirring among creole friars in the Colca valley (Marsilli 2005), independence uprisings began breaking out by 1810
in both northern and especially southern Spanish South America—in
Charcas (Bolivia), Paraguay, and Argentina as well as in the sympathetic
and economically linked southern coastal cities of Tacna and Arica.
Arequipeño general José Manuel de Goyeneche led royalist troops, many
of them Arequipeño *montoneros* (local irregulars drawn from the ranks
of urban plebeians and non-Indian rural smallholders), to put down an
insurrection in La Paz in 1811. In response to these uprisings, in 1810 the
viceroy of Peru had temporarily reincorporated into "loyal" Peru not
only Charcas but also much of Ecuador from La Plata and Nueva Granada, respectively—until such time as royal control in Buenos Aires was
restored, making "Peru" even larger than shown in fig. 3.1.

Mateo Pumacahua had served as a royalist military leader in the campaign against Túpac Amaru and again in the Goyeneche campaigns in Upper Peru. Though a loyal royalist, as prefect of the Audiencia of Cuzco he became upset that the progressive Spanish constitution of 1812 was not being applied in the colonies. He consequently led an uprising in late 1814 throughout southern Peru, attempting to apply those constitutional provisions by force. He attacked and occupied Arequipa for ten days in November 1814, but royalist forces chased him to Puno, where he was defeated; he was executed in Sicuani in 1815. The Arequipeño Pío Tristán was named president of the Audiencia of Cuzco in 1816.

The nature of Arequipeño involvement in the wars of independence is surprisingly little understood. Indigenous leaders and masses resisted Spanish rule yet maintained ambivalent relationships with creole leaders in Cuzco (Walker 1999); however, the consensus has been that Arequipeños were largely royalist until the last minute, when the Battle of Ayacucho made independence an unavoidable reality (Bonilla and Spalding 1972, 105). Subversive literature was being read, however (Arce Espinosa 2016). Refracting this through a social-class lens, Sarah Chambers (1999) discerned strong royalist leanings among the Arequipeño elite (particularly in leading families such as Tristán and Goyeneche), a revolutionary spirit in the middle class, and a careful neutrality among the rest of the population. These differences point to the nature of cultural citizenship and honor in regional society, themes that will occupy us ahead.

The late-colonial period was a time of deepening provincialism. Lima's creole elite remained rather royalist not out of deep Spanish sympathies but, rather, out of fear that a southern uprising might move the capital from Lima or, even worse, incite a general Indian uprising. Southern provincial creoles were more inclined to ally with the indigenous class to achieve their ends than were the socially more elite and distant Lima creoles.

> It seems clear, in fact, that the principal motive behind demands such as this [to move the capital from Lima to the interior, to either Cuzco or Puno] for the emancipation of southern Peru from the inefficient, expensive bureaucratic machine of Lima was economic dissatisfaction. . . . The economic life of the southern provinces was bound up essentially with agriculture, which clearly did not expand after 1784, and trade with Upper Peru, which, it was believed, could be restored to its former importance only by the reunification of the two Perus. (Fisher 1979, 239–240)

Despite these protonationalist yearnings, other than within the Confederation episode (discussed below), Arequipeño leaders made no political moves to consolidate any "Arequipa" larger than these colonial jurisdictions, thereby casting the die for a modern Arequipa without larger political ties to or claims on the Altiplano. Independence sentiment in Arequipa (and Cuzco) was more about separating from Lima than from Spain proper. It is somewhat ironic, then, that the formal declaration of independence by José de San Martín was made in Lima, rather than in the southern provinces that had more clearly fought for it.

Perhaps "pragmatic" and "opportunistic" better characterize Arequipeño ambivalence about the end of Spanish rule and the prospect of independence (Condori 2008), attitudes that not only are more understandable and were probably more widespread among Andeans, but were also less periodized than is typically acknowledged (Gootenberg 2004). At different times both royalist and independence forces received less support than expected from Arequipa. This indicated not just political ambivalence but also the generally reduced circumstances of the elites (merchants and *hacendados*) as well as of the general population—though all were temporarily overjoyed with the sudden influx of commerce in support of the now-Cuzco-based viceroyalty (Viceroy José de la Serna having fled Lima in 1821, moving the viceregal capital to Cuzco via Jauja)—a self-interested and perhaps fickle localism.

With the capture of de la Serna and the defeat of the Spanish military in 1824, as the highest-ranking military officer in the region, Tristán was named viceroy—a post he held for little more than a month before capitulating and managing an orderly transfer of powers to the independence authorities. With independence militarily consummated by 1825, Arequipa joined Peru, albeit with certain apprehension about the nature and direction of the new state—again, an ambivalence undoubtedly shared by people in other regions.

Ever pragmatic, many former royalist leaders in Arequipa changed loyalties as the new state emerged, but others fled to Spain. With the mission of orderly transfer accomplished, Tristán returned to Arequipa, where he had earlier been elected mayor (1808). Adopting republican ideals, Tristán was named prefect of the new Department of Arequipa (and later went on to be president of South Peru in 1838–1839 under the Confederation). Likewise, José Sebastián Goyeneche Barreda, the archbishop of Arequipa (and cousin of the royalist general José Manuel de Goyeneche), remained in Peru until 1859, well after independence, keeping his clerical post (eventually becoming archbishop in Lima) and maintaining his sumptuous residence near the main plaza in Arequipa as well as a country retreat in Sachaca—both now historical sites.

With some exceptions, independence led to the conversion of late-colonial intendancies into departments, partidos into provinces, and *curatos* into districts. During most of the colonial era, political Arequipa had corresponded to ecclesiastical Arequipa, the Bishopric of Arequipa having finally been separated from Cuzco in 1609. As we saw above, the Intendancy of Arequipa, created in 1784, continued the boundaries of the old obispado and audiencia (fig. 3.1) (Málaga Medina 1990). Though Arica pertained to the Intendancy of Arequipa, from 1680 the Corregidor de Arica had been under the authority of the Audiencia (later Intendancy, then Viceroyalty) of Charcas, setting the stage for the eventual separation of Arica from Arequipa and from Peru.

Independent Arequipa, now a department, included all seven late-colonial partidos (ex-corregimientos) of the intendancy. Over the course of the nineteenth and twentieth centuries, the four northern partido jurisdictions of Arequipa (Condesuyos de Arequipa, Camaná, Arequipa, and Collaguas [Cailloma]) were successively reorganized into the current eight provinces of the Department of Arequipa (La Unión, Condesuyos, Castilla, Caravelí, Camaná, Caylloma, Arequipa, and Islay), while the southern three partidos of the intendancy (Colesuyo, Arica, and Tarapacá) had a complex, chaotic evolution in the growing territorial disputes leading to and through the War of the Pacific and even after the 1929 accord.[5]

The relative geographic stability of the four northern sections of the colonial intendancy of Arequipa contrasts sharply with the volatility of the three southern sections. Boundary instability in the Atacama reflected imperial policy and the larger pulls toward emerging power centers and, with independence, the new polities of Chile, Bolivia, and Peru, far more than it reflected local interests in this suddenly strategic but sparsely populated, remote desert region. With independence, Colesuyo (Moquegua) and the old partidos to the south—Arica (including Tacna) and Tarapacá (including Iquique-Pisagua) became provinces of the Department of Arequipa, reproducing the outlines of the colonial intendancy. Tarapacá was sparsely populated, and until the nitrate boom it was of little economic interest; Arequipeño or Peruvian and Bolivian interest was focused on Arica, the better-populated, long-standing, and primary port for the Altiplano.

III. CONFEDERATION TO THE WAR OF THE PACIFIC

It is necessary to go into some detail on the confusing, at times frankly somewhat numbing, political and economic history of the Peru-Bolivia Confederation and the period to, through, and after the War of the Pacific—enough, anyway, to provide context for the central thrust of this chapter: Arequipeños' central role in regionalist jockeying and growing cross-class understanding of themselves as a culturally distinct region within the polities (i.e., "Peru") that emerged out of the colonial system.

The 1834 rebellion preceding the Peru-Bolivia Confederation, discussed below, inaugurated the more militant, heroic, antiauthoritarian, and anticentralist strand in Arequipeño regionalism so celebrated by later cultural entrepreneurs. The collapse of the Confederation a few years later effectively ended this early protonationalist effort for political autonomy, which then became a movement for regional autonomy within an emerging "Peru." The later debacle of the war with Chile further intensified regionalist loyalties and anticentralist sentiments.

A lot was at stake in the widespread felt need (at least among politically engaged members of postindependence society) to build some sort of Peruvian nation-state in a postcolonial vacuum of changing bureaucratic fields. Varying ideas about "Peru" circulated and informed the intensifying competition among regional elites for control of this new space, particularly farther into the nineteenth century as new resources were discovered in the Atacama Desert.

> The Spanish government had made little effort to carefully delimit the boundaries of its colonial possessions since most of them lay in remote and sparsely inhabited areas which were of minimal importance to the Crown. With the establishment of independent republics, boundary issues assumed a new importance as they now involved questions of territorial possession which did not exist when the entire area belonged to Spain. At the same time, the wars of independence generated or accentuated personal and regional jealousies and these rivalries hardened as states fought for political and economic advantage. Separatist sentiment in the south of Peru, and to a lesser degree in northern Bolivia and northern Chile, added another element of discord to an already inflammatory situation. (St. John 1994, 2)

While economic trends after independence seemed to be favoring the restoration of the old pre-Bourbonic unity of Charcas and Peru, overall demographic trends combined with political trends (described below) to work over the longer term against the south's desire for relative independence. Though it is hard to imagine that in 1828 the population of Lima (department) was scarcely larger than that of Arequipa—149,112 versus 136,812 (Basadre 1968, 167)—Lima's viceregal centrality continued. The south's share of total national population is estimated to have fallen, however, from about 52 percent in 1791 to about 40 percent in 1876.[6]

Upper Peru (Charcas) became independent in 1825, with Símón Bolívar himself declared its first president. Bolívar favored the new autonomous country (Bolivia), though as part of a great continental federation; a majority in the new country favored (re)incorporation into a greater (colonial-era) "Peru." Antonio José de Sucre, the hero of Ayacucho, became president when Bolívar left shortly after the creation of the country. Sucre, who like Bolívar favored an independent Bolivia, was in turn forced out in 1828 by the Peruvian army under Agustín Gamarra, who was intent on reincorporating Upper Peru into Peru.

Gamarra (born in Cuzco) and Andrés de Santa Cruz (born near La Paz but educated in Cuzco) were the two main actors in the events between independence in 1825 and the Peru-Bolivia Confederation of the latter 1830s. Both had risen through the ranks of first the Spanish royal army and then the independence army, largely via campaigns in what is now Peru. Though both considered themselves Spanish, they were proud of their maternal indigenous heritage. Both Gamarra and Santa Cruz agreed that Peru and Bolivia should be united, restoring the colonial unity that had prevailed for centuries, though they differed on whether Peru (Gamarra) or Bolivia (Santa Cruz) should be the center of gravity. Personal rivalry and these different views on Peru-Bolivia unity led the two into confrontation. From Colombia, Bolívar supported the alliance of Peru-Bolivia but pressed his case for a union of all Spanish-speaking South American countries as Gran Colombia, opposing a separate large, breakaway country of Peru-Bolivia.

Economic, social, and cultural relations between Peru and Bolivia were still relatively strong, at both elite and popular levels, so when the new Bolivian government deemed Cobija inferior to Arica as its principal port, in 1826 Peru offered Bolivia jurisdiction of the entire coastline south from the Sama River (18° south, about the latitude of Tacna city). This was later not ratified by the Peruvian congress. "While Bolivians continued to seek either the annexation of Arica or political union with Peru, Peruvian rejection of the 1826 pacts was a watershed event in the Atacama Desert dispute as it proved to be the only time the Peruvian government ever agreed to give Arica to Bolivia" (St. John 1994, 4).

Arequipeños were torn on the question of restoring formal union with Upper Peru. While independence for the south established long-sought Arequipeño autonomy from Lima, confederation threatened to put this new state under Bolivian authority. Federation or fusion of the south with Bolivia became matters of heated discussion (Quiroz Paz Soldán 1990, 443). While 1831 saw much movement toward cementing relations between Arequipa and Bolivia (ibid., 428–429), residents of the old southern partidos of Tacna, Arica, and Tarapacá were nevertheless mostly in favor of union with Bolivia and separation from "Peru"— marking their deep ties to the Altiplano and already cultural as well as economic distance from both Lima and a "greater Arequipa."

Arequipeños had supported the general Gamarra position—for a unified but Peru-centered country—even as they opposed Gamarra's continuing extralegal caudillismo, such as against Luis José de Orbegoso, who had been elected in 1833 to succeed him. In the 1834 civil war, this meant support of Orbegoso, despite the more obvious sympathies for Gamarra regarding union with Bolivia.[7]

As president of Bolivia, Santa Cruz had brought order to the new country through a series of administrative, constitutional, and financial reforms. Longing to restore the grand union of Peru and Bolivia, he saw his opening when Orbegoso was overthrown in a Lima-based coup by Felipe de Salaverry in February 1835. Gamarra, former president of Peru and long a proponent of unity, opposed former ally Santa Cruz's move, because he favored a single, greater Peru-based union. Santa Cruz and Orbegoso had joined forces, and war ensued between forces loyal to Santa Cruz and to Gamarra. Three key encounters in Arequipa defined the outcome—Uchumayo and Socabaya, fought in the Arequipa basin in February 1836, and a third, later naval battle off Islay. Victorious in Arequipa, Santa Cruz had Salaverry promptly executed there, without judicial process.

While supporting the reunification of Peru and Bolivia, most Arequipa leaders, such as clerics Francisco Xavier de Luna Pizarro and Valdivia, were initially suspicious of Santa Cruz, as his model both severed Peru into two states and placed both under Bolivian control. Though there was alarm over Santa Cruz's extralegal execution of Salaverry, the tide was shifting toward the Santa Cruz option, and both leaders and Arequipeños in general overcame their earlier reluctance to favor the establishment of a southern Peruvian state. After some initial hesitation, clerics Valdivia and Luna Pizarro strongly and publicly supported the Confederation of Peru and Bolivia—a symbiotic union of Peru, with its privileged economic position and access to the sea, and Bolivia, for its wealth of natural resources.

Again Arequipeños' pragmatism, legalism, and opportunism are apparent. From earlier defense of Oregoso as the constitutionally elected president of a unified Peru, despite implicit opposition to a confederation, Arequipa became the Peruvian region most strongly supporting the new Confederation with North Peru and Bolivia.

> The independence of the State of South Peru was received in Arequipa with joy and celebration, with festooned houses, cleaning of streets, night lighting and pealing of bells, during the day of April 2nd [1836]. Next day, an enormous crowd gathered at the main plaza and the plazas of San Francisco and Santa Marta, listening to the declaration of Independence to later erupt in enthusiastic cheers for South Peru. (Quiroz Paz Soldán 1990, 443)

With conflicting nationalist interests at play, regional leaders (including the father of Nicolás de Piérola) had been especially evident at the mid-1830s South Peru congress in Sicuani to organize the Confederation. Echoing the sorts of discussions among late-colonial administrators over how best to politically manage the large Altiplano, there was interest in incorporating the Department of La Paz into South Peru, but this did not materialize. There was also a failed move to separate the provinces of Moquegua, Tacna, and Tarapacá into a new Department of Santa Cruz (cracks in "greater Arequipa"). Though Lima had originally been proposed as the capital of the Confederation, delegates from Cuzco and Arequipa could not agree on the capital for the southern state. So important was the littoral, from an Altiplano (Bolivian) perspective, that Santa Cruz moved the new capital of the Confederation and of South Peru, apparently with the consent of the Sicuani congress, to Tacna shortly before the constitution took effect in May 1837.

Southern aspirations for political autonomy thus became fact with the creation of the Estado Sud-Peruano by the constituent assembly of Sicuani in March 1836, formed by the union of the departments of Arequipa, Ayacucho, Cuzco, and Puno. Bolivia formally merged with Peru in October to form by decree the Confederación Perú-Boliviana, and the constitution of the Confederation took effect the following May (1837). Orbegoso reluctantly became president of North Peru in August 1837.

 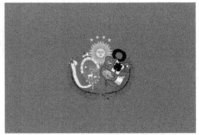

FIGURE 3.2

Flags of the Estado Sud-Peruano (left) and the Peru-Bolivia Confederation (right).
From "Republic of South Peru," Wikipedia, http://en.wikipedia.org/wiki/South
_Peru; "Peru-Bolivian Confederation," Wikipedia, http://en.wikipedia.org
/wiki/Peru-Bolivian_Confederation. Accessed 8 July 2013.

Ramón Herrera, followed by Arequipeño Juan Pío de Tristán, who had been the last Spanish viceroy, became the two presidents of South Peru, in 1837–1838 and 1838–1839, respectively. José Miguel Velasco became the only president of Bolivia, and Santa Cruz of the overall Confederation itself. New coins, stamps, flag (fig. 3.2), and coat of arms of South Peru were issued (North Peru kept the original red-and-white flag from Peruvian independence).

The Peru-Bolivia Confederation was the sole attempt after independence to reestablish the pre-Bourbonic political and economic unity of Peru and Bolivia. The new country was more popular abroad than at home, being quickly recognized by France, Great Britain, and the United States, who viewed a large, stable central Andean state very favorably for commercial concerns. The Confederation experiment was strongly resisted, however, not only by the Lima–north coast oligarchy, which had strong commercial ties with Chile and relatively weak ties with Bolivia, and by regional interests within Bolivia in Chuquisaca and Tarija, but also by Chile and Argentina, each of whom viewed the massive new state with alarm as a direct trade competitor. Anti-Confederation leaders, including Gamarra, fled to Chile and plotted their attack.

The oversized egos, influence, and shifting alliances of the network of specific personalities in this era of caudillismo surprise our modern sensibilities. It seems that caudillos, like Mongol cavalries invading imperial China, could take over but not govern the state (see Walker 1999, 225). The caudillo Gamarra in particular is usefully compared with Túpac Amaru, since both were Cuzco-based regional caudillos who anchored their anti-Spanish campaigns in deep attachment to Cuzco and its Inka heritage as they navigated sharp colonial racial categories. After Gamarra and Santa Cruz, caudillos often coalesced around Arequipa, since it was a major city and the principal adversary of Lima (in contrast to many smaller-scale caudillos in the interior and north of Peru) (see Walker 1999, 223). Race dogged these earlier serrano caudillos; Arequipeño caudillos and their liberal elite supporters were suspicious of the true loyalties of someone extolling his mixed blood. The military served, as it does now, as a key part of the bureaucratic field for a great mixing of people, upsetting as well as reinforcing racial and social divisions. Hence it is ironic that Gamarra served under Pío Tristán in the royalist army, only to later (1823) fight side by side with Santa Cruz against the Spanish army.

The late 1830s attacks on the Confederation saw the rather free movement of Chilean troops across Peruvian territory, especially in the valley of Arequipa. (The later Chilean invasion in the 1880s, and local resentment toward it, then, had important regional precedent.) Pacification of the Chilean force and the subsequent 1837 Treaty of Paucarpata (Santa Cruz had defeated Salaverry in Paucarpata hardly a year earlier) temporarily ended Chilean hostilities against the Confederation, but the Chilean president did not recognize this treaty, and Gamarra continued to conspire with the Peruvian opposition in exile. Chilean forces regrouped, again invaded, and the army of Santa Cruz was finally defeated in January 1839. After less than two years, North and South Peru were rejoined into "Peru," with Gamarra resuming the presidency, and Bolivia resumed life as a separate country.

Santa Cruz was seen in Bolivia as too much a lover of Peru, and in Peru as too Bolivian—an imperial dreamer longing for Tawantinsuyu-or colonial-scale unity (Basadre 1962, 435–436; 1977, 112). Coupled with this Janus-like curse, racial animosity toward Santa Cruz and Bolivians (and South Peruvians) was barely beneath the surface in North Peru, which saw itself as the rightful heir of Spanish viceregal authority over this territory. Too many forces conspired against reassertion of an Altiplano-based central Andean state with control across the full spectrum of coast to *yunga* ecozones.

The Confederation experiment had dissolved. But had an independent South Peru managed to maintain political autonomy (with or without Bolivia) for some while longer, it could perhaps have become its own country, with North Peru and Ecuador perhaps uniting into a separate country (Basadre 1977, 109–110). Occasional subsequent efforts to join

Bolivia with southern Peru, as in the mid 1840s and again in 1853 and 1860, were viewed primarily as Bolivian attempts to continue the larger Santa Cruz scheme, meddling in Peru's internal and electoral affairs (Basadre 1977, 113). Friction over monetary policies in the 1850s added to the distrust by Peruvians of Bolivian intentions.

In the wake of the political instability of the 1830s and with Arequipa's southern provinces slipping out of orbit, early in 1845 Pedro Gamio, rector of the Universidad Nacional de San Agustín, spoke of the damages wreaked on Arequipa:

> Since [18]34 Arequipa has lost much more than had been gained in the war of Independence. Victim always of its own efforts and always sustaining with its scarce resources combats and causes elsewhere in the republic, we see now nothing but a sad picture of misery and desolation. Its territory dismembered of provinces that used to belong to it, without capitalists, without commerce, without industry, with a petty piece of agriculture declining more and more every day, whose products are beaten out by foreign trade, nothing about prosperity remains for our Department but appearances [*ilustración*]. (Quiroz Paz Soldán 1990, 467)

During the virtual civil war of 1854–1858 Arequipeños rose up again in righteous cross-class anger against overweening Limeño centralism. The confusing details of all this mid-1850s caudillismo and civil war would be tangential to my analysis but for two reasons: it was this bloody period that was at the core of Valdivia's skillful rendition in an invented tradition of "Arequipeño rebelliousness" (Ballón Lozada 1996), and it was these events that served as the backdrop for cultural entrepreneurs such as the poet Benito Bonifaz, who urged on the "hijos del Misti" as he fought (and died) in these battles, and later Maria Nieves y Bustamante, whose 1892 *Jorge, el hijo del pueblo* (discussed in chapter 4) came to constitute one of the most important early literary efforts in the Arequipeño traditionalist canon. These authors lauded the heroic, unified response to injustice and tyranny as well as the civic-mindedness of everyday Arequipeños.

The story of Manuel Ignacio de Vivanco (whose name I could still easily make out written on a big boulder near Uchumayo—in 1979, over a hundred years later) runs right through this episode, illustrating the traits and influence of key caudillos on political and economic events of the period, the vagaries of popular support for various leaders, and key anticentralist themes picked up by later cultural entrepreneurs.

Though born in Chile and descended from the Lima aristocracy, Vivanco early on became something of a favorite son of Arequipa: he farmed in Majes, served in various battles in the region, and was named prefect of Arequipa after the collapse of the Confederation. He had served under Gamarra in the independence struggle, and with Ramón Castilla he had participated militarily under Gamarra to end the Confederation. But given his overly personalistic style and lust for power in the virtually anarchic situation of the early 1840s, Gamarra decided to deploy Castilla against him. Vivanco had assumed the presidency in 1843, but Castilla marshaled forces and, in defense of the constitution, defeated him in Arequipa at the Battle of Carmen Alto in 1843.

Vivanco retired to Ecuador, while Castilla temporarily assumed the presidency amid caudillo infighting; he reinstated the earlier-elected Manuel Menéndez and was then elected to the presidency in 1845 in a constitutional transfer of power. As president, Castilla was closely tied to the rising guano boom, which enabled him to initiate a series of railroad and development projects. He was succeeded in 1851 by José Echenique in the first direct elections and first peaceful transfer of power in Peru's Republican history. Yet though Castilla had earlier supported Echenique, he launched a widely supported coup in 1854 against him; Castilla was favored by liberals who wanted to end slavery, as well as by those with broader concerns about illicit enrichment from guano proceeds under the Echenique regime. Decisive military action in the central highlands resulted in Echenique's exile, this time to the United States rather than Chile. Castilla resumed the presidency from 1855–1862.

Vivanco had left for Chile after losing the election of 1850, but he was suspicious of Castilla's motives and apparent manipulation of anticentralist public opinion in Arequipa, since Castilla had commandeered the anti-Echenique sentiment and returned to power. Despite Vivanco's Arequipa ties, Valdivia played an instrumental role in rallying Arequipeños for Castilla, probably because of his attempts to control guano-related corruption and harness those funds for national development. From Cuzco, Castilla created a province in the Majes valley (perhaps in direct retribution against Vivanco, who had farmed there?); locals proposed it be called "Castilla" to honor the caudillo.

Vivanco had tried to regroup his loyalists on returning to Arequipa from Chile in 1854 to offer his services in the fight against Echenique, but friction with Castilla surfaced even as he finally submitted to Castilla's command. Vivanco is said to have written that Arequipa with its campiña was "like an eclogue [a pastoral poem] . . . a precious diamond surrounded by emeralds"; tradition has it that Castilla replied, "Bah, Arequipa is nothing more than a white burro in the middle of an alfalfa field" (Quiroz Paz Soldán 1990, 475). Vivanco retaliated to Castilla's slight by throwing his lot in with Echenique; popular resistance to Echenique's advances in Arequipa (against Castilla and the general popular uprising), led by Vivanco and General José Trinidad Morán, were fiercely resisted by a cross-class uprising and resulted in the wounding of Vivanco. Morán, Echenique's military aide leading the attempt to control the uprising, halted the attack rather than see Vivanco die; Echenique's resulting order to execute Morán exacerbated popular resistance and reinforced loyalty to Castilla, who defeated Echenique in Lima a month later. Vivanco fled to Chile.

Returning from Chile in late 1856, Vivanco regrouped and, with popular support in Arequipa, rose up to challenge Castilla, initiating a bloody civil war. Vivanco had popular support in Arequipa (though little in Lima or the north coast), largely because Castilla was coming to be seen from the south as having compromised his principles to continue Echenique's project of consolidating a Lima-based national aristocracy based on wealth from guano (Quiroz Paz Soldán 1990, 480–481). Castilla's troops encircled Arequipa for nine months but hesitated to attack, fearing too much bloodshed. Castilla finally attacked, broke through the trenches, and occupied the city, at great cost and with five thousand dead, including three thousand civilians (Quiroz Paz Soldán 1990, 485). Vivanco again fled to Chile, but returned yet again in 1863 to assume a role in a new government, only to be hounded out after a guano-related blunder and forced into exile yet again to Chile. He maintained support in Arequipa and, rehabilitated under the new Miguel de San Román regime, settled in Arequipa, and was elected senator, serving from 1868 to 1872. He left again for Chile for health reasons and died there in 1873.

It is hard from our vantage point to appreciate local Arequipeños' amazing ability to understand and navigate these personalistic interests, shifting loyalties, and mercurial rivalries. In addition, we struggle to realize how violent Lima-based political centralization in this nascent Republican phase was (five thousand dead in Arequipa!).

Further uprisings came in 1865, led by Arequipa prefect Mariano Prado, protesting the treaty signed (by Vivanco!) with Spain over control of the guano deposits of the Chincha Islands and forcing its abrogation. And again in 1867, Arequipeños rejected the secularizing elements of the proposed new liberal constitution of 1867 and took to the defense of their city as they successfully resisted the military assault by Prado's forces (their former prefect!).

Though Lima was commercially vibrant, it was more of an enclave than Arequipa—more closely connected with Valparaíso in Chile than with the interior of Peru itself, as described above. Economically, exports had continued in a colonial vein until the midcentury guano boom. State receipts from growing exports by the 1850s had enabled Castilla to end Indian tribute, abolish slavery, and begin the process of constructing railroads—all steps in the relentless political and economic consolidation of Limeño control of the national field.

IV. INVENTING THE AREQUIPA TRADITION: MELGAR AND VALDIVIA

By stitching together such events in early-Republican Peru into a narrative of loyalty to an emerging idea of "Peru" and of defense of constitutional processes, Mariano Melgar and Juan Gualberto Valdivia were key figures in the invention of a largely conservative yet populist tradition that became central to Arequipeño regionalism. Since Melgar died a martyr's death at a young age (twenty-five), it is to Valdivia we must mostly turn to understand the foundations of the Arequipa regionalist tradition. Francisco Mostajo best caught the importance of Melgar and Valdivia for Arequipeño traditionalism in his 1916 biography of Valdivia:

> ... that demagogue [Valdivia] was the strongest representative that Arequipa has ever had. Tumultuous Arequipa, revolutionary Arequipa, heroic Arequipa—that's Deán Valdivia. Like him fanatic; like him, exalted republican; like him, restless and rebellious; like him, brave and dark; like him, provincial to the core; like him, possessed of a blind faith in his historic destiny. . . . If Melgar represents sentimental, dreamy Arequipa, Deán Valdivia represents revolutionary and brave Arequipa. To the extent that he [Melgar] is like our sky and campiña in which youthful melancholy is dissolved, this one [Valdivia] is like our ragged mountains, in which there is the hint of cataclysm. (Quoted in Ballón Lozada 1996, 100)

95

It seems odd on the face of it, from our vantage point two hundred years later, to have Mariano Melgar (1790–1815) said to be near the origin of *lo arequipeño*. The precocious son of a middle-class Arequipeño family of Spanish descent, he had a relatively ordinary childhood—much time on the family's property in Paucarpata and schooling in classics at the progressive if severe Seminario de San Jerónimo (Miró Quesada Sosa 1998). He is most famous for romantic poems sent to "Silvia," an unrequited love of his youth. After two years (1812–1814) of university study in Lima, where he found inspiration in the brewing independence movement, he returned to Arequipa, where he conspired with like-minded independence compatriots. Rejected by the woman he loved because of family pressures (prefiguring the status distinction theme animating Nieves y Bustamante's *Jorge*), he joined the rebellion led by Pumacahua, but he was soon captured in Puno. His early death by firing squad after the Battle of Umachiri, near Ayaviri in western Puno, marked him as an early patriot and a martyr for independence (Miró Quesada Sosa 1998).

Although a romantic spirit and melancholic tone infused Melgar's poetry, it was the populist, utopian tenor of his writing that led to his being enshrined as a regional hero. "The Indian and the wise man in fond union, will govern you from now on" (cited in Poole 1997, 148). His poetry was finally published as a collection in 1878, on the eve of war with Chile (Basadre 1962, 2110–2111). He had set some of these to music in the form of the *yaraví*, a then-widespread Andean song form with Spanish lyrics but indigenous musical forms. Appetite for this music, closely associated with stirrings toward independence because it was a wholly Andean music, was common enough among the racially mixed urban middle sectors in Arequipa. But the appeal of the form was greatly enhanced by Melgar, given his heroic martyrdom and social rank, thus securing what later became the "mestizo" thread in Arequipeño identity and the localist symbolic importance of the *yaraví* (see chapter 4).

Juan Gualberto Valdivia (1796–1884) was born in Cocachacra, a small village in the fertile coastal sugar fields of the mid-Tambo valley. His humble origins, combined with the asceticism of his clerical calling, created in him a frugal habitus that meshed well with widely held regional values of pragmatism and the honor of everyday citizens.

Valdivia was an especially important figure in defining what would become Arequipeño traditionalism, not only because he lived through tumultuous events central to Peruvian nation building, but also because he was a prolific writer over a long life (eighty-eight years) spanning the period from independence through the War of the Pacific. Valdivia may have been the first to use the term "campiña" in writing (in 1847), referring to Tiabaya (Ballón Lozada 1996, 225). He embodied the engaged, civic-minded cleric; it was Valdivia who spearheaded a tradition of writing essays addressing current events and history and engaging in political propagandizing in journals, using *Escocia, Yanacocha,* and other typically short-lived journals to fan the flames of regional sentiment in opposition to haughty, Lima-based political and ecclesiastic authority. Many short-lived newspapers such as these circulated in the city, including also *El Calavera, El Zarriaga, El Ariete, El Aji Verde,* and *La Paliza* (the Museo Gráfico el Peruano's exhibition of these newspapers in the restored colonial mansion of Editora Peru can be seen at http://www.editoraperu.com.pe/sitios/museo/sbolivar/areq/1.htm). While he was reprimanded by his superiors by being denied promotion at one point, his very public scholarly, political, and teaching efforts secured his place in the regionalist pantheon as one of the fiery writers and orators representing the broader, nonelite populace.

Classically liberal, anticentralist sentiment welled up in his earlier writing, in relation both to the centralizing state and to the church and its role in maintaining Limeño centralism (Ballón Lozada 2000; see Pike 1967b). Starting in the 1850s, however, Valdivia launched a tirade against liberal tendencies in the church and the new Republic, shifting dramatically from his earlier favoring of liberal ideals (see Pike 1967b). He was fundamentally a political conservative, alarmed by growing poverty and opposed to the liberalizing tendencies of the emerging Lima-based plutocracy that blocked general and more just development.

Valdivia "played a transcendental role in the history of Arequipa between 1827 and 1868" (Ballón Lozada 1996, 15); he founded the Colegio de la Independencia (important for incubating future revolutionaries) on 15 July 1827 and was a central figure in the Republican reestablishment of the Universidad Nacional de San Agustín on 11 November 1828, of which he was the first elected rector. Sharing faculty and locale, the Colegio and the Universidad were virtually the same institution and were central to the development of the regionalist tradition;[8] Valdivia assumed the moniker "Deán" as a result of his long association with these two institutions. Both institutions were affiliated with the church; Valdivia opposed the anticlerical tenor of the 1867 constitution and supported the uprising that year led by Pedro Diez Canseco and Juan Manuel Polar.

Though there were colonial antecedents of Arequipeño regionalist insurrection against central authority, such as the 1780 Rebelion de los Pasquines, the revolution of 1834 has been said to mark the real beginning of Arequipeño regionalist sentiment (Quiroz Paz Soldán 1990, 431), for it involved the uprising by the broad mass of people for judicial and legal order against the ongoing irregularities of the military caudillos. These nineteenth-century populist stirrings featured an armed, cross-class populace, remarkable not just because they took place in the general context of authoritarian regimes then prevalent in the region (and the world), but also because they represent a very early postcolonial example of the blurring of racial categories in an emerging republican concept of citizenship—a theme that Jorge Polar, Francisco Mostajo, and later writers picked up and essentialized as the beginnings of an Arequipeño regional discourse about outmoded colonial racial categories (see chapter 4).

Valdivia's populist leanings are very apparent throughout his writing. In 1845, for example, echoing the despair of the university rector quoted earlier, he lamented the poor state of agriculture in the valley, due primarily to the import of cheaper wheat flour from Chile and Bolivia that had led to ruination of honorable small farmers:

> If one stops to think, that agriculture is the primary basis of public wealth, and that most merits protection! That the fieldworker is precisely he who eats bread literally wrapped in his sweat! That there, and in no other place, it's worth looking for the simplicity, the candor, the praises to God, the sweet marital love; in a word, innocence! What honor it would do a government to wipe his tears, that would melt God himself! Fellows [Arequipeños]: you know that I'm not writing a novel; rather I'm just lifting up a corner of the curtain that covers this picture of our disgrace, of our brothers. If your voice is worth something someday, realize that as far as this position, I lament my fellows and friends, the desolation of our common homeland. (Quoted in Ballón Lozada 1996, 159)

Here and in many other places (see Ballón Lozada 1996) Valdivia voiced the plight and anxieties of everyday citizens. In chapter 4 we will examine the intersection of this anxiety from below about exclusion from regional society in relation to the romanticizing of rural life by urban writers and painters.

By the 1840s Arequipa had begun to more clearly reorient itself toward the coast and to accommodate increasing foreign—especially British—domination of import/export activity. With growing obstacles to free-trade ties with the Altiplano, political instability, and growing national attention to the Atacama region, these middle decades of the nineteenth century were uncertain for Arequipeño commercial interests, which searched for additional and even new sources of export-led wealth (contrary to what is claimed in Wibel 1975). Foreign merchants married into prominent Arequipeño families, initiating a flood of European imports that was damaging local manufacture, creating tension between traditionally free-market-prone Arequipeño merchants and manufacturing interests favoring protective tariffs (see Hunt 1973, 107). Artisans, like Francisco Mostajo's father, were particularly hard hit by the import of cheap British textiles.

The series of revolutions, particularly 1834 and 1856–1858, described by Valdivia in his 1874 *Las revoluciones de Arequipa* and briefly summarized above, set the "revolutionary Arequipa" tone for subsequent, broadly popular uprisings against central rule, such as in 1930, 1950, and later.

> In her [the uprising] one can count many examples of popular participation, of the Arequipa people, of peasants like the attitude of the humble [plebeian] and peasant women, [for example in 1834] advising Santa Cruz about the movement of Salaverry's troops or when the same Santa Cruz, defeated, received aid of another peasant woman; in short, one could enumerate a series of examples that are valuable as symbols. (Valdivia, quoted in Ballón Lozada 1996, 25)

Jorge Basadre (1977, 102) argued that despite its idiosyncratic nature, Valdivia's *Revoluciones* was the first work in Latin America that portrayed average people ("gente humilde o anónima" [humble or anonymous people]) as main actors. What is important about Valdivia's citing the assistance that local peasant farmer-citizens gave to troops, however, is less the reality of this assistance (examples of which could undoubtedly be found in any number of armed conflicts) than the fact that Valdivia and later cultural entrepreneurs seized on these examples—in the context of lingering status concerns—to build a case for the "revolutionary, populist spirit" of everyday Arequipeños. Valdivia not only wrote about but also played a key role in the various regional uprisings of midcentury.

Basadre (1929, from "La multitud, la ciudad y el campo en la historia del Perú. Con un colofón sobre el país profundo," in Rivera Martínez 1996, 607–610) also argued that with all these regional uprisings, the middle third of the nineteenth century was the defining period for Arequipa. Though birthed earlier in the midst of chaotic nation building and the Confederation experiment, it was during this period before the War of the Pacific that regional elites, with substantial popular participation, mounted successive acts of resistance to Limeño efforts to consolidate control over the entire space we now know as Peru. The 1850s were particularly formative for the tradition, as ongoing troubles with Bolivia converged with the beginning of illicit profiteering by Limeño elites from the guano trade. There were armed protests in Arequipa each year during the guano boom years—the four decades between the collapse of the Confederation and the war with Chile (Carpio Muñoz 1990, 529).

While the decades between the Confederation and the war with Chile were politically formative, then, it is to the periods just before and especially after the war with Chile and the turn of the century that we must turn (in chapter 4) to fully grasp Arequipeño regionalism and the contours of the changing bureaucratic field within which it took form. For it was then that debates about the role of the state and national identity escalated. An emerging commercial elite was beginning to use the state to leverage revenues from guano to consolidate effective administrative control over Peruvian society around the growing north-coast economy of sugar. The mid-nineteenth-century consolidation of the state can be seen in various actions: Railroads were built to provide the beginnings of a national transportation infrastructure (albeit geared to the export economy) the Lima-Callao line, opened in 1851, was the first railroad in South America. A national telegraphy system was begun in the 1860s. The first good national census was carried out in 1876. The first full accounting of external trade finally appeared in the late 1890s (Bonilla 1980, 16). And systematic organization of the school system began about 1900 (see the discussion of Jorge Polar in chapter 4), with precedents from the constitutional reforms of the 1860s.

At the same time, the general focus of the central state on the north coast—the emerging dynamic center of the national economy—opened a space for the development of Arequipeño regionalist discourse. The clamor by regional elites dominated, and was, after all, for free trade and for recovery of the potential mercantile wealth to be had through control of trade in the central Andean space. Despite friction with this emerging guano elite, modernist virtues of order and progress clearly resonated with Arequipeño merchants and intellectuals in the general situation of recovery from the natural and political disasters. This is especially to be seen in the prominent role played by members of the Arequipeño and southern elites, typically as members of the Civilista Party, during re-

construction after the war with Chile, including Remigio Morales Bermúdez, Nicolás de Piérola, and Eduardo López de Romaña. Scarcity of
money in circulation inhibited commerce and increased the calls for a
national monetary policy.

V. THE WAR WITH CHILE

Guano wealth facilitated the development of Peru's first national bourgeoisie, finally, by the 1850s—a Lima-based aristocracy, inheritor of viceregal institutions, which became closely tied with a succession of caudillos. Enabled by both the Echenique and Castilla regimes, guano wealth
cemented Lima's national predominance (Bonilla 1974; Carpio Muñoz
1990, 508). As we have seen, their extralegal machinations led to a period of interelite conflict during the several decades after the Confederation until, by the 1860s and 1870s leading up to and during the war with
Chile, regional elites closed ranks with Limeño interests, largely under
the banner of the Civilista Party, to form part of the consolidating national elite.

Southern boundary disputes during the first two decades following
independence were fundamentally various attempts, alternately Peru
based versus Bolivia based, to restore wider, long-standing political links
in the central Andes more commensurate with the existing Altiplano-
centered economic and cultural space between coast and highlands. Embodying widely shared aspirations for central Andean political, economic, and even cultural unity, even in failure the Confederation cast
a long shadow over ensuing Arequipeño regionalist sentiment and long-
simmering Altiplano ethno-nationalism. We will pick up this thread after a brief review of political and cultural aspects involved in the tangle
of shifting boundaries in the Atacama, finalized by war and then diplo-
macy almost two centuries after the Confederation.

At the Sicuani Convention in 1836, representatives from Moquegua,
Locumba, Tacna, and Arica were all in favor of incorporation into Bolivia. While delegates had deadlocked on the creation of a new coastal
department, on the eve of official establishment of the Confederation a
year later, Santa Cruz decreed the creation of a Departmento del Litoral of the Estado Sud-Peruano, composed of Tacna (including Arica)
and Tarapacá provinces, with Tacna as its capital. (Moquegua was still a
province of Arequipa.)

After the Confederation collapsed, Gamarra, again president of an again-united Peru, again invaded a politically disorganized Bolivia in 1841 in an attempt to annex it, but Peruvian forces were defeated at Ingavi. The Bolivian government in 1842 made a military counterattempt to annex Puno, Tacna, Arica, and Tarapacá—the last military effort by either Peru or Bolivia to invade the other. Failing that, for maritime access the Bolivian government was forced to favor Cobija, its own port near Antofagasta in its old colonial partido of Atacama, since traffic from Bolivia through Arica (still in Peru) was declining by 1850. The southern border of Atacama, finally fixed at 24° south latitude by treaty with Chile in 1866 (fig. 3.3), had marked the northern limit of Chile until it began to reassert old colonial-era claims to this territory (St. John 1994).

The political, economic, and cultural situation in the Atacama was unlike that of the Altiplano. With poorly defined political boundaries and sparse population, indigenous or not, construction of cultural frontiers—felt loyalty to something larger—in the Atacama largely *followed* the imposition of state boundaries there. In the Altiplano and the adjacent Tambo valley, cultural frontiers long *preceded* the construction of state boundaries, as explored earlier. The Tacna/Arica question, plebiscite and all, was both a political and a cultural project in the making for the long century from independence to 1929, tied to Peruvian and Chilean nation building (Skuban 2007).

Various factors led to heightened Chilean interest in the then-Peruvian Atacama region, and debates about the causes of the War of the Pacific lie beyond our scope here. Geopolitical, economic, national political, and cultural reasons have all been proffered. By the early decades of the nineteenth century, as we have seen, improving sailing technology increasingly favored the faster maritime shipping routes around Cape Horn for export to Europe of quinine bark, guano, wool, and nitrate. Chileans had moved into the Atacama during a silver boom, coming to outnumber the sparse Bolivian or Peruvian populations.

Chilean and Bolivian interest in the coastal desert picked up with the discovery in the 1820s of nitrate and other minerals, and Tarapacá turned out to contain the richest nitrate deposits. Though *salitre* (saltpeter) began to be exported from the Tarapacá region in 1836, first from Pisagua Vieja, interest built dramatically in the 1870s, peaking in the 1890s. By the 1870s, as guano extraction in Peru began to decline, Chilean and Peruvian interest in the sodium nitrate mineral deposits began to intensify (Melillo 2012). This renewed interest in the Atacama's resources in the 1870s came at a time of general economic downturn; the global Panic of 1873 threw the increasingly export-driven economics of all three coun-

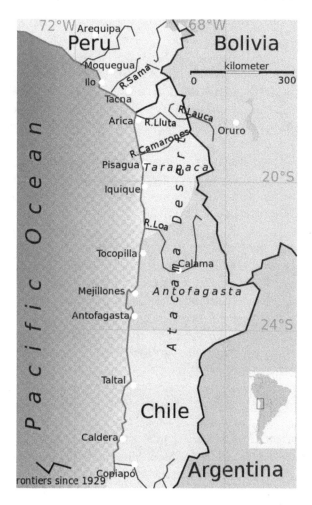

FIGURE 3.3

*Political geography of the Atacama in 1879, on the eve of the War of the Pacific. From "War of the Pacific," **Wikipedia**, http://en.wikipedia.org/wiki/War_of_the_Pacific. Accessed 7 January 2013.*

tries into a tailspin, stepping up Chilean economic interest in and war preparations for direct control of the Atacama (see Skuban 2007, 4–12). In sum, the Atacama deposits became increasingly valuable as North Atlantic demand for fertilizer, gunpowder, and other industrial uses of the chemical grew rapidly, and they were the most important in the world for almost a century.

As tensions with both Chile and Bolivia over control of Atacama re-

sources mounted in the ensuing decade, Peru took several bureaucratic steps to strengthen its control there. Ramón Castilla, hailing from
Iquique—deep in these soon-to-be-contested regions—as president of
Peru in 1855 separated Tacna into Tacna and Arica provinces. Understanding the larger geopolitics of the region, in 1857 the Castilla regime
created a Department of Moquegua, with Tacna as its capital, severing
Colesuyo (Moquegua) from Arequipa and uniting it with Tacna, Arica,
and Tarapacá provinces. Castilla had little love for Arequipa, as we have
seen; in fact, after defeating Vivanco in early 1858, he briefly had Arequipa demoted to provincial status. Peru in 1868 created a special Provincia Litoral de Tarapacá, separating it from (greater) Moquegua. Tarata Province was separated from Tacna Province in 1874; in 1875 Peru
elevated the provinces of Tacna, Tarata, and Arica, in combination with
Tarapacá, into the Department of Tacna, leaving the Provincia Litoral
de Moquegua (with Moquegua its capital) as its own unit. In 1878, Tarapacá itself was again separated from Tacna Department and elevated to
departmental status. All these jurisdictional changes both reflected and
widened fissures between Arequipa and its former southern provinces
and spelled trouble for Arequipeño elites still intent on maintaining control over these former parts of a "greater" Arequipa, especially Arica.

Some poorer Arequipeños traveled to the *salitre* fields for work. But
in general, Arequipeños were less involved in providing labor for the extraction of nitrate in the Atacama, let alone in working the offshore island deposits of guano, both of which relied heavily on imported Chi-
nese and blackbirded Pacific Islander laborers and poor Chileans who
streamed north to the Atacama from the central valley to work in the *salitre* fields (Melillo 2012). Indications are that smallholders here and elsewhere in the Andes largely resisted the lure of quick incomes that hid
the terrible working conditions and debt-peonage relationships central
to their operation.

Details about the actual military and political unfolding of the War of
the Pacific would, again, seem tangential to my argument, except for the
direct and indirect political and economic impacts the war had on Arequipa and the cultural effects on Arequipeños' sense of regional identity in relation to both state and nation. Coming on the heels of a decade
of rapid modernization and gathering national debate about nationhood
in Peru (reflected, e.g., in naturalist Antonio Raimondi's exploits and
writings and in Mariano Felipe Paz Soldán's 1877 *Diccionario geográfico*
and 1878 *Demarcación política*), the collapse in the face of Chilean invasion was all the more painful for Peruvians. In Basadre's evocative fram-

ing, this was a double crisis of the empirical existence of the state and of the country's social abyss—the lack of relationship between "el país legal" and "el país profundo" (between legal and "deep" [real] Peru) (Basadre 1962, 2313, 2315). "The lack of concern of the republican epoch for the Indian problem developed an absence of a national spirit in this mass of people, in spite of the great proofs of self-denial given by so many of them" (Basadre 1962, 2314).

In brief, faced with Chile's aggressive moves to take control of the Atacama region and its resources, Nicolás de Piérola launched a coup d'état in December 1879 while President Mariano Prado was traveling in Europe seeking funds for the looming war. Though hailing from Arequipa, Piérola's aim was defense of a political Peru, not advocacy of regional political autonomy. Politically ambitious, Piérola had made several coup attempts while based in Chile; defeating two British navy ships off Moquegua had boosted his popularity as a can-do caudillo. Once in power, however, Piérola badly mismanaged the defense of Lima during the 1881 Chilean invasion. He quickly left for Ayacucho, where he lamely called for the resuscitation of the Peru-Bolivia Confederation to fight the Chileans—southerners' historic ace-in-the-hole, fallback political position.

Unlike in the previous Chilean invasion during the Confederation years, however, Arequipa was not a scene of direct military engagement during the War of the Pacific. Though the war was about the far-southern coastal departments, the main damage to the country was in the center, both coast and highlands. After Lima fell, Cáceres had retreated to the country's rugged interior to mount a guerrilla war against the Chileans. Though this Breña campaign was a rather effective guerrilla war of attrition, the Chileans finally defeated Cáceres's force in the northern highlands in 1883. Cáceres later turned coat and betrayed his ragtag mestizo/indigenous army (Mallon 1983).

Francisco García Calderón (from Arequipa) had been elected president earlier in 1881 by the congress under Chilean occupation, but with Lima occupied, and being held in what was tantamount to house arrest, he refused to capitulate or agree to cede Tacna and Arica; he authorized his vice president, Lizardo Montero Flores, to move the Peruvian government out of Lima for the duration of the Chilean occupation. García was finally sent into exile by the Chileans. In an echo of Viceroy de la Serna's flight from Lima to Cuzco, after a brief period in Huaráz, Montero transferred the core of government to Arequipa in August 1882, not only because it was the second city of the country but also because it was strategically closer to Bolivia and somewhat distant from the Chilean-controlled coast (Carpio Muñoz 1984, 5). With little budget, no control over major parts of the country, and recognition from no foreign government but Bolivia's, however, Montero in Arequipan exile governed in name only.

Arequipa, then, abruptly served as the nominal national capital for over a year during the latter part of the Chilean occupation. The local population supported Montero by serving as soldiers as well as by contributing maize, wheat, and other necessities, tending to the everyday needs of the troops and the government (Carpio Muñoz 1990, 533). Arequipeños continued to imagine a unified Peru and Bolivia. For example, an anonymous broadside urging joint action with our "Bolivian brothers . . . peruvians and bolivians [sic], always united," was circulated in late September 1883 opposing the quisling government of the north, which was being recognized by the Chileans to sign a final peace treaty (Carpio Muñoz 1990, 534).

At the same time that Montero was transferring the government to Arequipa, Miguel Iglesias, military chief of the north, conspired with the Chileans to conclude the war by accepting defeat. With the Treaty of Ancón the Iglesias "government" agreed to end the occupation, just days before the Chilean army marched south to Arequipa to root out the Montero government. Faced with terrible odds, Montero (like Santa Cruz before him) finally fled under cover of morning darkness to Chiguata and Puno, leaving an outraged populace and demoralized army to face the Chileans. The provisional municipal government negotiated the best terms it could for a peaceful entry to the city, which was directly occupied by the Chileans for the ensuing two months (October–December 1883). Departure of the troops from the city (for a month's encampment down-valley in Tiabaya) was accompanied by the entry of authorities from the Iglesias government. In February 1884 the port and customs office in Mollendo were returned to the Iglesias government, and six months later Chilean troops finally left the country.

No battles took place in Arequipa or the south, unlike during the Chilean incursion of the 1830s. Yet civilians—e.g., the locally famous "six of Quequeña," who were captured and killed by firing squad—still harassed the Chilean occupiers. Though futile, this resistance by common people echoed the popular participation of earlier regional rebellions (e.g., in 1834 and 1854–1856) as well as peasant guerrilla uprisings in the central highlands during this war (Larson 2004; Mallon 1983), fueling regionalist sentiment and continuing the tradition that it was just such everyday resistance by ordinary Arequipeños, not the actions of the central government or regular military, that had finally forced the Chileans to leave.

Rioting erupted in Arequipa the day after the last Chileans departed Arequipa Department and Peru (16 August 1884); the rioters sought to annul the Treaty of Ancón. Troops loyal to the widely reviled Iglesias were defeated and expelled, and Andrés Cáceres, the hero of the sierra campaign, was proclaimed president. Cáceres regrouped in Arequipa and the following year marched on Lima, defeated the Iglesias forces, and took control of the reestablished government through hastily called elections in 1886.

In the wake of Chilean withdrawal, Peruvians fell to recriminations and attacks on other social sectors, often using still-circulating colonial racial categories (no "mestizo" identity yet!). Elites generally blamed the indigenous population for the defeat; Ricardo Palma famously summed up this attitude: "The principal cause of the great defeat is that the majority of Peru is composed of that wretched and degraded race that we once attempted to dignify and ennoble. The Indian lacks patriotic sense; he is born enemy of the white and of the man of the coast. It makes no difference to him whether he is a Chilean or a Turk. To educate the Indian and to inspire in him a feeling for patriotism will not be the task of our institutions, but of the ages" (Palma quoted in Larson 2004, 196). The landed oligarchy similarly blamed the broad masses of Peruvian society: "Peruvians were judged 'ungovernable,' a 'sick populace,' incapable of responding to the entreaties of the homeland, an entity personified in the 'cultured' class of the country [. . . in a] mixture of hatred, contempt and fear of the large property owners . . . toward the popular sectors. . . . [The] population of the former [coast] represented Western civilization, while the inhabitants of the mountains remained stuck in their primitive prehispanic and feudal world, due to their 'natural' inertia" (Larson 2004, 120). Limeños accused Arequipeños of cowardice for not standing up to fight the Chilean troops when they entered the city in 1883 and for generally failing to unite with the national cause by supporting Iglesias.

Nationalist fervor gripped the battered country. In a symbol of national pride, in the wake of the Chilean occupation the *chilena* dance was renamed the *marinera* out of distaste for the Chileans and to honor the marines who had resisted them. Some streets in Arequipa were renamed, and there was renewed interest in traditional dance and music, such as the *yaraví*.

While Arequipeños in general before the war had been indignant over the plunder of the nation's guano resources for private gain and associated political corruption, resentment exploded over the mishandling of the war with Chile. Arequipeño resentment had intensified with the government's failure to effectively confront the Chilean advance into the Atacama Desert—the initial "southern" phase of the conflict. Arequipeños and other provincial elites, as well as commoners and peasants there and around the country, accused the Lima aristocracy of being the primary agents of the country's humiliating defeat. Arequipeños were enraged at the inept and traitorous way the Lima/north coast oligarchy, especially Iglesias, had dealt with the Chileans, and the loss of national territory left widespread frustration and resentment, further fueling regionalist sentiment.

> The War and defeat were a corollary of fifty years of miscalculation and squander in the conduct of the Peruvian State and, the aristocracy as much as the Arequipeño people, lived denouncing and fighting repeatedly over these manipulations that permitted the transfer of Peru's guano wealth to the Lima aristocracy and the military strongmen, conductors of the State and THOSE TRULY RESPONSIBLE FOR ITS DEFEAT. The war wasn't lost in the military encounters, it was lost in the fifty preceding years in the intentional manipulations of the Peruvian political economy that made evident our republican immaturity. (Carpio Muñoz 1984, 23–24; emphasis in original)

With defeat in the War of the Pacific, Tacna (including Arica, Tacna, and part of Tarata provinces) and Tarapacá Departments were occupied by Chile. In the negotiations with Chile after the hostilities ended in 1884, José Antonio de LaValle conceded the loss of Tarapacá, reasoning that there were few Peruvians there, but he refused to allow Tacna or Arica to be severed from Peru (see fig. 3.3). By the 1883 Treaty of Ancón, Peru had ceded Tarapacá and allowed Chile to occupy Tacna and Arica for ten years, after which a plebiscite was to be held determining their final disposition.

Cultural memory of the Chilean occupation was still very much alive during my early fieldwork in Arequipa a century later. In 1979 (the first year of the centenary of the Chilean war) the inebriated mayor of Pocsi stopped me one day as I was riding through to Puquina on my motorcycle; he interrogated me about what I was doing, wondering rather hostilely if I were Chilean. While I took it as a left-handed compliment of my Spanish, it is also a good example of local cultural memory of the 1880s occupation and resistance, since Pocsi (containing Chapi) had played

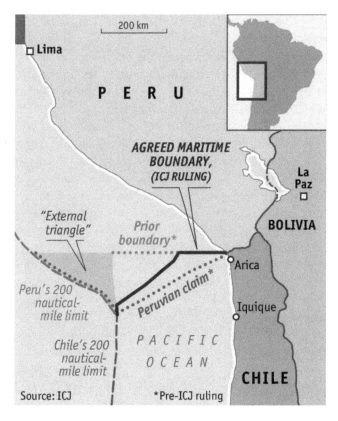

FIGURE 3.4
*Maritime dispute between Peru and Chile, resolved in 2014. From "A Line in the Sea,"
Economist, 1 February 2014, http://www.economist.com/news/americas/21595481
-heres-grown-up-way-settle-long-standing-border-dispute-line-sea.
Accessed 4 July 2014.*

a role in the regionally famous martyrdom of six villagers in nearby
Quequeña. This memory is kept alive not only by oral tradition but also
by street names and the monuments to heroes of the war that are seemingly everywhere in Peruvian cities, especially in the south. It is also sustained by periodic saber rattling, such as that in the late 1970s by the military regime of Francisco Morales Bermúdez over meeting the terms of
Peruvian access and port facilities at Arica, pursuant to the 1929 Treaty
of Lima, or more recently that over maritime boundaries left unresolved
until 2014 by the 1929 accord (see fig. 3.4).

This longest-running boundary dispute in modern South American
history has finally concluded as I finish this chapter in 2014, since the

maritime border had not been decided in the 1929 accord. Control of ocean territory did not emerge as an issue until later, in 1947, when Chile and Peru, in close succession, became the first countries in the world to declare two-hundred-mile maritime economic exclusion zones. Both countries had agreed to abide by the decision of the world court in The Hague, which was finally issued on 27 January 2014.

It is easy to overlook how deep emotions run almost a century and half after the War of the Pacific. Bolivian-Peruvian sentiment remains divided over both the Confederation project itself and the desirability of union (see Basadre 1977, 95). We forget that Chile controlled Tacna until 1929, so that for over forty years Peru's southern international border was much closer to Arequipa than it is today. With Arica and Tacna city occupied, Peru moved the departmental capital to Locumba and continued disputing control of Tarata. William Skuban (2007) describes the role of the highland indigenous population in the intriguing standoff in Tarata as Chile and Peru wrestled for administrative control there. Tarata was reincorporated into Tacna Department when, shorn of Arica, it was itself reincorporated into Peru by the 1929 treaty. In 1936 Moquegua was restored to departmental status and was split into two provinces when the right/north bank of the rugged Tambo drainage was separated and named Provincia General Sánchez Cerro, with its capital Omate, in honor of the recently assassinated president Luis Miguel Sánchez Cerro.

VI. EARTHQUAKE AND RAILROAD

Along with the Chilean occupation (1883–1884), two other pivotal events in the region revealed the intensity of Arequipeño regionalist sentiment in the latter third of the nineteenth century: the earthquake of 13 August 1868 and the arrival of the railroad from Mollendo on 1 January 1871. These three events were central in reinforcing Arequipeños' deeply rooted sense of isolation, alienation, and autonomous self-sufficiency from the capital.

While Arequipa is certainly a seismically prone area, as we learned, the great earthquake of 1868 (estimated to have registered 8.5 on the Richter scale) was devastating even by Arequipan standards. Centered off the coast of Tacna, the quake killed hundreds of people and created a huge tsunami that damaged coastal ports from Pisco to Iquique. The earthquake destroyed much of the city, toppling buildings and demolishing the main cathedral, which had just been finally restored from a damaging fire in 1844. This was a severe setback to Arequipeño elites' faltering hopes of keeping pace with north-coast economic and political growth.

For a city in such travail, the arrival of the railroad two years later could not have been better news. The economic revitalization spurred by construction of the southern rail line can hardly be overestimated: it consolidated Arequipa's commercial preponderance over other commercial hubs in the south and thereby its hegemony over the entire economic space of the southern highlands. Commercial houses concentrated in Arequipa and opened offices in towns and cities along the route. Although anchored in the wool trade, the railroad facilitated the expansion of wider market forces ever deeper into the highland and rainforest lowland interior.

Construction of the Arequipa railroad was the greatest state-sponsored public works project in Peru to that time, and it was done within budget and completed before the stipulated deadline. As minister of hacienda, Piérola had arranged the controversial 1870 guano contract. The resulting funds allowed resumption of the development of Peru's railroads, begun under Castilla in the 1850s. With the concession granted to the wildly entrepreneurial Henry Meiggs, who was fleeing creditors from San Francisco, the first part of the southern railroad was built from Mollendo to Arequipa in 1870–1871, with Chilean as well as Peruvian and Bolivian workers. Meiggs, well aware of the significance of the project and eager for future contracts, sponsored a gigantic gala celebration in Arequipa on New Year's Day 1871 to inaugurate the line. The festival featured dances, speeches, parades, and a several-day visit of President José Balta and his retinue, who had sailed south for the occasion. The southern line was completed to Puno in 1874, this time primarily with Peruvian and Bolivian workers (Basadre 1962, 1769, 1773) and without any inaugural event (Lévesque 2008, 59). Steamers and train ferries later connected with the Bolivian side at Guaqui, and the line from Juliaca to Cuzco, begun in 1872, was finally completed in 1908, making this the longest Peruvian rail line. The line had stopped at Sicuani from 1892 to 1908; so closely were Arequipeños identified with commerce that Sicuani merchants' key role in the wool trade led locals to call Sicuani the "Arequipa of Cuzco."

Juan Carpio Muñoz (1990, 512–528) has insightfully detailed key elements of the political and economic dimensions of this railroad project. The 1867 uprising against the illegal imposition of a new constitution was the culmination of a campaign started by Castilla (who died en route from Chile), and successfully toppled the Prado regime and propelled Pedro Diez Canseco into the presidency for a third interim term in 1868. Diez Canseco (who was Castilla's brother-in-law), along with Juan Manuel Polar and Juan Gualberto Valdivia, had led the city council in supporting the 1867 uprising. (As a young soldier, Diez Canseco had earlier supported Gamarra in opposition to Cáceres's Bolivia-centered Peru-Bolivia Confederation.) Polar had served as plenipotentiary minister to Bolivia (1859) and to Chile (1859–1862) during the Castilla regime and personally knew Henry Meiggs and his enviable construction record there. Even before arriving in Lima to take office, from the port at Islay, Diez Canseco wrote to Meiggs inviting a proposal to build the train through Arequipa.

English commercial pressure was portending an enormous shift of Altiplano commerce southward toward Cobija, and the expanding nitrate exploitation by Chileans, with British backing, further threatened Arequipa's commercial position. A similar coast-interior rail line was started in Antofagasta (then in Bolivia) in 1872, tied to the *salitre* exploitation; it eventually reached La Paz in 1913. All this led to growing anxiety among commercial elites over the development of an export market in southern Peru and to their avid support of the southern railroad. The railroad opened up possibilities for the long-hoped-for recovery of mining as well, as ore could be shipped to port for export.

Construction of the line in southern Peru cemented Arequipa's commercial fortunes in relation to its old economic hinterland; one can hardly imagine merchants' and regional elites' relief as the wool trade continued developing even during and after the ensuing war. Carpio Muñoz (1990, 512–528) argues that the 1867 rebellion aided regional elites' effort to have the southern rail line put through Arequipa, since the national government's plans were tending to favor Arica and Tacna—then still part of Peru.

The railroad was the beginning of the concentration of commerce in and through Arequipa and along the rail line and therefore of the marginalizing of towns and trade fairs, such as at Cailloma or Vilque, respectively. *Arriero* culture was reconfigured with the advent of the railroad in the latter nineteenth century; for example, after the mid-1870s the export of alpaca wool shifted from *arrieros* to the railroad station at Sumbay (Manrique 1986, 201). My Sabandía informants' father had worked as a muleteer between the gold mines at San Juan de Oro and the rail connection near Azángaro in the 1930s. *Arrieraje* then declined dramatically with the advent of highways and trucking after the 1930s. Llama drovers continued on the vertical exchange networks, but those networks were now much more local in nature than before and were confined to more isolated areas like the Cotahuasi valley (for the rock-salt trade), the Colca valley, or the upper Tambo (Love 1988; see Carpio Muñoz 1990, 526).

VII. THE WOOL TRADE

While the apogee of regionalist sentiment must be understood in relation to the growing centralization of power in Lima in the latter part of the nineteenth century and at the turn into the twentieth, culminating with the twin regimes of Augusto Leguía, before we turn to these matters we must close this chapter by examining the wool trade and its importance for Arequipa. Since the wool trade played such an important role in the social history and culture of Republican Arequipa and was at the heart of the later nineteenth-century pattern of largely foreign-controlled import/export firms, I will elaborate this story here even though it takes us well into the first three decades of the twentieth century and to some matters that might have been saved for chapter 4.

The auspicious economic developments just discussed came alongside global and general national economic downturn in the 1870s and of course political reversals during and after the war with Chile. The one bright spot for Arequipeño aspirations during these problems, then, was the wool trade, though wealth from wool export did not have such a decisive impact in the south as export-generated wealth had in the north coast or other parts of the country (Flores Galindo, Plaza, and Oré 1978).

Though wool is a far more renewable product than guano, the wool trade did echo the guano trade in providing the basis for commercial revitalization in the south after the war and in opening up a series of economic opportunities in the waning decades of the nineteenth century. Chilean occupation and military action had not reached the producing zones of the southern highlands, and Arequipeño merchants simply warehoused wool during the months of Chilean occupation before resuming export in 1884.

Wool, first of sheep and then of alpaca (and llama), had begun to be exported just before the independence wars. Exports increased steadily until the global financial panic of 1873, when international (largely British) demand dropped by 40 percent (Bonilla 1973). While overall demand did not recover to those levels until after 1910, exports of sheep wool—which could be replaced by wool from other, cheaper sources such as New Zealand or the United States—dropped far more than did exports of alpaca wool, available only from the Andes.

There were two main sources of wool: lower-grade sheep wool from highland haciendas, and higher-grade alpaca wool from mostly indigenous communities and smallholders. Unlike export sectors in other parts of Peru during this period (guano, mining, sugar, cotton), relations of production were never rationalized and brought under the supervisory control of merchant capital, owners of the large haciendas. Wool production (especially that of alpacas) remained largely in the hands of *comuneros* (members of indigenous communities) and smallholders, and wool already circulated in highland precapitalist exchange circuits before these smallholders were brought into export markets (Orlove 1977). Haciendas were largely in the hands of or closely allied with absentee urban-based Arequipeño merchant landlords, who also pursued other economic activity and invested wool wealth into other pursuits, including rural retreats in Sabandía (e.g., those of wool merchants William Stafford and Guillermo Ricketts) and Tingo.

Though local effects of the wool trade in Cailloma were significant (Manrique 1986), highland Arequipa proper played a small role in the overall story of wool export; Puno and Cuzco were far more important overall (Burga and Reátegui 1981; Jacobsen 1993; Thorp and Bertram 1978; Orlove 1977). The 1867 Bustamante uprising in Huancané was a precursor to periodic uprisings in the southern highlands as the wool trade intensified and, especially with the presence of the railroad, haciendas expanded against indigenous landholdings and firms' advance agents fanned out to interact directly with Indians selling wool.

Despite the general world and national economic slowdown in the last several decades of the nineteenth century, then, the period 1873–1919 was overall one of general expansion for indigenous producers as well as for commercial houses in Arequipa. Like Arequipeño middlemen and wool processors, indigenous producers were very much affected by the post–World War I market downturn, which underwrote general indigenous tensions and uprisings in the early 1920s.

Economically dependent on wool production that was largely in the hands of indigenous workers but socially distant from them, Arequipeño elites were unable to respond quickly to market openings and encountered general limits on overall growth of the trade. The collapse of mining and hacienda activity in the south in the early Republic had restored

to Indians a measure of control over basic resources. Thus puna grazing communities had more leverage on wool buyers than might be imagined from classic Marxist readings of the "Indian problem" (Gootenberg
1991a).

It was not until late in the nineteenth-century wool trade that Arequipeño elites consolidated large estates in Puno (Jacobsen 1993). Wool export in the south through Arequipa to Mollendo and Islay connected
Altiplano producers with the world market and further developed a
mercantile elite in Arequipa that pressed for free trade and relative regional autonomy. Hopes for political stability to foster regional economic growth fed elites' demands on the central state to normalize constitutional rule and liberalize trade.

Transformations of highland society during the peak of the wool
trade have been well studied (Orlove 1977; Bonilla 1973; Flores Galindo
1977; Burga and Reátegui 1981). On the ground in highland communities, local political control by *mistis* rested on their prior role as advance
agents of the wool trade and their associated financial acumen, their
marrying into local communities, their social capital (ties to Arequipa),
and their command of Spanish. By the 1930s local leaders (*varayoc*) were
all but subservient to such *mistis* (Manrique 1986, 203).

World War I was a defining period for Arequipa's economic fortunes.
First, mining shifted focus. The Atacama saltpeter trade, over which so
much blood had been spilled, went into decline with German development of synthetic nitrates (via the Haber-Bosch process) shortly after the
war ended. Germany had depended on this process, which they developed for agriculture and munitions during the war, though the United
States and Britain remained tied to Chilean sources of natural mineral
nitrate. Copper replaced nitrate as the economic lifeblood of this now-
Chilean desert region, but in southern Peru this occurred only after
Chile had returned Tacna in 1929. The first large copper mine in Peru, at
Cerro de Pasco, began operation in 1906 (Lévesque 2008, 89), but mining in the south came much later: Toquepala, the first large copper mine
in the south, commenced operations in 1960. In Chile, the big Atacama
copper mines, such as Chuquicamata, began after Chilean consolidation
of control by the 1880s. "La fiebre del oro rojo" (red-gold fever) brought
many small miners from Chile to the new northern territories, adding
to the Chileanization of the far north (Skuban 2007); corporate development really began about 1910.

Second, having resumed earlier production levels by the start of that decade, the wool trade was greatly stimulated by Allied demand for wool during the war for uniforms and other clothing. With war's end, however, wool export suddenly declined, parallel with nitrate and guano export (though this had less direct effect on Arequipeño merchants). Total freight, the bulk of it wool for export, fell from 137,520 metric tons in 1918–1919 to 128,338 metric tons in 1922–1923 (Lévesque 2008, 76; Thorp and Bertram 1978).

The construction of Ferrocarriles del Sur (the Southern Railroad) had consolidated the regional hegemony of the Arequipeño oligarchy. Renewed commercial activity stimulated by the railroad was in the hands of largely foreign commercial houses and was oriented to the coast for export rather than to the mining interior, which benefited Arequipa's growth against that of Cuzco. This trade was centered on Arequipa and brought products from Bolivia and even Argentina. Some dozen commercial houses grew up, increasingly tied to the wool trade, mostly in English hands but also French and German, such as those of Gibson, Stafford, Iriberry, Braillard, Gibbs, Múñoz-Nájar, Ricketts, Emmel, and Forga (Orlove 1977; Flores Galindo, Plaza, and Oré 1978, 57; Burga and Reátegui 1981).

As the twentieth century progressed, Arequipeño commercial capitalists found themselves opposing the ongoing concentration of wealth and power in Lima yet in sympathy with an urban-industrial bourgeoisie intent on reforming the traditional large-estate system on the north coast. With a decline in exports from the south, principally wool and leather, Arequipa's commercial interests increasingly clamored for a "rationalization" of agriculture (e.g., Belaúnde [1915] 1963), meaning implementing policies favoring easier credit and stimulating investment in irrigation projects. Though campiña farmers exported 20,000 kilograms of guiñapo (corn mash for chicha) to Puno in 1891 (Polar [1891] 1958), for example, highland markets continued to remain relatively closed or undeveloped. Subsistence production on community and other lands combined with undercapitalized and poorly managed haciendas constituted strong barriers to market penetration.

Always dependent on external trade more than were other regions of the country, Arequipeño aristocratic families were therefore less xenophobic. By the early twentieth century, foreign wool merchants wound up marrying into or being displaced by a native Arequipeño bourgeoisie, which in 1887 had organized itself into the Cámara de Comercio de Arequipa (Chamber of Commerce). Other institutions linked to this class were founded during this period of reviving economic fortunes, including the Club de Arequipa (1871) (the first elite social club in the city), the Banco de Arequipa (1871), the Jockey Club de Arequipa (1876), and the Sporting Club Internacional (1894) (Carpio Muñoz 1981–1983, 18).

While it is claimed, given all this, that Arequipa represents the clearest case in Peru of oligarchic class hegemony over a regional space (Flores Galindo, Plaza, and Oré 1978), as I seek to demonstrate, the popular underpinnings of regional identity have generally been overlooked. Regional elites surged to prominence (and took Arequipa with them) in the nineteenth century with the growth of commercial capital, particularly linked to the railroad and the wool-export trade. Descendants of these families, among others, continue as important members of the commercial elite of Arequipa.[9]

Yet this regional elite found itself split between authoritarian/conservative and liberal/free market political visions of *peruanidad* that had framed debates within Arequipa and the nation struggling to define itself after the Chilean war. Liberals sought to establish a new oligarchy in power (Walker 1999, 145), whereas conservatives leaned toward maintaining the privilege and power of the landed aristocracy. Manuel Pardo's founding of the Civilista Party in the mid-1870s had middle-class aspirations in mind even as the movement fundamentally advanced the interests of the landed oligarchy. *Civilismo* (the national political movement tied to the Civilista Party) successfully fended off clamors for change, largely from below, during the "aristocratic republic" period from the end of the war to the 1920s.

It was not until Piérola's defeat of Cáceres in 1895 that stable civilian rule was firmly established. Despite his blunders during the war with Chile, Piérola, the "democratic caudillo," was elected president and governed from 1895 to 1899; his close association with the landed oligarchy ushered in a period of rehabilitation and reform after the war—though with an autocratic approach not well suited to the growing democratic urges of the early twentieth century. This was a movement seeking to create a strong state committed to modernization. But by the beginning of the twentieth century it had split into two wings—one compromised with the old elite and committed to the continuation of economic growth based on foreign investment; the other more committed to modernization, an end to corruption, and a strategy of national growth. The individual who came to represent this more radical wing was Augusto Bernardino Leguía y Salcedo, though Leguía never questioned the central role of foreign capital in the process. He was elected to the presidency for the first time in 1908 and returned to power again via a coup d'état in the momentous year of 1919.

While Arequipeños generally welcomed the stability brought by Civilista Party rule, it came at a heavy social and political cost, particularly in growing state centralism. Anticentralist sentiment simmered in the early decades of the twentieth century, which saw heightened labor activism, decentralist politics, and indigenist sentiment, advanced as well as reflected in literary and artistic circles (Deustua and Rénique 1984, 47). Economic fortunes waxed and then waned in the first decades of the twentieth century. Regionalist sentiment in Arequipa intensified by the 1920s, a decade characterized by a perfect storm of autocratic rule, labor unrest, and rising racial tension during the Leguía years—themes to which we turn in chapter 4.

In sum, the tumultuous century from independence to the 1920s saw the nationalist aspirations of some Arequipeños turn fairly quickly to regional trade and development interests. Having by the 1840s abandoned the possibility of outright political secession and sickened by the bloody battles of the 1850s, Arequipeño elites' fundamental, long-standing commercial vocation between interior and coast led them to focus on continually espousing free-trade policies, carving out the best defense of regional interests possible within the framework of a rapidly consolidating, Lima-based Peruvian state. This was clear enough in the strategic insistence of Pedro Diez Canseco (1868) on getting the southern railroad built through Arequipa rather than Arica (Carpio Muñoz 1990, 510).

This fundamental shift is also signaled by the prominence of the feeling, apparent from the 1830s and in the writings of Valdivia, that the fundamental Arequipeño political interest was the proper rule of law in an emerging Peruvian state. Emblematic of this is the sharp contrast between Iglesias's traitorous dealing with the Chileans and García Calderón's refusal to capitulate to them. The frustration was with Limeño political intrigue and ongoing corruption that was holding back economic development and the benefits of modernity. Witness the degree to which Arequipeños of means traveled to the United States and Europe and were entranced by the latest fashions (see chapter 4 on photography and styles of consumption) and the newest technologies (again, see chapter 4 on electrification, public transportation, and waterworks). Consumers increasingly emulated European fashions, especially British but also French (Orlove 1997).

With the centripetal force of unity against a common aggressor—first the Spanish in the 1860s, then the Chileans in the 1880s—regionalist sentiment had shifted decisively from political to cultural terrain. In chapter 4 we will turn to examine how this cross-class, popular involvement informed the anticentralist politics and literature of the decades from 1890 to 1970. Of central interest will be how the region's now emblematic mestizo figure was constructed by several well-placed cultural entrepreneurs, chiefly urban middle-class intellectuals, via print media, as a new, post–War of the Pacific, postcolonial racialist way to conceptualize regional identity and inform decentralist politics. Accused by centralists of promoting instability, many regionalist intellectuals looked to rural smallholders as the very embodiment of an imagined stable and authentically Peruvian community.

FOUR

LITERARY REGIONALISM

Browning, Secularizing, and
Ruralizing Regional Identity

> *Widespread assumptions of congruence between ethnicity*
> *and "objective culture" are in both cases shown to be cultural*
> *constructions themselves.* **Talk about culture** *and culture*
> *can here, perhaps, be distinguished in roughly the same*
> *way as one distinguishes between the menu and the food.*
> *They are [both] social facts [but] of different orders.*

THOMAS HYLLAND ERIKSEN,
ETHNICITY AND NATIONALISM, 1993, 101

While plebeian Arequipeños' sense of regional identity was connected with Marian devotion, with its deep pre-Hispanic and colonial roots, and was practiced in muleteers' and emigrants' long journeys across cultural frontiers and political borders, republican ideals of citizenship and civic virtue began to strongly inflect regional popular culture after independence. Arequipeño cultural identity in Republican Peru was deeply affected by regional elites' early postindependence aspirations for relative political and especially economic autonomy, epitomized by the strong support Arequipeños gave to the Peru-Bolivia Confederation and reignited in the wake of the war with Chile. These elite demands quickly became reframed as "decentralist," focused on getting the national government's attention to regionally specific needs and aspirations. Popular participation in frequent regional insurrections against Lima-based caudillos characterized the period between the Confederation and the war with Chile, validating everyday Arequipeños' ongoing demands for participation as full citizens of the imagined regional community. Championed by Valdivia and others, remembering those valiant years of collective struggle developed into a shared history, an invented tradition cultivated by key cultural entrepreneurs, passed down by families, and reproduced through educational institutions like the Colegio de la Independencia and the associated Universidad Nacional de San Agustín.

Given the ongoing vitality of racialized stratification in postcolonial Peru, we now turn to the postwar (1890s) through 1970s experiment with a discourse of mestizaje, which came to lie at the center of Arequipa's regional identity. After the war with Chile and through the first half of the twentieth century, questions of citizenship and national identity became more urgent, particularly in Arequipa, where locals had largely stopped identifying as Indian and the reality of a mixed-race urban plebeian population was now undeniable (Chambers 2003, 42). Faced with continuing central-state intransigence blocking a variety of social reforms, key regional intellectuals and decentralist politicians in Arequipa engaged these debates by drawing on the reservoir of popular sentiment and identity in the valley and on the regionalist tradition invented by Valdivia, Melgar, and others over a century of anti-Lima struggle. Populist rhetoric increasingly colored their portrayal of regional identity, even as urban plebeians and smallholders themselves largely remained on the sidelines of this cultural production.

The construction of Arequipeño traditionalism by regional intellectuals—the main focus of this chapter—was set in regionally specific contexts that shaped how the broader early twentieth-century debates on the "national problem" were understood. Of primary importance was Arequipa's location near and strong ties to the Altiplano, which meant that the national question was in turn unavoidably tied to the "Indian problem"—how to bring indigenous populations of the southern highlands into the mainstream of evolving national culture (e.g., Guinassi Morán 1908, 51–63). Mestizaje, I argue, was a discourse experimented with by local urban intellectuals as a way of making sense of Arequipeños' geographic, cultural, and linguistic hybridity and political "in-betweenness."

Arequipa's long history of oligarchic control and working-class debility conditioned a broadly cross-class consciousness, whose concerns were now being articulated by a string of largely urban middle-class politicians and cultural entrepreneurs. Drawing on the shared sense of cultural citizenship, already established and practiced in pilgrimage and developed in nineteenth-century struggles, people variously situated in regional social space could identify and imbue an ambiguous "mestizo" identity with multiple meanings without having to directly address fundamental social divisions within regional society or actually deal with the central national problem—how to extend citizenship to the country's

indigenous majority. Emigration, industrialization, and highlander immigration had by the middle of the twentieth century begun to fundamentally change the context of campiña-anchored regional identity and
the contours of the fields within which actors moved, attenuating these
concerns and generating the deeply *nostalgic mood* that came to characterize Arequipeño regional identity by the latter twentieth century.

Many of the writers, artists, and musicians whose work I describe in
this chapter were in touch with and were certainly influenced by *indigenista* currents in the arts. But as we will see, *indigenismo* was almost entirely an urban-based, largely literary movement engaging centralist/de-
centralist politics of the period (Kristal 1987; Walker 1989), having little
to do with indigenous politics (or culture) per se. Flying under different
colors, it was really a debate about national identity, about the nature and
future of Peru both as an imagined community and as a heterogeneous
society experiencing an increasing pace of industrial development, social dislocation, and authoritarian regimes tied to the old order, blocking
change and serving the narrow interests of landed oligarchic privilege.

While commercial elites had earlier led regionalist sentiment in the
national field, battling against extralegal caudillismo, their move by later
in the century to broadly incorporate into an emerging national elite under the banner of *civilismo* left this sentiment of citizenship in the imagined community of Arequipa largely in the hands of second-class citizens, primarily urban, and their intellectual representatives whom I
examine in this chapter. These everyday Arequipeños had strived for
position in a postindependence regional field still marked by the very
exclusionary Spanish concerns with respect (*dignidad*) and status authority (Chambers 1999). Despite the legal abolition of Spanish colonial
distinctions in the nineteenth century, the strengthening bureaucratic
field, informed by liberal political thought drawing on European and
North American models, compelled the need to create citizens subject
to equal treatment by law. Such modern notions of citizenship resonated
strongly with regional intellectuals, as we will see.

In this chapter I explore the main symbolic content and contours of regional identity developed and consolidated by a new generation of modernist cultural entrepreneurs—writers, painters, and musicians, some
of whom were active politically, mostly in the first three decades of the
twentieth century. Whether or not they used the term itself, they essentialized regional identity as fundamentally *mestizo*, anchored in the practices and customs of urban plebeians and, especially, of rural smallholders of the valley, who came thereby to be emblematic of regional identity.

What these cultural entrepreneurs meant by various claims of Arequipeños' mixed race, and what those claims signified, is the principal thread of my analysis in this chapter. While there were "mestizos" identified as mixed racial types in various censuses of the late-colonial and early-Republican periods, as we learned, there was no "mestizo culture" until the late nineteenth- and early twentieth-century developments I describe in this chapter (Chambers 2003).

It is hard to bring into focus a period like this, situated between the present and considered history, a twilight no-man's-land of time (Hobsbawm and Ranger 1983)—far enough back in time to be out of living memory, yet close enough to still resist pressures to construct an orthodox, canonical reading of people and events. Yet lying beyond ethnographic reach, as noted in the preface, I am therefore somewhat uncomfortably forced to rely primarily on interpreting what was printed and painted (and read and appreciated) to understand discursive trends and content during this period.

Arequipa's distinct regional identity, oddly populist yet conservative, grew out of Peruvians' prolonged difficulty in building a new nation out of Spanish colonial and indigenous political and cultural elements. Arequipeño intellectuals and politicians had by this period long since given up the idea of formal political autonomy (Gootenberg 1991b), and so were generally less interested in breaking up the institution of the state per se than in developing an idea of "Peru" inclusive enough for a somewhat more diverse set of social and political actors to find a place. Given their strong ties to plebeian life and their intermediate location between coast and highlands, Arequipeños' experience in an orderly, functioning society (i.e., one not riven by class or other sectarian tensions or incorporating gross social inequality) seemed for these intellectuals (e.g., Teodoro Nuñez Ureta) to be much more relevant to the mass of Peruvians than did either Limeños' experience in the foggy coastal capital or peasants' experience in remote highland villages. While regionalist stirrings against the center had been common enough throughout the country's history, anticentralist sentiment had been strongest in Arequipa, and this intensified in the political, economic, and cultural wreckage after the disastrous war with Chile.

After the war a new generation of intellectuals debated how best to pick up the pieces and reconstruct the country. Modernist ideas flourished among the "Generation of 1900"—a national group of intellectual "aristocrats who identified with the oligarchy" (N. Miller 1999, 152). Lead by Arequipeños V. A. Belaúnde and Francisco García Calderón, they searched for ways to go about the long-overdue reform and renewal of the political and educational systems. *Tertulias* (informal, artistically informed meetings to discuss current affairs) flourished in regional institutions like the Academia Lauretana in Arequipa (Ballón Lozada 2000), as well as in the capital, such as the Club Literario in Lima (Basadre 1962, 2846–2847).

Manuel González Prada—a leading, Lima-based agitator against established political power—became a lightning rod for controversy about the role of the indigenous and popular classes in these debates about nationhood. His anarchist, political, anticlerical, liberal, literary, and yet patriotic ideas were very influential (Basadre 1962, 2854, 2856).

> The most trenchant critique of the old order came from the poet Manuel González Prada [who] exposed the moral degeneration of the old ruling class and set it against a picture of "Indian Peru," which was both romantic and idealized. . . . Despite his reputation as a defender of the indigenous population, however, González Prada clearly saw the decay of Peruvian society as [stemming from colonial practices] corrupting both rulers and ruled; though he laid the responsibility firmly with the powerful, he never saw the indigenous people as potential subjects of history, capable of bringing about change through their own actions. (González 2007)

González Prada, like many urban intellectuals after him and even *indigenistas* of the 1920s and 1930s, never visited the sierra, reminding me of several leftish upper-middle- and upper-class Arequipeño city friends who had been to Miami, London, or Paris but never (until recently) to the Colca or Cotahuasi valleys.

A central idea emerging in this period was that at the heart of Peruvian identity was the undeniable reality of racial hybridity. In the complex racial labyrinth of postcolonial Peru, diverse perspectives on this "reality" led "mestizo" to be a usefully ambivalent concept with which a broader spectrum of people could identify, both socially and politically. As we will see, for most Arequipeño writers "mestizo" really meant *criollo* (Peruvianized Spanish behavior and mentality), while for fewer others "mestizo" meant *cholo* (associated with upstart immigrants from the Indian countryside who didn't know their place).[1] The 1940 census confirmed what many were already coming to think—that the country was no longer primarily Indian but was, rather, mestizo (Klarén 2000, 285).

While elsewhere in the country mestizaje became connected with explicitly political movements—especially the Alianza Popular Revolucionaria Americana (American Popular Revolutionary Alliance; APRA), in Arequipa this perspective was given voice in the decades between the Chilean war and the 1970s by a somewhat diverse set of several key intellectuals—the earlier ones more from patrician families (e.g., Maria Nieves y Bustamante and Jorge Polar, and somewhat later Victor Andrés Belaúnde), then increasingly figures with more middle-class origins (those primarily examined in this chapter, Francisco Mostajo especially), but then later again figures from the upper ranks of regional society (Manuel Bustamante de la Fuente and José Luis Bustamante y Rivero). I argue that these figures all, in their own ways, seemed compelled to describe the city and the landscape in grand and evocative ways and to portray Arequipeños as a hybrid sort of people in deeply local and telluric, place-bound terms, as a response to their lived social experience in the city and in the context of an unrelentingly authoritarian national political culture. They built on the rebellious, anticentralist Valdivia/Melgar identity established in the mid-nineteenth century, described in chapter 3, to recenter regionalist sentiment toward symbols and practices associated with the urban plebeian and, especially, rural smallholders in the valley, whom they saw as models for authentic Peruvian identity.

The image of the rural, smallholder, mestizo Arequipeño—both white *and* Indian, hardworking, practical, decent even if bawdy, proud, but above all entrepreneurial and with a can-do attitude—served as a trope for a progressive, pragmatic, even modern identity around which Peruvians (if they would only get on board) could rally and to which they should aspire. "Indians" could not serve this discursive function, given the deeply racialized wider culture that regarded them as unreliable, even lazy, and associated with a failed past. Indians, in short, were incapable of undertaking the hard work of forging a nation.

Recentering traditionalist discourse in these directions had three links with regional culture that played to national concerns:

• Taking pride in *lo nuestro* (our own local identity) downplayed the more overtly Spanish aspects of Arequipeño life and of Peruvian culture (a necessary task for constructing a postindependence national identity).

• The anticenter struggles of everyday Peruvians had broadened the space for intellectuals' work in developing an inclusive national identity (at least beginning to address the place of the then-indigenous majority in national society).

• Ordinary Arequipeños' aspirations to honor and citizenship in the imagined regional community were acknowledged in a regional social contract pointing to a broader, more inclusive, modern sense of citizenship.

Evoking idealized traits of plain-talking small farmers and matronly picanteras, then essentializing them as "authentic" and characteristic of all "true" Arequipeños, was the heart of the contributions these cultural entrepreneurs made to the regionalist tradition. Though not uncontested from either left or right, this imagery became the dominant way urban Arequipeños came to think about themselves—a hegemonic structure of feeling (Williams 1977) at the core of Arequipeño identity. Drawing upon the symbolic power of the essentially peripheral, anticenter identity of rural peasants in the valley of Arequipa—already in place from the earlier colonial, pilgrimage-based identity—was a template at hand for dealing with the identity vacuum at a national level and, for those more engaged with decentralist politics, for navigating the inherently strained state-region relationship intensifying during the *civilista* period and coming to a boil during the 1919–1930 Leguía dictatorship. For Mariano Lino Urquieta, Francisco Mostajo, and Antero Peralta, this was about fighting back against antidemocratic authoritarians. For conservative V. A. Belaúnde it was a moral imperative to develop a coherent national identity. Oligarchic repression of these movements and developments characterized this entire period; Leguía exiled many of these poets and writers, including even Belaúnde, and later, General Manuel Odría toppled Bustamante y Rivero in a 1948 coup and sent him into exile.

I. SOCIAL, ECONOMIC, AND POLITICAL DEVELOPMENTS AND CONTEXTS

Despite some encouraging developments (the railroad, the wool trade at times), from the 1830s Confederation episode through various anticentralist caudillo movements to the War of the Pacific and on to the post–World War I collapse in the wool trade and the Great Depression we find trends generally inimical to Arequipeño commercial and political interests. The nation had been humiliated by occupation and loss of territory, and the Atacama region's new riches had slipped out of reach of Arequipeño (and Peruvian) commercial interests. Faced with the continuing inability of the Limeño/north coast oligarchy to consolidate legitimate power and project a common sense of *peruanidad* (see Cotler 1978), particularly in the wake of the disastrous experience with Chile in the War of the Pacific, by the turn of the twentieth century many in Peru, especially from Arequipa and elsewhere in the south, came to think that championing some sort of culturally hybrid mestizo identity was a prerequisite for overdue national cultural integration.

The "Indian question" dogged all postwar attempts to (re)construct some shared national identity. While highland indigenous engagement with the larger national economy generally grew slowly and unevenly, as we have seen, Indians in the south living at higher elevations (i.e., on the Altiplano) practiced pastoral livelihood strategies that were already strongly connected with the wool trade. As a result, seemingly intractable questions of citizenship that remained unresolved nationally broke through the surface of political and intellectual discourse in several indigenous movements and in the words of spokespeople in the south in these decades.

Anxiety over this subjectivity was particularly acute in Arequipa, given its proximity and juxtaposition with the nearby indigenous highlands, and was shared across classes: by commercial elites, ever anxious about threats to commerce and the fragility of trade; by middle sectors, such as urban artisans and shopkeepers, and by the urban working class, all of whose livelihoods were directly affected by the pace of commercial activity; and even by rural smallholders, who were indirectly affected by commercial vitality and who, like urban plebeians, continued to regard themselves as full citizens in regional society.

Various intellectuals tried to make public sense of this dynamic, complex situation. The cultural entrepreneurship I describe here depended heavily on the availability of print media in the city of Arequipa, which in turn depended on wide circulation among a literate urban public that was capable of reading and understanding printed (and painted) works and for whom the imagery resonated.

The strong presence of the Catholic church informed this situation, just as literate clerics like Chávez de la Rosa, Luna Pizarro, and especially Valdivia had earlier played key roles in politics and education, and they wrote a lot for wider, popular audiences. These "second wave" regionalist intellectuals were mostly anticlerical, however, tending to play down everyday Arequipeños' vibrant Catholicism (cf. N. Miller 1999).[2] While the importance of print media and literacy were evident even in the 1780 poster rebellion and in Valdivia's prolific writing in local newspapers in the mid-nineteenth century, it was during the literary turn in the early

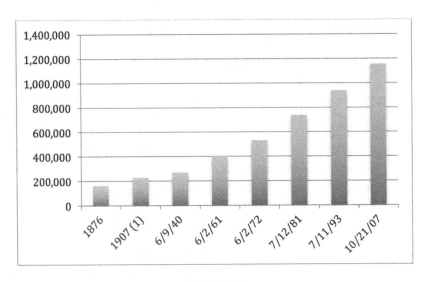

FIGURE 4.1

Population of the Department of Arequipa, 1876–2007. From "Regions of Peru,"
Statoids, http://www.statoids.com/upe.html. Accessed 15 June 2013.

decades of the twentieth century that regional identity as we now know
it crystallized.

Arequipeño writers' sense of their city as a confined social space, a
virtual *aldea* (village), was certainly incubated by the general lag in Peruvian demographic growth, which continued until the mid-twentieth
century, when Peru's population grew from 6.2 million (1940) to 23 million (1993). Though Arequipa's population began to grow at this time as
well (fig. 4.1), it is important to keep in mind how small the city was until the 1950s, when the central city hardly covered more terrain than it
did in 1920 or even in 1820 or earlier—a grid of roughly 15 × 15 blocks,
surrounded by cultivated land. Until the construction of Puente Grau in
1882, there was still only the early colonial Puente Viejo across the Rio
Chili. It is not entirely without reason, then, as we will see in closing this
chapter, that old-time Arequipeños still wax nostalgic about the intimate
city that Arequipa once was, lamenting the way everything has seemed
to change from the 1950s on.

By the early 1890s the effects of the war were subsiding (recall that
the south had been spared direct damage), and productive activity was
resuming in southern Peru. Commercial activity picked up, aided by
strengthening ties with Bolivia, given the Chilean seizure and continuing control of Arica. But within two decades a railroad line had been

constructed up to La Paz from Arica, a follow-up to the reconfigura-
tion of relations between Chile and Bolivia. Arequipeños' commercial
connections with Bolivia declined after that, and with this the regional
space under Arequipeño oligarchic hegemony was reduced from "el sur
andino" to "el sur peruano" (Flores Galindo, Plaza, and Oré 1978, 59).

> Regional precapitalist sectors managed to affirm their existence while
> threatened by oligarchic-monopolist capital and the growing state
> centralization. This fact is evident in the demands of the commercial–
> large landowning bourgeoisie of Arequipa, that constituted the most
> powerful group in the region. Their projects of decentralizing admin-
> istrative, credit and public expenditure, along with the modification
> of the traditional political economy that favored agro-mineral ex-
> ports, signaled their antioligarchic bourgeois intentions. To the extent
> that these demands coincided with those of the middle and popular
> sectors of that important city, the bourgeoisie was capable of combin-
> ing them to become the hegemonic factor of local society (Caravedo
> 1978). Nevertheless the political support of the *civilistas* and popu-
> lar sectors of Lima, along with other coastal cities, thwarted these re-
> gional efforts. (Cotler 1978, 230–231)

As we learned in chapter 3, the economic fortunes of the Arequipa region came to depend primarily on fluctuations in the alpaca- and sheep-
wool export market (Thorp and Bertram 1978, 62–64), which dominated
the regional economy from before the war with Chile until the rise of
copper mining and wider industrialization in the 1960s under the first
regime of Fernando Belaúnde Terry. These fluctuations had important
effects among indigenous populations linked to the wool trade, as we
will see.

Because Arequipa was still hardly industrialized, other than the
wool-processing facilities, such as the Huayco factory, and the brewery, a
working class was only beginning to form and conceive of itself in class
terms. We forget that Arequipa, like most of the country, was still profoundly rural in the early twentieth century (Deustua and Rénique 1984,
16). In Lima, by contrast, overt class conflict was beginning to emerge,
with a rising tide of labor unrest and strikes, even riots, since the 1890s
in Callao and Vitarte, especially among textile workers in the period
1915–1919. Because the regional economy was dominated by mercantile
rather than industrial capital until the 1960s, capitalist class relations remained generally underdeveloped in Arequipa (Love 1989).

Intensifying race and class issues thus framed the work of intellectuals in these decades, especially the "Generation of 1919," which included such figures as José Carlos Mariátegui, Jorge Basadre, Victor Raúl Haya de la Torre, and Alberto Sánchez (Chavarría 1970, 277) on a national level. "The 1919 generation questioned the nationalism of the [Generation of 1900], particularly their traditionalism and lack of commitment to action" (Chavarría 1970, 278); unlike the earlier writers, the members of the Generation of 1919 came from middle-class and provincial rather than aristocratic backgrounds. In addition, these intellectuals saw themselves as social critics independent of both state and church, unlike V. A. Belaúnde, for example (see N. Miller 1999, 6).

Universities began growing, largely by accepting students from middle- and lower-middle-class backgrounds, and university reform was in the air. Inspired by the Russian Revolution and subsequently fueled by the Great Depression beginning in 1929, many university students at San Marcos and other universities in the 1920s became more politicized and began to join left, anticentralist political and cultural movements. Growing out of the University Reform movement, the González Prada popular universities were an attempt to extend the benefits of education to the poor and marginalized in Peruvian society.

Arequipeño regionalism became more defined, public, and intense as the Peruvian state consolidated and its power intensified during the "patriarchal republican" period of 1890–1930. Much of this political-literary energy intersected complexly with, and in a sense was eclipsed by, developing Aprista, Communist (Partido Comunista Peruano; PCP), and populist movements in the middle to late 1920s and the 1930s (Jansen 2009), a period of rapid economic and political change in Arequipa and the nation. All these matters came to a head during the eleven-year dictatorship of Augusto Leguía (1919–1930), a period characterized by increasing centralization in the executive branch, continued government spending on public works (though marked by corruption), and growing external debt. Domestic agricultural and industrial production stagnated, and the government's focus was on Lima and north-coast agricultural exports rather than on the development of an internal, national market. "The result was a recession of the regional economy . . . which received little or no relief from Central Government, since . . . the determinants of economic policymaking in those years did not include any desire to alleviate regional inequalities, nor any interest in fostering the sort of diversified, inward-directed economic growth which might have benefited at least some of the declining regions" (Thorp and Bertram 1978, 66). After an initial phase of support for middle-class aspirations (N. Miller 1999, 66), the regime dedicated itself primarily to defending dominant north-coast *exportador*-class interests against a rising tide of unrest among both urban textile workers and rural cane, wool, and other producers. Persecution of these efforts by the Leguía regime in 1924 inflamed progressive sectors and contributed centrally to the formation of the APRA Party (Klaiber 1975). APRA subsequently developed a strongly mestizo narrative, portraying "'the people' as national protagonists, embracing Jose Vasconcelos' ideas of mestizaje, and envisioning a continental movement to construct 'Indoamerica,' a mestizo continent" (Itzigsohn and vom Hau 2006, 206, citing Peter Klarén's 1977 work "The Social and Economic Consequences of Modernization in the Peruvian Sugar Industry, 1870–1930").

All these developments sapped investment and threatened the freetrade interests of the Arequipeño commercial oligarchy, and therefore the broad urban and rural sectors connected to ongoing commercial vitality. Faced with few other economic prospects and no political openings, Arequipeño elites continued to clamor for state support of infrastructural development, modernization of agricultural production, and open trade policies to expand the internal market in the southernhighlands economic space they strove to manage. The construction of highways to both Lima and Puno in the 1930s led to a growth of trucking and some growth of this internal market, but export and other agricultural policies emanating from Lima lagged behind the economic developments that the south was experiencing. The impending loss of Tacna and Arica to the Chileans in 1925–1926, culminating in 1929, was ominous, and when US investors pulled out in 1929, the effects of worldwide depression were made more severe.

By 1930 the Decentralist Party under Sánchez Cerro demanded political and economic autonomy, which they saw as necessary to continue local development and expansion of the regional market (Rénique 1979). Despite the populist rhetoric of Sánchez Cerro, who led the coup that took down Leguía in the 1930 revolution from Arequipa, oligarchic and/ or military control of the state continued. Though Sánchez Cerro was originally from Piura and was hailed as the "first mestizo president of Peru," his military regime, and then that of Óscar Benavides, continued the repression of Apristas and of left movements generally. Military intervention in national politics continued throughout this period.

Benavides had intervened against Billinghurst (1914–1915), who had been supported by a growing labor movement, and again governed from 1933–1939 after Sánchez Cerro's assassination.

Political repression of reformist movements in the name of national order continued through the 1960s via a succession of military and conservative civilian regimes. This trend was briefly interrupted when distinguished legal scholar Arequipeño Bustamante y Rivero, who had been instrumental in the 1930 coup against Leguía, was elected president in 1945 via a coalition of moderate and left political parties—only to be deposed in a 1948 coup by General Odría. Military seizure of the state in the 1930s and oligarchic recapture of the state apparatus after World War II under the Odría dictatorship (1948–1956) blocked alternative projects (see Itzigsohn and vom Hau 2006), including the Arequipeño version of nationalism. Such repression again prompted popular uprisings in Arequipa in 1950 and 1955 that were spearheaded by its commercial elite (Caravedo 1978) and that in 1950 involved Francisco Mostajo as symbolic leader. Though Fernando Belaúnde Terry was elected to the presidency in the early 1960s, the military again promptly intervened, bringing us to the 1980s and the general close of the period under examination in this chapter.

II. REINVENTING THE REGIONALIST TRADITION

Given the overwhelmingly Spanish, colonial, and commercial character of Arequipa, why was a (re)invented tradition centering on symbols primarily associated with "mestizo" small farmers, symbols that were at first more feminine than masculine, used to press the case for Arequipeño exceptionalism in the national field? Who built this tradition, and when? And whose interests were served by it? Who thought (and thinks) of themselves as members of an imagined community thus conceived?

In this first half of the twentieth century, and particularly in the 1920s and 1930s, then, Peruvians were repeatedly faced with the specter of social upheaval and spreading violence, both in Lima and Puno. The central problem seemed to be a continuing lack of national resolve to confront perennial—indeed mounting—social and national identity problems. An explosion of intellectual work around these matters—much of it regional—characterizes the first three decades of the twentieth century (Deustua and Rénique 1984). What is interesting about the Arequipa case is the ways that regional intellectuals chose to work in the cultural field—the reconfiguring of nineteenth-century developments and ideals—because of the near impossibility of working in more overtly political ways, given the long succession of militarily supported authoritarian regimes representing oligarchic interests.

Arequipeño civic and commercial leaders found themselves in a predicament: with so much trending against their interests, and given a distant, corrupt state that wouldn't intervene to sustain growth, what to do? Along with members of the regional elite, in generations as different as those of Victor Andrés Belaúnde and José Luis Bustamante y Rivero, aspiring middle sectors felt boxed in by a repressive Lima-based state and faced with the twin prospects of labor conflict on the coast and race war emanating from the nearby highlands. The ongoing sense of Peru's weak national culture and very divided society after the 1880s debacle with Chile spurred a search for authentic local traditions that could serve as a template for a truly national culture. Given the legacy of failed attempts at regional political autonomy in the south, the reestablishment of some hegemonic identity around which people nationally could rally and regroup became even more pressing. With his "Queremos Patria" (We need a national identity) concluding his speech opening the 1914 academic year at San Marcos (Belaúnde 1987, 130), V. A. Belaúnde voiced a widespread feeling that resonated strongly and across classes, especially in the south.

A majority of the Arequipeño cultural entrepreneurs significant for the regionalist tradition came from middle-class or even plebeian origins and/or had political sympathies with popular sectors; some (e.g., Urquieta, Peralta) were politically active. Unlike on the north coast, a hegemonic regional landed oligarchy had not formed in Arequipa, so the commercial elite in Arequipa did not need to confront this political bloc (Carpio Muñoz 1981–1983, 51); rather, they absorbed the few *hacendados* and made them a secondary ally, and middle-sector interests generally corresponded with those of the commercial elite. In a parallel movement, a group of artisans (including Mostajo's father), mindful of the direct threat posed by the importation of cheap manufactured cloth (see below in this chapter), mounted a political campaign in the form of the Liga Independiente that, after internal struggle, transformed into the Partido Independiente—the first entirely nonaristocratic political movement in Peruvian history (Ballón Lozada 1992, 52–53).

Prominent regional intellectuals such as Maria Nieves y Bustamante, Jorge Polar, Francisco Mostajo, and Teodoro Núñez Ureta, and to a

lesser extent Percy Gibson, César Atahualpa Rodríguez, Alberto Hur-
tado, Guillermo Mercado, and many others, looked to the image of hard-
working, honest locals as progressive, incorruptible, and therefore sta-
bilizing role models for the region and, by extension, the country. They
produced poems, novels, essays, songs, and paintings that extolled these
purported qualities and even romanticized ordinary folk, especially the
campiña smallholder.

My central assertion in this and the next chapter is that though smallholders, picanteras, and other plebeians were often the key symbols and
primary bearers of this structure, they themselves played virtually no
role in the construction of this imaginary. The bulk of this cultural production was about viewing the countryside from the perspective of the
city (Kristal 1987)—rural Arequipa seen through an urban lens. Intellectuals of this tumultuous period, such as Mostajo, Belaúnde, Gibson, and
later Núñez Ureta and Peralta, went to great lengths to evoke such rustic
and popular figures and scenes as the *picantería*, the *lechera* (milkmaid),
and the rural smallholder, as well as urban popular elements, in their
contributions to defining *lo arequipeño*.

Picanterías were the principal social arena where intellectuals and
others from rising urban middle-class and professional sectors mixed
with local artisans and farmers in traditional peri-urban districts like
Cayma (with its vestiges of colonial pilgrimage), Tiabaya, and Yanahuara. Imagery from these picanterías was far more prominent in most
of this writing (e.g., Mostajo [1924] 1956) than was imagery from more
distant parts of the campiña. (I explore the gendered dimensions of picanterías and regional culture in chapter 5.)

The invented tradition I describe in this section came to have a recurrent undertone of nostalgia, particularly by the mid-twentieth century,
lamenting the apparent lack of leaders and patriots of a caliber like that
of the heroes of the nineteenth-century struggles on which it was built.
While this tradition urging people to rise up against injustice reaches
back to the late-colonial period and coalesces with Valdivia, as we saw
in chapter 3, in the hands of Jorge Polar, Francisco Mostajo, and others
it becomes a major theme tying together diverse experiences and mold-
ing them into a common frame opposing political and economic centralism with authentic national spirit. The qualities of the plebeian/rural
everyman extolled in this tradition, often explicitly labeled as mestizo,
became a trope for a shared national identity (cf. Martínez-Echazábal
1998). The foregrounding of these populist elements had as much to do
with elites' political opposition to Limeño centralism as with plebeians'

success, through intellectual interlocutors, in forcing open the closed social ranks above them in regional society.

I describe this tradition and its main protagonists at some length in this chapter, but I harness key concepts, largely from practice theory, to analyze it more explicitly in chapter 6. The tradition was passed down both institutionally and through families, directly including many of these writers. Two of the leaders of the 1867 uprising, for example—Pedro Diez Canseco and Juan Manuel Polar—were, respectively, Victor Andrés Belaúnde's maternal grandfather and Jorge Polar's father. Arequipeño traditionalism was reproduced not only by such direct descent from illustrious earlier Arequipeños, however, but also through a new generation of intellectuals with more modest social origins and through the practices of several notable institutions, primarily educational, that served as training grounds for inculcating that traditionalism. These include the Colegio de San Jerónimo (founded 1619, reorganized 1802) and the Academia Lauretana (founded 1821), from which rose the Colegio de la Independencia (1827) and the associated Universidad Nacional de San Agustín (refounded as a republican institution in 1828). (We examined Valdivia's role in these latter two institutions above in chapter 3.) The university and the academy had even formally merged for a while in 1846 (Quiroz Paz Soldán 1990, 468). Along with the Colegio de Abogados, these secondary schools and the public university—long run by Jorge Polar—served as the principal nodes around which Arequipeño traditionalism developed, since across social classes most of the cultural entrepreneurs discussed next were trained and/or taught there. For example, aristocratic former president Arequipeño Francisco García Calderón, who had refused to cooperate with the Chileans or to surrender Tacna and Arica, returned to Arequipa after his brief tenure as president during the Chilean occupation of Lima and served on the faculty of the Colegio de la Independencia, where he himself had studied.

Regarding the Colegio de Abogados, it is important to note that *abogado* was in Peru a more general professional distinction than mere lawyering. Study of the law had been a key path for social mobility and an emblem of status in colonial Arequipa (Wibel 1975, 162), and in provincial towns such as Arequipa, having a law degree was almost prerequisite cultural capital for participating in this literary-based tradition, *tertulias*, and educated circles. The central locale of Arequipa's Colegio de Abogados—now prominently featuring a life-sized portrait of Francisco Mostajo—has long served as a principal setting for important conferences and workshops.

A. *The Traditional Story Arequipeños Tell Themselves*

The story most Arequipeños tell themselves is this: Unlike other Andean cities, Arequipa was fundamentally Spanish in origin (three of Francisco Pizarro's original thirteen conquistadors—the "Trece del Gallo"—resided here). It was not built on a large indigenous city, nor was there a large indigenous population in the valley, that population having been much reduced by natural disaster shortly before Spanish arrival. Consequently, founding settlers had to learn and share agricultural techniques with the few locals who had survived, had to make the desert bloom through the hard work and sweat of their brows. Poor Spaniards worked on small estates in the campiña, and some miscegenation with local indigenous populations gradually occurred over the centuries. These rural smallholders were primarily poor Spanish, with some mixing with local indigenous populations. Late eighteenth-century immigration and intermarriage of Basque and other northern Spanish merchants, as well as nineteenth-century immigration and intermarriage of British and other European merchants tied to the wool trade, only enhanced this hybrid vigor and entrepreneurial spirit. These sturdy, proud, entrepreneurial everymen, like urban merchants, shared a desire for the freedom to work hard and make something of themselves and their society.

It is a fairly coherent story, actually, and while not quite ethnic, in the sense of being a discourse of shared descent, I heard it more or less in this form from a variety of people in the city, from my key informants in Sabandía, and from several other of the many farmers I interviewed from Chiguata to Tiabaya. It is anchored in the Valdivia tradition as well as in the lived experience of everyday urban dwellers and rural cultivators in the valley, and its canonical nature suggests it was primarily produced, refined, and transmitted in the key institutions cited above. The Spanish conquest is even projected back onto the Inka, since (according to the poet Garcilaso de la Vega) the traditional story relates that the name "Arequipa" derives from Quechua *Ari-quepay* or *Ari-quepari*— "Quedaos, si os está bien" (Stay and reside, if it please you)—as Inka Mayta Cápac was said to have told his troops in their apparently peaceful takeover of the valley (see Polar [1891] 1958, 11). The name, then, was a clear (if mistaken, as we learned above in chapter 2) reference to the especially fertile and agreeable characteristics of the valley, recently depopulated by an earthquake. The Spanish arrived by the mid-1530s, founding the city on 15 August 1540, but because of the depopulation, they were not obliged to conquer a local population and had little indigenous labor to rely on. Pizarro's vision was to establish a Spanish city that would be an administrative center and entrepôt for the entire central Andean interior from Cuzco through Collao (the Altiplano) to Charcas. The dry, temperate climate was stimulating and conducive to the hard work of laying out a city and farming the valley lands.

What is emphasized in this story is the hard work of the early Spanish farmers and the current mestizo smallholders in making a hostile land produce, given the lack of Indian labor in the valley. That an extensive system of terracing and canals was already in place, or that the indigenous inhabitants had to be dispossessed of their land, is hardly mentioned in the conventional story. Campiña imagery, so important to the traditionalist narrative, captures this harmonious human, workaday landscape. People quickly came to admire and even cherish the verdure of the countryside, with its early-established, harmonious mix of Andean and Iberian crops: sheep, cattle, wheat, barley, broad beans, squash and various other vegetables, alfalfa, various vine and tree fruits, potatoes (especially the *chaucha*), and of course maize. Periodic earthquakes and volcanic eruptions (especially in 1600) forced locals to redouble their efforts and rebuild their city, thus forging the hard-working, independent spirit that characterizes Arequipeños to this day. Volcanoes inspired a rebellious, courageous spirit (see, for example, Guinassi Morán 1908, 38–50).

This discourse prevailed in the absence of a more indigenous identity. In the Arequipa basin and in the city, the early erosion of *curaca* (Spanish-recognized Indian authorities) authority and the alienation of Indian lands (see chapter 6) had resulted in extensive miscegenation and cultural assimilation in Arequipa over the long colonial period, laying the objective foundation for a later discourse of mestizaje. Giving up "Indian" status was certainly accelerated by Castilla's abolishing of tribute in 1854 (the mining *mita* having been abolished in 1812); there was now no need to continue to expect the state to reciprocate with defense of communal land in exchange for labor tribute. Whether through sale or theft, by the middle of the nineteenth century there was virtually no communal land in the valley left to redistribute (Chambers 2003, 40). This legal change might be said to mark the beginning of the possibility of developing a mestizo identity, since Indians were no longer tied to legal subordination. Prior to 1854 there had been some incentive to maintain "Indian" identity, even if that was offset by having to continue to pay a head tax. But after 1854 the incentives to publicly maintain an indigenous identity were gone, and with *curacas'* authority having already been generally undermined by independence, the push was on for ordinary Arequipeños to identify as "citizens." Acculturation, along with a discursive silencing of Indians, ensued, and "Indian" Arequipeños just seem to fade away in the basin.[3] After the war with Chile some urban intellectuals—especially those with kinship or other ties to plebeians and small farmers (such as Mostajo)—began to recognize and extol the mixed ancestry of everyday Arequipeños.

B. Novelistic Treatment

Even in the late colonial period we find some early examples of writing in the traditionalist style—stirring descriptions of the beauty of the campiña, the orderliness of the city, and the hard work of early Spanish in making the desert bloom (e.g., Echeverría [1804] 1958). Juan Espinosa ([1839] 1996) noted in a rather romantic vein how hard the rural inhabitants worked on their smallholdings and how colorfully they dressed: "Go out to the countryside, you'll see the beautiful red and yellow skirts, that form the most beautiful contrast with the perennial green of the campiña."

MARIA NIEVES Y BUSTAMANTE (1861–1947)

Post–War of the Pacific reflection on the tumultuous caudillista era between the Confederation and the war with Chile marks the takeoff of literary regionalism. Maria Nieves y Bustamante's 1892 *Jorge, el hijo del pueblo* is a founding document capturing and establishing the sentiment of and aspiration toward regionalism,[4] drawing from the 1851 and 1856–1858 regionalist struggle of Vivanco against Castilla. Though fictional, *Jorge* sticks close to historical events of the era and reveals much of sociological interest about the everyday lives of average Arequipeños in the middle third of the nineteenth century. It bears comparison with Clorinda Matto de Turner's better-known 1889 novel *Aves sin nido*. Both deal with a love made impossible by social conventions of the day—though more class, in *Jorge*, than race, as in *Aves*. Along with Matto de Turner, Nieves was one of the few women to break into elite literary circles.

> Peru features the singular characteristic that the novel form was most assiduously cultivated by women. In the case of Clorinda Matto de Turner, the regionalism that appeared connected with realism came to be, in an effort of literary democratization, about the people, about

the Indian within a romantic sentimentalism and with a sense of idealization and protest. (Basadre 1962, 2959)

In Nieves y Bustamante's *Jorge*, earnest commoner and artisan Jorge falls in love with beautiful aristocratic Elena, but her mother forces her to marry a better-placed but manipulative Alfredo Iriarte. Elena dies before Jorge learns that he is of honorable (if illegitimate) birth after all, but with her dead he turns his passion to defending Arequipa from Castilla's troops. Drawing details from Valdivia's *Revoluciones* and from interviews with people who lived through the 1854–1856 period, Nieves denounced the insanity of war, the social differences between the aristocracy and the commoners, and the oppression of women. She delineated at least three aspects of the theme of honorable citizenship and the hybrid mestizo character of everyday Arequipeños: first, the lingering colonial status distinctions between the elites (particularly Iriarte), who dismiss local people as *cholos*, and the humble everyman, who is always, like Jorge, portrayed as an "honorable *artesano*"; second, the very Catholic, Marian sense of selfless martyrdom; Elena's mother dies in poverty, at the last minute repenting of her mistake in forcing her daughter to marry someone she didn't love; third, the honor that inheres in every true citizen; unlike the self-centered Iriarte, Jorge fell in battle, selflessly fighting for the people.

Among many interesting details of life in the mid-nineteenth century, the scene at the end of volume 1 has Jorge with friends drinking and singing; their song turns to a sad *yaraví*. Nieves may have had in mind a specific *chichería*—La Sebastopol in San Lázaro (Arce Espinoza 2009). The friends toast, clinking glasses, though there's no mention of the *challa* toast—tossing some to the ground to "pay the earth" before drinking the rest and passing the bottle, a common feature of drinking in countryside taverns. Even a century later, nightly beer drinking was almost mandatory among local farmers at the shop at the main crossroads in Sabandía, across from my house. Such a trivial slip reveals the author's (gendered) social distance from the lives of real rural folks—again, part of the tradition's urban view of the countryside.

C. *"Scientific" Folklore*

In the latter nineteenth century the study of folklore was becoming professionalized in academic settings, in complex conversation with racialist thinking of intellectuals from Herbert Spencer to Charles Darwin. Folklore societies were founded in various parts of Europe (such as Scandinavia and the Balkans) and in the United States, tied in large part to the building of distinctive national identities. Two schools emerged— "scientific" and "romantic" (Mullen 2000). In Norway, for example, struggling to define itself against Sweden, "certain aspects of peasant culture were thus reinterpreted [by members of the city bourgeoisie] and placed into an urban political context as 'evidence' that Norwegian culture was distinctive, that Norwegians were 'a people' and that they therefore ought to have their own state" (Eriksen 1993, 102). Urban and rural Norwegians consequently belonged to the same culture and had shared political interests.

Developments in Peru paralleled these efforts—all symptomatic of growing interest and anxiety about national identity, as well as of a shift of regional sentiment toward the cultural sphere and away from actual efforts to seize control or alter the form of the state. This was new, since all this would have been at sharp odds with the cosmopolitanism of Arequipa's colonial elites (for example, of men like Goyeneche or Tristán). Before such stirrings around a shared national identity, "the idea that the aristocracy belonged to the same culture as the peasants must have seemed abominable to the former and incomprehensible to the latter" (Eriksen 1993, 102).

JORGE POLAR (1856–1932)

The decades after the war with Chile were filled with soul-searching about "Peru"—its history, its purpose, its future, its failures, its potential. Various intellectuals and public figures in Arequipa, as elsewhere in the country, joined this debate. In Arequipa, few figured more importantly in this period than Jorge Polar Vargas, who reworked and harnessed the regionalist narrative begun by Valdivia and Melgar into an optimistic, can-do postwar reconstruction effort. An early positivist and modernist, he argued that hard-working, mestizo Arequipeños were just the sort of Peruvians uniquely equipped to undertake this national task.

The son of Juan Manuel Polar, who had been part of the 1834 uprising and who later occupied high positions in government in the mid-nineteenth century, Jorge Polar was steeped in regionalist thinking. In addition to this direct family tradition, he was educated at the Colegio de la Independencia and UNSA. He pursued law, and after earning two doctorates (political science and history) at San Marcos in Lima (1899), he returned to Arequipa to become director of the Colegio de la Independencia and later a member of the faculty and rector of UNSA. He was an Arequipan delegate to congress from 1899 to 1907 (representing Cailloma) and served in the Superior Court of Lima (1907–1916). Polar was also minister of public education (*justicia, instrucción, culto y beneficencia*) between 1904 and 1906 under the Civilista José Pardo y Barreda regime. Strongly influenced by positivism and addressing the reconstruction of the country after the war with Chile, Polar undertook the first university reforms in Peru in 1895 in Arequipa (Chavarría 1968, 193) and then nationally while minister. Aggressive reformer of education that he was, interestingly Peru's first strike by university students occurred in Arequipa in 1907.

In this milieu, Jorge Polar's best-known work—*Arequipa: Descripción y estudio social* ([1891] 1958) is notable for striking a modernist, positivist, yet warmly lyrical stance. He began writing the book in 1890 when he was director of the public library, before he had spent time in politics in Lima (Arce Espinoza 2003). At the orders of the provincial council, he had an official portrait of Melgar brought from Lima. *Descripción* is a virtual poetic almanac extolling the mestizo virtues of Arequipeños and the extraordinary beauty of the place itself. Widely read at the time, Polar's work served to define *lo arequipeño* and, along with Nieves's *Jorge*, served as a foundational literary expression of the cultural reformulation under way in the region during the period between the War of the Pacific and the post–World War II era of big changes in population growth and industrialization.

Both the content of his 1891 text and its organization merit a somewhat extended examination for its foregrounding of place-linked symbols and elements in the regional culture. About a third of his book describes the rural districts, the people, and the valley and environmental features. Polar was not quite ready to abandon the reality of race; nevertheless, for him the objective racial mixing among everyday Arequipeños was a historical product, creating a space for the cultivation of virtue. His evocation of mestizaje prefigured national debates across Latin America several decades later (see Telles and Flores 2013, 418).

For Polar, "the heart of the Peruvian homeland lives in [Arequipa]" (Polar [1891] 1958, 149). Arguing for a loosening of constricting colonial racialized status distinctions, he noted, "We're now quite far from the colonial era and Spanish civilization, so we're able to begin something new, distinct and original" (ibid., 183). "Arequipa now has, within its influences of race, delineated its almost formed individuality, its personality as a people, as a city" (ibid., 184). Characteristics of the local, free-holding campiña farmer are important to the overall (re)formulation of Arequipeño identity. "All that's great and noble in our revolutions, pertains to the people of Arequipa. . . . One's not born at the foot of a volcano in vain" (ibid., 150, 151).

It is Polar's emphasis on the scientific reality of Arequipa's essentialized, naturally mestizo character that is most important here.[5] Mestizaje is not just a possible ideal; it is a living reality in Arequipa. The admirable qualities of the first Spanish conquerors—"heroic fantasy, impulsive wanderings, adventurers, romantics" (Polar [1891] 1958, 115)—didn't leave much of a trace, unfortunately. For Polar, "to have been colonized by a race that declined [in the seventeenth and eighteenth centuries] was the immense, irreparable disgrace of America . . . they were born old, tired and decadent" (ibid., 117).

Like the Spanish, however, the indigenous peoples of Peru were also lacking important character traits.

> That which the quechua [sic] lacked, was, above all, character, his long, his age-old indifference for any sort of individual independence, had produced a profound atrophy of his will. . . . The Indian labored like a passive wheel of a mechanism, who didn't know any other activity except to eternally turn in circles. . . . The Indian didn't and couldn't have security and sovereignty over himself, in whom will had been tenaciously and heavily repressed, by a social organization in which the state was everything, and the Inka was the state. This was the radical flaw in ancient Peruvian society, in other ways so admirable and beautiful. . . . The Indian has resistance bordering on heroism; but initiative, action, spontaneous individual impulse, independence—these he lacks. (Ibid., 119–120)

In a fascinating section on what modern science can tell us, Polar engaged ideas of racial degeneration and social Darwinism (though not the biological science behind them) then circulating in North Atlantic intellectual circles to argue for a doctrine of hybrid vigor holding that the combination of two races can produce a race of people better than either one. But apart from Arequipa this was not the general case in Peru, because one race was superior and the other inferior:

> The modern sciences of man—Anthropology and Sociology—prove, or a bit less, that the product of a mixture of two races that find themselves at different levels of civilization, that is, the mixture of a supe-

rior with an inferior race, is always weak, always incapable of fighting for life, for progress. (Ibid., 120)

So should the Spaniards have just eliminated the natives here, as the English did in North America, he wondered? If the Spanish brought passion but not the necessary will and individual self-control, is the situation hopeless? Given his positivist orientation, Polar argues that the Arequipeño people are up to the task.

> The product of this mixture, the Peruvian creole, who is, almost exclusively, the inhabitant of the valley of Arequipa, then should carry in his blood, in his nerves and brain the stamp of his origin, he ought to be on fire, a dreamer, fickle, turbulent, romantic, these racial qualities modified by the influence of the environment where he has lived. (Ibid., 124)

Polar elaborates his long analysis of Arequipeño mestizaje by examining these "scientific" aspects, veering toward a sort of environmental determinism. Hence Polar's careful, even statistical, measurement of the chemical properties of spring water, district populations, the height of mountains, and the number of children of various categories in the orphanage. (One can almost imagine him being a fan of phrenology.) For example, he discusses at length how the local diet—of meat, potatoes, maize, vegetables, and a lot of water (in soups)—characteristic of the "the poor and working people," provides all that is necessary for good health except calcium. But this is provided by maize, particularly in the form of widely consumed *chicha* (ibid., 126–127). This balanced diet leads to good health and provides the basis for Arequipeños' noted ability to work at all elevation levels: "Woodcutters and charcoal makers spend nights, in whatever season, at 12 to 14 thousand feet elevation, suffering snow, wind and extremely low temperatures. Muleteers constantly travel from the hot valley climates to the rigor of the puna, with no unhealthy effects" (ibid., 127). Likewise, the region's excellent climate—abundant sun, pure air, electrically charged atmosphere (from the dryness)—are very healthful (in an almost medieval sense of balancing of humors: not too hot or too cold, too wet or too dry), stimulating physical and intellectual development. Concluding with a flourish, "Y bien se ve, que hija de la soberbia montaña es esta comarca" (and so we see, what a child of the proud mountain this region is) (ibid., 145).

But when one grasps the moral defects in the generally healthy, balanced Arequipeños, one sees the need for further improvement. White immigration would help: "One understands the necessity of reconstituting our population in the highest classes by means of immigration of the strong races, and drawing ourselves near, as much as possible, to nature" (ibid., 134). The volcanic passion of Arequipeños has a certain romantic appeal, but it has always led to ruin and destruction (ibid., 145). Arequipa's intense Catholicism is not an intolerant, violent religiosity, and its occasional excess is a consequence of a living moral spirit and a volcanic fervor (ibid., 148).

Modernism, with its positivistic, scientific worldview, influenced regional intellectuals besides Polar, such as Mariano Rivero and Francisco Mostajo. Intellectuals of this turn-of-the-twentieth-century Generation of 1900—students of Polar's at UNSA—engaged with regional issues and aspired to understand the politics and history of their region in such terms.

In the hands of Polar and his contemporaries, elegiac descriptions of the heroic struggles of nineteenth-century heroes against seemingly overwhelming political odds were read onto the idealized traits of the campiña farmer struggling against seemingly overwhelming environmental odds. Fusing modernist sensibilities and "scientific" analysis with traditionalist rhetoric and imagery, this fighting resolve and entrepreneurial spirit were invoked as essential traits of Arequipeños in the ongoing struggle to define Peruvian identity.

I quote Polar at some length, not only because his is the foundational version of the mestizo discourse emerging in this period, but also because he occupied such influential educational positions both nationally, as minister of education, and regionally, as a professor of literature and philosophy and a rector at UNSA and at the Colegio de la Independencia. He influenced many students, and his 1891 work deeply shaped literate Arequipeños' understanding of and love for their region. So central is Polar's *Descripción* to the regionalist tradition that the book was reprinted thirty years later (in 1922) during the height of the Leguía dictatorship and again in 1958 in the wake of the Odría dictatorship.[6]

FRANCISCO MOSTAJO (1874–1954)

Apart from Polar, arguably the key person in the intellectual and literary life of Arequipa during the first half of the twentieth century was Francisco Mostajo, an organic intellectual of astonishing productivity. He was particularly important in giving voice to the dreams and anxieties of the nascent urban middle class in a city experiencing growing modernization pains, appreciative of the heritage of popular engagement with the civic life of the city, with a certain nostalgia for the order and simplicity of the plebeian and rural life in and around Yanahuara and Cayma, where he lived most of his life. Given his working-class origins, Mostajo's writing is much more anchored in the lived realities of plebeian Arequipeños than is that of anyone else of his era—certainly more than that of Gibson or even Polar. Mostajo was also the least nostalgic of his peers.

Mostajo was a boy through the Chilean occupation and grew up in the postwar reconstruction period. He was a disciple of Polar at UNSA (he dedicated his thesis to his "maestro el galano prosador y eximio filósofo Jorge Polar" [professor the gallant prosist and eminent philosopher Jorge Polar]). Hector Ballón Lozada (1999) argues that his work can be periodized into political (early), folkloric (middle), and historical (later) periods; he was at the peak of his literary powers in that middle period— roughly the 1910s and 1920s. While the various writers analyzed above, and even those who came after Mostajo, contributed in many important ways to the construction of Arequipeño regionalism in its classic, peak formulation, it was Mostajo (and Polar) who had the greatest impact— not least because Mostajo stayed in Arequipa, while the others, almost without exception, left, either voluntarily or forced into exile.

Mostajo's father Santiago had played a key role in the organizing activity of the Sociedad de Artesanos, establishing a Centro Obrero about 1903—more a mutual aid society than a class-conscious workers' association. Though this movement and Mostajo's involvement in it peaked about 1906, it left a strongly populist and political imprint on him. Shaped by their labor politics in this earlier phase and heavily influenced by Polar, Mostajo and Urquieta played major roles, chiefly as journalists, in fomenting the image of the urban artisans and rural smallholders as embodying the hard-working qualities of everyday mestizo Arequipeños.

Mostajo straddled both the generations of 1900 and 1919 and was central to the construction of an essentialized mestizaje for Arequipa. It was Mostajo who charted the least literary course, differing from the more strictly literary impulses of, say, Guillermo Mercado or Percy Gibson, with his broader, more populist vision of a deeply rooted, mestizo identity for Arequipa. Very much a public intellectual, Mostajo combined his populist leanings with fiery oratory, informing his strongly folkloric interests in the 1920s, unequaled by anyone else in this period.

While his writing from the earlier *librepensador* (freethinker) days and his work with Urquieta, an avid decentralist, are much more polemical, political, and anticlerical, his middle-period writing (Urquieta died in 1920) involved a turn to folklore and history, marked by a distancing from politics and a more conservative, nostalgic posture as he aged. His *San Gil de Cayma: Leyenda folklórica arequipeña* (Mostajo [1924] 1956) epitomizes this turn. Here, he was especially inventive in the ways he tapped plebeian and rural lifeways and imagery and connected them to regionalist sentiment. The first half of *San Gil* was published in the local paper in 1924, and the entire work, somewhat amplified, was serialized in the regional agricultural magazine *La Campiña* in 1929–1930 and was later elaborated in several versions. In *San Gil*, Mostajo was deeply concerned with rescuing "all the folklore of Cayma, widespread in our campiña." He explored the magnetic appeal of Cayma as a preferential place for burial by local residents of La Chimba (today's Yanahuara, Cerro Colorado, and Cayma districts), tapping into the early lore about the appearance of La Candelaria in association with a cemetery there.

In a 1940 introduction to the book, Mostajo reflexively situated himself: "Even though I'm the key promoter of modernism in Arequipa, my poetic essence is wholly romantic, by reason of my social origin, my temperament and the spirit of the times." He waxes eloquent about Cayma, arguing forcefully that in its soul the indigenous spirit is still present and that this is essential to understanding "lo arequipeño." The 1956 edition (from which I draw) contains not only a thirteen-page prologue by Manuel Suárez Polar, the five-page 1940 preface by Mostajo, and the fifty-three-page poem itself, but also sixty-six pages of notes on history, geography, social conditions, and so on; a nine-page "interview" with "a contemporary of San Gil"; an eighteen-page "Sátira Mestiza"—a series of imagined encounters with distinguished early Arequipeños—and, finally, sixty-eight pages of ethnographic "notes" on Cayma.

Long-lived and prolific, Mostajo was by orientation anticlerical, with an even more prodigious output of written materials than Valdivia or Polar. As astute an observer of local folk culture as Mostajo was, with his fierce anticlericalism he either did not pick up on or chose to understate the importance of folk Catholicism to campiña dwellers, particularly to the working poor, or of pilgrimage to either the Virgin of Characato or the Virgin of Chapi. Pilgrimage to the Virgin of Cayma had apparently subsided by his time, perhaps because of its proximity to the city.

A deeply historically minded observer of local culture, to all varieties of ahistorical localist pride, Mostajo had this to say in 1915 (note the wistful tone about an Arequipa already passing away; cf. Williams 1973):

One shouldn't be surprised that we emphasize the Arequipeñist note. It's necessary not to tear apart our character as a people. Arequipa's decline coincides with this coming apart. Love of homeland, national sentiment, must be awoken and intensified, for without it a people is destined to be run over or surpassed by other peoples of [stronger character]. This deep, strong love of the land is fully lacking in Peru, our spirit full of anxiety over the Chilean damage and the cholo of the Altiplano. We're a bunch of mestizos fallen out of love with what we have, without fiery pride about who we are, with the energetic sentiment of our land, our race, our collective identity, the history which surrounds us with its force. In any Chilean or Bolivian national spirit is affirmed. The Peruvian comes up blank. And this inferiority in the very fiber of our civic bond can cloud our future and make Peruvians like the last Moorish king of Granada [ruler of nothing, looking back with a sigh at what was lost]. Some response is needed to nationalize instruction, nationalize our behavior, nationalize our life as a people . . . raising the flag on our life as a people. And fiestas like the workers' [ms. break] mental states, it determines directions and renews in its innocence a good radical sediment. Afterward none of this is provincialism or fear of change. No. A laggard provincialism is for the troglodytes. Fear of change is for imbeciles. So love of one's homeland [is] the origin of national sentiment, the base for patriotism that is necessary even now in the midst of international barbarity, uplifting of the collective personality or masculine pitch, not meticulous and without stupid village-level egoism, without inveterate slowness, but rather its nature is assimilationist, open, progressive, comprehensive. Provincialism is like an animal instinct, unconscious, but regionalism on the other hand, is consciousness of our educated selves. Thus we applaud without reservation our compatriots who have the cult of Arequipa, which they always must proclaim, like the Cervantes hero of age-old form, "the most beautiful." (Mostajo's 1915 speech commemorating the tenth anniversary of the Workers' Social Center, and noting the participation of Jorge Polar, cited in Ballón Lozada 1992, 158–159)

Mostajo came to define and even embody the Valdivian populist, feisty part of the regional tradition; in his introductory essay to *San Gil*, Suárez Polar called him a "bull dog" (in English). Mostajo's place in Arequipeño traditionalist sentiment has grown since his death. Ballón Lozada and Carpio Muñoz, among others, elevated his standing in ongoing discussions in the region about identity, and his writing informed much of this and addressed key questions head-on. Since he was so prolific and long-lived, and since he remained in Arequipa and was such a public intellectual, his vision of *lo arequipeño*, building on Polar's, became primary in the tradition.[7]

Mostajo, then, played a key role in consolidating, popularizing, and transmitting the traditional story of Arequipa. Careful in his detailed studies of local life and culture, Mostajo recorded his observations in works scattered in various short-lived periodicals. Though his ideas were influential, largely through his personal ties with many people in Arequipa, his legacy remains relatively unknown, extremely fragmented, and, until recently, out of reach of average readers (Ballón Lozada 1999, 2000; Compañía Cervecera del Sur 2002).

In addition, because he did not hold an academic post or public position, Mostajo's influence was more personal and charismatic than institutional. Though he excelled at law (with all that *abogado* entailed culturally), in Arequipa's highly class-stratified and status-conscious society, Mostajo's non-upper-class background dogged him throughout his career. He relied for a living on meager proceeds from his many articles, poems, and editorials in local magazines.[8]

Though Mostajo was lionized even in his later years, and has certainly been celebrated since his death, Polar probably had the greater impact on regionalist sentiment, since he was centered in the educational establishment, where he influenced many people, had social capital from his class position, and was very politically connected. Local universities played a key role in training administrators and intellectuals around and through which the regionalist narrative developed (see Domingues 2006, 543). This included training schoolteachers and transmitting local heritage and pride of place to the broader populace.

Because he had the strongest social ties with plebeian Arequipa, though, Mostajo's vision was also the most sociopolitically informed. Given his time in rural Puno, Mostajo's comments about the nature of Arequipeño society become all the more intriguing—particularly since his masterpiece *San Gil* was written in a period when he spent some time in Huancané. The other cultural entrepreneurs in this apogee phase of regional discourse were at some remove from plebeian Arequipeños', let alone highland indigenous people's, lived reality, permitting them to make unwarranted assumptions about the homogeneity of everyday Arequipeños (and highlanders) that had the local effect, as Aurelio had discerned and instantiated (see chapter 5), of making the horrible mistake of confusing honorable campiña farmers with landless workers—of failing to recognize social distinctions that plebeians and rural dwellers themselves made. Plebeians' "identity" was not based in their "plebeianness"; rather, it was all about membership in regional society as citizens—a very modern conception of self forged in the nineteenth century and drawing, as we have seen and as I develop in chapter 5, on attitudes across classes even from late-colonial Arequipa.

Other regional intellectuals contributed in this more "scientific" folkloric vein. Alberto Ballón Landa, brother of the then archbishop, for example, enunciated the mestizo essence of Arequipeños and similar conservative themes in his 1908 essay "Estudios de sociología arequipeña: Discurso preliminar" (Ballón Landa [1908] 1958, 81–123), which won first prize in a competition sponsored by the Centro de Instrucción (one suspects Jorge Polar's influence here) on the theme "Causes for which Arequipa, since the end of the eighteenth century until the middle of the nineteenth, produced so many illustrious men?"

In Ballón Landa's essay we see a very clear distillation of major ideas in the conservative thread of mestizaje in Arequipa at the beginning of the twentieth century: an amalgamation of racialist if not racist, Spencerian, progressivist ideas about hybrid vigor and other benefits to come from the mixing of races, though always with the Spanish element dominant. Quite like Polar, Ballón argues that Arequipa's greatness was the product of racial mixture and the environment:

> We see in the dreamy spirit, the burning imagination and the adventurous character of the Spaniard, united to the pure, sweet sentimentalism so perfected in the quechua, [sic] [that] place the Arequipeño on the road to philosophical speculation and contemplation of beauty. . . . We quickly see the conditions of Arequipa and convince ourselves that just about everything has been propitious for intellectual development . . . The climate . . . The environment . . . Life's comforts . . . The beauty and poetry of the panorama. (Ballón Landa [1908] 1958, 96–97)

It was the greatness of the Inka (not the Altiplano, note) that was the indigenous contribution to the Arequipeño spirit, he argued. "The legacy left us by our [Spanish] ancestors was, well, of nobility and distinction" (ibid., 97). Great church leaders of the late-colonial period, especially Archbishop Chávez de la Rosa (who reformed and improved the Colegio de San Jerónimo), prepared the way for the great intellectual opening that came with independence, which opened the shackles placed by colonial restrictions upon the intellectual development of Arequipa. "In every Peruvian, who is a mixed personality, we see the indian [sic] and we hold him in contempt, we see the iberian [sic] and we distrust him" (ibid., 109). But all the fighting among caudillos in the mid-nineteenth century had had a negative effect on the development of this latent talent. Furthermore, growing utilitarianism and selfishness were sapping the souls of the citizenry and making them slaves of materialism. Corruption by political maneuvering was affecting individual psychology. Peruvians couldn't advance without perseverance, but too often people seemed to want immediate gain and gratification.

Ladislao Cabrera Valdez, in his 1924 "Los primeros españoles en Arequipa" ([1924] 1958, 19–26), added an interesting note to this largely conservative thread extolling a very white sort of mestizaje: in the same way that trusted agents of Mayta Cápac residing in the valley requested the emperor to come and found a city in Arequipa, so a few early Spanish settlers residing in what is now the San Lázaro area of central Arequipa requested of Pizarro that he found a city in Arequipa. (Arequipeños seem always to have been forced to depend on an outside authority!)

D. "Romantic Folkore" (including Indigenist and Vanguardist Writers, Painters, and Photographers)

While Polar's and even Mostajo's understanding of regional society was anchored in a modernist, "scientific" mode, notwithstanding Mostajo's admission of romanticist leanings, most of the cultural entrepreneurs involved in constructing this mestizo version of Arequipeño traditionalism worked in a more romanticist vein (see Cornejo Polar 1998).

Along with a flood of new styles, fashions, and technologies following on the arrival of the railroad and the postwar economic recovery (e.g., hydroelectrification of the central city by the turn of the century), new intellectual and artistic currents were sweeping into Arequipa in the first decades of the twentieth century. Percy Gibson and César A. Rodríguez were two of an entire generation of Arequipeño writers prefiguring and then making up the indigenist and vanguardist movements in literature and the arts. Ties with intellectual developments in Lima led many to leave Arequipa (including not only Gibson but also Alberto Hidalgo and Belaúnde, discussed below), where many became active in university and left politics.

Other Arequipeño vanguardists included photographers, especially Max T. Vargas (1874–1959). Vargas was instrumental in bringing photographic technique to southern Peru (as well as to La Paz, Bolivia), documenting quotidian Arequipa in landscapes and portraits of both upperclass and common citizens. He could be considered the founder of documentary photography in the central Andes, though little is actually known about his life and training. He was part of the Centro Artístico in the 1890s and ran his own studio in the 1910s and 1920s. He deeply influenced a subsequent generation of photographers, including Juan Manuel Figueroa (Poole 1997, 174–175) and brothers Carlos Vargas (1885–1979) and Miguel Vargas (1887–1979) (unrelated to Max Vargas), who apprenticed in his studio.[9] Martín Chambi, born in Puno in 1891, also studied under Max Vargas in Arequipa from 1908 to 1917, when he left for Sicuani and later Cuzco.

Arequipeños of means quickly came to consider being photographed a valuable way to record their status in accordance with new North American and European consumption styles.

The presence of a creole society proud of its colonial past, and desirous of immortalizing that social status in images; but above all, the establishment of an international oligarchy that arrived at the White City in the middle of the nineteenth century, for the exploitation of the mineral ores and to invest in infrastructural development, like the railroad or the telegraph. Photography was a sign of scientific progress for these powerful economic classes, and a visual guarantee that they were living in European and North American style, also in the dress and public appearance. The Vargas and Martín Chambi framed this cosmopolitan context generated in the southern Andes, that had no comparison in any other city in Peru. (Balda and Latorre 2014, 8)

CÉSAR ATAHUALPA RODRÍGUEZ (1889–1972)

Rodríguez graduated from the Colegio de la Independencia in 1906, but his graduate career in Lima was cut short by economic difficulties. He returned to Arequipa, and after working odd jobs became director of the Municipal Library for over four decades, from 1916 to 1959. His 1930 poem "Ciudad de Piedra" powerfully evokes Arequipeños' mestizo essence. "The only objects that say anything in Arequipa are the bells and the liquid green of the fields. . . . Arequipa is the suffering [doliente] workshop of the most pure mestizaje in the country" (Rodríguez [1930] 1958, 125). Being one of the few of these cultural entrepreneurs who stayed in Arequipa, as long director of the public library he played a key role in cultivating the traditionalist narrative in literary and intellectual circles there and (at least in the early 1930s), linking these interests with decentralist politics (Deustua and Rénique 1984, 103). (It was Percy Gibson who gave him the "Atahualpa" moniker.) He was on the Cuarto Centenario board in 1940 (see below) and was part of the organizing committee for the 1958 republication of various key texts in the traditionalist narrative (Bermejo 1958; Polar [1891] 1958).

PERCY GIBSON MÖLLER (1885–1960)

Gibson is perhaps the most interesting of these romantic folklorists for our purposes here. The Gibson family, one of the most prominent Arequipeño wool merchants, played a key role in forming the Sociedad Ganadera del Sur, and they attempted to modernize their large hacienda in Puno. Despite his relative privilege, Gibson studied at the general public Colegio de la Independencia—an autodidact who did not complete his university studies. A contemporary of V. A. Belaúnde, after a precocious early period in Arequipa he left for Lima, where he moved in literary circles. He was a curator at the National Library, where he was very influenced by Director Manuel González Prada. He returned to Arequipa for another decade (roughly 1915–1925), then returned to Lima before leaving in the early 1930s for the United States and Mexico and later Europe, where he spent most of the rest of his life, in Britain, France, and Germany with extended family.

Gibson was arguably Arequipa's major poet of the twentieth century and particularly of the 1915–1925 period, when he and Rodríguez were the prime movers of the bohemian Aquelarre arts group. Although the group existed for only a few years and did not have an impact comparable to that of the Grupo Colónida in Lima, it stimulated artistic activity in Arequipa in the following decade. The Aquelarre group was intensely modernist (railing against the ignorant, anti-intellectual stupidity all around them—e.g., Rodríguez's essay in *Aquelarre*, no. 2), decidedly anticlerical (witness the group's name, which means "the coven," which they took because they gathered only in the moonlight, originally on a hill in the valley that was associated with various folk superstitions), and deliriously romantic. In this mix the traditional countryside became both template and resource for working out the strains inherent in the heady, confusing mix of contemporary Peruvian life.

Literary regionalism of this period was decidedly secular, even anticlerical, especially for the romantics, downplaying the religious element in people's identities and practices and in the landscape. These *libre-*

pensadores emphasized the picantería rather than the pilgrimage as the most important collective experience lying behind Arequipeños' mestizo essence. Most of these writers were committed, explicitly or not, to building a modern sense of nationhood, so such backward, irrational, and non- (even anti-) modern, quotidian elements as regular devotion or saint's day festivities, let alone pilgrimage, hardly appear. (The very Catholic Belaúnde was the major exception in this entire group of urban intellectuals.) While their anticlericalism never amounted to a full-scale attack on the church (as it did in Mexico, Colombia, or Chile), that was probably due not only to the relative strength of the church in Arequipa but also to a tacit compromise between liberals and conservatives that characterized Peruvian sentiment on the matter (Pike 1967a).

Detractors on both the political left and right might well have considered Gibson and others of his generation to be bohemian idlers lost in an aesthetic fog, disconnected from the wider politics swirling about them. Yet they were rather tightly connected with city and provincial politics; Gibson was on the city council, and Rodríguez headed the Municipal Library, among other engagements. Arequipa's confined social space meant that the intellectual circles there were intimate and overlapping; everyone knew everyone else. Both Mostajo and Polar wrote in *Aquelarre*, no. 4, for example, though Mostajo later declared, as the movement had matured, "Vanguardist poetry doesn't move me; but neither does it scandalize me: I understand it. I believe it won't last" (Mostajo 1928).

Getting past his early days as a dandy, and despite his class position, Gibson played a key role in bringing the lifeways of the hard-working, humble, rural workers and urban plebeians (though he hardly knew them) into literary and intellectual circles. Reacting to the aping of foreign consumption styles by Arequipeño high society, captured by Max T. Vargas's portrait photography, he wrote, "¡Yo soy arequipeño del cogollo, valeroso, nervudo, de meollo volcánico, fantástico, potente, *y lo mismo que yo es cualquier criollo!* Soy autónomo, altivo, independiente, *mis maestros son el campo y la cumbre*: por eso en mi cerebro hay savia y lumbre . . ." (I'm Arequipeño to the core, gallant, sinewy, of volcanic marrow, fantastic, powerful, *and the same as any other creole!* I'm autonomous, haughty, independent, *my teachers are the countryside and the peak*: this is why there's wisdom and light in my brain . . .) (Gibson 1916; emphasis added).[10]

In collections of poems from 1916 and 1928, Gibson described the Arequipeño landscape in transcendental terms, seeing the most universal

FIGURE 4.2

*Campiña work party, ca. 1920. From https://plus.google.com/photos
/113518930836788618970/albums/5498831386660455265/5514417068607358946?banner
=pwa&pid=5514417068607358946&oid=113518930836788618970; site discontinued.
Accessed 23 July 2013.*

in its specifically local features (e.g., his poem "Los Trigales" [The wheat
fields]). "There are moments in which one is uncertain if the poet is singing of the mountains and valleys or if these are not rather a pretext to
treat much more important themes" (Armaza 1960, 26). Yet however
much he extolled commoners' simplicity and humility, Gibson's distance
from the lived countryside (e.g., fig. 4.2), typical of *indigenista* writers
generally, is evident in his work. For example, in "El Cholo" (1928), he de-
picts proud but humble, melancholy Arequipeño mestizo peasants:

EL CHOLO

La chacra, cholo y chola, y olla y tacho
ella hace chicha, el riega su maíz;
con sombrero faldón, poncho y caucacho
vegeta como el hongo en su raíz.

Ramada, y tardecita del poblacho,
Canta su amor erótico, infeliz,
entre sentimental y entre borracho,
con gotas de sudor en la nariz.

Triste cholo llorón, alma doliente,
quechua andaluz, pesar y frenesí
la voz ronca y cascada de aguardiente,

gime con su vihuela el yaraví,
y melancolizado de poniente
el cree que la vida "es, pues, así".
("El Cholo," *Mundial*, 31 December 1928, cited in Rivera Martínez
    1996, 423–424)

THE *CHOLO*

Field, peasant, and wife, cooking pot and ladle
she makes *chicha*, he waters his maize;
with peaked hat, poncho, and boots
growing like a mushroom on its root.

Bowered, and late from the village,
Singing his erotic love, unhappy,
halfway between sentimental and drunk,
with drops of sweat on his nose.

Sad crying *cholo*, suffering soul,
Quechua Spanish, heavy and frenzied
hoarse voice and torrent of cane liquor,

He wails the *yaraví* with his guitar,
And saddened to put it
He believes that life "is, well, like this."

PAINTERS

At the heart of Arequipeño regionalist sentiment in this era, then, was
romanticist writing of various genres, often poetry. Nevertheless, several painters contributed important imagery that came to form a canonical part of the tradition. With mass education, at least in the cities
(and especially in Arequipa), literature had become more accessible to
more people than painting—a theme that centrally preoccupied painter
Teodoro Núñez, who quite deliberately shifted his work from caricature
and portrait to mural painting so as to have his work more accessible to
broader segments of Peruvian society.

JORGE VINATEA REYNOSO (1900–1931)

Jorge Vinatea formed part of the indigenist current in Peruvian painting
in the 1920s, focusing in his short life on colonial houses and life in the

campiña of Arequipa (Villacorta 1971) but also on rural life in Puno and Cuzco and on caricatures of various political figures in Lima, where he lived much of his twenties. He studied at the Colegio de la Independencia before emigrating to Lima to pursue his career.

His 1930 *Arequipa* (fig. 4.3) is emblematic of this indigenist tradition, emphasizing the quotidian elements of life in the valley. Here Vinatea defines the iconic symbols of regionalist identity—the dark-skinned mestizo everyman with his poncho and mule (not a burro, signaling that he is an *arriero*) and shows them against a panoramic background of campiña, white stone city, and the Misti volcano. A *jarra* (a typical large drinking glass remarkably like an Inka *q'ero* drinking vessel) and a pitcher of *chicha*, a plate of *cuy chactado* (a local delicacy of fried guinea pig flattened with a large stone), and red and green *rocoto* chilies complement a crucifix and lit candle on the rough-hewn, handmade table above two *joras* (large clay jugs characteristic of Andean *chicha* making) and guinea pigs scurrying in the darkness on the floor. One presumes the book on the table is a Bible, but in any case the man's literacy is implied.

FIGURE 4.3

*Jorge Vinatea Reynoso, **Arequipa**, 1930. From "Jorge Vinatea Reinoso (1900-1931)," Art Experts, http://www.artexpertswebsite.com/pages/artists/reinoso.php. Accessed 28 January 2013.*

FIGURE 4.4

Jorge Vinatea Reynoso, **Chacareros de Arequipa,** *1927. From "Jorge Vinatea Reinoso (1900-1931)," Art Experts, http://www.artexpertswebsite.com/pages/artists/reinoso .php. Accessed 28 January 2013.*

(Though this is probably not meant to be a literal perspective, the angle of view is from Antiquilla just south of Puente Bolognesi, the old colonial bridge.)[11] His 1927–1928 painting *Chacareros de Arequipa* (fig. 4.4) enunciates similar themes of rural campiña life, centered on a gathering (informal market? Sogay village?) around *chicha* of dark-skinned men and women at a rustic picantería.

TEODORO NÚÑEZ URETA (1912–1988)

The painter Núñez, like Vinatea (and Mostajo), was of middle-class social origin (his father was a petty merchant) who also favored depictions of quotidian life in the city and the countryside. He studied at the Colegio de la Independencia and at UNSA, where he rose to chair the art history and aesthetics program from 1936 to 1950. Despite holding this post, he spent the majority of his adult life in Lima, where he was direc-

FIGURE 4.5A

Teodoro Núñez Ureta, **La ciudad de Arequipa,** *1950. Mural in Hotel Libertador.*
From "Murales," Teodoro Núñez Ureta: A 100 años de su nacimiento,
http://www.teodoronunezureta.com/murales/.

FIGURE 4.5B

Teodoro Núñez Ureta, **La campiña de Arequipa,** *1950. Mural in Hotel Libertador.*
From "Murales," Teodoro Núñez Ureta: A 100 años de su nacimiento,
http://www.teodoronunezureta.com/murales/.

tor of the National School of Fine Arts from 1973 to 1976. He was perhaps Peru's best-known muralist—Peru's Diego Rivera, one might say. A
postindigenist painter and writer with populist leanings and left political
orientation, though no party affiliation, he was the bane of the various
dictatorial regimes he lived through; Sánchez Cerro had him deported to
Chile in 1933 for participating in a student protest.

But such a bare biographical sketch barely begins to capture the many
influences on his rich and complex life, nor the wide impact he had on
painting, primarily through caricature and murals, and on wider society through his careful observations and running commentary on the
types of people and customs of his life and times. (In this sense he bears
comparison with Martín Chambi.) He was a much beloved public intellectual who stood up to authoritarian impulses and in his own being
searched for Peruvian national sentiment through his painting. Impelled

by the national question, he not only documented but loved his people, his landscape, and his country. Drawing on his Arequipeño roots, his life and work encapsulate much of the complex movement and change under way in Peru during the mid-twentieth century—emigration from the countryside to the cities, popular classes increasingly insisting on full recognition as citizens—all in the extraordinary yet everyday ordinariness of his people. These themes all come out of the populist tradition in Arequipa into which he was born and of which he was so celebrated an exponent, observer, and participant. His best (and best-known) murals of life in Arequipa are in the Hotel Libertador (the former Hotel de Turistas) in Selva Alegre in Arequipa, painted between 1948 and 1950 (figs. 4.5a and 4.5b).[12]

MUSICIANS

While most of the cultural production during this episode was literary, musicians (as well as painters) also played a part. Benigno Ballón Farfán (1892–1957) was the most prominent Arequipa exponent of traditionalism in music. Ballón, like Mostajo, was steeped in popular culture. He and his small group played for a variety of social occasions, including funerals, which took him to various campiña villages and to urban neighborhoods. While Ballón's quickly became the best-known of these groups, it was not uncommon for small musical groups to so perform. Within his prodigious repertoire, one of Ballón's most popular songs was the *pampeña* "Rio de Arequipa," written about 1950. The *pampeña* dance form is Altiplano in origin, but it takes its name from the Pampas of Miraflores—that "Indian" district on the eastern outskirts of the old central city.

Arguably the best-known exponents of Arequipeño traditions in music were the Hermanos Dávalos—José and Víctor. Born in the 1920s, they grew up in the plebeian downtown, sons of a musician and a picantera. They grew up steeped in the music and culture of the picantería and the working-class milieu, and both attended high school at the Colegio de la Independencia. They got their break on Radio Arequipa as teenagers in the late 1930s, grew in popularity in the 1940s, and then moved to Lima, where through radio, frequent performances, and a voluminous discography in the 1950s and 1960s, they became emblematic of *musica criolla*, especially Arequipeña. The YouTube video of their version of Ballón's "Río de Arequipa" (https://www.youtube.com/watch?v=6aKSKHIHyVg) is accompanied by campiña photos and images from Núñez and Vinatea.

Friend Roberto Damiani shared with me his love of this traditionalism. He had a small country bungalow—a *dacha*, one would say—where he grew *lacayote* and other traditional crops. We made several excursions to the countryside, especially Quequeña, his favorite campiña village. Back at his home near the train station, he pulled out old LP records of *yaravíes*; he was especially fond of the Trio Yanahuara (even more than the Dávalos), a group widely esteemed for capturing this song form's gripping, melancholy tone. Much of this music is now available on the web; for example, on YouTube you can hear their interpretation of Melgar's "Desde tu Separación" (http://www.youtube.com/watch?v =jV7UN8WWY5M), with regional photos, or "Lamento del Misti" (http://www.youtube.com/watch?v=76QQ534H6CM). *Charango* (Andean lute) master Angel Múñoz Alpaca "El Torito," who founded the trio, was born in Yanahuara in 1928 into an agricultural household. An autodidact, he was a particularly beloved interpreter of Arequipa's nostalgic musical tradition.[13] He had studied at the Colegio de la Independencia before moving to Bolivia and later to Buenos Aires and Lima. See his YouTube video *Corazón Mañoso* (http://www.youtube.com/watch?v=tq _m6bLi_2Q) and *Lamento del Misti* (fox Incaico [central Andean foxtrot]). As one commenter wrote, "Hace llorar a cualquier arequipeño" (It makes any Arequipeño cry).

Like Don Angel, pianist and composer Jorge Huirse Reyes also had strong ties to the Altiplano and Buenos Aires. Born in Puno in 1920, he trained in Bolivia and then resided in Argentina. There he met Arequipeño Enrique Portugal, whose ties to Arequipa are yet another indication of surprisingly vital and ongoing Altiplano connections among certain sectors of regional society, particularly cultural entrepreneurs. Múñoz, Huirse, and Portugal were all part of the expatriate community in Buenos Aires active in the 1940s.

The availability of recordings (and traveling performances) enabled people to gather and listen to the music even when away from Arequipa and strongly contributed to the development of nostalgia. Huirse and Portugal's *pampeña* "Montonero Arequipeño" has become a staple in the traditionalist repertoire (see, for example, the video at http://www.you tube.com/watch?v=B01sHrddJ5I). *Montoneros* were irregular troops— unorganized peasants, guerrillas really—who had fought against the Spanish in the wars of independence (akin, for US readers, to the local farmers who were colonial irregulars against the British in New England) and, more important, against the Chileans during the War of the Pacific. Though one is tempted to see in the *montoneros* the sort of rural banditry described for the southern highlands or in Brazil, Basadre (1962, 576) perceptively argued that *montoneros*, more typical of Lima and the north coast, were less a sign of the countryside organizing against the city as of the violence of the city affecting the countryside.

E. Post-Boom Exponents of the Mestizo Tradition

JOSÉ LUIS BUSTAMANTE Y RIVERO (1894–1989)

Though ten years younger than Belaúnde, Bustamante y Rivero was similarly well positioned socially, had a long life, and was politically engaged. He served on the UNSA faculty from 1922 to 1928 and 1931 to 1934 and stepped into decentralist politics in writing the proclamation that Sánchez Cerro used in launching the coup against Leguía in 1930.

Beginning in his university years in Lima, he composed poetry and folkloric writing about Arequipa, earning recognition in 1918 for his poem "Ciudad que fue" dedicated to old Arequipa. Echoing Polar and so many others in the tradition, Bustamante y Rivero extolled the essential mestizo character of Arequipa:

> These figures . . . reveal as well how the conquerors neither avoided contact with the indigenous race nor maintained respect for them in the hierarchy of caste separation, rather they mixed and confounded in good number with the locals, so as to give birth to *the best achieved mestizaje of the country, the most industrious of the colonial era, the most characteristic of the Republic and personified in the creole or "cholo" Arequipeño figure.* (Bustamante y Rivero [1947] 1996, 618; emphasis added)

He was elected president after World War II in a coalition with APRA; during his short tenure as president, his chief minister was Rafael Belaúnde Diez Canseco, grandson of President Pedro Diez Canseco, brother of Víctor Andrés Belaúnde, and father of future president Fernando Belaúnde Terry. During the 1960s he served on and later chaired the International Court of Justice in The Hague, after which he served in the Peruvian senate.

As president, Bustamante y Rivero was opposed both by the landed oligarchy and by a large faction of the military, which finally under General Odría overthrew him and sent him into exile in 1948. In 1956, freshly back from exile in Argentina after the *ochenio* (the eight-year Odria dictatorship, echoing the popular term for the Leguía dictatorship), Bustamante y Rivero's "Arequipa y su destino histórico" (1958, 144–146) contains perhaps the clearest statement in print of Arequipa's purported mestizo identity. On the city's 1957 anniversary, Arequipa had two problems, he powerfully asserted: increasing immigration from the Altiplano, which was overwhelming this "diminutive oasis" (*diminuta vega*), and declining commerce, which was further isolating "the noble southern capital." It merits an extended quotation, as it echoes Polar in bookending, six decades later, the major themes in the regionalist tradition that consolidated in the period after the Chilean war:

> Arequipa arrives at its new anniversary [1957] in circumstances little short of a historical crossroads. Lethal danger looms over the noble southern capital, ready to be ambushed by hidden and curiously contradictory sociological forces—overpopulation and isolation. Which is to say expansion and decadence. On one hand, demographic congestion from the Altiplano is knocking over the small oasis of Arequipa with its famished overflow. On the other hand, progress signals new routes to market for products of Cuzco and Puno that skip the stop in Arequipa. This trapped city finds itself on the edge of two problems: misery and loneliness. In the face of these, it should already have rallied itself; but, truth be told, neither the Government nor the country have understood its drama. We hope they'll understand; but in the meantime, Arequipa is maintaining its alert, vigilant attitude, trying to figure out means of overcoming the danger. It is this attitude that leads to its old traditions.
>
> Life was never easy for the man of Arequipa and wealth was never just given. But in its austerity, never relenting, lies precisely the secret of its virile talent; and the difficulties of the daily struggle just to live gave spirit to its character and persistence to its purpose. This oasis that Arequipa is has been isolated before; but the arequipeño muleteer, in his eagerness for contacts, forged roads toward a world with the hooves of his mules. Water allotment was scarce and the river's flow miserly; but the mystical tenacity of the workers gave opulence to the fruits and the shining gold of the wheat fields. El Misti's volcanic convulsion spoke in earthquakes; but Arequipa spread out at the feet of the colossus never knew fear; and the volcano taught its attributes to the people; fiery within and magnanimous in its power. The noise of factory machines was not pleasing to the people; but a vigorous manual artisanry cured leather, hammered tools, sculpted rock and raised cathedrals. The same as today, a nucleus of indigenous people settled in these lairs that Garci Manuel de Carbajal would select

for the foundation that 15th of August, fed by a select group of peninsular founders; but due to the numerical predominance of these latter, people never meanly discriminated by color or eluded racial contact; the strong chemical impulse of the people, perhaps an unconscious consortium with telluric factors dominated the biological problem of mestizaje until obtaining in the "cholo" the highest expression of this admirable symbiosis in which both the qualities of indigenous reminiscence and white Spanish ancestry interpenetrate. In this way, due to a constant struggle and greater refinement, this tiny oasis on the edge of the sierra came to constitute a center of civic consciousness which was forging a republic over a long century [since independence]. Used to dealing with adversity, [life in] the oasis was sober. The ordered restraint of existence infused in the spirit of its people adherence to law, which means order and action; the figure of Law grew in the Arequipeño soul like a reaction of sanity to the awkward rudeness of presumptuous and passionate caudillismo or inconsequential frivolity. But the serene equilibrium of this juridical vocation—forever the repository of contrasts!—also knew to break out in raptures of passion. To erect barricades in those civic tumults symbolized the intent to construct a nationality out of the coarse paving stones of dictatorships. And so, in a perpetual trance of fighting against narrow things and ideas, over many years Arequipa made its hard but sure trajectory without giving up.

So this sort of complex of adverse factors weighing on its future is nothing new. We're dealing here with a new formulation of something natural to Arequipa's history: the constant rising above obstacles that again challenge the resilience of the people. This time the crisis is profound and the causes that present themselves [are] more complex than in other times. This is why I've recently stated the problem of Arequipa is a national problem and thus needs to be faced with national criteria, without regionalist bargaining that takes away collaboration for a city that constitutes one of the clearest bulwarks of our national civic spirit. But, before and above everything else: the solution to that crisis is within Arequipa itself, in her hidden conscience of her historic mission, in the constructive will of her men, in the nerve they display in dealing with hostile fate, in their imaginative power to think of new saving conceptions [fórmulas salvadoras], in their capacity to make real their old traditions, that qualify and consecrate the city whose permanent destiny goes beyond temporary contingencies and adversities.

So for all this on this anniversary the men of Arequipa should affirm and reunite in one unanimous vote that is at the same time a promise: fight to survive. And not just by any means, but upright, as in the old days. There's only one Arequipa; one yesterday, one always, suffering but stoic; poor, but whole, liberal and flexible within her austerity; rough in the field, learned in the forum, epic in the uprising. The children of Arequipa are called—overcoming whatever obstacle—to convert this heritage into a perennial legacy for the future. No crisis can frustrate such a noble task.

ANTERO PERALTA (1900–1980)

By the 1960s the demographic growth of Arequipa, resulting largely from rapidly increasing, largely Puneño immigration, was impossible to ignore (fig. 4.1). With the regionalist tradition now well established, writers by this time were turning very nostalgic as the Arequipa of their childhoods was undergoing irreversible social and demographic change. So a final set of sources useful for making sense of the content of Arequipeño regionalism, and in particular for capturing the dominant nostalgic quality, is the several memoirs published by various Arequipeño literary and intellectual figures in the 1960s and 1970s.

We will examine below Victor Andrés Belaúnde's writing—especially his memoirs—but for now we will turn to Antero Peralta Vásquez's intriguing *La faz oculta de Arequipa* (Peralta Vásquez 1977) to close out this presentation of key intellectuals who played a role in constructing the mestizo tradition of *lo arequipeño*. Peralta held a philosophy post at UNSA and was a founder of the Frente Democrático Nacional, a party of Christian Democrats, Apristas, and other progressive elements that reached its apogee with the election of Bustamante y Rivero as president (1945–1948). Peralta later became the "patriarch" of *aprismo* in Arequipa (Soto Rivera 2005, 35).

Faz is an eccentric text that speaks directly of the populist image underlying the official, conservative image of Arequipa—the "hidden face" of Arequipa. I take this as typical of a number of texts from the 1960s and 1970s, memoirs mostly, which take nostalgic looks back at a mestizo, village Arequipa said to be vanished or vanishing. They provide a further literary reflection on the image of *lo arequipeño* constructed in the first few decades of the century. The wave of such works (e.g., Zevallos Vera 1965; Velasquez C. 1976; Gómez G. 1977; Ricketts Rey de Castro 1990) at this time is best understood as a camouflaged creole response at the literary, intellectual level to challenges posed by the rising tide of serrano immigrants from Puno and Cuzco that revealed the whiteness undergirding assertions about Arequipeños' fundamentally mestizo essence.

In *Faz*, Peralta (like his memorializing contemporaries) emphasizes place (*terruño*) and the role of Misti as symbol of Arequipa. Peralta speaks of *mistianidad* (Arequipeño mestizaje), symbolically launched by a young liberal party member (representing the "new" thought of liberals like Mostajo) from Puno who lit a fire on 1 January 1900 atop Misti to welcome in a new era (Peralta Vásquez 1977, 51). Later that centennial year, though, the archbishop said mass at the summit (Carpio Muñoz 1981–1983)—Arequipa conservatives reclaiming the mountain, symbol of Arequipa.

Noteworthy elements of Arequipeño regional identity continue to include the beauty of sky, climate, and Spanish architecture; Catholic religiosity; and a psychological propensity to explode, to become irritated at slights (the last typically attributed to the volcanoes and the desert dryness). Also emphasized is the picantería—the very cradle of this regionalist spirit (which I analyze at length in chapter 5).

> Cradle of poets and jurists, of saints and beautiful women . . . of hearty peasants toasted by the sun and unwashed artisans fatigued by the monotony of their work, of laborers and employees at the ready in belligerent unions and large-scale merchants and industrialists, organized in chambers [of commerce], who wrongly represent and direct society. Arequipa is disposed to incorporate her singularity to the present age. . . . Enchanted city, where everyone wants to remain. But, disgracefully, since the workable land is scarce and the environment for larger business limited, it is difficult to develop a career here. As a result, few are the foreigners who put down roots here and many the Arequipeños who "throw themselves out in search of life." . . . Not without reason was it said that when Roald Amundsen arrived at the South Pole he was surprised to see the red flag of an Arequipeño picantería flying. (Peralta Vásquez 1977, 58–59)

III. "MESTIZO" TRADITION SKEPTICS

Progressive agents within the urban middle and upper classes had advanced this conception of the modern Peruvian self as a sort of mestizo everyman, epitomized in imagery associated with everyday Arequipeños, and this understanding became dominant in writing and thinking about the Arequipa region in the first half of the twentieth century. The whole notion of a prototypical citizen of a modern nation was being tried out in this Arequipa mestizo discourse.

This was new. Central was the fuzzy claim that Arequipeños were essentially, objectively hybrid in nature, the product of a cultural, linguistic, and biological mixture of Spanish with local indigenous populations. This promised to be a model for developing an authentic national spirit, and in one form or another, this was the thesis of Polar, Gibson, Rodríguez, Mostajo, and many other leading intellectuals of the era, as well as of Bustamante y Rivero and later writers, especially Peralta.

In the hands of Melgar and Valdivia, the version of lo arequipeño in the early republic was about the poor but honorable citizen of an imagined community of Arequipa; race was at most in the background or was, at least, implicitly Spanish. Race entered this picture as the place of Indians in the national culture became a more pressing issue, both culturally and politically—issues still far from settled in Peru, as recent violence over oil and gas exploration in the Amazon and mining in various parts of the highlands makes clear, as well as in the Arequipa region itself.

Mestizaje was Arequipeño intellectuals' response to the "Indian question," adapting to an indigenist discourse increasingly circulating not only broadly in Latin America, especially in Mexico, but also in Peru—specifically in Puno (Deustua and Rénique 1984, 50) and Cuzco in the early decades of the twentieth century. Influential as these writers advocating Arequipeño hybridity were, though, not everyone agreed that this defined who Arequipeños "really" were; for all its intensity, this discourse was marginalized, if not rejected, by various other intellectuals and was, in any case, submerged by larger events in the national and international fields from 1930 to 1960.

Other voices argued that in reality little biological mixing had taken place in Arequipa, and some even denied that there had been much cultural or even linguistic mixing at all (see the discussion of loncco in chapter 5). Arequipa was and had always been fundamentally Spanish, such critics argued—an Iberian island in a southern-Peruvian Indian sea. Despite the hybridity imagined by some, Arequipeños were as far from "Indian" as were most Limeños or others tied to national society. All this spatialization of race changed with the choloization of the coast (Quijano 1967) and the desborde popular (Cotler 1978)—the massive mid-twentieth-century emigration from the countryside to the cities, which of course only intensified nostalgia in these generations for Arequipa de *antaño* ("Arequipa of old"—i.e., the "good old days") (e.g., Santos Mendoza 1996; Valdivia Rodríguez 1989).

The key cultural entrepreneurs examined above had an outsized influence on this discourse, illustrating how holders of cultural capital can have major cultural and even political impact in smaller social spaces. While some came from well-placed families (e.g., Gibson, Polar, Bustamante y Rivero), by and large these men were the sons of the urban middle class (e.g., Rodríguez, Vinatea, Ballón Farfán, Núñez, the Dávalos brothers). Mostajo was probably the member of this set from the lowest social class, making his achievement all the more notable and important, as I have argued.

Of course, what is important is not some illusory biological reality but, rather, the fact that influential Arequipeños in this period came to think this way, identifying themselves, smallholders, and/or others as "mestizo" (even if they didn't use the specific term) and extemporizing on the qualities of regional character and on the conditions that gave rise to it. Many wrote that the desert and the mountains gave a stamp of place to this identity. But however "brown" the imagery, the Spanish element is always primary in these depictions; while campiña *chacareros* were said to be mestizo, they were finally always more white than brown (Mostajo's 1918 "Palique Linguistico" newspaper article, cited in Ballón Lozada 1999, 74). For example, "Arequipa has the faith and grace of an Andalusian city. This is the Spanish input. But in perfect blending with the native traditions of her earthy bowels" (Zeballos Barrios 1978).

Writing near the end of this period, Peralta (Peralta Vásquez 1977) synthesizes this discourse, arguing that while *mistianidad* had changed over the years ("like all living things"), taking different forms in different historical periods, underneath these surface changes lay some Jungian essence (ibid., 13). Here Peralta seems to be channeling Polar's positivism, almost a century later. Architecture reflects many of these changes: graceful Spanish-inspired houses of *sillar* (local white volcanic building stone) with interior courtyards were giving way to more uniform, North American–inspired rectangular concrete buildings. For the Aprista Peralta, the heart of *mistianidad* is customs from its agrarian sector (ibid., 15). He speaks in a populist vein of "two nations" in Arequipa: "the [nation] of the leaders of industrial companies and the advanced students that march in the respective paths, more or less, and the [nation] of artisans, laborers and peasants that are almost always outmoded . . . of the masses left behind, of haggard mentality, who give, nevertheless, the tonic of originality in their forms of living, that is, their cultural style" (ibid., 17). "In the veins of the traditional Arequipeño there's nothing but a mixture of two bloods. More copper than silver in skin color and more Hispanic than Indian in spiritual profile. . . . The insignificant minority of white elements in the Misti population is on the verge of being totally absorbed by the indigenous race" (ibid., 59). Peralta notes that Bustamante y Rivero (with whom he had been politically allied) had argued that mestizaje in Arequipa proceeded gradually, so that only the most removed districts—Pocsi, Quequeña, and Yarabamba—maintained an indigenous stamp, so that "in Arequipa 'the best achieved mestizaje of the country' has been produced" (ibid., 60).

The substitution of "*cholo*" for "mestizo" furthers the semantic "browning" of this discourse. While "*cholo*" broadly refers derogatorily to people of indigenous background trying to make their way in urban and/or white social spaces, in its use in traditionalist writing (see Gibson above, now Peralta) it is charged positively. Many *cholos* have risen to occupy important positions in society, Peralta notes: "The new cholo [he's a bit ambivalent here] . . . is more indigenous than mestizo," but that would be but a continuation of the proud independent spirit of the neighborhood gangs of yesteryear and the sort of middle-class man who has led the region for the last fifty years. Zevallos continues in this vein:

> Four and a bit centuries of civic life have made Arequipa a bulwark of Peruvianness and an authentic exponent of mestizaje and of American culture. It constitutes, within the national boundary, the best achieved synthesis of American creole [reality] and the expression, full of hope, of the America that all peoples of the continent desire to be and have been heroically forging, as in Arequipa, [where we] have been birthed with the striking bravery of the peninsulares [Spanish], white-skinned, inveterate materialists in their plunder and sublimely spiritual in front of the altar, and with the untamed power of the Indians, copper-skinned, generous in their riches and stoic in sacrifice and in creative work. (Zevallos Vera 1965, 5–6)

Given its ambivalence, however, "*cholo*" can just as easily be negatively charged, since in and underneath these diverse perspectives in early twentieth-century Arequipeño discourse about mestizaje lay continuing and strongly racialist, even anti-indigenous sentiment—barely below the surface in Belaúnde's work, much more buried in Mostajo's (see below and chapter 6 on Huancané). The continuing vitality of these racialist undercurrents was still evident, for example, in the scarcely veiled slurs thrown about locally in the 2001 presidential race among candidates Alejandro Toledo, Lourdes Flores, and Alan García, as well as in the revealing comment a friend's daughter made as we were viewing the more colorful dancers (who happened to be from Puno) in the 1997 annual patron-saint-day parade (a new cultural frontier in the very heart of urban Arequipa): to my enthusiasm she replied, "Ah, es la misma cholada" (Ah, it's just the same upstart Indians).

Several key intellectuals and major sectors of society were skeptical that this "*cholo*/new mestizo citizen" had any objective reality. Critics on both the right and the left were unconvinced that Arequipeños, let alone other Peruvians, were fundamentally mestizo or even should be. Behind these critiques were ideologies arguing more or less consciously or explicitly that colonial racialized categories remained applicable to Peruvian reality—that Indians were a nation apart. For some on the right, this meant they were unreliable, even lazy, and unable to become modern citizens—at least any time soon. For others on the left, this meant they were holders of traditions on which authentic Andean socialism could yet be realized.

VICTOR ANDRÉS BELAÚNDE (1883–1966)

The major regional figure largely unpersuaded by this mestizo rhetoric was arguably Victor Andrés Belaúnde. Belaúnde played a central role in making public, through his many writings, a patrician view of the major outlines of the regional identity prevalent from the 1880s to the 1970s. Unlike most of the writers I examine, such as Mostajo, who remained provincial, Belaúnde's prominent position in Lima and foreign intellectual circles assured that his conservative message was widely heard and read, though unlike either Bustamante y Rivero or Mostajo his ideas did not circulate much outside of academic and intellectual circles. He was a vocal and principled representative of progressive Catholicism and of the commercial elite of Arequipa, and he was conservative in his defense of relatively liberal ideals.

Belaúnde was born into the Arequipeño aristocracy. He was the grandson of President Pedro Diez Canseco, who had been part of the 1834 and 1867 rebellions and three times president of the country and who had built the boulevard from Arequipa to the local elites' summering spot at Tingo. Arequipa was then still a small, provincial city, and its elite families were very closely connected, with much intermarrying. Belaúnde's father knew and was a disciple of Dean Valdivia at UNSA, owned important properties in the Majes valley, built a commercial house that grew with the wool trade, and founded the Catholic newspaper *El Deber*, the oldest continuous newspaper in southern Peru.

Uprooted by an unjust legal action by the state against his father, young Victor's family abruptly moved to Lima in 1900 when he was seventeen, and he entered the Universidad Nacional Mayor de San Marcos. Certainly part of his deep-seated distrust of the centralized state stems from this unjust treatment of his father (and mother). As a member of the Generation of 1900, Victor Andrés joined Francisco García Calderón Rey (son of the ex-president, who spent much of his adult life in France) and José de la Riva Aguero y Osma, among others, in an intense desire to help reconstruct the country after the War of the Pacific. Belaúnde, in particular, "spent the greater part of his life casting about for a cultural definition which would explain his elusive postulate of *Peruanidad*" (Chavarría 1970, 270). Historically minded and progressive university students in Lima (especially San Marcos), as well as in Arequipa and Cuzco, began a more active engagement with various injustices in the social life around them.

The period from 1895 through at least 1908 was one of profound optimism. This mood ended, however, when, during Leguía's first government (1908–1912), student leaders (e.g., Riva Aguero) were arrested and the clamps were put on social-reform movements. In a famous lecture at San Marcos in 1914, Belaúnde criticized such personalistic leadership styles, which, combined with economic pressures on the middle class and the moral crisis of the ruling elite, threatened political stability and the still fragile sense of shared national identity.

Borrowing a page from Polar, Belaúnde was a central figure in the university reform movement in Peru, an experience with profound implications for his intellectual development and later career. The idea was to convert the university system into a tool for national integration, to be accomplished by breaking down the barriers to higher education for the growing urban masses, primarily in Lima. Most of the students in the Popular Universities in Lima (including the one in Vitarte) were Spanish-speaking mestizo workers affiliated with organized labor (Klaiber 1975, 702). Indigenist sentiments were certainly present. The first Universidad Popular (UP) established outside Lima was in Arequipa, in January 1922, though it was closed in Leguía's general shutdown of the UPs in September 1924. Belaúnde was sympathetic to these movements and protested Leguía's antiuniversity policies; in response, Leguía, having returned to the presidency in 1919 by coup to fend off Civilista Party resistance, closed down San Marcos in May 1921. Belaúnde (strongly Catholic) and other moderates found themselves caught in the middle when the UPs (and Haya de la Torre) led a movement to protest Leguía's and the church's 1923 effort to have Peru dedicated to the Sacred Heart. Belaúnde went into exile, first in Uruguay and France, but he spent the remainder of the 1920s in various academic positions in the United States.

Belaúnde was chief promoter in his generation of an export-oriented but conservative and Catholic formula for national development. His 1915 *La cuestion social en Arequipa* is a central document, written when he was thirty-two. In it he reveals key elements of his vision of Arequipa as source and model for solving the national question, so paramount in the decades following the debacle with Chile. He was disdainful of the self-serving oligarchy ruling the country, which, while hardly a criticism of a white elite, nevertheless constituted a space for voices from below— and from a key representative of the regional oligarchy. "Among us lives a feudal regime . . . but now without religion, without poetry and without glory [as in the middle ages]" ([1915] 1963, 117). Likewise, he strongly condemned the growing presence of foreign capital that drained off rather than worked to build the wealth of Arequipa (and the rest of Peru). With the growth of the population over the same extension of cultivated land, emigration of native talent and loss of local control were inevitable.

Belaúnde's strongly regionalist sentiment is evident in a passage remarkably similar to the 1845 laments of the UNSA rector and Valdivia:

> We see, then, a tragic exodus unfolding. Villagers abandon their old and traditional dwellings, leaving their motherland to undertake the route south, to suffer a doubly sad exile, because they come to realize that that soil [Chile] was once ours. They don't give their energies to the land of their birth, rather they give it to foreign companies and capital, in this way contributing to the growth of a country that isn't theirs. [After failing in the city] they will have to return home, tired, perhaps ill, in the same condition in which they left; to the sadness over the time spent will be added that of the silence of the village bell tower, deserted mute streets, and barren fields left longing for their loving care. (Ibid., 126)

He extolled the place of the indigenous populace in making colonial and Republican Peru possible, from working the fields and mines to serving as soldiers in the fight with Chile. "It's no exaggeration to say that, without the indigenous, our fields would be dried up, our mines deserted, our flocks abandoned, our barracks empty, our nationality extinguished" (ibid., 118). Despite the appreciative tone, though, there is little mestizaje evident here.

Belaúnde highlights the egalitarian nature of an earlier Arequipa, pointing to the fundamental role of individual families, especially small-holders, though again, hardly in a mestizo vein. "Arequipa was a white democracy, with a tiny slave population. . . . It's surely the quality of our population, their egalitarian tendency, individualist by race, affirmed by small property, that has determined their unique participation in the development of Peruvian democracy" (ibid., 122). He portrayed Arequipa as "a democratic and middle class city: 'Arequipa did not have . . . Spanish titles, nor a social hierarchy constituted by extensive properties and lucrative encomiendas, characteristic of other Peruvian cities'" (Flores Galindo 1977, 15, citing V. A. Belaúnde 1960, 234). His few comments about the wider valley population, let alone the urban working class, reflect his social position, urban focus, and boyhood experience.

> This tiny oasis, limited and we might say familial, accents its human character in the face of the horizontal infinity of the sand dunes and the vertical infinity the mountains suggest. Man feels more united to his piece of earth and at the same time experiences with more intensity that feeling of limitation which [some] saw as the basis for religious sentiment. (Belaúnde, quoted in Peralta Vásquez 1977, 64)

Leaving aside, for a moment, the reality or desirability of developing a mestizo identity, a common thread through both scientific and romantic writing about the essence of Arequipa was that Arequipeños' ongoing resistance to Limeño intrigues and interests turned on questions of honor rather than on similarly narrow, if regionally different, questions of self-interest. In successive rebellions, we see a history of military honor, courage, and *hidalguía* (gentlemanliness) in the nineteenth century—the Valdivian thread in regional identity.

This code of honor carries on from the Spanish colonial period, but now has both Republican and Catholic aspects and plays out in a bureaucratic field dominated by a dishonorable landed oligarchy. Belaúnde is critical for grasping the cross-class emphasis on the importance of honor and virtue, representing as he does most clearly the urban commercial elite that most strove for distinction in the emerging national field. The clear picture is one in which leaders (for example, his grandfather Pedro Diez Canseco) are measured by the yardstick of a patriarchal set of values, leaders who with probity and honesty followed their duty to God, country, and family. Grace and honor were symbolized by mastery of horse riding and by cattle breeding, all very Spanish (Indians were forbidden to own horses during colonial times).

Writing his memoirs toward the end of his life, well aware of the sociopolitical context of the authoritarian regimes dominating national political life in much of the first half of the twentieth century, Belaúnde reminded his readers of the heroic stature of Arequipeños of an earlier time:

> I evoke those beautiful civic times of Arequipa, the Arequipa of legend, of bravery and rebellion. How I'd like to live via the imagination in the marvelous epoch from [18]30 to [18]60. The people formed one unity, beating their chests impelled by one sole interest and ideal, the glory of the land and prestige of their city of birth. With social classes united, they could carry out [the various rebellions and uprisings]. I'm not sure if all these commotions were justified and had good results, I just know that they were beautiful; and that's enough for me. I know they were idealistic and disinterested; the gentleman and the worker grabbed a rifle and went together to the barricades. The woman of this city, the woman of this race, of this land that has produced the most refined type of maternal, self-sacrificing [woman], enthusiastically intervened in the fight. What's happened to the current epoch!" (Belaúnde [1960] 1967, 76–77)

The settled, ordered life was (always) already passing away (see Williams 1973):

> At the end of the last century life in Arequipa had changed. The city started to modernize and predominate over farming. Our ancestors had fewer distractions in the city. They rarely traveled. They were tied to the land, they were sustained in her and they found in that environment health, peace and an instinctive aesthetic emotion. The lands belonged to the neighbors in Arequipa and were cultivated by them. The small property regime that had predominated in Arequipa had consequences not just in the social order affirming its democratic tendency, but also in the economic order, maintaining a tight linkage between the city and countryside. (Belaúnde [1960] 1967, 62)

Belaúnde, then, embodies the conservative, aristocratic side of these post–War of the Pacific conversations, brushing aside more explicitly racial themes in painting a picture of postwar Arequipa as an almost-classless society with a unified culture. This timeless, Arequipa *de antaño* or Arequipa *antigua*, good-old-days theme, always including a roster of Arequipeños *destacados* (illustrious), was exemplified by Belaúnde. His writings appeared in two major sets, including both works from the early decades of the twentieth century and later reflections in old age in midcentury. The first, *Meditaciones peruanas*, was a collection of writings and speeches from 1912 to 1918 that circulated widely in intellectual circles in those years in Lima and Arequipa. These materials were first collected in a 1932 book, publication having been delayed by Belaúnde's 1921–1930 exile, but then prodded by and in response to charges by Mariátegui ([1928] 1971, 100–101) that Belaúnde's Generation of 1900 was fundamentally colonialist and oligarchic.

In a little-known 1918 letter, Belaúnde astonishingly prefigures Mariátegui's critique of some years later about the nature of "regionalism" in Peru as mere camouflage for continuing control by local warlords (*gamonalismo*). In it he went way beyond extolling Arequipeño civic culture as a decentralist recipe for national restoration (and in the process he strongly opposed the creation of a decentralist party per se). Rather, he incisively tied local provincialism to autocratic centralism ("régimen personal en colaboración con el caciquismo provincialista") as two sides of the same coin, each propping up the other (Belaúnde 1918).

The second set of writings, where the nostalgic tone predominates, is in the form of memoirs from the late 1950s and early 1960s, written late in life after a long and distinguished international diplomatic career. The two-volume *Trayectoria y destino: Memorias* appeared in 1967 shortly after his death. In these tomes Belaúnde reflects back, from the vantage point of forty years later, on a long life and especially on the tumultuous period of the first three decades of the century. Naturally optimistic, Belaúnde confessed that nostalgia was his primary experience in life (Pacheco Vélez 1967, xiv)—a nostalgia that was a product both of his long absence and international career and of his class position and Catholic values, which led him to emphasize decentralist and regional specificity in his desire for cross-class unity and harmony in the face of a rapidly changing Peru (Pacheco Vélez 1978).

Arequipa de mi infancia ([1960] 1967) consists of Belaúnde's clear recollection of his earliest days there. His assistant Pacheco noted that he consulted virtually no other sources than a small notebook of his own jottings. So this is very much a memoir in the strictest sense, very personal "memories from a life" or "memos to self" rather than autobiography. *Infancia* constitutes a reflection back from a great time distance, and as such it presents the post–War of the Pacific Arequipa in which he grew up very much in terms of the movement of his Generation of 1900 to regenerate the country and construct a coherent *peruanidad* around which the nation could rebuild. (Reading Belaúnde recalls for this North American student an almost Jeffersonian ideal of sturdy yeoman free-holding farmer-citizens.) Here he yields some ground on the question of Arequipeños' "mestizo" identity:

> In the Peruvian panorama, Arequipa has the character of a city of synthesis. It's highland by geography and coastal from the ethnic and social point of view. She represents the union between the coast and the sierra; between the white, the mestizo and the aborigine. Peruvianness is embodied by these Andean cities who with their strong Iberian seal dominate the highland landscape. . . . The soul of Arequipa carries the indelible seal of integral Peruvianness. Iberian in its faith and customs, it had to adapt its economy to the lands both directly exploited and those with which it traded. . . . For this the yaraví is at the same time brother of Spanish and echo of indigenous songs. Two souls have melted in it to make it more representative of Peruvianness. (Belaúnde (1960) 1967, 13–14)

Belaúnde is important at this point, for he was well placed enough to be able to excoriate the idle rich for not working hard like the Arequipeño everyman—though this is much more a critique of the landed oligarchy than of Arequipa's regional commercial elite. While it might have been inconceivable for most elites in Peru to consider that they shared citizenship with plebeians (let alone with Indians), it was this fragility, this vulnerability of elite Arequipeños, their anxiety about commercial ruin, plus their lived experience together in this *diminuta vega*, that made them (e.g., Polar, Gibson) much less resistant to a discourse of mestizo inclusion.

CUARTO CENTENARIO TEXT OF 1940

Despite the prominent roles of César A. Rodríguez, Manuel J. Bustamante de la Fuente,[14] and José L. Bustamante y Rivero on the organizing committee for the four-hundredth anniversary of Arequipa's Spanish founding, the *chacarero* imagery and symbols associated with urban plebeian and rural livelihoods are almost entirely absent from the *Arequipa: Homenaje en su IV centenario* booklet sponsored by the Banco

Popular del Peru (*Arequipa* 1940). Directed by aristocrat Eduardo López de Romaña, son of the early 1900s Civilista Party president, this publication was an effort by the regional commercial elite to tell the "white" story of Arequipa. (This tells us either that Rodríguez and Bustamante y Rivero were silenced, which is unlikely, or, more probably, that they and the committee had little to do with actually writing the booklet.) A competition at this time led to the selection of Ballón Farfán's "Himno de Arequipa" as the "official hymn" of Arequipa.

Arequipa: Homenaje en su IV centenario is a text of great interest, an attempt to leverage industrial development in Arequipa after the spurt in the 1930s of import substitution industrialization.[15] A commercial focus dominates the presentation, which seems clearly aimed at a foreign, largely business and even tourist audience. Despite some relevant passages referring to folkloric elements of everyday life in the countryside (e.g., "the land of the yaraví reflects in her artistic treasure"; *Arequipa* 1940, 13), the dominant theme is the Spanish heritage of the city; for example, referring to the *sillar* architecture, it notes, "Tourists arriving to Arequipa get the strong impression of her Spanish heritage," and the Plaza de Armas is "of typical Andalusian conformation" (ibid., 16). "Toward the provinces of the Department, leaving the city, Paucarpata, Characato and other places display grating, churches, decorations and facades *of pure Spanish conception elaborated by the indigenous hand*" (ibid., 16; emphasis added). Mestizaje gets barely any mention; for example, in describing the artwork of the Iglesia de la Compañía, the spectacular Jesuit church on a corner of the main city plaza, it says, "In her altars and ornamentation in general, the plateresque style dominates categorically. But in truth, it's that this is not the work of authentic aboriginals. It's rather the capacity of the mestizo intelligence that in Arequipa rapidly rises to the level of being the most well-bred companions of the conquistadors and colonizers" (ibid., 20).

The commercially linked regionalism behind this intriguing document paints a picture of Arequipa as fundamentally Spanish, and it also, unlike the cultural entrepreneurs discussed above, draws a department-wide picture of Arequipa. The guide mentions many opportunities for the enterprising businessman, though with no mention of the already-developing dairying. The productivity of the entire department is extolled, not just the fertility of the campiña, and is claimed to be especially productive for wheat—all of which would change in just a few short years with the post–World War II dairying boom and growing industrialization. The map included is particularly rich in stereotypical imagery, symbols of the entire department from an urban elite vantage point—an echo of yesteryear's "greater Arequipa." For example, much more is shown of the Ocoña/Cotahuasi valley than might be expected, and settlements from Acarí and Yauca on the north, from Camaná to Orcopampa, and from Mollendo and La Punta to Cailloma are all mentioned. Yet Chapi is not mentioned, again pointing to the fundamentally popular, plebeian nature of pilgrimage there. There are fascinating details represented: rural workers are shown on burros near Atico, plowing with *yunta* (ox team) and sowing seed near Chuquibamba, and picking fruit (apples?) off trees near Aplao; it shows women and men planting potatoes near Salamanca; a man weaving at Cotahuasi; another man with *yunta* near Orcopampa; miners at Cailloma and Cerro Verde; two men reaping wheat at Chivay (with cattle grazing nearby); somebody peering through a telescope in Cayma (the Harvard telescope in Carmen Alto); swimmers at Yura, Jesús, and Tingo; statues of Melgar and Francisco Bolognesi at Arequipa; and the odd mermaid figure with a trident seated on a strange fish in the ocean at the elite summering spot of Mollendo. Many physical features from throughout the department are identified, from the Pampa de Cerrito and the Rio Chala in the north through Laguna Parinacochas (Ayacucho) and Acocoto (near Orcopampa), to the Pampa de Humala with a flying condor near Chivay (so the condor theme is not just recent!), the Rio Colca, "El Misti 5781 m." (the only elevation shown), the Rio Chili, to the Pampa de Islay, the Rio Tambo, the Pampa del Meadero, and the Islas Guaneras.

Continuing with the content analysis of the 1940 document, it is peculiar that under *periodismo* (journalism) no mention is made of Francisco Mostajo, who was then the most active journalist in Arequipa and probably founded more newspapers (however short-lived) than anyone else in the first half of this century—again evidence of the elite stamp of this document. We have seen how important print media were for the construction of regional identity, and how Mostajo in particular exploited and relied for part of his income on these outlets.

What all this points to is the degree to which Arequipa's identity was contested, however indirectly. This 1940 document helps us nail down the content of the dominant, hegemonic rhetoric in Arequipa during the period, rhetoric that was very different from the mestizo tradition being crafted by middle-class and left intellectuals. That such an important figure as Mostajo was systematically left out and that the more conservative, Catholic elements of regional society, architecture, and culture were systematically emphasized (e.g., the principal newspaper in Arequipa noted was the Catholic daily *El Deber*) is evidence of this point.

JOSÉ CARLOS MARIÁTEGUI (1894–1930)

The views of the regional aristocracy were voiced by Belaúnde and were central to the 1940 text, never buying in to the idea that Arequipeños were fundamentally mestizo, but on the left there were others equally critical of mestizaje. While Gibson and other poets were extolling Arequipa's purportedly mestizo essence, José Mariátegui was analyzing Peruvian society and supporting university reform and indigenous and labor movements in the years leading up to the founding of the Peruvian Communist Party (and his early death).

Mariátegui addressed the regional question in the sixth of his 1928 *Seven Interpretive Essays on Peruvian Reality*: "Regionalism in Peru is not a movement, a current, a program. It is nothing else but the vague expression of some discomfort and discontent" ([1928] 1971, Essay 6). He conflates regionalism with *gamonalismo*, arguing that regionalism was basically a smokescreen for continued political, economic, and social domination by local, rural, sierran, feudal, landed oligarchy outside Lima.

Yet it was Mariátegui (above, chapter 1) who had argued that there was a "natural" region in southwestern Peru. Like Belaúnde, he noted that Arequipa, surrounded by deserts, mountains, and the ocean, has a marked oasis-like quality that strikes all observers and visitors. Until completion of the railroad, Arequipa was a relatively isolated place, and this objective reality certainly provided a basis for the regionalist sentiment said to have prevailed in Arequipa since its Spanish founding—and perhaps even during the Inka or earlier periods as well.

Notwithstanding, Mariátegui's critique of regionalism centered on the lack of mass participation in anticentralist political movements—a position foreshadowed by Belaúnde (1918), as noted above. He saw federalism as a superstructural phenomenon and decentralism as hollow rhetoric echoing independence-era ideals but without popular involvement or support. By the racialized, anti-serrano imagery embedded in traditionalist discourse, Arequipa was unable to take on the mantle of all anti-Lima provincial resentment. Hence Mariátegui's contempt for such regionalist sentiment, since there was neither working-class nor indigenous social participation or movement in Arequipa.

The decentralization problem and modernization more broadly could not be solved before addressing both the "Indian problem" and the agrarian question. Existing inequalities were anchored in the backwardness of the sierra and in the forms of servile labor that persisted there.

> The Peru of the coast, heir of Spain and the conquest, controls the Peru of the sierra from Lima; but it is not demographically and spiritually strong enough to absorb it. Peruvian unity is still to be accomplished. . . . Instead of a pluralism of local or regional traditions, what has to be solved is a dualism of race, language, and sentiment, born of the invasion and conquest of indigenous Peru by a foreign race that has not managed to merge with the Indian race, or eliminate it, or absorb it. (Mariátegui [1928] 1971, 164)

Given the central importance of Huancané in the 1923 uprisings in Puno, Mostajo's statement bears comparison with Mariátegui's views on this same event. Mariátegui saw in the events of Huancané not an atavistic rejection of the neocolonial order but, rather, the possibility of an indigenous Andean socialism built on what remained of indigenous communitarianism. Mariátegui saw mestizaje as, in effect, a fundamentally conservative plot to weaken the best chance Peru had to reach socialism. The indigenous population had to become persons fighting not for the Indian but (guided by the proletariat) for socialism (see Manrique 1999, 80).

In the end, owing largely to Jorge Polar's central place in the educational establishment and regional society and to Mostajo's prolific writing and public persona, it is fair to say that the "scientific" folklorists—Polar and Mostajo—had the biggest impact on the hegemonic sense of regional culture. This is evidenced by the quite stereotypical account of Arequipa's history and nature that was recounted to me by so many people in so many parts of the city and countryside. Of course many of the progressive cultural entrepreneurs advancing this mestizo discourse were also "contested" through direct state repression. It is telling that the Colegio de la Independencia—that main incubator of anticentralist thought—was attacked by Odría's troops and sympathizers in the June 1950 uprising, and many members of the faculty departed. As we learned, most of the cultural entrepreneurs examined above, amid generations of students, studied or taught at the Colegio as well as at the Universidad de San Agustín.

FIVE

PICANTERAS AND DAIRYMEN

Quotidian Citizenry

Oye, Tomás—somos agricultores, no campesinos
(Listen, Thomas—we're farmers, not peasants).

AURELIO APOLO, PERSONAL COMMUNICATION

The campiña is small enough that from certain vantage points—certainly from the slopes of any of the three volcanoes, but also from closer in, too, such as in Cayma or Sachaca, less in Yanahuara (where what is now the most visited observation area is located, ironically)—one can take in the whole basin in one exhilarating, panoramic view. When you see it bounded on one side by three impressive volcanic peaks and on the other by rocky desert hills, it is not hard to quickly come to feel that the whole settled basin is one living, pulsating *aldea*—the sense Belaúnde captured in his evocative memoir *Arequipa de mi infancia* ([1960] 1967), quoted and discussed in chapter 4. Belaúnde was most impressed by the valley's sensory unity—of sound, of light, of motion—symbolized by the daily cycle of ringing bells in each of the village and city churches. Obscured by urban intellectuals' generally pastoral, bucolic representations of the region, however, were the daily struggles, local social distinctions, back-and-forth movement within as well as in and out of the valley, and, above all, the varied conditions and aspirations of the smallholders and plebeian residents themselves.

The literary regionalism I examined in the previous chapter painted a picture of Arequipeño identity as being exemplified in the characteristics and embodied in the practices of urban plebeians and rural smallholders in the campiña outside the urban core, portraying them as hardworking, rustic, simple, and entrepreneurial, and as "mestizo" (though generally excising their typically deep Catholicism). These qualities were symbolized by particular sorts of plebeian dwellers, more rural than urban—milkmaids, picanteras, muleteers, and rustic farmers—and by the foods they ate and the way they spoke and dressed as well as by the land-scape itself, the product of a harmonious synthesis between these people and the particularities of this mountainous desert oasis.

As I noted in the preface, however, there was a curious disconnect be-tween these images, intended to portray a vital, living, albeit "disappear-ing" tradition, and what I directly experienced with the purported bear-ers of these traditions, though I lived among them for almost two years in three very open, representative campiña communities, with daily ob-servation and interaction, and interviewed a random sample of over a hundred farmers. Picanterías seemed almost a thing of the past, the dress and speech of local farmers were hardly different from what I saw and heard throughout various parts of the city itself, and, above all, these rural dwellers were by and large well integrated at all levels (social, eco-nomic, political) with life in the city. And I never heard a single *yaraví* sung or played, except in a touristic venue well after my main fieldwork period.

Informed by reading Raymond Williams's *The Country and the City* (1973) well after my main fieldwork period, I explored the nature of this disconnect, including the irony that so much of the folklore and local history of the campiña that was said to be disappearing came just as some smallholders themselves were moving to take a central role in re-gional identity as owners of fighting bulls and fine Peruvian *paso* breed of horses. As a tradition of an already-disappearing countryside was gripping (and being reinvented by) urban intellectuals, very quotidian concerns animated the lives of these very smallholders and urban ple-beians, who continued to see themselves as quite regular members of re-gional society. As exemplified in Aurelio's admonishment quoted in the epigraph to this chapter, it was clear that without exception, the many farmers I interviewed presented and understood themselves as full, in-tegrated members of regional society. I elaborate this crucial point in chapter 6 (section C).

Clearly, a lopsided "conversation" was taking place between the self-appointed represeners of this "disappearing" tradition and these every-day Arequipeños themselves, one in which they were talked *about* but not, apparently, much *with*. I learned that farmers themselves in effect resisted the objectification inherent in this writing and painting about them, however sympathetic it may have been and from which they drew a certain delight. It also reframed my understanding of bullfighting, which I learned was a largely post–World War II tradition coming largely after the main florescence of literary regionalism described above.

Before we can close with a more theoretically driven examination of this multilayered irony, with all its discursive intersections (which I take up in chapter 6), we need to understand the lives and interests of small-holders themselves. My obvious focus more on valley farmers and less on urban plebeians is both a response to the general depictions examined in chapter 4 and a direct result of my fieldwork focus. Since it was not until well after my fieldwork period that I came to realize the nature of this ur-ban imagining, as I discuss at some length in the preface and elsewhere, I did not undertake a careful study of urban plebeian aspirations and motivations, either then or more recently. As I elaborate in this chapter, I also focus on rural smallholders because the main development in re-gional identity after the exhaustion of the main 1890–1970 period of ur-ban intellectual cultural production was bullfighting in the countryside, and no such parallel development in urban plebeian life emerged.

What can ethnography tell us about rural smallholders' lives that will thereby inform our overall examination of why urban intellectuals were writing about rural dwellers in these ways in the first half of the twenti-eth century? What we will discover in this chapter is that smallholders' own concerns, anchored in a quotidian rhythm of dairying and cash-cropping, family, church, and village life, were much more integrated with urban life and that smallholders were insistent on their cultural citizenship in regional society—that there was ongoing, everyday resis-tance to various attempts to exclude them from regional society using outmoded divisions of caste and class as well as more modern notions of "peasant folklore."

I. BACKGROUND

It became conventional anthropological wisdom that smallholder sur-vival throughout the Andes was predicated on access to a variety of eco-logical zones (e.g., Brush 1977). Under the verticality model (Murra 1975) such multizone complementarity was seen as the heart of *lo andino*, the Andean way of adapting to the extraordinary environmental complex-ity of these neotropical highlands. We are now in a radical rethinking of that paradigm, as noted above (chapter 2)—a long-overdue conversation among linguistics, archaeology, and cultural anthropology focusing on the deep relationships between material and cultural processes.

What interzonal exchange there was in southwestern Peru has long since been affected by the close associations among local, regional, national, and international commercial circuits, as, for example, with muleteers' often long-distance travel. Reconfigured by the railroad and then long-haul trucking, drovers adapted their routes even as interzonal trade declined overall (Love 1988), though I saw several Salinas-based llama drovers pass through Sabandía during my main fieldwork period.

But while some communities continued to assert interzonal rights—for example, to harvest guano on coastal islands after independence—most campiña smallholders seem to have given up this presumably pan-Andean multizone strategy by the mid-nineteenth century (Galdos Rodríguez 1985). Although this coincided with independence and the loss of formal legal protection of Indians by the crown, Indian landholdings had been whittled down in a long series of expropriations by Spaniards of lands and resources (see chapter 6), including those managed by colonists from other ecozones.

This suggests that the hold of a multizone adaptive strategy—though clearly deeply embedded in long-standing practices—is less part of some timeless Andean cultural essence than a more conscious, rational response to prevailing political economic, cultural, and ecological conditions (e.g., van Buren 1996). The relatively early abandonment in southwestern Peru of this multizone strategy suggests that occupational, educational, legal, and commercial ties to Arequipa city had long strongly affected rural households' livelihood strategies (see Wibel 1975).

Smallholders with freehold tenure overwhelmingly dominate agriculture in the campiña—11,415 hectares in the early 1970s, constituting 35 percent of the cultivated area of the entire Quilca and Tambo River drainages (ONERN 1974, 752). Farms of less than 5 hectares constituted over 90 percent of all farms in 1940 and 1955, covering 58 percent of total hectarage (in 1955), and they constituted 94 percent of all farms in 1974, covering 57 percent of total hectarage (Love 1989, 110). In 1974, 88 percent of the farms controlling 43 percent of this area were under three hectares in size, data little changed from earlier studies or estimates from the nineteenth (e.g., Kaerger [1899] 1979) and twentieth (Mostajo Chávez 1942; Love 1989) centuries. Remaining farms were almost all in the 6–20 hectare range, with virtually no farms in the valley over 20 hectares in size. Though urban encroachment on cultivated lands has dramatically increased in the last several decades, the smallholder land-tenure pattern itself remains little changed.

Ideal growing conditions for a variety of midaltitude crops prevail in the valley, which stretches from 1,700 to 3,450 (mostly 2,200–2,600) meters above sea level. While rivers on the coast are notorious for unpredictable changes both of course in their riverbeds and of volume of flow, long hindering more water-intensive sugarcane production in favor of grapes, the basin of Arequipa was early noted for its abundant water supply, particularly relative to the limited land base, and for the year-round sunshine that supports very high agricultural productivity per unit area. Though there are problems with inadequate water supply in some campiña districts (e.g., the southernmost areas) and though little excess water is available to enlarge the cultivated area in the valley itself, generally there is not a huge problem with access to water for irrigation on either side of the Rio Chili, for example, in Sabandía or in Huaranguillo. (This is rapidly changing with increasing aggregate and per capita urban water consumption.) Consequently, valley smallholders had less need for access to multiple zones or for communal water management organization in order to sustain their family farms. Periodically supplying workers to clear portions of canals was the main water-related task reported by my key informants in Sabandía, for example (a particularly well-watered zone, to be sure).

Land scarcity, on the other hand, has been a pressing matter in Arequipa since the late-colonial period. Fully 93 percent of cultivators in my three study districts farmed properties smaller than a third of a hectare (Love 1989, 114b, citing 1972 census data), which covered about 47 percent of the total cultivated land in these three districts. In 1940, 36 percent of farm households were renting the land they cultivated (Mostajo Chávez 1942); this had declined slightly by the late 1970s.

Even in the mid-nineteenth century, state-supported expansion of the agricultural frontier through irrigation works on the La Joya and Santa Rita de Siguas pampas was becoming a top priority for regional elites. By the late twentieth century, in a bid to shore up support for the military government's agrarian reform, Juan Velasco Alvarado, in October 1971, himself inaugurated the long-dreamt-of Proyecto Majes in a stirring speech in Arequipa's Plaza de Armas.[1]

Expansion of the agricultural frontier outside the traditional campiña proper now dominates the region. Population estimates for 1990 show about as many people in the Proyecto Majes and the other recently developed irrigation projects, including those in the older, adjacent valleys (La Joya, Santa Rita de Siguas, Vítor, San Juan de Siguas, Pedregal, and Santa Isabel de Siguas) northwest of Arequipa city, as there are in the traditional campiña districts themselves (Paucarpata, Sabandía, Characato, Mollebaya, Quequeña, Yarabamba, Pocsi, Chiguata, Polobaya, Yura, Tiabaya, Sachaca, Uchumayo, and Socabaya). Many of the districts of the traditional campiña were rapidly urbanizing (or suburbanizing) even in the 1970s; since my sample then was drawn from a universe of small-holders, rather than residents overall, it was and is increasingly difficult to tell what proportion of total district populations are actually engaged primarily in rural livelihoods, even in fairly rural districts.

The ongoing plausibility of Arequipeño mestizo identity into the late twentieth century was linked to two basic facts about regional agriculture. First, regional elites' wealth had long come from agricultural holdings in lower valleys outside the campiña, not in the campiña itself, so there was no pressing struggle that might have led to a more classed conflict over land, water, or other productive resources in the valley.[2] Second, the transition of campiña peasants into local market-oriented farmers was relatively seamless in the nineteenth and early twentieth centuries and again in the post–World War II growth of dairying in the region. As had been the case with the wool trade before, the rise of commercial dairying failed to transform relations of production in the city's immediate countryside. Minor social differentiation among campiña small-holders by emerging capitalist relations of production was offset by their ability to rely on the cheap labor of highland immigrants to work their campiña *minifundios* (Love 1989).

Ongoing *minifundismo* both fed urban intellectuals' imagined bucolic mestizo countryside and grounded smallholders' persistent claims to full citizenship in the imagined community of Arequipa. Interpreters—literary, musical, or artistic—developed and used material about, though not by these smallholders or plebeians, who themselves were less concerned about representing themselves in the developing national field than with making a living and actually achieving and maintaining position in regional society.

II. QUOTIDIAN CAMPIÑA

In the predawn cold, family members stir, dress, and walk to the nearby stall where they and/or hired workers start the day's round of milking cows. *Porongos* (large metal milk jugs) of warm milk, steaming in the chill dawn air, are set on the roadside for the Leche Gloria truck to pick up as it labors along rural roads around the broad valley in its daily circuit. Anacleto comes walking down from his home in Yumina with his burro loaded with small *panes*, fresh out of his rustic oven, selling them along the way but mostly delivering them to the several shops along the main road, their shelves already lined with batteries, sodas, small factory-made cakes, cookies, and beer. The morning traffic jam of animals and vehicles builds as teens jostle to move small herds of cattle to their plots up toward Yumina or Coripata, staking them for the day, before they get back to school in the village center or, if older, take the rickety bus to high school in Arequipa. Once settled, a quiet, bucolic landscape prevails, punctuated by trucks rumbling through town carrying agricultural products—for example, seasonal crates of prized *chirimoyas* from Omate and Quinistaquillas—to or from towns into the southern campiña and beyond. Later in the afternoon, children return from school for the evening commute of herds back to stalls and corrals near or connected to their houses. Milk from evening milking keeps cool overnight in the Andean chill for pickup the next morning. Cows lowing, dust, fresh milk, earthy smells, bright sun, and crystal-clear running water in grassy, *molle-* (tree-)lined *acequias* (canals).

So unfolded a typical day in Sabandía, where I lived for almost a year. Similar patterns and scenes repeated in Chiguata and Tiabaya—my two other study districts—as well as in villages around the campiña. On a two-week or twenty-day schedule, men bearing shovels and picks trudged up to headwater plots to manage their *turno* (ration) of water, deftly opening and closing small check gates to allow water to flood terraces. On a more seasonal cycle, fields would be plowed with a team of oxen pulling a scratch plow through the fertile black soil. Teams of harvesters would be employed to plant potatoes, onions, or other crops and then later to weed and finally to harvest them. (Cuadros's brother had told me that locals considered wheat, maize, and potatoes to be "masculine" crops, while onions and garlic were considered "feminine" crops. The former could be worked by peons with little supervision while owners gathered to drink *chicha* in the afternoons, whereas the latter required more labor and supervision.) These day workers, picked up at various checkpoints near *pueblos jovenes* (recent invasion settlements) around the valley (Gómez Rodríguez and Love 1978), often demanded and got a ration of *chicha* for a midday break from the day's toil in addition to a meager cash wage. On key feast days, Chapi pilgrims streamed through Sabandía on foot and in vehicles, though the weekly movement to mass at the small church down toward the small town plaza along the road was less noticeable.

Recalling Raymond Williams's puzzlement over romanticized depictions of his own country childhood, one doesn't have to spend much time in campiña villages to witness the myriad ways this bustling, workaday rural world is and has long been tied to the city. Building materials—*si-llar* blocks quarried from across the valley near Yura, bricks from a growing number of kilns built out toward Yarabamba in unirrigated flats between irrigated stretches of farmland, or the manufactured zinc-plated tin roofs that have almost completely replaced traditional ichu-grass roofs—are delivered and construction proceeds. Dates on some homes in virtually every campiña village indicate something of a spike of construction in the early decades of the twentieth century. Rebar in unfinished building sticks out everywhere into the clear blue sky, reminders of long-term family-building (and tax-avoidance) strategies. Day workers and locals alike move about, beginning and ending various tasks in the brilliant sun. On weekends ice cream vendors walk out to campiña villages like Sabandía and Characato, their canisters somehow managing to stay cold even as the heat of the day grows. By the 1970s cultivation practices had been thoroughly influenced by modern agro-chemical materials and practices; for example, every farm family I interviewed purchased synthetic fertilizers and pesticides. Though everyone knew natural guano was better for the soil and for the plants, not once did I see anyone using it, as it had become prohibitively expensive.

Of course some of these features are more recent (post–World War II) changes, though such infrastructural developments as electrification and transportation (fig. 5.1) are older than most people realize. Nevertheless, the relative isolation of campiña cultivators was vastly overemphasized by the early twentieth-century cultural entrepreneurs we have examined (e.g., fig. 4.4, which shows locals in a scene that could just as well be from the 1700s as the early twentieth century), particularly in the nearby districts, such as Cayma and Yanahuara, that they most favored (they mostly weren't traveling out to more remote villages like Sogay or Mosopuquio). Carpio Muñoz (1981–1983) shows 1860s photographs of presumably rural market vendors having set up shop right in the center of Arequipa, in the Plaza de Armas, and we certainly see then-current manufactured clothing styles worn by rural workers from the 1910s and 1920s (e.g., in fig. 4.2)—near the apogee of traditionalist cultural production.

While urban intellectuals, poets, painters, politicians, and others developed an imagined regional identity essentializing the "mestizo" nature of Arequipeños, the purported bearers of this imaginary—urban plebeians and, especially, rural smallholders—continued their quotidian lives largely disconnected from such concerns. However sympathetic these intellectuals' portrayals of rural livelihoods were, they were typically not well grounded in the everyday realities of these people. Of all

FIGURE 5.1

Electric tram near Paucarpata, in the valley of Arequipa, ca. 1940.
(Reproduced from Morrison 2004.)

the cultural entrepreneurs we examined, only Mostajo—and Valdivia before him—seems to have had direct, more-than-casual experience with rural dwellers. Belaúnde and Gibson were perhaps the most socially distant, reflected in the former's idyllic descriptions and the latter's romanticized imagery. Distinguishing a traditional, idealized Arequipeño everyman (or everywoman in some iterations, as we will see) did not map well onto plebeians' and smallholders' experience or understandings of themselves.

All this early twentieth-century reification of local "traditional" rural culture was taking place parallel with peoples' actual lives and with their periodic pilgrimage to Characato and Chapi. Not to make too much of it, but echoing Belaúnde's observation (quoted in chapter 4), pilgrimage may usefully be understood as a *horizontal* weaving together of urban and rural, in the process reproducing the imagined community through periodic shared experience, while trade and other ties with Altiplano and coast constituted a *vertical* relationship, experienced less as community than as individual *arriero* and *comerciante* (merchant) encounters with typically racialized others in higher or lower communities. Bumping into my good friend and Sabandía neighbor Juan López Apolo in Juliaca, for example, made me realize that his buying cattle there, dressed as an Arequipeño farmer replete with broad-brimmed hat, made him almost as culturally out of place as I was.

Like the city with which the countryside was so tightly connected (see Ødegaard 2010, 9), the campiña was not composed of some undifferentiated mass of typical smallholders, as the cultural entrepreneurs' imaginary implied. Just under the apparently uniform surface of campiña *minifundismo* was and is social, economic, and other complexity—ties of kinship and shared Hispanic ethnicity, along with all the accoutrements of everyday life, from love and honor to domestic violence and petty thievery and a variety of occupational and related material pursuits.

We learned that the general pattern of *minifundismo* had not changed in a long time, and since these land-tenure figures are broadly representative of overall campiña patterns, they indicate that smallholder survival has long been far more a matter of maintaining access to off-farm employment in the city than of having access to other ecozones—perhaps a new form of "multizonal adaptation." It was common for farmers to send meat, beans, maize, big squash, and potatoes every couple of weeks to family in Arequipa or even Lima and for family members to come out on the weekend to do farm work. With this mutual subsidy from urban ties and employment, as well as a generally favorable local urban market for their foodstuffs, smallholders could devote the investment necessary to maintain the terracing and irrigation infrastructure in their areas. Arequipa has featured less abandonment of terracing than have comparable areas of southwestern Peru (Donkin 1979; Mitchell 1985). Skilled stonemasons (*pilcadores*) for these terraces are a campiña specialty in high demand. In sum, the vast majority of campiña households in my 1978–1979 sample had members engaged in off-farm employment, almost entirely in or toward the city center.

Certainly a key reason for this tight urban-rural connection is that distances between campiña villages are not great; hardly twenty kilometers separate any two villages in the valley (except Polobaya and Chapi), and (again except for Polobaya and Chapi) no village is more than twenty kilometers from the city center. Transportation within the valley was improving by the early twentieth century; Arequipa city's system of horse-drawn tramways, begun in 1873, was electrified in 1913 by W. R. Grace and Company and ran until 1966, when it was finally outcompeted by gas and diesel bus transportation. The first line ran between the historic city center and Tingo; lines were built to Paucarpata and Yanahuara by the 1930s (Morrison 2004) [fig. 5.1].

With completion of the main coastal Pan-American Highway in the 1930s, campiña farmers became even more commercially organized in response to the expansion of the internal market in the southern highlands and to Lima (Love 1983, 85). Campiña smallholders seeking to expand to meet demand for vegetables, fruits, and fresh milk for newly opened Lima and Puno markets, as well as for the growing urban population of Arequipa, did not have to compete with an entrenched landed oligarchy. Rather, they had to compete with a sea of smallholders generally unwilling to sell lands in a situation of land scarcity. The perennial problem of partible inheritance, with too much subdividing of arable campiña land, creates a positive feedback loop with villagers' insistence on maintaining social ties to the city to keep access to employment and services for themselves and, especially, for their children. *Minifundismo* is symbiotic with the city—both a product of and maintained by these close urban ties. Hence Belaúnde's urging to rationalize regional agriculture (chapter 4) to make it more commercially competitive in an expanding national market and the huge appeal of the irrigation projects out west in the desert pampas.

With such improved local, regional, and national transportation, the survival strategies of households from ever-farther-flung districts came to rely on urban-related incomes. Access to these jobs typically required more social than economic capital—networks of kin and friends—so getting and maintaining such ties was crucial. Often a family would have a son or nephew working as a *taxista*, who would ferry relatives or goods to and from market on weekends or while off duty. These close rural-urban ties also tell us that post–World War II urbanization was thus not just a consequence of in-migration by Puneños; it was also in part the result of the construction of second houses in the city by campiña families.

Smallholders throughout the valley sent children of all ages to the city for schooling, even from well beyond the valley. Schoolchildren regularly commuted on the local buses (ironically, repurposed Bluebird-type US school buses, though now mostly replaced by faster *combis* [minivans]) that ply the maze of narrow roads in the valley. A girl I met in 1976 in Mollebaya, for example, who couldn't have been more than ten, took a bus to school in Arequipa each day. Her aunt tended her after she got back home as she minded the store; her mother was off working in Tacna. On a trip out to Puquina in 1979 I wound up visiting a family whose several children all spent the week in school in the city, returning on weekends. This was true of many farm families in Chiguata too. Most farm families from Sánchez Cerro province of Moquegua (the right/

north bank of the rugged Tambo drainage)—clear out to Omate—have homes in Arequipa.

Another of the many factors binding together rural and urban Arequipeños across the imaginary divide constructed by traditionalist entrepreneurs was their shared experience as emigrants. With so few employment opportunities in this "diminutive oasis," upwardly mobile middle-class young Arequipeño professionals, like so many of the cultural entrepreneurs earlier examined, too often had to emigrate to Lima or abroad to pursue their careers. The draining off of aspiring Arequipeños is actually a very old process; a study of *encomendero* (labor-titled) elites in early colonial Peru found that moving to Lima was essential for real upward social mobility (Bronner 1977). As Belaúnde had lamented, for the working class (as well as for professionals), there simply were not enough jobs in the region, no coastal plantations to migrate to, few big mines (until lately) in which to find employment.[3]

A key indicator of the strong ties between city and countryside was the lack of developed village marketplaces. I was stunned by the lack of active village markets in any of my three study districts—Sabandía, Tiabaya, or Chiguata—though, oddly, there was an occasional attempt by an enterprising nonlocal to open a stall or find customers. It was clear that most households provisioned themselves from the city (this may date from the 1930s with the opening of the tram), and none locally sold any fruits or vegetables either. Most of the 118 households in my stratified random sample of campiña smallholders were centrally dependent on the commercial sale of crops—chiefly onions (especially in Tiabaya) or dairy cattle, as well as potatoes, maize, a few other food crops, and milk. Few had a small house garden (*huerta*) for various herbs, fruits, and some vegetables.

Yet another indicator of the close ties between city and countryside in Arequipa was the centralization of police and political figures in the city. Local, village-level political authority was very weak; in none of the three villages in which I lived and worked was I ever directed or urged to contact the mayor or any other local official, nor was I ever introduced to one. At my initiative I met the *juez de paz* (justice of the peace) of Chiguata, a kindly older gentleman who performed several political roles there.

With all these ever-tighter ties between city and countryside in the valley, then, rural dwellers like Aurelio (quoted in the epigraph) had every reason to take umbrage at any depictions of them as simple, isolated peasants. Central to Arequipeños' collective self-understanding is the hardscrabble, populist, entrepreneurial quality emerging from this shared social matrix that is fundamentally foreign to some invented rural/urban divide that objectifies rural dwellers.

The tension between urban imaginings of campiña smallholders and farmers' own sense of themselves as fully equal members of regional society intersects the curious story of the "*loncco* Arequipeño." The prototypical Arequipeño everyman, particularly in many recent versions of "typical" life in the valley, is said to be the *loncco*—like the farm couple depicted in fig. 1.2, or like the men in knickers and women in *polleras* (full gathered skirts) depicted in fig. 4.2. In the last several decades *loncco* has come into much wider use by tourist agencies to refer generally to local smallholders and their folkloric speech and lifeways. Yet while the term is by now well known by most Arequipeños, nobody seems to quite know where it came from or to whom it actually refers.

Loncco was used by hardly any of the early twentieth-century cultural entrepreneurs discussed in chapter 4. Since Mostajo had the closest ties to actual rural life in the valley, we can turn to him for help. In 1942, in his introduction to "Cuentos lonccos," he observed that "the countryside has continued without genuine expression in the literature" (Mostajo, quoted in Compañía Cervecera del Sur 2002, 240–241). The Quechua term *loncco* itself refers to a "dull, unpolished knife-blade" and is therefore a disparaging term connoting "useless, rustic, rough in manners." When used in reference to people, it connoted socially crude, rural illiterates—something like "hillbillies" for North Americans.

Loncco stood in a contrasting pair with *ccala*, or city folk (perhaps analogous to the *runa/q'ara* distinction made by Quechua speakers in Cuzco [Allen 2002]). *Ccala* is Aymara for "wall," signifying the urban Spaniards (and later in-marrying foreigners), who lived behind walls made of noble material. Mostajo insightfully linked this term to the rebuilding of the city after the disastrous earthquake of 1786 with *sillar*—the white volcanic tuff for which the heart of the city is now so famous. The *ccala* perspective is well represented in Belaúnde's *Arequipa de mi infancia*, section 3, "Naturaleza, contorno y confín" ([1960] 1967, 45–67), where the various districts around the central Cercado District are all seen in terms of the country houses there owned by distinguished families of the center.

In the hands of *chacareros* themselves, *loncco* was a sarcastic term for someone from their midst who had mixed it up with the city folk—someone who was putting on airs. It was thus a locally owned, rural term, so to speak, and this may explain why hardly any of the writers we have examined actually used or understood it. For example, showing his social distance, Belaúnde never used the term in his memoirs, utilizing instead "campesino" (e.g., [1960] 1967, 64) to refer to local farmers—a term, like *loncco* itself, that rural dwellers would certainly have rejected, just as Aurelio had with me.

Mostajo's clarification of both these terms seems not to have had much impact, however. There is an entire cottage industry in recent decades devoted to "*loncco*" speech and cuisine, with books of poetry (e.g., Núñez Pinto, n.d.), CDs, and YouTube videos (e.g., *La ruta del loncco*, at http://www.youtube.com/watch?v=bFw-MQHT9XQ&feature=related). This whole "Ruta del loncco" (Bedregal La Vera 2008) business, tied to growing campiña tourism—double-decker buses now take tourists on a rural circuit—continues to perpetuate the idea that *loncco* is a local generic term for a *chacarero* or local smallholder farmer. It isn't. So even though smallholders are sometimes loosely referred to as *lonccos*, my smallholder friends—for example, the López family—emphatically rejected the idea that the term applied to people like them. Though it glosses with both *characato* and *chacarero*, the use of *loncco* in relation to yeoman, middle-level propertied smallholders is inappropriate.[4]

It is certainly true that everyday campiña speech has many local terms of Quechua, Aymara, and even Pukina origin. Much of this debate about the "essence" of *lo arequipeño* winds up turning on language as a key indicator of mestizaje. Gibson and Mostajo both focused on these *Arequipeñismos* as Quechua-influenced localisms characteristic of the traditional yeoman farmer—residue of the essence of *lo arequipeño* (e.g. Carpio Muñoz 1999). The distinctive speech of locals was a key marker of regional identity, captured in the *loncco* materials cited above. Many Quechuaized localisms do survive, evidence of an older linguistic, perhaps even cultural mixing. These linguistic matters have been exhaustively explored and documented by Juan Carpio Muñoz (e.g., 1999). A common local term from Quechua, for example, is "topo"—the basic unit of areal measurement still used in the campiña, both in the vernacular and in legal documents. A topo is equivalent to one-third hectare $(3,333.00 \text{ m}^2)$ or 0.815 acres.

In sum, the key point is not that this sort of cultural and linguistic mixing didn't occur—of course it did. There is enough (and had to be enough) of an objective basis for such mixing that the idealized and stereotypical mestizo imagery proffered by late nineteenth-century and early twentieth-century cultural entrepreneurs was plausible. Rather, the issue is the extent to which these criteria characterize a culturally distinct category of people rather than, as smallholders themselves would have it, barely differentiated rural dwellers aspiring for full membership in regional society.

III. PICANTERAS AND MILKMAIDS

Though traditionalist imagery during the first half of the twentieth century was relatively gender balanced (see, e.g., the poem by Gibson quoted in chapter 4 and figs. 4.4, 4.5a, and 4.5b), most urban writers, musicians, and artists focused on the central role played by picanteras. These matrons were often said to be the main bearers of traditional culture and were portrayed as being as much or more at the center of traditional Arequipa regional identity than were the male farmers going about their everyday tasks. As we will see, traditionalist imagery became more masculinized, and gender even more salient, starting in the 1950s.

Early twentieth-century cultural entrepreneurs frequented picanterías, which became popular local "taverns" that incubated a bohemian, democratic space in still-status-conscious Arequipa and that served for many of them as metaphor for a more egalitarian general culture. As esteemed musician Benigno Ballón Farfán trenchantly observed, the picantería was "the real university of the people"—a democratic space that fostered much of this modernist-yet-traditionalist worldview. The poet Guillermo Mercado was accorded the privilege of having his own table at the famous picantería La Josefa in Antiquilla (on the La Chimba side of the old colonial Puente Bolognesi). The musician Ballón frequented La Josefa as well as such picanterías as El Pacai in Alata, Las Moscas in Zamácola, El Timpu de Rabos on the way to Cayma, and La Mundial and La Palomino in Yanahuara (Arce Espinoza 2009).

Women were restricted by patriarchal custom and division of labor to culturally approved roles tied to domestic tasks. Even aristocratic women were constrained, as illustrated in *La Monja Gutierrez*—the story of a nun intent on escaping from a monastery (Bustamante de la Fuente 1971)—and as depicted in Maria Nieves y Bustamante's *Jorge, el hijo del pueblo* ([1892] 1958) as well as in her own life.

Managing picanterías and selling and delivering milk in the city were two culturally approved roles, however, that featured strong, independent women managing small businesses (figs. 4.5a and 4.5b)—public spaces where women were in charge (see Weismantel 2001). These tropes were based on social reality, and in the hands of cultural entrepreneurs they signaled that, so to speak, "our women are not licentious or irresponsible, but industrious and thrifty," tying to the "honorable artisan" theme discussed in chapter 4. The literary focus on the picantería also gave voice to the actual aspirations of such women, connecting with broadly understood plebeian concerns with being recognized as honorable citizens of regional society.

> That which hasn't changed a bit is that the world of picanterías was, is and will always be a matriarchy. The seasoned universe of pots and fires is dominated by women. The 1940 census registered 663 women and 67 men working in picanterías. But even more, Velmy Villanueva, proprietress of the "Cau Cau" picantería indicated that cooks' great fear was to not have daughters and thereby to not be able to pass on their culinary secrets. (Rocha, n.d.)

Picanteras made the *chicha* and *picantes* (spicy tapas-like dishes) in what amounted to a logical outgrowth of the domestic tasks already established and assigned in the prevailing sex/gender system. "The *suysuna* (sieve for the *chicha* must) was hung in whatever corner of the kitchen, along with the *fucuna* (bellows for the fire) and the *tokpina* (stoker for the charcoal) . . . 'Poison that doesn't kill, fattens'" (Peralta Vásquez 1977, 40).[5]

Traditional foods, especially drinks—e.g., fig wine and *chimbango* (fig liquor) in Uchumayo—continued to be produced around the campiña. But local cuisine pivoted fundamentally on *chicha*, served in the picantería, more characteristic of urban plebeian districts (fig. 5.2) than of country villages. A fairly set arrangement of foods by time of day and day of the week had developed by the twentieth century, and this pattern more or less carries over into our day in the hole-in-the-wall eateries all over urban Arequipa and, more recently, in the countryside restaurants that have exploded in Tiabaya, Sabandía, Characato, and elsewhere catering to urbanites looking for a weekend escape to fresh air and countryside, and even to foreign tourists. Lunches were "a full plate of soup (*chaqui* on Mondays, *chairo* on Tuesdays, *pebre de gallina* on Wednesdays, *blanco de cordero* on Thursdays, *cazuela* on Fridays, *alocrado* on Saturdays and shrimp soup or *puchero* on Sundays) along with a 'fino' or second ('*chanfaina*' of chunks of lamb, *kauchi* of sheep's head, etc.). And to top it off a large glass of chicha" (Peralta Vásquez 1977, 35; see Cornejo Velásquez 2006). Adobo (spicy pork stew), after marinating all Saturday night was served on Sunday mornings after early mass;

FIGURE 5.2

Chichería arequipeña, 1920. From https://plus.google.com/photos /113518930836788618970/albums/5498831386660455265/5503496006981247922 ?banner=pwa&pid=5503496006981247922&oid=113518930836788618970; site discontinued. Accessed 23 July 2013.

one woman's adobo, on the corner of the plaza in Cayma, was especially sought out during my dissertation years.

More tied to place, women came to symbolize tradition in this earlier phase of traditionalist discourse. The matronly picantera was mother to weary workers and, in the eyes of sympathetic literary modernists, manager of a social space crucial for incubating and nurturing democratic society. Basically functioning as neighborhood taverns frequented by all occupational groups, these picanterías leveled social differences and were key sites of emerging civil society.

> In the picantería every day the taciturn worker and the talkative artisan, the scheming notary and the troublemaking lawyer, the stingy merchant and the scoundrel of a property owner, the hacienda owner and the peon, the worker and the employee, "the large and the small," men, women and children, everyone, without distinction of social position or color. (Peralta Vásquez 1977, 30)

At around the time Peralta is remembering (the early decades of the twentieth century), virtually everyone in Arequipa drank lots of *chicha*; picanterías were common right in the center of the city. "It was the popular restaurant of the epoch . . . within reach of the pockets of the poorest" (ibid., 35). "Workers, seated on the edges of their fields, did honor with the chicha glass with the solemnity of a priest drinking the sacred wine in sacrifice on the altar" (ibid., 31). "The picantería was . . . the forum where public intrigues were worked out, with complete impudence" (ibid., 31). Political uprisings began and ended in the picantería, birthdays and religious holidays were celebrated in the picantería, godparents (*comadres* and *compadres*) rendezvoused in the picantería. "In it Eros was incubated to the sound of yaravíes being sung . . . with as many crying [as singing] the song" (ibid., 33). "[In sum] . . . the cholo arequipeño, the 'characato,' is by any standard made of *guiñapu* [corn mash for chicha]" (ibid., 37–38).

The *yaraví* song form as we know it is said to have originated with Mariano Melgar, who combined the indigenous *huarari* with Spanish sentimental verse in composing love poems to Sylvia. The form is said to have quickly come to typify plebeian and rural life, its melancholy content reflecting the subordinated class position of campiña *loncos* (Carpio Muñoz 1976). To the extent that there is any class content in the *yaraví* oeuvre (which is much less than claimed by Carpio, as is evidenced by the lyrics of the songs in his own songbook), it has to do with ruralites' feeling shut out of the urban prosperity, which wasn't translating into improved fortunes for them.

Yaravíes—laments about lost love, loneliness, and deprivation—became more widely popular after the war with Chile, when nationalist fervor was running high and the national question was becoming paramount (Carpio Muñoz 1976). By the 1920s radios were widespread enough that musical groups singing *yaravíes* could be widely heard, even by people who couldn't attend live performances in theaters. While there are indeed rural and urban-plebeian origins to this song form, by the early twentieth century it seems to have become, to the contrary, a style largely for urban middle-class consumption. The melancholic mood also meshed well with emigrants' nostalgia for the homeland, a theme that became central to the tradition by the mid-twentieth century.

Don Antonio Pinto of Sabandía averred in a March 1997 interview that in the old days (which would have been roughly the 1920s), bands of musicians from the city (especially Yanahuara) were hired by *ccalas* for their country soirées. (He may have been recalling stories told him about the latter part of the nineteenth century as well.) Belaúnde confirms Don Antonio's memory, since Sabandía, with its old mill, had witnessed before Belaúnde's time (i.e., in the 1880s) a *ccala* scene of "creole dances

[and] rural banquets" (Belaúnde [1960] 1967, 61). "The rocky slope of So-cabaya, the Sabandía mill and the pear orchards of Tiabaya were famous as places of excursion, amusement and romance" (ibid., 62).

Picanterías, *yaravíes*, *chacareros*—the whole scene encapsulates an ur-ban view of a village-level universe in a rapidly transforming regional society:

> A classic chichero told us recently: "Chicha used to be (so good) you'd take off your hat. It was pure. Not like now that's pure goo added to the remains of beer. So much red maize used to be grown to make *gui-ñapu*. Now there's no red maize and no *guiñapu*. Now chicha is just bad beer. It used to be hardly any kalas [*ccalas*, see above] that didn't go to the picanterías, but even they drank chicha at home. Today kalas focus on drinking who knows what kinds of hideous foreign drinks. The real Arequipeño, fed on chicha since he came into the world, you can tell a mile off, by the uneven shoulders: the right bent by the jug of chicha carried below and the left up high due to the plate of picantes he would have carried in his life." (Peralta Vásquez 1977, 33–34)

For political liberals like Peralta and most of the literary modern-ists, then, picanterías became central symbols of the purportedly fun-damentally democratic spirit of everyday Arequipeños. They were pub-lic spaces in which social tensions could be worked out in civil discourse rather than in the violent movements characteristic of the coast or the highlands; "there weren't labor agitators then putting ideas of social re-venge in their heads," wrote Peralta (ibid., 35) (an odd thing for the don of *aprismo* in Arequipa to be writing!). In sum, picanterías symbolized the mestizo essence of Arequipeño culture, since as Polar had argued de-cades earlier, *chicha* itself was a key symbol of the indigenous traits so harmoniously fused in the soul of the Arequipeño.

Picanterías like the ones Peralta and others describe began to disap-pear about midcentury, though there has been something of a resur-gence in the last decade or so as people seek the "country experience" in a more touristic sense. How can we best understand this decline (un-til recently) of the picantería in Arequipa? Picanterías were marginal to polite, aristocratic society; as with tavern culture in many societies, they were frequently associated with fighting, domestic violence, sex, and in-toxication. Pressure against public drunkenness was evident even early in the Republican period, when *chicherías* (as they were formerly called) came to be called "picanterías" as a way of sprucing up their public image (Chambers 1999, 191). In the countryside, however, picanterías were afternoon watering holes for the more prominent local farmers.

Though many factors are involved, the postwar rise of dairying certainly contributed to the decline of picanterías, since people had to be out bringing cattle home from the fields and milking them rather than congregating in picanterías at the end of the workday drinking chicha or *cerveza* (European-style factory-made beer). But the decline was due to more than that, since these twice-daily milking tasks fell mostly on hired serranos or women. The daily round of tasks didn't seem to keep some local dairymen from congregating almost every day at the shop at the main crossroads in Sabandía to drink *cerveza* Arequipeña when I lived there.

Drinking *cerveza* seemed to be supplanting chicha drinking as a marker of cattle owners. Also important were consumption styles imported from abroad, appropriate for new generations aspiring to be more trendy by drinking beer rather than chicha (Orlove and Schmidt 1995). Beer drinking became associated with new prosperity, as exemplified by the prominent sponsorship of local bullfights by the local brewery.

In addition, declining maize production with the post–World War II intensification of dairying and the consequent spread of alfalfa cultivation also hit picanterías; land devoted to maize declined precipitously as many campiña cultivators shifted from cultivating maize to raising alfalfa for their own or others' dairy cattle (see Love 1983). Declining supply put upward pressure on the price of maize, making it more expensive for the average worker. While picanteras could have simply purchased maize for brewing, falling demand from changing consumption styles as well as rising prices seem most responsible for the decline.

As Arequipa industrialized, more employment options opened for women, which also added to pressures on picanteras. By midcentury most were older women, like those extolled in recent literature (e.g., by Peralta) but unlike those featured in fig. 5.2. Urbanization was pushing the rural working class out from the urban center.

At its heart, Arequipeño traditionalism was fueled by urban middle-class nostalgia in a time of dramatic social change for a settled, ordered way of life perceived as slipping away (see the analysis in chapter 6). For Arequipa's urban middle sectors and for most literary figures, traditionalist imagery in this peak period was feminized—personal and familial, with images of milkmaids and motherly picanteras constituting reassuring anchors against the onrushing tide of impersonal forces associated with market, class, and bureaucratic state.

This imagery was linked to the projection of a "mestizo" identity onto regional society, as we saw in chapter 4. Mestizaje, of course, implies miscegenation between castes. Gender and race are thus fully entangled in all this evocation of chicha and picanteras. Despite all the rhetoric about matronly virtues, this is a latter-day revisionist take on the ribald nature of the picantería to which Peralta hinted (above). The bawdy nature of picanterías was part of its working-class culture—hence the general disrepute of picanterías in politer circles of regional society.

The bawdy nature of the picantería was brought home to me during my main fieldwork in Sabandía, where the lone picantería (usually closed) along the main street was run by "las texanas"—so nicknamed by locals, drawing on some then-popular US television western. The nickname carried the sense that the sisters were tough but flirtatious, as they often joked with me in these ways. Though it was irregularly displayed, mostly on weekends for the growing local tourism, the traditional small red flag hanging out on the street told passersby that they had chicha. (They now have a spacious, full-fledged picantería catering to weekenders and tourists in the heart of the village.)

The *lechera* (milkmaid), a peasant woman who milked cows and then delivered milk to urban households in the mornings on her burro, was also prominent in the more feminized symbolism characteristic of this period (fig. 4.5b). As with the picantera, evoking the lechera in literary regionalism was both a reflection of a nostalgic yearning for a simpler, premodern time and a way of highlighting the hardworking local smallholder. Like the picantera, the lechera represented the country in the city (Bustamante y Rivero [1947] 1996, 629)—the seamless unity of city and countryside, refracted through a popular lens. Though lecheras were entrepreneurial, this imagery is again also very domestic, reminding us of the gendered roles that placed women as symbolic nurturing figures for war- or work-weary men.

Picanteras and lecheras also symbolized the boundaries of plebeian social space: popular spaces or plebeian nuclei within the city in the first (see Weismantel 2001), the boundary of the city in the countryside in the latter. Like the notaries who would sit in the main city plaza with heavy upright typewriters, stacks of *papel sellado* (official paper for legal purposes) at their sides, picanteras and lecheras symbolized the boundary between plebeians and power (see Coaguila 2008).

Literary regionalists tended to domesticate Valdivian images of women fighting alongside men, instead tying them to the home and hearth (especially some writers toward the end of the tradition, such as Peralta) and portraying them as maternal. It may not be too much of a stretch to think that they imagined picanteras and milkmaids as biological re-producers of new citizens of the imagined community. However central this symbolism was for all the cultural entrepreneurs evoking the val-ues of citizenship embodied in the picantería, the imagery of the pican-tera (who received far more attention than the lechera) is fundamentally about women's matronly role in creating and managing a space, a thresh-ing floor where males could work out the meanings of citizenship.[6]

In sum, highlighting the centrality of picanteras and milkmaids in the literary regionalist tradition points to several larger gender issues at stake in the construction and reproduction of subnationalist discourse. In the original Valdivian formulation of regional identity, women were portrayed as active participants in the caudillo struggles; consider, for example Valdivia's recounting of a rural woman's heroic informing of Santa Cruz, or Mostajo's story of "La rabona," which highlighted the ac-tive role that women traveling with soldiers had played in these subna-tional struggles. While women were indeed portrayed in this discourse as key symbols of regional difference, most of the literary regionalism of the early twentieth century domesticated and confined them to com-fortable, quasi-domestic spaces—as the main bearers of this (reinvented) tradition.

IV. HONOR AND THE MASCULINIZATION OF REGIONAL IDENTITY—FROM CHACARERO TO BULLFIGHTER

Emigration from this small, familial oasis—overwhelmingly by young men seeking their fortune in the city or abroad, whether in Lima, Chile, Buenos Aires, or Europe, depending on their social class—is a main thread in the story of Arequipa. The *arriero* culture is usefully seen as a precursor of this masculinized "traveling Arequipeño" imagery, mocked by dancers in Pisac (above) or evoked in the *Montonero Arequipeño* who, tired from battle, returns to "his *morena*" (his woman) (discussed above in chapter 4). As the bulk of the exponents of the literary regionalist tra-dition either left voluntarily or were forced into exile, its main tone be-came increasingly nostalgic and began to run out of steam after midcen-tury (e.g., Belaúnde [1960] 1967; Peralta Vásquez 1977).

In the latter half of the twentieth century symbols of this subna-tional identity underwent a further masculinizing shift. Where the early twentieth-century imagery depicted the traditional Arequipeño as both

honorable and hardworking—whether women as milkmaids and picanteras or men as farmers and *arrieros*—by the second half of the century
the imagery had recentered on the male owner of fighting bulls (*arrieraje* having gone into decline decades earlier). Though food remained a
key locus of regional identity, milkmaids, picanteras, and *arrieros* moved
to the background in regional identity, nostalgic symbols of an already
"disappearing tradition."

The emigration (voluntary or by exile) of most of the early twentieth-
century cultural entrepreneurs (Mostajo and Rodríguez notwithstanding) and the departure of most aristocratic families from direct involvement in valley agriculture (Belaúnde [1960] 1967) opened a space
in regional society for the rise to prominence of an even more masculine imagery, directly associated with the rapid emergence of a dairying elite among farmers in the valley. Already closely integrated with regional markets, valley agriculturists quickly shifted from a broad array
of staple crops toward dairying with the 1940 establishment and subsequent growth of a Carnation Milk Company evaporated-milk plant
(Love 1983). Carnation's entry into regional agriculture, warmly received
by regional elites clamoring for investment in the regional economy,
also opened up a space into which even some *mayordomos* and tenants
moved into prominence in regional agriculture as property owners in
their own right.

Faced with the collapse of wool and other trade in the 1920s and 1930s,
Arequipeño elites strongly favored import substitution industrialization
as well as foreign-financed industrialization. Leche Gloria—the Carnation Milk Company's local affiliate—was primary among several food-
processing plants established in the valley during the 1930s and 1940s
(Love 1983). The elites' focus was all about attracting foreign capital, as
evidenced in the 1940 Cuarto Centenario tract analyzed in chapter 4.

Dairy farmers grew out of the general social matrix of rural smallholders, particularly those with ties to the cattle business. While oxen
had long been used for plowing and even hauling, the focus of cattle raising was producing milk and making cheese and butter; Pérez Wicht was
one of the better-known brands. With Carnation's entry, a larger market for fresh or (canned) evaporated milk rapidly developed. This meant
importing Holstein cattle, a breed known for higher milk (but lower fat)
production, and improving herds through artificial insemination and
better husbandry practices directly or indirectly tied to milk-company
programs.

Male cattle had long been bought up by traveling buyers from valleys throughout the region (see section "V. An Ethnography of the Particular," below) to be slaughtered for meat and hides for leatherworking. Some intentional fattening of young bulls (*toretes*) was practiced locally, but with the advent of trucking, by midcentury cattle buying spread to more distant valleys. Mostly bulls were loaded into trucks and hauled to the slaughterhouse. It was but a few short steps from these long-standing practices first to selecting out the stronger bulls for bullfighting (see below in this chapter) and then to intentionally raising prize bulls via artificial insemination from champions.

As farmers' activities quickly reoriented toward milk cattle, a full-blown "cattle complex"—a whole culture of raising and training bulls for bullfighting—rapidly emerged (fig. 5.3). Engaged in what was now the most obvious rural activity in the countryside, dairy farmers adopted the traditionalist mantle, as it were, and by the late 1940s the urban appetite for and love of the countryside was already shifting to focus on bullfighters as the main bearers of tradition, with their distinctive and dramatic bull-on-bull fighting and love of horses. Owners of fighting bulls are often featured in the local patron-saint-day parade (15 August) (which the local Lions Club began in the 1960s), resplendent with their fine *paso* horses and (coastal) *marinera*-style *charro* dress (a rather Spanish, seignorial style characteristic of the north-Peruvian coastal estate owners and managers) (fig. 5.4).

After describing the excitement and all that goes into bullfighting, we will examine in more detail the crucial role, both direct and indirect, played by the Leche Gloria (Carnation) evaporated-milk plant in the development of this aspect of regional culture. For, quite unexpectedly, it was Gloria's economic empowerment of the rural dairymen that further masculinized smallholder-related imagery and enabled its move to the center of regional identity.

A. Peleas de Toros

Bullfighting (as *peleas*) is specific to the campiña of Arequipa, not found until recently even in adjacent valleys like the Colca or the Tambo, nor even in such cattle-intensive Majes communities as Pampacolca or Viraco. Instead of a matador with cape and sword confronting a charging bull, in the campiña bull fights bull. It is very picturesque and full of emotion and excitement (fig. 5.3); excellent videos have been produced by the Asociación de Criadores, Proprietarios y Aficionados de Toros de Pelea de Arequipa (Association of Breeders, Owners and Fans of Are-

FIGURE 5.3
*Poster of a **pelea de toros**. Photograph by the author.*

quipa Fighting Bulls; ACPATPA) (see below), but the fights are also view-able, yes, on YouTube (e.g., *Tiempo de viaje: Toros de Arequipa*, at http://www.youtube.com/watch?v=qL2bSn5A4lU).

From elks to warthogs, sparring male animals are a fixture of many species' territorial mating rituals. Yet oddly enough, bull-on-bull fight-ing similar to Arequipa's is found in few other places in the world. On Sumatra, peasants outside of Bukittinggi at the base of Mt. Sorik Merapi train their water buffaloes to fight other bulls, and bull-on-bull fight-ing is also found in Cheongdo-gun in southeastern South Korea. While there are undoubtedly other examples to be found, it is a curiously un-usual sport—perhaps reflecting an uncommon social matrix of relatively egalitarian, propertied owners involved in status-group competition that sustains it.

Though prominent in regional folklore now, *peleas* were surprisingly not part of the traditionalist narrative until the mid-twentieth century. Though *peleas* almost certainly emerged out of the many ways men validate their place in local society through competitive display, games, or consumption (e.g., sporting competitions, dress, or drinking), perhaps well back into the nineteenth century (though probably not into the colonial period; see Motta Zamalloa 1979, 24; Céspedes Carpio 2010), the earliest-known public recognition of a bullfight was on 10 May 1881 in the Pampa de Miraflores (Carpio Muñoz 1981–1983, 60).[7] It is tempting to link the public emergence of *peleas* to the threats to honor posed by the War of the Pacific, with citizen locals as the main carriers of republican virtue. In any case, there is no mention of *peleas* at all in Belaúnde's detailed memoir about his 1883–1900 Arequipa childhood (Belaúnde [1960] 1967), and *peleas* do not figure in Maria Nieves y Bustamante's 1892 *Jorge, el hijo del pueblo* or in poetry of the 1920s–1930s (Gibson) or in other writing of the period (e.g., Mostajo [1924] 1956). Even more curiously, *peleas* are not mentioned in *La Campiña*, a magazine of the 1920s–1940s that circulated widely in the region. The magazine catered to prosperous members of regional society with the means to improve agricultural practices, since it regularly featured ads about the latest agricultural machinery, animal-husbandry tips, and dress styles, along with poetry (often poems by the Leguía-approved poet José Santos Chocano (N. Miller 1999, 67), for example) and news about recent laws or government policies of relevance. Mostajo wrote regularly for this magazine. This striking absence additionally points to both the recency and the very rural, smallholder origins of *peleas*.

Peleas both constitute and symbolize newly empowered smallholders' attempt to break into regional status circles. As we have learned, and as Don Aurelio had admonished, valley smallholders and urban plebeians were anxious about being mistaken for mere campesinos and thereby excluded from the field of "honor" developed in Arequipa after independence. Some well-placed members of the regional elite—Polar and Mostajo especially—had come to recognize the honor of rural smallholders, especially compared to highland Indians (see Chambers 1999, 180), however cloaked in the romanticizing nostalgia of traditionalist rhetoric. But in the Republican era even elites' honor had to be primarily validated in behavior; it could not just rest on inherited status or rank—thus the importance of performing one's status to validate it. But as we shall see, it takes quite an investment to acquire, maintain, train, and transport a prize fighting bull.

A typical *pelea* has several elements: a sponsor, a dedication, a set of judges, an audience, a charitable purpose, and, of course, the bulls, their owners, and handlers (Motta Zamalloa 1979, 67–81; Céspedes Carpio 2010). Bull owners are typically in the ring directly encouraging their bulls; until very recently, apparently, there were no absentee owners of bulls, and there are still few. Masculine virtues—rational, hard, cold, decisive, calculating—are much in evidence. In the 2014 example shown advertised in fig. 5.3, the *peleas* were sponsored by the Municipality of Socabaya and were held in the Menelik stadium in Socabaya devoted to *peleas*. Each *pelea* is dedicated to someone important, such as the president of FONGALSUR (Fondo para el Desarrollo de la Ganadería Lechera del Sur [Southern Dairy Development Fund], the regional dairymen's cooperative); proceeds usually go to some worthy public cause.

ACPATPA was formed in 1986 explicitly to preserve the "tradition." They sponsor the official *peleas*, even though there are still illegal or unauthorized *peleas*, which ACPATPA thinks of as local, preliminary *peleas* leading up to the grand, official *peleas* they sponsor. There is a *pelea* somewhere in the campiña every weekend, often on Sundays, and bigger ones are held periodically. The biggest *pelea* is said to be the one held annually on 15 August at Cerro Juli, the regional fairgrounds, on the city's feast day. Edwin Gómez, ex-president of ACPATPA, told me, however, that the biggest *pelea* is always held at Easter (pers. comm., 12 July 2005), a tradition started in Sabandía (see below in this chapter).

The regional agricultural association (Sociedad Agrícola del Departamento de Arequipa) had by 1920 begun to organize and to recognize the best fighting bull with a silver medal (Lazo Carpio 1996, 31). ACPATPA emerged in the 1990s to represent this status group of prosperous cattlemen who now carry much of the symbolic weight of campiña traditionalism. *Peleas* constitute a regionally specific form of status rivalry among members of this emerging dairying elite, who attained their positions by converting newfound income from the cattle-buying and dairying business into cultural capital, displayed in *pelea* performance. I harness practice theory to analyze this development in chapter 6.

Bull owners' performance of their masculinity is revealed in many ways, most of them evident on the YouTube video cited just above. Men, both owners and managers, encourage, prod, and guide the bulls during the fighting, sometimes stroking the bulls' genitals or passing a young cow in heat to stimulate them to fight. When this happens it produces in the audience both ribald laughter at its sexuality and dismay that the owner had to stoop to such tactics, so timid, so un-*bravo* was his bull. There is much sexual joking among both owners and spectators, and a losing bull is shouted down as a coward. For Arequipeño aficionados,

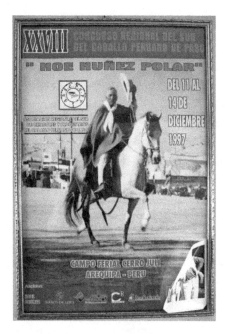

FIGURE 5.4

*Broadside of campiña cattleman on Peruvian **paso** horse. Photograph by the author.*

mostly of the urban plebeians, *peleas* are a microcosm of struggle over honor and what it means to be Arequipeño. A typical match features a lot of barely concealed betting. When bulls don't fight (which is surprisingly often), people take it as metaphor for Arequipeños' no longer having "fighting spirit" (see Céspedes Carpio 2010).

The masculine names of bulls emphasize their fighting prowess and notoriety, and naming is a developed art full of allusions and double entendres. A somewhat random list of names from recent *peleas* includes Alcapone, MacGiver, Stalin, Saca Chispas, Alemán, Nunca es Tarde, Fumanchu, Vikingo, No Me Mates Cobarde (You Won't Be Able to Kill Me, Coward—probably my all-time favorite), Athletic Peru, Cataclism, Fury, and Black Assassin.

While all campiña smallholders think of themselves as *agricultores*, "farmers," and most definitely not *campesinos*, which connotes "peasant," as Aurelio had insisted, those working exclusively with animals constitute a separate stratum, an esteemed subset of *ganaderos* (cattlemen) (see fig. 5.4). There is a close, personal association of maleness between an owner and his bull, who responds to his owner's voice and has both a fighting name and a personality. Being so closely associated with their animals, dairymen are not only close to their bulls but also symbolically "closer to the earth" (Orlove 1998). Bull owning reinforces male ties to land, since landed males stay put and fight if necessary. This feature makes them ideal symbols of homeland, for it contrasts sharply with the alienating experience of emigration. It dovetails with the major themes of the Valdivia and mestizo phases of regional tradition, evidenced in the lyrics of Portugal and in Huirse's 1950 *pampeña* "Montonero Arequipeño" (above, chapter 4), which says, "You've fought in the militia, for your division and caudillo, but now you must return to your woman." Cattlemen also have a wheeler-dealer reputation that feeds into the masculine bravado.

The emphasis on the family names of specific owners in the programs produced for these *peleas* is another indication of these status concerns. In the campiña, the long-standing emphasis on family honor meshed with landholding gave rise to a tradition that carries to the present day. This close association between patrilaterally extended families and places lies at the heart of the very personal sentiment people have with the campiña, and it is expressed in the general association of patronyms with particular places and villages. In Sabandía, for example, "los Santos" owned the lands in the saddle between the main road through town and Yumina, while "los Fernández" owned land nearer the main road and the church as well as the broad shelf of land just before the final ascent to Yumina. The site where an odd Italian hermit lived for many years, back behind Yumina toward the river, was "El Moyo." Even though the López family had owned the land near the center of town for decades, locals still referred to it as "donde los Cuadros" (from Juan Cuadros, who had long owned these parcels and from whom the López family had purchased them). The campiña is thus a landscape of memory, so while patronymic place-names associate masculinity with landowning, they are also often signs of "what happened here" rather than simply names of points demarcated in abstract geographic space (cf. Basso 1996).

Concern with status is also reflected in dress. Every morning in Sabandía, almost like clockwork, Don Elisbán Fernández used to walk from his house near the plaza to the small shop run by his wife near the (empty) market, down the main road through Sabandía, in his lumpy pin-striped suit and campiña sombrero—the classic gentleman farmer by status, however much or little wealth he may actually have commanded. Campiña farmers, even those who do not trace descent back to the nineteenth century or farther, continued this tradition, together forming a distinctive status group within regional society. Concern with honor links tightly to pride in legitimate citizenship in the imagined community of Arequipa, as we have seen.

The reputation of a family name and the inviolability of one's home were central Republican principles (Chambers 1999, 181), and they meshed well with prevailing ideals in rural Arequipa, where *minifundista* family ownership of land and family honor were paramount. Rómulo del Carpio, president of FONGALSUR, for example, was at great pains in my interview with him to make sure that I noted that he was a "del Carpio," not just a "Carpio." "De Dios"—as in "Juan de Dios"—was a polite way of noting someone's illegitimate birth.

The current focus on prize bulls grows directly out of the association of campiña *ganaderos* with cattle buying in the highlands and with the mule trade since the colonial period. Despite these deep roots, *peleas* intensified at midcentury not just with *ganaderos'* increased and regular income from Leche Gloria, but also with increased immigration by poor serranos, who constituted a growing rural wage labor force that made accumulation by smallholders possible (Love 1983). Honor-driven status concerns easily meshed with the ever-present desire of plebeians and smallholders to be considered as full citizens of the imagined regional community and were thus easily naturalized and woven into these now very public spectacles extolling regionalist identity.

So prominent is this bull-and-horse stratum in contemporary rural culture that I could almost have titled this book *Of Horses and Bulls*. While the symbolic presence of Peruvian *paso* horses in Arequipeño traditionalism is linked to upper-class nostalgia for a landed-gentry, seignorial way of life, associated with the coast, the symbolic presence of the bull represents the rising class of prosperous agriculturists, made possible by Leche Gloria and the irrigation projects of La Joya and Majes. *Peleas* are therefore more popular and broadly enjoyed by plebeians, whereas horse riding is more elegant, formal, and anachronistically patrician (recalling "José Antonio" as sung by famed Peruvian singer Chabuca Granda).

Campiña farmers internalized this perhaps overdue recognition and turned their growing wealth from the shift to dairy farming (Love 1983) toward the cost of maintaining conspicuously costly fighting bulls and *paso* horses—much as people in core developed countries might convert economic wealth to such seemingly irrational consumption choices as traveling to exotic places or buying fancy cars, fine art, or expensive breeds of dogs or racehorses. Many of these upwardly mobile rural smallholders moved into prominent positions in regional society in the latter part of the twentieth century, the most prominent example being the takeover of Leche Gloria by the Rodríguez Banda company.

B. Leche Gloria

The rise to prominence of this masculine imagery, centrally tied to bull-fighting, is directly associated with the emergence of a dairying elite in the valley, which is in turn closely tied to Leche Gloria, a Carnation Milk Company evaporated-milk plant. Faced with 1920s and, especially, De-pression-era collapse of trade, regional business leaders such as Busta-mante y Rivero, Bustamante de la Fuente, and others strongly favored import substitution industrialization and state stimulus during a pe-riod of slack exports to turn around the regional economy. Leche Glo-ria, the US-based Carnation Milk Company's local affiliate, was pri-mary among several food-processing plants established during and after World War II.

Unlike other regional elites, Arequipa's had been especially open to foreign involvement in the regional economy, particularly from the wool period forward. The presence of non-Spanish European surnames, es-pecially British, among elite families in the nineteenth century is nota-ble. In the 1920s, though, it seems that these intermarried members of the merchant oligarchy became somewhat nervous about further foreign investment, seeing that foreign capital entered Peru to develop activities that would otherwise have been developed by local capital (Thorp and Bertram 1978, 143; Belaúnde [1915] 1963). This attitude may help account for Leche Gloria's significant post–World War II effort to integrate itself into the regional culture by stimulating and supporting cattle breeding and *peleas de toros*—foreign (US) capital lured to Arequipa in a climate of some mistrust and suspicion. In any case, Leche Gloria was given a warm welcome. Leche Gloria sponsored a cattle fair in Vallecito in Au-gust 1940—the four hundredth anniversary of the Spanish founding of Arequipa—and again in October that same year with a silver trophy cer-tified by President Prado (Lazo Carpio 1996, 15, 17).

Agro-industry, along with export of fishmeal, copper, and other raw materials, led Arequipa to become the industrial focus of southern Peru from the 1950s onward (Chávez O'Brien 1987, 35). It is during this period that we see increased internal migration both of Puneños and Cuzque-ños toward Arequipa, as well as of Arequipeños toward Lima. The Parque

Industrial dates from the early 1960s, during the first government of Francisco Belaúnde—the first real effort by the central state to invest in and stimulate regional development outside Lima. The oil-linked beginning of economic recession in the central capitalist countries in the mid-1970s, along with the policy preoccupations of the then-current military regime, caused a retraction of state support of regional development in the 1970s, initiating yet another crisis for the regional economy of the south. In the 1970s Leche Gloria began to diversify into canned fish, oatmeal, and coffee, and in 1978 it changed its name to Gloria SA.

Some campiña smallholders leveraged their ties to this rapidly developing dairy sector. Vito Rodríguez Rodríguez is a prominent example. Along with his parents and his brother Jorge, he had founded a trucking company that had become Gloria's main transportation arm. In 1986 their company—Rodríguez Banda—with support from the García regime's nationalist policies requiring partial foreign divestment, became majority shareholder in Gloria and, shortly thereafter, in Nestlé, which had operated primarily in Cajamarca. Gloria continued its expanding control of milk production in Bolivia, Ecuador, and now Argentina, and in recent decades it has continued diversification into chocolates, ice cream, pharmaceuticals, cement (Cemento Yura), fertilizers, paper making (*bagasse*), plywood, and north-Peruvian-coast cane sugar.

As noted earlier, the ongoing vitality of Arequipeño mestizo identity is due in no small part to the relatively seamless transition of campiña peasants into farmers, and this is predicated on key transportation and other developments in valley agriculture. Leche Gloria's twice-monthly cash payments enabled local dairymen to purchase consumer goods and to convert this increased income into status longings, materialized in the actual practice of bullfighting. (I elaborate on this conversion of capitals in the concluding chapter.) Again, Leche Gloria's rise (like that of the wool trade before it) did not transform relations of production in the countryside; to the extent that campiña smallholders experienced differentiation by emerging capitalist relations of production, this was offset by the immigration of highlanders to labor on campiña *minifundios* and by expansion into the irrigation projects (Love 1989, 2005).

In sum, enabled by the developing dairy industry, local farmers adopted the traditionalist mantle, as it were, emerging as the main bearers of tradition with their distinctive and dramatic bull-on-bull fighting. With regular reenactment of stereotypical symbols in a dramaturgy of bulls and men, by the 1970s bullfighting had moved to central position in regional symbolism. In sum, *peleas* are both a new tradition and an ongoing performance of Arequipeño identity, though now with small-holders themselves more centrally in charge of their own representation.

V. AN ETHNOGRAPHY OF THE PARTICULAR:
FEDERICO LÓPEZ APOLO

I close this chapter with the story of a particular and remarkable man, Federico López Apolo, one of my key informants during two years of fieldwork and a long-term friend since. Examining the particular has become a useful way of getting underneath the over-large categories into which it is easy to slide, particularly in a monograph like this one centering on broad patterns and the *longue durée*. Examining one key person's life history illuminates the complexities and local contexts that defy simple generalizations about such a regional cultural scene (Abu Lughod 1991).

Though he has resided elsewhere for long periods, Federico considers himself a native of Sabandía, where he was born in 1925, where he has lived the bulk of his life, and where his parents, grandparents, and great-grandparents were born and lived. He finished the tenth grade (*cuarto año de comercio*) at the Colegio Mercantil de Arequipa, then after a few years he worked as an employee of the Hacienda Picotani, northeast of Lake Titicaca in Puno. Though he was a hardworking, highly regarded employee, even being offered double salary to stay, he left after a year to work for his uncle—buying cattle in Ilave, then fattening them for sale and transport by truck to Arequipa and Lima. For the next eight years he would spend six months in Ilave (from 6 January, Three Kings Day, to 30 June), on the southwest side of Lake Titicaca, then six months (from July to December) buying cattle in Santo Tomás in Chumbivilcas, Chuquibambilla, and Viraco, a cattle-raising town on the slopes of Coropuna volcano in north central Arequipa Department. A childhood illness kept him from ever having children, but he cared for a cousin there who wound up working in the mines in Madrigal. After a dispute over payment with his uncle, Federico returned to Sabandía in 1958, where with his savings he began his own career as a cattle buyer, sending his brother Rómulo to Lima, in part for health reasons, to receive cattle he would send for slaughtering there.

At the time of my first actual interview with him (May 1978)—a bit awkward, since we had already gotten to know each other—Federico, along with two brothers, owned 33.64 topos of land in Sabandía, in various parcels inherited as well as purchased in 1956, 1966, 1968, 1972–1973, and 1976; they also later purchased land in the newer La Joya irrigation project northwest of the valley. Alfalfa for grazing cattle is the primary crop grown on all their parcels (six cuts per year; he would occasionally buy alfalfa forage in Quequeña, where it was cheaper), though a few other crops—pumpkins (*zapallo*), maize, potatoes, or barley—were sometimes rotated in on the field near the main spring in Yumina. Watering times vary for each parcel, but are generally set an amount of water every thirteen days, managed by a hired *camayo*. Synthetic fertilizer (urea, two bags [at 480 soles] for each topo) and insecticide (about twice per year; the price skyrocketed in the mid-1970s) were purchased from FONGALSUR. He had a total of eighty head of registered Holstein cattle (of which twenty-four were cows producing about 290 liters of milk per day, though milk production varies greatly by season), for which he had taken out a loan of 480,000 soles from the Banco Agropecuario. The number of bulls for *peleas* varied from three to seven.

I had rented the old Cuadros house as a base for my exploration of valley smallholding. My landlady, married to a prominent professional in the city and living in a fine Victorian mansion in Yanahuara, insisted on prompt payment of the monthly rent; she would carefully count out change, then give me a receipt while I waited in the shadowy parlor. This directs our attention to a key element of regional culture, a certain severe, Catholic habitus of thriftiness, if not stinginess. Arequipeños, whether "elites" or regular members of regional society, were so dependent on trade that they were always anxious, directly or indirectly, about the threat of commercial ruin. Belaúnde is key here in noting that Arequipeños were "todos hidalgos . . . dineros menos" (all gentlemen . . . except for money), as mentioned above. Even Flora Tristán noted Arequipeños' impecunious ways.

A wonderfully generous, humane individual with a salty demeanor and vivacious laugh, Federico befriended me early on as I explored the Sabandía countryside. The family's small milking stall was near the house I had rented, and he invited me into the corral one day as I walked by on my way down a country lane toward the recently restored colonial wheat mill.

I ran by him and Juan some of the rather unsophisticated questions I was developing as part of my survey instrument of campiña smallholders. As we got to know each other over the ensuing months, I was learning a lot about the ins and outs of managing a scattered set of smallholdings in this part of the campiña—the frustrations and tradeoffs in managing a small herd of milk cows, a few fine *paso* horses, and fighting bulls—and about managing the longer-term serrano laborers who supervised the milk stall and herd or the day laborers doing various cultivation tasks on the fields, such as up on the parcel near the main spring in Yumina. I had been taken aback by the living conditions of the young Cuzqueño couple managing the milk stall, who Federico had once insisted play the *quena* (Andean flute) for me in a rather strained stereotypical performance, but I later learned that Federico had given them land and a few milk cows to get them on their feet.

I was struck by how casually Federico and Juan seemed to keep track of their money flow. Their shirt-pocket accounting led me to realize that campiña smallholders, unaccustomed to a regular cash flow like the one Leche Gloria provided, really didn't quite know how much income they had (see below in this chapter). Time was measured by which president was in office. It also made me wonder about the effectiveness of the state tax system.

I also learned about the important role campiña dwellers had played as muleteers. Federico's and Juan's father Manuel López (who had the same hearty laugh and twinkle to his eyes as his son Federico) had worked as a teenager for six years in the *salitre* fields of Tarapacá (1907–1913) before becoming a muleteer in the 1920s and 1930s, transporting agricultural and some manufactured goods not only toward the coast (to coastal estates in the Tambo valley and Moquegua) but also to the sierra and on to Tirapata and the *ceja de selva* (high mountain forests) in eastern Puno on long trips (twenty-five to thirty days round trip) for *goma* and *caucho* (wild rubber products) (the Japanese were very involved in this traffic). He invested in buying cattle in the highlands, which enabled the family to begin purchasing land in Sabandía. Manuel was later mayor (*gobernador*) of Sabandía, and his wife (Federico's mother) sold meat in the market (replacing her own grandmother). Manuel described the campiña in those years (1920s–1930s) as being dominated by a few richer families who had *obligados*—people obligated to work for them at whatever task on a yearly contract, paid in kind as well as with a small wage. While these were mostly Arequipeños from local areas, living in rustic huts (*chozas*), some were children from the sierra sent by their parents, practically as indentured servants, to learn Spanish while working for next to nothing.

I also learned about the close social as well as economic ties rural smallholders had with urban life. Federico once attended a meeting with three ministers (of agriculture, food, and economy and finance) and the head of Leche Gloria, who was close friends with the minister of *alimentación* (food). I would run into Federico in the central city occasionally—at the main post office or near the main San Camilo market. A younger brother lived in a new development on the edge of the city (his wife worked and the children went to school in the city). In their old, battered, but eminently serviceable Chevy pickup, they would get supplies at the FONGALSUR office, run tools or workers up to Yumina, or haul bulls to *peleas* around various parts of the valley. Urban-rural ties are strong in the valley, and local smallholders who attended the Colegio de la Independencia or UNSA were exposed to the folkloric currents I have outlined. Federico would walk with his friends to the tramway stop across the river toward Paucarpata (fig. 5.1), while his brother Juan, twelve years younger and from all angles a typical campiña youth, studied anthropology, including archaeology, at UNSA in the 1960s. We had many long conversations about rock art, about the Wari and Tiyawanaku influences on Arequipa, and about archaeological aspects of his travels to the Altiplano and elsewhere in the highlands buying cattle. He was always keenly interested in the latest findings.

Mayordomos had played a major role in campiña life, named by urban families to manage the valley properties. (There are actually four levels of people who care for others' *chacras* (fields): *administrador, mayordomo, encargado,* and *cuidante.*) With partible inheritance, these properties would be split up among heirs, leading to the *minifundista* land-tenure system so characteristic of the campiña. Little land was for sale, and with high demand, prices were generally high. While some urban aristocratic families had purchased small estates for summering (the Ricketts, for example, who had told me that as children they would ride by mule to spend several months in their rural retreats), with their departure from direct control, even if not ownership of campiña properties, local families like the López family bought in with money from a variety of activities. For example, when Juan Cuadros died in 1973, Federico, a shirttail relative of the Cuadros family, purchased various properties from the heirs, both right in the center of Sabandía and in Yumina. The Cuadros heirs had decided not to continue in farming or cattle but, rather, to pursue urban professions. Like the Cuadros, Manuel and (later) his sons Federico and his brothers had done well enough from the *arriero* trade and cattle trading to afford such prime parcels. Cuadros himself had earned his wealth from buying cattle in Puno to sell to Lima and then investing in several estates in Moquegua—not so much from managing his small campiña parcels.

High land prices in the campiña made raising beef cattle there uneconomical—hence the focus on traveling to buy cattle elsewhere, reserving campiña parcels for dairy cattle. When regular income from dairying started to flow with Leche Gloria's entrance into the regional economy in the 1940s, some local cattle owners stepped up their focus on raising and fighting prize bulls. Federico's uncle Hector López was the one who had brought the famed bull Menelik to Socabaya (where the bull's mother came from and where there is now a huge stature of him at the main entrance to the town) from Siguas as a young (three-year-old) bull. Before he became superfamous, Menelik passed through several hands in Sabandía, including those of Félix Santos. He didn't fight for several years, but then he was put in the *cancha* with El Tigre, who belonged to Don Luis Alberto Guillén in Lambramani. He then fought a bull belonging to Angel Rodríguez on the field of Carlos Sánchez up toward Yumina. Menelik was still young.

In 1962 Federico decided to start moving in these circles; with his experience in the cattle business, he had a well-developed eye for the weight and condition of a bull. He was asked by a Cuadros relative to be part of a three-person committee heading up the organization of the annual *peleas* on Easter. All funds raised from admission were to be devoted to rebuilding the village church; the colonial wood altar had burned in 1956, and the building itself had been destroyed in the 1958–1960 earthquakes. The tradition of holding fund-raising *peleas* on Easter began in Sabandía; I attended the Easter *pelea* in 1978, and it was indeed spectacular and well attended. Federico adroitly sold some land and bred bulls, acquiring notable fighting bulls to eventually become a well-known, indeed emblematic, "local farmer."

One day Juan asked me if I might bring them a metal detector on my forthcoming trip back from the States. This came up one afternoon as they were talking about the colonial Jesuit treasure that they were sure lay on the downslope edge of the campiña at the base of the arid stony hills still draped in white ash from the 1600 Huaynaputina eruption—precisely near what had once been the Jesuit estate of Huasacache (which had been owned by the Goyeneche). I asked how they were so sure, and why they would want to make such an investment. (My question was about the rationality of such an investment, not about whether they would reimburse me! Of course nowadays they could buy a detector on the Internet and have it shipped to their door.) Juan assured me that on some evenings you could make out a glow from the buried treasure—burning either gold or silver, depending. Jesuit treasure stories persist among campiña farmers, even though there is no record of such an accumulated treasure and despite the tendency of the Jesuits to invest and use their gains, not save them. Stories like these date from the expulsion of the Jesuits and the hope that because they were forced out, some of their enormous wealth must have been left behind.

On a return visit a few years after my main fieldwork period, I was again surprised when Federico mentioned his desire to have me pick up a western US–style (*tejano*) cowboy hat next time I was returning from the United States. (I was starting to get used to being a mule for various friends.) Accustomed to regarding the wide-brimmed straw hat as a nonnegotiable "traditional" part of dress, anchoring campiña identity, I was shocked; it just didn't make sense. Hats are ubiquitous in the Andes, not only to protect the head from the intense tropical sun (or rain or cold), but also to mark local identity. Since pretty much everyone wears hats, they serve as an important common denominator for symbolic communication—of community membership, social status, or geographic origin. Headwear is therefore often the most distinctive part of the traditional dress. Federico and Juan pointed out pictures in a Sears-type color catalog they had come by; they wanted one in beige and the other in gray. They also wanted to get one as a gift for Don Antonio Pinto—a village patriarch—to be given to him by his daughter Josefina.

Later, understanding better the field of honor in which campiña smallholders moved and their consequent motivation toward competitive display, linked to maintaining honor in regional social space, such incidents came into focus. Why wouldn't they want the distinctive accoutrements of the horse- and cattle-based lifestyle they recounted seeing on television westerns, or the possibility of riches unobtainable by other means without the latest metal-detection technology?

Honor and social position are paramount among Arequipeños *netos* ("real" Arequipeños). Bulls' names capture this concern with maintaining status. For example, Federico named one of his prize bulls Rommel, after the German general, and another Gardel, after Carlos Gardel, the famed, suave Argentine tango singer who died in a tragic 1930s accident at the peak of his career. Honor needs to be reproduced through performance, however, and hence the importance of periodic bullfighting, where a bull is really only as good as his last match. Such need for recurrent public recognition also played itself out in the nightly drinking at Julia's shop next to the market. I fell in and, inept as I initially was, barely extricated myself from the carefully orchestrated masculine bravado, where each one buys a bottle (though it seemed I often woke up realizing I had bought more than the others) and takes his turn in down-ing a shot of beer and passing the glass—always, however, after carefully paying the *challa* toast to the earth by throwing to the ground the lit-tle bit remaining in the cup. (A friend paid a *challa* toast to a field before planting broad beans (*habas*), but I don't know if this is a local custom; he had come from Puno as a teenager.) I was surprised that Federico and Juan did not participate in these nightly performances, until I realized how deft they were at not being near the market at the close of day to get pulled into such honor bouts.

Such an insider account reveals the positioned nature of the bearers of this bullfighting tradition, and shows that as with other aspects of the tradition, there is no single complete insider account of *peleas*. Federico's life story shows one route into the bullfighting circle: converting eco-nomic capital (literal *capital*, in this case, since these are heads of cattle) from cattle buying and dairying into cultural capital from raising fight-ing bulls for status competition in regional *peleas*. Owners of fighting bulls are now the very embodiment of the campiña smallholder—and therefore of general Arequipeño traits (cf. the description of the *majeño* dancers in Mendoza 2000), since they are masculine, proud, courageous, symbolically associated with animals or depicted riding horses, and en-gaged with local food. But there are also personal qualities at the core of this, for Federico's brothers—equally engaged in managing land, dairy cattle, and labor—are not such public owners of fighting bulls.

SIX

SOCIAL GENESIS, CULTURAL LOGIC, AND BUREAUCRATIC FIELD IN THE CHANGING AREQUIPEÑO SOCIAL SPACE

If politics is the ground upon which the category of the nation was first proposed, culture was the terrain where it was elaborated, and in this sense nationality is best conceived as a complex, uneven, and unpredictable process, forged from an interaction of cultural coalescence and specific political intervention, which cannot be reduced to static criteria of language, territory, ethnicity, or culture.

GEOFF ELEY AND RONALD GRIGOR SUNY,
BECOMING NATIONAL, 1996, 8

In this concluding chapter I move to a more theoretical plane for tools to understand both the content and the timing of the emergence and waning of Arequipa's remarkably intense regional identity. To review: this subnational identity, originating in an Altiplano-linked system of pilgrimage with strong pre-Hispanic and colonial roots, initially developed shortly after independence containing certain aspirations for political autonomy (the Peru-Bolivia Confederation). This exceptionalist discourse had settled into a regionalist mode by the mid-nineteenth century around surprisingly strong cross-class resistance to the emerging Lima-based postindependence Peruvian state. Then in the decades between the war with Chile and the 1970s, prevailing regional identity shifted from political to cultural terrain in a burst of cultural production using symbols associated with an "already-disappearing" traditional, plebeian, and rural way of life—an urban-based discourse cognizant of the cultural hybridity embodied in the practices of these everyday Arequipeños. In the regional social space of the Arequipa valley, experiments with a discourse of mixed race attempted to resolve on cultural terrain the continuing inability to achieve consensus about the identity of "Peru" on the national level. After the failure of the decentralist charge against the central state, which peaked in the early 1930s, questions of state and national identity remained unresolved, and by the mid-twentieth century the central symbols of regional identity had passed to economically emerging valley landowners and narrowed around their invented tradition of distinctive bull-on-bull fighting. The twists and turns in successive iterations of a nevertheless surprisingly coherent, deeply populist discourse around "the Independent Republic of Arequipa" complexly intersected a remarkably intransigent series of regimes controlling the central state, emerging modern understandings of citizenship, growing engagement with modern globalizing forces (particularly transportation and communication), and the penetration of the regional agricultural sector by multinational capital.

Broadly, the conventional framing of Arequipa's intensely regional identity (e.g., Flores Galindo, Plaza, and Oré 1978) is anchored in a rather uncritical representation of the perspectives of the commercial oligarchy, making for a seemingly straightforward account: a regional commercial aristocracy, beset by declining economic fortunes (especially with the decline of the wool trade), fanned local resentment at the slow pace of economic activity to make sense of its misfortune at the hands of the powerful and wealthy but misguided, even corrupt, Lima-based national elite that had come to control the postindependence state of Peru. Following this line of inquiry, we see the state tighten its grip on decentralist stirrings, either indirectly by oligarchic regimes or directly through a succession of military regimes. While challenging extralegal maneuvering and guano-era corruption, the regional commercial elite in Arequipa had nevertheless long since largely fallen in line and become part of the *civilista*-anchored national oligarchy in control of an emerging Peruvian state; alternative visions of the nation itself—as well as of the relations of areas and peoples outside the capital with the central state—were blocked, undeveloped, absent, and/or severely marginalized (cf. Itzigsohn and vom Hau 2006) until the brute class tensions of the mid-twentieth century could no longer be contained, forcing Velasco's military to seize control of the state and impose a corporatist solution to finally address fundamental social and political contradictions. In short, Arequipeño elites, sidelined or co-opted in this centralizing process, expressed their resentment in an invented tradition of regionalist exceptionalism. The purportedly elite core of this resentment can be chalked up in part (perhaps in large part) to the postcolonial lack of communal organization and political voice on the part of popular sectors, who were fragmented in the city and the *minifundio* land-tenure system of the val-

ley and falsely conscious of their real class situation. Against a sea of rising indigenous movement in the nearby highlands, Arequipa atavisti-
cally remained the "white city," so-called both for the *sillar* architecture
of its urban core and for its overwhelmingly Spanish, anti-indigenous,
deeply oligarchic cultural inheritance.

This line of analysis is not so much wrong as it is very incomplete and
one-sided, missing the most interesting parts of this largely untold story.
Such a class-focused, elite-centered reading of the regional social formation doesn't much help us account for the main elements of regional
identity, especially as it coalesced primarily in early twentieth-century
regionalist discourse: Why were *rural* symbols given so prominent a
place in the traditionalist story? Why was it *modernist middle-sector intellectuals*, not elites, who were most behind Arequipeño traditionalism?
Why was a discourse about mestizaje so central? Or, especially, why does
the traditionalist narrative have such strong *populist* roots? Perhaps most
important, this instrumentalist view misses the *cross-class nature of regional identity*, which has given Arequipa such a broadly shared, conservative (and rather misunderstood) image as a sort of crypto-racist society lacking in class consciousness (e.g., humorously, Acevedo 1981).

What we learn from a deeper analysis of the conditions giving rise to
this traditionalist discourse connected with regionalist exceptionalism
is that while its main builders were urban intellectuals, mostly from the
middle sectors, in the small social space of urban Arequipa many were in
touch with (or even came from the ranks of) everyday Arequipeños and
from Arequipa's more populist traditions, and they responded in their
art to continuing pressures from below for inclusion as full, honorable
members of regional society. By incorporating popular conceptions of
citizenship in regional society into their cultural production, these intellectuals built a relatively stable vision of regional identity in the shadow
of the state (N. Miller 1999), a vision that was not at odds with elite interests, had some local footing, and served as a trope for a more genuine
"Peruvian" citizenship (cf. Mallon 1995, 311)—even as it failed to gain political traction in the national field.

Such cross-class resonance and responsiveness to pressures from below, from Valdivia to Mostajo, marks the long and surprising staying
power of the story of "the Independent Republic of Arequipa." Anchored
in widespread folk Catholic pilgrimage and practice, urban plebeians
and valley smallholders already understood themselves as part and parcel of the imagined community of Arequipa, however blocked they were
by lingering class or status privileges. Having no distinct communal or-

ganization, leadership, or particular social movement per se, however, they were therefore relatively voiceless politically. Pressure from below is evidenced not only throughout the uprisings of the middle of the nineteenth century, but also in the continuing participation of everyday Arequipeños in cross-class civic uprisings through to 1950 and 1955, for example (Caravedo 1978), and to the broad 2002 protest against the Toledo regime's attempt to privatize the regional electric company. Nevertheless, social class and more narrowly party-based politics after the 1970s increasingly colored the frequent popular strikes and demonstrations by teachers, truck drivers, government employees, farmers, and others, from general strikes during the late 1970s that I witnessed to the 2010 protests against the Tia Maria mine in the Tambo valley.

I. THE SOCIAL GENESIS OF REGIONALISM: SHUTTLING BETWEEN POLITICAL AND CULTURAL TERRAIN

Such key concepts as social space, field, forms of capital, symbolic power, and imagined community—primarily from the corpus of Bourdieuian practice theory—serve as tools to help us understand prevailing ideas about the social construction and reproduction of national and regional identity and how these illuminate the cultural politics of regionalism in Peru.

A. The Social Construction and Reproduction of National and Regional Identity

Drawing on primarily European models of nation-state formation, our modern era is said to be characterized by a widespread longing of peoples everywhere to become "national" (Anderson [1983] 1991, 3). While our felt need to be part of groups certainly draws on our species' deeper sociality and harkens back to an older meaning of "nation" (Latin *natio*, "birth, origin"; "breed, stock, kind, species"; "race of people, tribe"), as Hobsbawm explored (1992, 2), Benedict Anderson zeroed in on the role of (print) media in fostering this modern sense of belonging to a community larger than the one made up through immediate face-to-face interaction, the community that preindustrial peoples everywhere experienced as their primary reality. Examining the emergence of a shared idea of European identity, Anderson generalized to posit that, though anchored in some local sort of shared culture, via evolving media technologies people in the modern age came to share language and symbols, in the process imagining themselves as part of something larger and mobilizing and self-identifying on that basis in a more abstract, "national" way.

Careful reading of the political and cultural history of any modern nation-state reveals that the ties of national sentiment to the state form of polity are at best provisionally stable, no matter how successful the modern state's efforts may be to monopolize the use of symbolic power as well as actual coercion. While the post–World War II world seemed to have settled down to a conventional set of about two hundred distinct, seemingly stable "nationalities," renewed nationalism of recent decades has upended this seemingly steady nation-state order and taken many politicians, scholars, and others by surprise (Delanty and Kumar 2006). From eastern Ukraine and Crimea or Chechnya, to the Basque provinces, Bretagne, and Rio Grande do Sul, to apparently faux or failed states currently under devolutionary pressure, such as Iraq and Libya— what are the stories of the many "national" aspirations (some of them now resurgent) that failed to materialize politically as "proper" nation-states? How were such subnational sentiments reproduced during periods of central-state control of national culture? These pre- or nonstate identities clearly can command substantial loyalty; witness the passion some people still have around the ideas of "Yugoslavia," "Israel," or even "the Soviet Union" (Brubaker 1996).

We now understand that national identity, however solid in appearance—even in "strong" states—is a more recent and always contested construction that has involved the suppression of some regional (and class, gender, age, and other) identities in favor of others, typically by using the state machinery to impose a particular vision—the legitimacy of that imposition being predicated on the strength of the state's claim to represent the interests, even if perhaps not the culture, of the broader population. Whether symbolic or physical, violent suppression of regional and other recalcitrant minorities seems, then, to be a central feature of all modern nation-states (Rey [1969] 1976), as in the making of modern France, Spain, or the United Kingdom. As Gellner (1983, 1) crisply noted, "Nationalism is a theory of political legitimacy, which requires that ethnic boundaries should not cut across political ones."

"Since nationalism is a modern phenomenon which has unfolded in the full light of recorded history, the 'ethnogenesis' of nations lends itself more easily to investigation than the history of non-modern peoples" (Eriksen 1993, 101). But most human societies did not achieve national status (in the modern political sense), even if they may have aspired to it. Why, then, do subnational identities—larger than local but smaller than national—continue to thrive, many of them having failed in their aspiration to become national or to coalesce as polities?

Bourdieu's linked concepts of field, social space, and symbolic power help us get at some central questions: in the midst of this unsettled situation, who primarily carried and fought for these subnational longings, and why? Identifying these social carriers helps reveal how it is that some identities come to be regarded as legitimate and incorporated into the lore of an imagined national community, whereas others are suppressed or marginalized through symbolic and even physical violence (Bourdieu 1994), or simply never coalesce in narratives or metaphors with sufficient plausibility to attract loyalty (Fernandez 2000). When and how are subnationalist movements, such as Arequipa's, sometimes "cultural" but at other times "political," and how is this related to the size and nature of the field in which they pretend to operate?

Or, to cut to the chase: *how* are subnational identities in larger states generated and reproduced, deprived as they are of the mechanisms— school curricula, military conscription, control of the means of violence, the ability to issue currency, taxation, control of interstate migration, and the like—that states have to build or enforce loyalty and identification in their subjects? In Arequipa, this points to the crucial role and social location of cultural entrepreneurs, tied to regional educational institutions, in the relative vacuum of the central state's symbolic power.

In Peru, intransigent oligarchic control of the state during the 1880–1960 period continued to block even moderate reforms (Itzigsohn and vom Hau 2006)—for example, state investment in development outside the capital—rendering the state's control of the national field more obviously coercive and thereby illegitimate.

> Contestations over national belonging are, on one hand, struggles for access to citizenship, and on the other, they are struggles for recognition in the symbolic imagery of the nation. The latter also entails a voice in the debate over the cultural order and the cultural politics of the state. . . . We argue that nationalism is a consciously articulated ideology put forward by the state or by social movements in order to legitimate authority, mobilize political support, and achieve social control. At the same time, nationalism is a cultural script with almost self-evident plausibility that provides a lens through which

common people frame their social relations and construct solidarity in their daily habits and routines. (Itzigsohn and vom Hau 2006, 196)

The state's continuing inability to project a plausible idea of "Peru" as a widely shared, collective identity—one that lagged behind other parts of Latin America in the early decades of the twentieth century (N. Miller 1999)—combined with state coercion to create a space within which a subnational identity flourished in Arequipa. The Arequipa case is particularly interesting in this regard, since we see "regionalist" sentiment strengthening during periods of increasing (typically militarized) central-state power (e.g., 1915–1950 or 1968–1980), then waning otherwise—reflecting at least in part the central state's ongoing inability to legitimately produce, control, and effectively wield the main symbols of national identity.

Since politics always has an instrumental as well as a symbolic aspect, symbols have the power of creating loyalty and a feeling of belongingness (Cohen [1974] 1996, 371). By examining the social genesis and cultural logic of the symbolic forms that both inform regionalist sentiment and camouflage the state's apparently mandatory violence toward nondominant movements, anthropologists therefore have a lot to offer.[1] Social context and cultural logic both matter: symbols of subnational identity can be reproduced through a variety of local practices (e.g., bullfighting) and remain "cultural" (see Fernandez 2000, 129), yet at other times they can be mobilized for specific political ends (emulating "heroic" local heroes of yesteryear) and, dragged onto the state bureaucratic field, become "political."

What Arequipa's cultural entrepreneurs of the main 1890–1970 apogee of regional identity did, as we will see below, was to reconfigure the cultural script largely developed by key predecessors in the middle of the nineteenth century to address mounting problems developing from elite intransigence toward the resolution of two major problems: the lack of a collective sense of belonging (see Belaúnde's "Queremos Patria" speech; [1915] 1963) and the inattention of the state, with all the resources at its command, to the legitimate material and social needs of citizens outside the capital. But these regionalist entrepreneurs did so sotto voce, on "cultural," not "political" ground (hence Mariátegui's disgust with "regionalism," which he thought blocked an authentic class- or ethnic-based social movement of national integration; [1928] 1971).

Though the traditional story of Arequipeños' descent from Spanish founders and the racialized nature of its cultural boundaries might suggest it, regional identity here is only very weakly "ethnic"—it is not really characterized by a metaphor of shared common descent, a myth of common origin, or an ideology encouraging endogamy. Unlike "tribal" or "ethnic" identities—long anthropologists' main focus—the "regional" idea is complexly intertwined both with the sediment of earlier state formations and with the actual state as current controller of some territorial unit. These matters circle around the question of how identity both informs and is shaped by political processes in an emerging bureaucratic field (Bourdieu 1994).

Arequipa is an especially appropriate case in which to examine these issues. While the process of nation building in postindependence Spanish America is a major theme in Latin American historiography, the development of subnational communities has been a far less comprehensively examined phenomenon, despite its pervasiveness. Hinging largely on methodological differences, historians and anthropologists have tended to approach the study of such subnational communities rather differently.

Historians have typically focused on the more overtly political aspects of subnationalism—as more or less direct efforts to maintain autonomy by challenging the centralizing processes in emerging state systems (leaders of anticenter revolts usually leave documents). This has been the primary focus, for example, of (mostly Arequipeño) historians examining the remarkably active political history of Arequipa—the success or failure of those more overtly political uprisings.

Anthropologists, on the other hand, have typically (over)emphasized the primordial quality of subnational identities—seeing them, for example, as deeply rooted legacies of precolonial identities, embedded in deeper cultural logics (Appadurai 2013), and paying less attention to the political and economic contexts and processes affecting these identities. As I noted in the preface, the overarching concern to define *lo andino* as a specifically Andean set of beliefs and practices dominated anthropological work in the Andes during the latter twentieth century—mirroring inside the academy the peripheral wisdom promoted by regionalists such as those we are examining here (Fernandez 2000).

Understanding the place and importance of locals' agency got buried as a result. As we have seen, Arequipeños' strong regional pride has manifested itself in various ways, at times in overtly political uprisings from the late-colonial period to date, at other times sublimated into various cultural forms seemingly distant from the central processes of unequal power and wealth that animate them. Conventional approaches in both history and anthropology have thus been inattentive to how people—whether cultural entrepreneurs in the earlier twentieth century or owners of fighting bulls in the later twentieth century—navigate these legacies. Taking a longer view of this subnational identity, we see Arequipeños shuttling back and forth between political and cultural terrain: in one place or time they may formulate their aspirations into "culture," and then, at later points in time or in other places, actors variously situated in social space may draw on these banked symbols as cultural capital and actually *use* these cultural materials in their ongoing efforts—"political," finally—to make sense of their place in the evolving, enlarging fields of which they are a part.

In short, not enough attention has been paid in anthropology to the ongoing *construction and reproduction* of subnational identities—the practices that sustain and reproduce them within the general processes of modern nation building. The preoccupation of modern theories of development with the nation-state as the primary unit of analysis, and with the European nation-state as the model (N. Miller 1999, 12), has certainly hampered such inquiry.

There is thus much to learn from the Arequipa case about the cultural and historical bases of subnationalist sentiment—in many ways the residue of past sociopolitical formations—now precipitated out in "culture." Since studies of regionalism generally adopt a within-state focus, the Arequipa case is additionally salient since the focus of its regional identity has been tied to state boundary making and jurisdictional matters that existed from the very first years of Spanish conquest but that especially emerged in the late-colonial period and intersected the longest-running boundary disputes in South American history—reminding us generally that boundary tending is important and that regions can also entail supranational (Warleigh-Lack 2006) boundary disputes with unresolved irredentist claims (consider, e.g., Bolivia's continuing claim to the Atacama littoral).

So it is not much help to claim that these subnational identities are more primordial, "driven underground" during periods of state building only to reappear later when central-state control relaxes or reconfigures. The basic question is still how these identities are reproduced during their long periods of dormancy or subordination and then used in relation to the state's national cultural projects. In the long history of southwestern Peru, what caused regionalist sentiment to flare up in certain social spaces (e.g., urban but not rural Arequipa) and historical periods but not in others? As an anthropologist interested in the relevance of this political and geographic history for understanding regional culture, my focus is on the wider contexts of peoples' subjectivity that is only at times explicitly mobilized as "political."

An important way these cultural materials have been politically mobilized is in periodic debates about regional reorganization of the state, a recurring topic in the political culture of Peru, from the earliest days after independence (e.g., from 1823 to 1834), during the Confederation experiment, and again in the 1870s (Basadre 1962, 2051), as well as more recently, since the end of military rule in 1980. These debates involve more or less explicit, perennial claims about the state's inability to inclusively represent the reality of a diverse country (Gutierrez Paucar 1990). The overriding idea has been to consolidate the departments of Peru into some more administratively workable system of formal regions (e.g., Montoya 1980; Tamayo Herrera 1988)—an attempt to bring regions more clearly and systematically into the state bureaucratic field.

Regionalist sentiment in Arequipa reached a peak in the early twentieth century, in reaction to Civilista Party and Leguíista centralism. It reignited in response to the corporatist model of the Velasco and Morales regimes in the 1970s, with all its centralized reform policies, evocation of Túpac Amaru, and reformulation of mestizo identity (Fisher 1979).[2] And it grew again in the 1980s when Arequipeño leaders resisted García's (1985–1990) *aprista*-linked regionalization scheme.

In recent times, political regionalism was most energetically advanced in Peru by the APRA Party after the strongly corporatist, centralizing military regime (1968–1980) in the 1980s under Alan García, which developed a scheme to divide the country into twelve autonomous regions (fig. 6.1). Decentralization (and mestizaje) have been major themes of this party since its origins (Víctor Haya de la Torre, 1931, cited in Lozada Stanbury 1988, 11).

Arequipeños' perduring sense of region remains evident even across these episodes and schemes. Of the proposed administrative divisions (regions) of Peru under a revised scheme proposed by the Fujimori administration in 1992, again, as in the earlier APRA scheme (fig. 6.1), only Arequipa, Lima, Loreto, and Ucayali departments initially maintained their former departmental boundaries as regions. La Libertad (Trujillo) was involved in boundary disputes with neighboring San Martín and Cajamarca departments. Tellingly, then, aside from the two large, sparsely populated eastside forest departments, only Lima and Arequipa

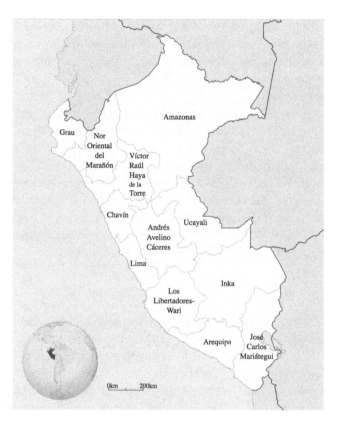

FIGURE 6.1

*APRA 1980s regionalization scheme. From "Regions of Peru (1989)," **Wikipedia**,
http://en.wikipedia.org/wiki/Former_regions_of_Peru. Accessed 8 September 2012.*

maintained their departmental outlines through these recent regionalization schemes (see Hudson 1993, 224).

Regionalization returned yet again in the early 2000s after the Fujimori regime, when the Toledo regime attempted to restart national debate about a more efficient reorganization into regional administrations.
A 2005 referendum on the matter was rejected by voters in every department except Arequipa, where the idea of an Arequipa region was supported. The fact that reorganized "regions" have now, thirty-five years
after the Velasco regime, broken down to be the same as former "departments" (albeit with changes in funding procedures) testifies to the
enduring power of long-established political boundaries around which

culture—living subjectivities—has coalesced. Arequipeño regional-ist sentiment has remained surprisingly intense and constant across all these episodes, confirming how well anchored and how unusually broadly shared in regional social space Arequipa's regionalism is.

As I bring this long project to a close, there is again another pendu-lum swing toward interest in regionalism, though this time in reaction to the seeming failure of the decentralization effort launched in 2002 by the Toledo regime. Peru's increasingly mining-dependent political economy again upset the provisional balance of power between strong center and weak peripheral regions. The situation with the regional government in Ancash in early 2014 demonstrates the perils of insufficiently remuner-ated and insufficiently trained local and regional political leaders, who are too often susceptible to the temptation of huge sums of money flow-ing from globally linked mining into local governments.

B. State and Region, Culture, and Politics

Whether worked out at the national or the regional level, then, debates about identity are always already both cultural and political, though participants and observers usually separate these moments in time and space. Variations in outcomes depend on the relative strength of the state in both material and symbolic terms, in the latter aspect centering on struggles for control over the production of "tradition" in relation to the legitimate exercise of symbolic power.

We learned from Hobsbawm and Ranger (1983) that making some-thing "traditional" usually results from decipherable processes both more recent in time and more instrumental in purpose than most peo-ple imagine. To make a discourse "traditional" is to wall it off from criticism, to naturalize it, so that it sinks into people's tacit, taken-for-granted knowledge about themselves and others, knowledge that lies just beyond the reach of living memory or critical reflection.

How people come to adopt particular identities—their sense of be-longing to a collective subjectivity—sheds light not only on the cultural dimensions of political and economic forces shaping development tra-jectories, but also and at a deeper level on general cultural processes af-fecting self-identity (Eley and Suny 1996, 8). The Arequipa case illustrates that literature and popular culture are among the key terrains on which the cultural memory of regionalist as well as "national" discourse is both reproduced and contested.

Following Pierre Bourdieu, it is critical to my analysis to connect the "subjectivist" moment of describing the symbolic, meaningful content of this regional identity with the "objectivist" moment of delineating the historically and spatially specific webs of interaction and fields of power within which this identity was constructed and made meaningful (Bourdieu 1989; Roseberry 1995, 160). Bringing both these moments into the same analytical frame helps us understand how the past constrains what is possible for agents in reproducing and reinventing identity, since each successive generation draws on the pool of symbols available to them, and with these symbols as a reservoir of possibilities, people imagine, revise, and so construct anew what it means, in this case, to be Arequipeño. But this takes place in a social space, where the forces of history— categorized into "political," "economic," "social," etc.—affect peoples' ability to imagine alternatives, and in fields increasingly dominated by the centralizing state (Bourdieu 1994).

At the center of the rather long, thick description in previous chapters has been my effort to locate the production of Arequipeño regional culture in social (including economic and political) as well as environmental space. Since at least the Middle Horizon this social space has been characterized by regular interaction with people of adjacent environmental zones, especially the Altiplano, as well as with agents of distant power centers. (Arequipa historically has never been the power center of any space it claimed to control, other than perhaps briefly during the Peru-Bolivia Confederation and again briefly but inconsequentially during the War with Chile.)

People's interaction in social space pivots in fundamental yet complex ways with "environmental space"—itself a way of talking about the particularities of the biological and physical processes characteristic of a place, with which people must deal and which both provide them with certain opportunities and place certain constraints on their social practices and their meaning making. The primary environmental opportunity afforded by these neotropical highlands, especially the central Andes, is the amazing proximity of different yet adjacent, altitudinally arrayed environmental zones that allow locals access to a great variety of relatively nearby resources. (Altitudinal zonation is of course so prominent in the tropical Andes that an entire model of *lo andino* was constructed by anthropologists and historians some decades ago, as discussed.) Environmental constraints are also obvious; for example, Arequipa is located in one of the most tectonically active regions on earth, and the fact that it sits at the northern edge of the world's driest desert makes access to water for irrigation critical for survival as agriculturists and makes crossing intervening, unpopulated deserts so central to the Arequipeño imagination.

Intersections among structures in these two broad categories of spaces—social and environmental—provide basic starting points for making sense of the bounded matrix within which people's actions and understandings result in the evolution of a regional culture. The surprising geographic isolation of Arequipa, for example—its often-remarked "oasis-like" setting at the base of three huge volcanoes—came to be seen by locals across classes both as the source of their unity and collective destiny as a people (e.g., Bustamante y Rivero's eloquent speech quoted in chapter 4) and as a constraint and boundary: to really succeed in life one had to emigrate from this *diminuta vega*.

Yet how that isolation was experienced varied widely among social classes. Elites in the colonial period moved in intercontinental orbits, throughout Latin America and Europe—within the larger field of the Spanish colonial empire—and were fundamentally tied to political and economic processes dominated by the colonial state. It was therefore not much of a shift for such late-colonial figures as Tristán, Goyeneche, and even Pedro Diez Canseco to engage the emerging center of power in Lima in the reconfigured bureaucratic field after independence, nor for Arequipeños from elite families (e.g., Piérola, López de Romaña) to play such central roles in the aristocratic state after the war with Chile (1884–1930). At the bottom end of the social order, Indians' movements were tightly circumscribed through a confining system of racial categories and poverty that tied them to land. "Mestizo" became a way in which socially as well as geographically middle sectors could make sense of their position in relation to both these polar positions in the wider fields within which everyday Peruvians were being swept up.

Though "these people are social personae whose very identities and practical orientations are influenced by [such] spaces in which they have been socialized" (Lomnitz-Adler 1992, 18), the production and reproduction of these social spaces in turn result from peoples' practices. The continuous making and remaking of social space through practice is fundamentally understood and done culturally, through the making and remaking of meaning, especially utilizing symbols that stand for the imagined community of which people think they are a part. So our attention must turn to the nature of the processes involved in the ongoing production of the dominant symbols and metaphors that people use to make sense of who they are.

In analyzing Arequipeño *regional culture*, then, it will be helpful to disentangle "region" and "culture" in relation to the nature of the social space within which people interact, guided by the tenets of practice theory. We are necessarily looking at the ways structures of these different social (political) and environmental spaces are themselves hierarchically organized and intersect in a particular place. So armed, we can begin to make some headway in understanding different yet deeply intertwined aspects of this dialectical relationship between people's practices and the social spaces in which they occur.

Since regions are by definition situated not just in geographic space but also in social (political) space, to understand what "regions" mean to actors requires understanding how variously positioned local actors are affected by and in turn reproduce the state (cf. Fernandez 2000, 130)— what Bourdieu (1994) calls a "bureaucratic field." It is crucial to realize that groups in such regional fields want to name themselves, to mark their own distinction as legitimate actors. But the regional field is by definition affected by the larger national field within which it occurs, so we must understand local practices in relation to these larger, evolving political and economic processes.

Lurking in the background here is the question of how it is that the boundaries of a nation-state come to take on a facticity and political reality that mere regions within state machinery lack. We are dealing with varying degrees of autonomy in distinguishing regions, countries, nations, and states, but can any general statements be made about the processes that lead to the "hardening" of some boundaries into "countries"—the jurisdictional tightening of cultural frontiers into political boundaries (cf. Sahlins 1989; Kroneberg and Wimmer 2012)?

The state-region tension is of central practical as well as theoretical importance here. Regimes in control of the state as a bureaucratic field have crucial powers unavailable to other social actors: the ability to impose categories, such as political boundaries or citizenship, within which people think as well as act. As noted above, not only through laws and policies, and not only through control of deadly force, but also through educational training, military conscription, issuing of passports and other credentials, etc.—those who control the state apparatus are in a stronger position to project their vision of division onto others, not least by defining who can be citizens in a process that reconstitutes the self and homogenizes local identities within a larger abstract nation. In short, agents in control of the state have more power, both physical and symbolic.

As an abstraction, the state disembeds local knowledge from particular contexts (Giddens 1990), which is how and where people actually experience life. Fighting back against these dissociative tendencies, then, is part of the regionalist discourse—hence the crucial importance of telluric symbols, which are by definition tied to a place. In all iterations of the Arequipeño traditionalist discourse, symbols associated with locality— plebeian picanterías, the Misti volcano, and rural places and lives—play a key role because they are (or are represented as) symbolically *immobile*, in the sense of being tied to people making their livelihood, indeed having been born, in a *place* (literally "indigenous").

And yet it is the crossing of those boundaries created by emphasizing telluric symbols that is at the heart of Arequipeños' regional identity— an identity that is therefore both local *and* national (and therefore relevant to the "national" problem, as Zevallos Vera 1965 had noted [above in chapter 1]):

> But any either/or formulation misses that ambivalence which is a marked characteristic, if not a source of energy, of peripheral societies and their peripheral wisdom: the desire at once to escape the identity constrictions of boundedness and, at the same time, to celebrate and privilege the separate identity that it confers. (Fernandez 2000, 132)

We will return to the importance of constructing and crossing these boundaries below.

Since the very concepts—the very language that we deploy to think about region—are already so inflected by the state form, it is useful, then, to pause for a moment to interrogate commonly used terms that so closely associate (sub)national identity with place. "Country," for example, comes to English ("district, native land,") through French from the Latin "(*terra*) *contrata* '(land) lying opposite,' or '(land) spread before one,' from L. *contra* 'opposite, against'" (http://www.etymonline .com/index.php?allowed_in_frame=0&search=country&searchmode =none, accessed 2 September 2012). This suggests that "country" took on a sense of lying not only opposite a city (Williams 1973) but also opposite a polity—in a more political sense, similar to the sense that *pays* (an ecclesiastical and taxation unit) has in France (which was directly transported into Spanish as *país* and then *pago*) and to the sense of the origin of "pagan"—places and the people who occupy them as lying outside the bounds of proper, civilized society.

In the same measure as the state centralized in Lima and national life came to be represented by both abstract and Lima-based symbols, the intensity of sentiment and focus on these immobile, anchored-in-place, non-Lima symbols grew. Analogously, it seems each generation conceives of the past not only as more settled and ordered, but also as always already passing away (Williams 1973). Images of rural, country life are particularly drawn upon to highlight problems with a more urban, unsettled present, leading to an "emotionally plausible," hegemonic structure of feeling (Williams 1977). Traditional rural Arequipa is always already disappearing for the urban writers we have been examining. Even by the 1880s *fiestas campestres* (country parties) around Christmas, New Year's, and Reyes Magos (Three Kings Day, or Epiphany) in Los Perales in the District of Tiabaya were described by Polar ([1891] 1958, 62) and Belaúnde (1987, 56–59) as vanishing. The stability and uniqueness of the campiña countryside anchored regional culture.

The consistent evoking of images associated with the countryside makes the regional emic concept of campiña crucial. The Spanish term *campiña*, like its Italian and French cognates, comes from Latin *campus*—open, flat country (especially near Rome)—and from this we get our English word "campaign," referring explicitly to the sense of open country suited to military maneuvers (German *kampf* also derives from the same source). In Arequipa, however, "campiña" evokes a bucolic, worked landscape resulting from a harmonious blend of human labor and natural fertility.

Both "campiña" and "country(side)" contain the idea of a place viewed from the city. What about the word "region"? *Región*, like "regal," again comes from Latin *regionem*, "direction, boundary, district, country," in turn derived from *regere*, "to direct, rule" (see Williams 1985, 264). From this Latin origin, and the analogous ideas of *suyu* of the Inka and previous central Andean states (Bouysse-Cassagne 1986, 201), it appears that early in state formation the concept of region was tied to state arrogance or myopia once thought characteristic primarily of modern states (Scott 1998), pointing to the antiquity of the state-region relationship explored in chapter 2.

The very term "region," then, has baked into it from the start a certain jurisdictional tension with states "above" and local identities "below"—part of the hidden discursive power of the state as bureaucratic field (Bourdieu 1994). Regionalist discourse is therefore an ongoing commentary on and site of potential resistance to or difference from both the state and its projects, and potentially as well from the city. But these forms are contingent, since without agents to act on this discourse there is nothing in the concept itself to suggest what factors lead some regionalisms into active antistate or anti-imperialist stances, or even armed struggles, particularly in a postcolonial and now digital world of resurgent subnationalism (as in the ex-USSR, Syria, Iraq, or ISIS), whereas in others, like Arequipa, regionalism early lost its nationalist impulse and settled into a struggle over the proper course of nation building (Marchand, Boas, and Shaw 1999).

As to the "culture" of regional identity, we are trying to get at how imagined communities get mapped onto political and geographic space, and in the process to find out why some symbols from the entire repertoire of available symbols become dominant in discourse about regional identity. Though long dismissed as overly simplistic, Marx's famous dictum in *The Communist Manifesto* that "the ruling ideas are the ideas of the ruling class" nevertheless continues to hold considerable sway, since it directs attention to who controls the means of idea production and then, of course, to how that is related to who holds control of the means of production. Since this practice is fundamentally political (Appadurai 1986), I take the task of this cultural analysis to at heart be a Gramscian effort to understand *whose* imaginaries become dominant among the entire set of understandings that such a large and diverse regional population has about itself.

Sandwiched between the state and the local, then, largely lacking the institutional means by which to propagate and reproduce regional identity—given all that, what institutions, processes, and people keep regionalist subjectivity going? To claim that they are merely frustrated national projects, vestiges of past political struggles, is to miss the agentive dimension, social origins, and institutional location of *cultural entrepreneurs* and the ongoing performance of regional identity by various actors.

II. THEORIZING THREE KEY EPISODES
IN REGIONAL CULTURAL HISTORY

Resisting the temptation to move toward some metanarrative about the long evolution of regional identity in Arequipa, and having developed key concepts to serve as useful tools to help us understand the origin, successive iterations, and staying power that successive cultural entrepreneurs have tapped to reproduce and reconfigure this regional identity, I conclude by analyzing three key episodes in the long evolution of regional identity:

236

- Early-colonial Marian apparitions and the 1640s response of Indians in Characato to usurpation of their land

- A main second section examining the 1890–1970 apogee of modern regional identity during which an urban-based discourse of mestizaje was attempted

- A closing third section on the post–World War II rise of wildly popular, rural-centered bull-on-bull fighting now at the core of regional identity.

A. Marian Apparitions; Characato and Chapi in the 1600s

What is important for present purposes is to acknowledge that in the Arequipa region deeply syncretic processes were at work that early laid the foundation among rural and plebeian Arequipeños for a shared regional identity on which postindependence work by urban plebeians and sympathetic urban intellectuals rested. By as early as the mid-seventeenth century a regional system of Marian worship was coming to define the greater Arequipeño imagined community for everyday Arequipeños—a space developed with and against the Spanish crown's bureaucratic field, and a social space traversed by merchants and muleteers that was much bigger and more deeply anchored in indigenous culture than is commonly imagined now, let alone by the urban intellectuals of the early twentieth century.

The dispossession of Indian lands and labor had already begun in the very first decades after conquest, as Spaniards established *encomiendas* and increasingly took over lands around the urban core, however much opposed by the crown on paper, marginalizing Indians near the city into peripheral barrios and *rancherías* (unlike what happened around Cuzco) (Quiroz Paz Soldán 1991, 21).[3] The crown's creation in 1565 of the corregimiento system was a direct challenge to local Spaniards' political power, in Arequipa and throughout the viceroyalty. *Vecinos* (landed Spanish citizens) of Arequipa pushed back against crown dilution of their control of this vast region, and by 1580 they were petitioning Viceroy Toledo to reassign to Arequipa (Cercado) all the Corregimiento de Characato y Vítor—the main seat of indigenous political authority in the region—and even the parish of Pocsi, of the Corregimiento de Colesuyo. But with the crown's defense of Indian interests, Arequipeño leaders were successful only in acquiring lands of La Chimba and Paucarpata (Málaga Medina 1975). By 1637—sixty years later—however, the entire

Corregimiento de Characato y Vítor was finally reincorporated into the Corregimiento de Arequipa (Espinoza de la Borda 2003, 190), indicating the extent of Spanish usurpation of valley agricultural lands.

These changes in the objective social order were both provoked and accompanied by changes in subjectivity, with Indians increasingly over the colonial centuries passing into "mestizo" status within colonial caste categories, especially as they moved to the city.[4] We see little trace of indigenous political actors in the valley after independence, which is when the tradition of "the Independent Republic of Arequipa" begins to be developed. Yet, given the legal status within the Spanish imperial structure that *kuraka* leaders of *repúblicas de indias* enjoyed and exercised, it can't have been much before the end of the colonial period that the system of caciques and *cabildos de naturales* (indigenous community councils) broke down.

Given the importance of the folk practice of Candelaria worship and given the way regional identity has been anchored in pilgrimage to several Marian shrines in the valley (chapter 2), it is revealing to more carefully analyze the nature and timing of Marian apparitions and the development of pilgrimage.

Practice theory helps us connect the seemingly separate movements of early-colonial land dispossession and Marian apparitions. As we learned, there had been a long struggle underway between local, decentralized participation in pilgrimage and the increasingly concerted efforts of central ecclesiastical authorities over who would control the great symbolic power of the Virgin—tenderly called "La Virgencita" by locals.[5] Fostered by Catholic priests of several orders intent on Christian conversion and proper religious instruction, indigenous devotion to La Candelaria spread in the early- to midcolonial period throughout the region of Altiplano cultural influence—roughly the boundary of the Tiyawanaku state/confederation—centering on Copacabana. This old cultural geography in a new guise represents an exquisite example of syncretism in the Andes—an intensely popular, "bottom up" effort to maintain social position in the abruptly emerging power fields of the Spanish colony as well as the construction of a hybrid culture to make it all work meaningfully.

Despite broad cultural similarities among most examples of Candelaria worship in this vast central Andean space, the timing, location, and cultural content of these several local Marian apparitions cloud this straightforward correspondence, revealing insights into the important and early dynamics of pressures from below on forming regional identity. We learned, for example, that Mary's apparition to muleteers in Cayma associated her with a cemetery and somewhat later with earthquake, that her apparition to the monk in Characato associated her with light and her apparition later to locals there resulted in her association with water, and that her apparition to muleteers in Chapi associated her with a volcanic eruption and then somewhat later with water. What might we learn about the complex relationships among political, economic, and cultural processes in early-colonial Arequipa from the timing and cultural content of these apparitions?

It seems clear that the earliest Marian apparition in the valley—to highland Indians accompanying Spaniards in Cayma in the mid-1540s—represents an initial connection by Collaguas there of Spanish developments in Arequipa with Altiplano cosmology—the burden of interpretive labor (Graeber 2015, 67) being thrust on the conquered. "Arequipa"—the coastwise region "behind the mountains" (behind the southwest Peruvian volcanic chain)—was associated with the setting sun and death. So associating Mary with the cemetery seems pretty clearly to be an early attempt by Indians to synthesize indigenous with Spanish cosmologies and, in the process, to gain some relative legitimacy in the rapidly emerging postconquest society.[6]

After what is apparently a long pause of about a century, the seventeenth century is marked by several new Marian apparitions in the valley. I of course make no assertion about their veracity—about what people actually experienced, perceived, or thought; that is not my focus and in any case appears to be irretrievable. Rather, I interpret these as attempts by local indigenous inhabitants to fuse their local understandings about water, earthquakes, and volcanoes with key Spanish symbols, especially Marian ones, and thereby assert their legitimate status in regional society against increasing threats from urban Spanish. The interests of local clergy and *corregidores* intersected these bottom-up indigenous interests in complex ways that bear closer scrutiny.

For example, in the "1640s" a monk in Characato "discovered" the five-decades-lost "sister" to the image at Copacabana. Established in 1541, Characato was the head of the Corregimiento of all Indians in the valley and the Quilca/Chili watershed to the coast. Note the close timing ("1640s") of Mary's apparition in Characato with the crown's final relenting (1637) to Arequipeños' ongoing pressure to reabsorb Characato y Vítor into the Corregimiento of Arequipa. Chipping away at the boundaries of corregimiento jurisdiction was tantamount to regaining control of Indian labor and, by extension, Indian land.

It is not hard to connect mounting threats to indigenous lands, labor, and authority with the way this apparition suddenly elevated Characato as a key Catholic site, leveraging crucial Spanish symbols to reinforce the status privileges of indigenous there. That the image was discovered by a monk (perhaps indigenous himself) also suggests a close association between Indians and at least some members of the religious orders—a way that Indians could gain social position by using such spiritual and institutional symbols to fight for position within the system of colonial racial categories, as well as a way for the *corregidor* of Characato to resist Arequipeño threats to his authority and power.

That the Characato image of La Candelaria had been (or was asserted to have been) carved by the same Titu Yupanqui who carved the image at Copacabana points to ongoing Altiplano understandings and social ties (recall that Indians of Chucuito had been resettled in Characato, as had other valley Indians after the 1582 earthquake and the 1600 volcanic eruption). That Characato became a major element in regional culture speaks to the successful meshing of these popular belief systems and practices in the context of Spanish institutions. As capital of the corregimiento and located near major pre-Inka and Inka cult sites on the slopes of Pichu Pichu, Characato would have been precisely the campiña village that best represented indigenous interests in the region. With this recognition and ensuing pilgrimage to Characato, we should not be surprised that a more proper church was built between 1650 and 1670. Mary's association with the miraculous spring fifty years later (1686 or "1690s") points to locals' insistence on their legitimate practice and belief as well as the "domestication" of her into local understandings of water ritual (see Poole 1982).

The somewhat derisive epithet "Characato," still thrown by outsiders at Arequipeños but worn proudly by them, stems from their centuries-long devotion to this early Candelaria pilgrimage site. The moniker (largely spoken by Limeños) may also be tied to the efforts of Juan Manuel Vargas, a priest of the Parroquia of Characato in the 1840s (when regionalist sentiment was really beginning to stir against Limeño intrigues) who promoted its special status in Arequipa for having a Candelaria Virgin (see Belaúnde 1987, 137). Vargas (Belaúnde's great uncle, interestingly) drew upon already-long-established traditions surrounding the Virgin of Characato, whose sanctuary had become a focus of devotion for pilgrims attracted by the many miracles with which she was credited (Málaga Núñez-Zeballos 2011).[7]

Devotion to La Candelaria—now the very symbol of the region ("La

Mamita de Arequipa")—has its origin in these early-colonial disputes pitting the Spanish city against the "Indian" countryside. The bifurcation between city and countryside is strongly inflected by social class, represented symbolically by locals' ongoing pilgrimage to villages out in the valley, where La Candelaria is worshiped, rather than to the succession of "official" patron saints representing the city. This political and social gulf became symbolized by locals in the *ccala/loncco* contrast (discussed in chapter 5).

Mary's apparition to muleteers in Chapi similarly entailed a contest between local understandings and colonial political and economic processes. Early-colonial jurisdictional tensions around Colesuyo continued for decades as corregidores of Chucuito, Arequipa, Ubinas y Moquegua, and Arica fought over control of this ethnically complex region (Espinoza de la Borda 2003, 184–188), itself the legacy of pre-Inka political boundaries that had shifted to ethnic identities linking west-slope villagers with the Altiplano, as we learned in chapter 2. Again, the blurry boundaries of Inka Kuntisuyu probably reflect that empire's very recent arrival and therefore incomplete attempt to reorganize these cultural frontiers into the new state's geographic projection.

The Corregimiento de Colesuyo was finally severed from Chucuito in 1627 (Espinoza de la Borda 2003, 188). As with Characato in 1637, local indigenous leaders, probably in connection with political (*corregidores'*) and ecclesiastical interests, moved their resistance to the state from political to cultural ground, linking memory of the recent, spectacular eruption of Huaynaputina with Marian apparition, giving origin to Chapi worship. Put too crudely (and requiring further research), we might understand this as locals' syncretic understanding that the volcano's eruption in 1600 was divine wrath for the dismembering of their subjective "ethnic" unity with the Altiplano.

Cultural ties of popular sectors with each other continued, however, encysted in a galaxy of Marian worship that extended throughout the old Tiyawanaku sphere of influence. These subjective ties were held by Indians, though by the late-colonial period, after whatever Altiplano ties that still reverberated in the midcolonial period had been severed, these understandings had apparently been transformed from an Altiplano sensibility to a narrower Arequipeño sensibility—fueling locals' increasing focus on their rightful citizenship in the imagined community of Arequipa, and on a par with the loss of "Indianness" by campiña dwellers.[8]

Pilgrimage to Mary's desert shrine at Chapi supplemented and then gradually stood in for pilgrimage to Characato, though locals see all the

Candelarias as sisters. As noted above, well into the twentieth century Characato was the primary destination for pilgrims among the three, apparently until the back-to-back earthquakes of 1958–1960 destroyed the temple there. Since then, and along with improved transportation, Chapi has become central to the Arequipeño pilgrimage system.

B. Arequipa, 1890–1970: Moving Regionalist Sentiment from Political to Cultural Terrain

Throughout the long first century of the country's postindependence life, Arequipeños had repeatedly called into question the legal and moral basis of Limeño power, threatening it with both pen and sword. While the intellectual life of Arequipa developed impressively through the nineteenth century, centering on regional pride against Lima, it achieved a remarkable coherence and focus in the 1890–1970 period. With both state and national identity slow to develop in such a huge, geographically and socially diverse country as Peru, the bureaucratic field was relatively weak, and there was room for the work of cultural entrepreneurs—especially in the crisis period immediately after the war with Chile. Arequipeño mestizo traditionalism—the key early twentieth-century "middle" phase or apogee of regional sentiment in my analysis—involved the working out of "modern" political subjectivities (remembering that key entrepreneurs, Mostajo especially, were strongly positivist and anticlerical) intertwined both with wider globalization pressures and with deeper colonial racial categories and pre-Hispanic layers of identity, in dialogue with popular sectors in regional social space. By the 1920s this sentiment rapidly intensified, though within a strongly centralizing state that co-opted some intellectuals (N. Miller 1999, 65–66) and instituted real reforms in rural life with a "pro-Indian" policy that received support from key intellectuals (e.g., José Angel Escalante in Cuzco) or that was leveraged by indigenous leaders in the southern highlands (N. Miller 1999, 153). Key Arequipeño writers, artists, and musicians—cultural entrepreneurs working within the regionalist genre—reconfigured meanings established decades earlier in the caudillo period to continue insisting on an alternative vision of national identity, one more open to popular pressures for inclusion and culturally hybrid under a discourse of mestizaje. This played out largely on the regional rather than the national field, however.

Since Arequipa had early failed to become the center of a state broadly conforming to its understanding of itself as a major political player

(Gootenberg 1991a) (or, rather, to the conceptions of some members of the political and cultural elite, such as Pío Tristán) in the broader central Andean space, the Arequipa case takes us straight to two related conceptual matters at the heart of these questions about nationalism, regionalism, and modern citizenship: the ontological status of entities named by historians, politicians, and poets as historical subjects (e.g., the history of "Peru" [Thurner 2008] or "una teoría sobre Arequipa" [a theory about Arequipa] [Quiroz Paz Soldán 1991, 240]) and the related question of the relationship between political boundaries and cultural frontiers—between the territorial state and the imagined communities within which people live and move and have their being (Lomnitz-Adler 1992).

The first question—of "Peru" as a national entity—is of course the "national question." By the turn of the twentieth century, postindependence Peru was thought by many to be a still largely unamalgamated country with no unity and no apparent direction in history. The humiliating experience of the war with Chile led to national soul-searching about identity, history, and politics. It is no accident that two of Peru's most perceptive analysts of these matters—Mariátegui and Basadre—emerged during this period, and both were from the far south, Moquegua and Tacna, respectively. The south was a volatile region in which "Peru" (or "Bolivia") was more dream or imagination than reality. Intellectuals like Basadre and Mariátegui, along with Belaúnde, Bustamante y Rivero, and other Arequipeños, imagined and described an "invisible patria"—something more than the European-inspired state-building ideals of early independence leaders, an imagined community anchored in the social experience and understandings of its people (a history not just *of* but also *for* Peru [Thurner 2008]). Regional intellectuals in Arequipa—Polar especially—began examining folklore and popular culture in the 1890s (Ballón Lozada 1999, 8–9) as a way of anchoring these identity aspirations and claims.

The second, related matter—relations between state and nation—is really the question of political legitimacy. The continuing unwillingness and inability of Lima-centered regimes to acknowledge, let alone incorporate, demands from different sectors and regions of the country (Mallon 1995) left gaping spaces for the persistence of alternative cultural identities—"racial" or "indigenous" in parts of the highlands and eastern lowlands, "class" in labor stirrings in Lima and along the north coast, "regional" in Arequipa and other parts of the territory—even as these alternative visions were repressed when they threatened Limeño power and state interests. The increasing salience of race and class in Peru contrasts with the situation in neighboring Ecuador or Bolivia, where politics centered on highland capitals has taken a more polarized, explicitly ethnic cast (Burga and Flores Galindo 2001). Again, it is no accident that Basadre and Mariátegui were active in the 1910–1950 period, when these matters of identity, politics, class, and ethnicity were coming to a head.

A key question here is why it was primarily urban middle-class intellectuals who tasked themselves with working out these frictions between state and nation. The real puzzle about Arequipa's intense, widely held modern regional identity is why the regionally hegemonic commercial oligarchy, overwhelmingly urban and of Spanish descent, did not come to dominate its cultural content. Revisiting the puzzle that launched this monograph: why was so much prominence accorded to the purported characteristics of the urban plebeians and rural smallholders, yet so little to the qualities of the commercial elite itself—the objectively dominant class in regional social space? While it is true that Arequipa's commercial elite was not able to finally consolidate its economic and political control of southern Peru until the latter part of the nineteenth century with the railroad and wool trade (Flores Galindo 1977, 16; Orlove 1977), commercial interests have nevertheless been central to Arequipa's economic life for a very long time—whether Spanish under the Habsburgs, creole under the Bourbons in the nineteenth century, or Basque, English, and other foreign interests in the nineteenth and twentieth centuries.

The short answer is that demands from below for inclusion in regional society were strong and largely consonant with middle-sector and elite interests in commerce (with elites' interests being unmarked and doxic)—all united around a cross-class discourse that elevated regional over class, ethnic, or gender identities. Under the influence of key cultural entrepreneurs, largely through print media, Arequipeños by the early twentieth century had come to understand themselves as occupying a cultural space framed by the two major poles of national identity—Spanish (coastal) and Indian (highland). This cultural frame corresponded with the preexisting unity of the broad mass of regional society, generated through historical processes examined above and reproduced in pilgrimage. Urban middle-class, politically liberal cultural entrepreneurs mapped their understandings both of the national question and of these issues of political legitimacy onto regional social space, elevating rural smallholders as representative everyday Peruvians ready for the tasks of citizenship.

Most of the regional commercial elite had long since given up fighting Limeño centralism, instead joining elites in Lima and the north coast in the national project even as they attempted to steer economic policy toward the interests of the southern commercial oligarchy in the emerging national context. Their regional hegemony was based both on commerce and on wealth that still came primarily from productive estates in coastal valleys or (later) the puna, not from direct control of property in the valley or city (Flores Galindo 1977), where there was little class-organized struggle over local productive property itself.

Save for Belaúnde, Bustamante y Rivero, Gibson, Polar, and a few others, all the voices in the explosion of regionalist cultural production from 1890 to 1970—those most pushing a cross-class, often mestizo discourse—were from the middle sectors, including painters Núñez and Vinatea and writers Mercado, Rodríguez, and (especially) Mostajo. With the growth of a recording industry and communication media in the 1930–1960 period, musicians—Ballon Farfán, Los Dávalos, the Trio Yanahuara, and others—increasingly added their voice to this regionalist yearning. These cultural entrepreneurs mostly grew out of the broad mix of popular culture in the city, so closely tethered to the countryside, and collectively they gave voice to and in turn projected into the national field these broadly popular concerns with gaining and keeping recognition as honorable members of regional society.

On the face of it, the regionalist tradition constructed in the wake of the war with Chile in opposition to growing Limeño authoritarianism seems to have flowed seamlessly out of earlier postindependence national struggles and into the current regional cultural formulation featuring bullfighting and *paso* horses. But we "must be careful to neither overemphasize nor underemphasize historical continuity with such cultural projects" (Tambiah 1996), since it is clear that cultural entrepreneurs had interests (sometimes political) that led them to draw selectively on local cultural materials of varying historical depth.

So though the Valdivia, Mostajo, and current iterations of regionalist identity deal with similar cultural material, anchored in the lifeways of rural smallholders and urban plebeians and their aspirations to be understood as full members of the imagined community of Arequipa, I will now attempt to show that despite these similarities, these were in fact three somewhat different projects involving struggles for distinction in somewhat different emerging fields. For analytical convenience I will rather crudely simplify and distinguish these as the "Valdivia" (1840–1880), "Mostajo" (1890–1950), and "bullfighting" (1950–present) versions of regional identity.

The first ("Valdivia," examined in chapter 3) was an urban intellectual project engaging long-running debates about political centralism in a context of postindependence state formation, cresting in the revolts of the 1850s. The second ("Mostajo"), though again an urban-intellectual project, was more centrally about middle sectors' anxiety about the growing problems—labor unrest on the coast and resurgent Indian unrest in the highlands—threatening nation building in the post–War of the Pacific context of soul-searching about *peruanidad* and the Indian question (this section and chapter 4). The third, "bullfighting" (next section and chapter 5)—a more decisively rural project—played even more in a regional rather than a national field and was more about locals' understandings of their place as honorable citizens in a now-industrializing regional society. Even though all three are constructed from similar cultural materials and broadly incorporate demands from below, only in the latest iteration are locals themselves more agentive about these representations.

Other than within the brief Confederation episode, Arequipeño leaders made no moves to consolidate any political "Arequipa" larger than the colonial intendancy, itself a jurisdiction deeply rooted in earlier highland understandings of spatial relationships among coast, west slope valleys, and Altiplano. Despite postindependence aspirations, the die had therefore been cast for a modern "Arequipa" without larger political ties to the Altiplano. Commercial elites were primarily concerned that whatever nation-state coalesced in this space—whether some bigger central Andean state, a confederation, or a reorganized "Peru"—would be capable of assuring legal footing for owning property and for fostering tax, fiscal, and other policies favoring free trade.

With the collapse of the Peru-Bolivia Confederation and the ensuing slow consolidation of the Lima-based state, regional elites turned to engaging the emerging national field for the most favorable policies for regional commercial development. Their "withdrawal" from regional social space, combined with the relatively light impact of the war with Chile, created an opening for urban intellectuals, overwhelmingly from middle- or working-class backgrounds, to project to a widely literate urban public a much more populist version of regional identity. Arequipa's pronounced "mestizo" regional identity, constructed by these urban cultural entrepreneurs primarily during the 1890–1970 period, was built around the image of the plebeian smallholder in the valley as a sort of prototypical Peruvian everyman.

Late nineteenth-century commercial expansion had been facilitated by the railroad, largely centered on the wool trade. Encouraged by the renewed opening of vigorous trade with the Altiplano, regional elites pursued new opportunities in brokering import and export between coast and interior. Prominent families sold agricultural land but kept campiña properties as rural retreats, especially in Yanahuara and Cayma but also in Sabandía and Tingo, favorite summering spots.

This economic quickening both strengthened regional elites and also facilitated their integration into the national project, closing the door on "revolutionary Arequipa" and any direct elite participation in regionalist sentiment. That now fell to middle sectors. As Basadre notes:

> It was exhaustion, the advent of new, more practical generations, the general ambience of the country, the railroad to Mollendo that put Arequipa in contact with the external world and accentuated centralism, that extracted Arequipa from its revolutionary life. That spirit wasn't totally lost, however, and even though the Chilean occupation had been carried out without resistance, it was a foreordained disgrace; and in her fighting attitude in 95 and in popular agitators like Urquieta, Málaga, Mostajo, [and] Meneses the men of steel of another time lived on intermittently. (Basadre 1962, 610)

By 1910, however, economic, political, and social conditions, both national and regional, had deteriorated, and Arequipeños, particularly the urban middle sectors in Arequipa city, felt pinched and anxious. By the 1910s the anemic regional economy was reminding many upwardly mobile Arequipeños of a long-standing local truth: to succeed professionally or economically, one had to emigrate. While these were hardly new impulses in Arequipa, they now took place in a more strongly centralized state field. Lima was of course the destination of choice, but Arequipeños had a long tradition of scattering all over Latin America and even Europe. This had been the social space for the offspring of elite Arequipeño families from the late-colonial period, but it now increasingly became the case even for members of the middle sectors seeking professional careers. This outward drain led Percy Gibson (1916) to anxiously write, "Arequipa, what's the matter? What ails you? Why do your children march bleakly to foreign lands looking for sustenance but feel nostalgia for your meadows [campiña]?"

The post–World War I wool crisis brought a sudden downturn to what had only a few decades prior been relatively auspicious economic developments. That crisis, coupled with the authoritarian rule of Augusto Leguía, followed by the financial, commercial, and employment catastrophe of the Great Depression, led to a pervasive sense of disaster. Anxiety developed not just among the commercial elites but also among everyday rural and urban Arequipeños whose trades—from a variety of agricultural foodstuffs to construction and retail commerce—were tied to commercial prosperity.

These developments put the newly emerging middle sectors in a particularly precarious position. Lying between the class extremes of the regional landed and commercial oligarchy strongly tied to the fortunes of the wool trade and national economic processes, on the one hand, and the rural-cultivators-cum-urban-artisanal-workers (the *ccala-loncco* binary discussed above and below), on the other, this middle sector was made up of "master artisans, small merchants, doctors, professors, pharmacists, lawyers, small business services: hotels and the like, horse stables, carriage shops, labor recruitment for the south [nitrate fields], nearby valleys and even Madre de Dios; picanterías; functionaries and office employees; university students; etc." (Carpio Muñoz 1990, 548).

In turn, the distance of the central state and regional elites from these matters of seemingly local and regional concern, particularly from 1915 to 1930, created a relatively large social space still weakly dominated by the bureaucratic field (a "weak" state) within which local intellectuals could move and experiment—witness the variety of positions and aesthetic forms tried out in Arequipa in those years. Perhaps the key difference between Arequipa and other Peruvian regions is the periodic episodes when local intellectuals tried to move these matters from cultural terrain back onto political terrain—however blocked or repressed. Though the events of the mid-1850s or of 1930–1931 (Deustua and Rénique 1984), for example, were hardly radical political movements as on the north coast, they were political manifestations of deeply cross-class sentiments about state and nation.

While wool merchants were facing a serious downturn after World War I, then, it was the middle sectors who during these first several decades of the century experienced ongoing struggle with the rapidly rising cost of living between 1915 and 1920 and relatively flat incomes—a precarious material position threatened by instability on a variety of fronts (Belaúnde [1915] 1963). Middle sectors came to be tied closely to employment in export-dominated commerce and state bureaucracies (especially the military after midcentury). Their economic fate was therefore particularly subject to the ebb and flow of national and international business cycles.

1. LABOR UNREST ON THE COAST

Though the Peruvian labor movement had its beginnings in the 1850s among Callao dockworkers, it was largely disconnected from growing organization among urban artisans. By the 1870s there were artisans' unions in Lima, Cuzco, and Arequipa (Basadre 1962, 2045). Artisans organized quickly after the war with Chile to defend and advance their interests, with support from various intellectuals such as Ricardo Palma and Manuel González Prada (Basadre 1962, 2857). But cross-class ties between intellectuals, mostly middle class, and artisans and members of the working class were few (Basadre 1962, 2959). Workshop-schools were established in Arequipa, Cuzco, and Puno in the 1880s.

Identification with the valley's long-standing *minifundismo* and general stasis in the basic pattern of productive arrangements in the region thwarted the development of class consciousness, however, leading to a marked reluctance for, and even opposition to, broader class-based movements that began to emerge elsewhere in Peru in the 1920s and 1930s. With some notable exceptions—such as Francisco Javier Gómez de la Torre Pereyra, arguably Peru's first advocate of working-class solidarity (Ballón Lozada 1992, 170–171) and who had served as UNSA rector in the 1930s—politically left class-based movements, like early *aprismo* or Mariátegui's Peruvian Communist Party, did not gain much of a foothold in Arequipa.

Strikes at textile mills in Lima in the 1910s and 1920s, combined with the rapid politicization in the 1920s of university students and factory workers by class-based parties such as APRA, then the PCP, contributed to a growing anxiety about unwanted social upheaval rather than change through civil discourse. The fragility of Arequipeños' sense of social order is revealed in Mostajo's turn from his earlier active politics by the 1920s, as well in Peralta's observation (chapter 5) that "[in the picanterías] there weren't labor agitators then putting ideas of social revenge in [people's] heads" (Peralta Vásquez 1977, 35).

Peralta's comment draws our attention to local intellectuals' fear of unwarranted social unrest if class-based labor movements got out of hand. Labor tensions thus framed part of Arequipeño anxiety in these years. There were active anarchist elements in Arequipa by the turn of the century, but little socialist movement developed until the 1920s (Ballón Lozada 1992). There was a 1902 railroad and port workers' strike (in Arequipa I presume; Ricketts Rey de Castro 1990, 197), perhaps in sympathy with the multinational working-class culture developing in northern Chile (Skuban 2007, 169), where some Arequipeños had gone to work. (Chilean *salitre* workers had gone on strike in 1907, effectively birthing the Chilean labor movement [Melillo 2012, 1048–1049].)

Relatively unindustrialized, and with the indigenous population in favor of an expanding wool trade (on their own terms), there was little working-class sentiment in Arequipa or in the adjacent highlands. It was urban petty artisans, like Mostajo's father, who had been the more radical element in the political decentralism linked to Urquieta and Luis Guinassi Morán (Ballón Lozada 1992; cf. Colque 1976). Like rural smallholders, urban artisans were directly exposed to the market, but unlike smallholders they had no subsistence base on which to fall back in hard times or down-market cycles. Moreover, being largely self-employed, they had no immediate enemies to fight; they had to direct their anger more against the whole system (see Collins 1994, 106).

The earlier democratic rhetoric of Urquieta and decentralists resounded with a surprising number of Arequipeño business and political leaders of the time, even if their protosocialist ideas not so much. Along with the continuing entrenchment of narrow-minded interests in control of the state and the church, foreign economic domination (e.g., the Peruvian Corporation) was holding back Peru's progress (Guinassi Morán 2008, 101–103). These middle- and even upper-class sectors were strong backers, finally, of Sánchez Cerro's 1930 coup against Leguía; in July 1931, the Liga Autonomista was formed in Arequipa, with Gibson and Rodríguez part of the executive committee, along with members of the commercial elite such as Manuel J. Bustamante de la Fuente and other strong regionalists such as Francisco Mostajo. Bustamante y Rivero wrote Sánchez Cerro's proclamation launching the coup. But national turmoil and state repression of class-based movements rapidly overwhelmed regionalist sympathies, reflected both in the tense 1931 election of Sánchez Cerro as president over Haya de la Torre and in a subsequent three decades of military rule through periodic coups and violent repression of labor unrest.

2. "RACIAL" UNREST IN THE HIGHLANDS AND ALTIPLANO

The "Indian question" became a more salient element in ongoing liberal-conservative debates about the national question after the war with Chile. These debates did not just involve passive postwar reflection on what had transpired in resisting the Chilean invaders. As we saw above in discussing Mariátegui (and as we will discuss again below), these debates were also influenced by periodic indigenous uprisings in the first decades of the twentieth century, particularly in the southern highlands.

The abrupt decline of regional commercial prosperity after World War I (Burga and Reátegui 1981; Painter 1991, 88–89) affected herding communities and intensified these questions in the 1920s, when dozens of indigenous uprisings raised alarm bells in conservative Arequipa. Wool merchants' immediate frustrations meshed with more general anxiety about the seemingly irresolvable "Indian problem." With deep roots in colonial racial categories, widespread if typically latent fear (reflected in periodic reports in the local papers) existed among most urban Peruvians as well as among estate owners of incipient race war (*sublevación general*), particularly emanating from Puno.

The Arequipeño merchant elite brokered precapitalist systems of production with an international market, but they were surprisingly weak relative to the neocolonial social order of the Altiplano (Jacobsen 1993, 10). Even limited attempts to respond to market demand with expansion of hacienda control over grazing lands met with both passive and active highlander resistance (by both *colonos* and *comuneros*), ranging from defense of traditional grazing rights on haciendas (Burga and Flores Galindo 1981, 115) to peasant/indigenous uprisings, such as the famous Rumi Maqui movement in 1915 and the more general uprising of 1920–1923. The collapse of the wool trade had affected everyone involved, from indigenous producers and hacienda workers to collectors (*rescatistas*) and intermediaries all along the supply chain to Arequipa factories and commercial houses.

While the collapse of the wool market directly informed their economic situation, indigenous producers perceived little threat from foreign imperialism per se and hence had little sympathy for APRA or PCP organizing in highland areas affected by the wool trade (Jacobsen 1993). Indeed, some peasant communities in the 1920s had effectively limited hacienda expansion onto communal lands by adroitly working direct connections with President Leguía (Alvarez-Calderón 2013).

Mariátegui considered the 1915 Rumi Maqui uprising in Puno to be akin to the Bolshevik revolution in Russia—a class-based uprising in the least expected part of the country (Flores Galindo 2010, 164), harbinger of larger incipient class revolution. He argued that while the uprising was new, as revolution, it was also old, as indigenous tradition—not an atavistic rejection of the neocolonial order but an indication of the possibility of an Andean socialism built on what remained of indigenous communitarianism. Whether Rumi Maqui was just one person or, as Flores Galindo suggested, a collective pseudonym, the uprising fueled debate over the Indian question.

Given the central importance of Huancané in the 1923 uprisings in Puno, Mostajo's observations bear comparison with Mariátegui's views on this same event. For Mariátegui, narrowly political decentralization, with resulting provincial autonomy, would only strengthen the hand of the *gamonales*. For Mostajo, who had intensely explored the language, culture, and history of the Arequipa region as a space where racial and national frictions might be worked out, the "Indian problem" was not this at all. Mostajo distanced himself both from Lima-based "literary *indigenismo*" and Mariátegui's socialism, arguing that neither understood the Indian in his real situation.

> What's happening in Lima [*indigenista* writing] is literary. It is necessary to get right down to the Indian. To know his intimate needs. To live with the Indian so as to perceive his emotions, his aspirations or concerns (*negaciones*), to intuit his thoughts, in short, to live near the Indian to comprehend completely and fully grasp the profound reforms that are needed in the political order, to reclaim him from his incapacity. Generally speaking I'm not of the belief that in the Indian a new consciousness has emerged, like some claim, who know things from afar and second-hand. I've lived a long time in Huancané, at the center of the indigenous mass, and my opinions are the fruit of my direct observations. ("Una visita a don Francisco Mostajo" 1927, 20)

3. ESSENTIALIZING A PROTOTYPICAL PERUVIAN EVERYMAN IN THE AREQUIPA SOCIAL SPACE

"A nation exists from the moment a handful of influential people decide that it should be so, and it starts, in most cases, as an urban elite phenomenon" (Eriksen 1993, 105). Subjectively, for reasons just advanced, drawing on long-standing patterns Arequipeños came to conceive of themselves as a kind of citizen fundamentally different from those of the very different worlds of Lima and Puno. Cultural entrepreneurs constructed a tradition in which they thought of themselves as inherently hybrid or ambiguous, and their experiments with a discourse of "mestizo" traditionalism became a central thread in regional identity—one inclusive enough in its ambiguity for people from various social situations (several class positions) to identify and imbue with multiple meanings without having to directly address fundamental social divisions. Locals who aspired to membership as honorable citizens of regional society could also understand this as still inclusive of their own mixed folk culture (and biology) while distinguishing them from Indians—again, useful for its ambiguity.

Arequipeños, then, came to define the boundaries of their imagined community against two "others," symbolized by Lima and Puno. While they were anxious about rising labor unrest on the coast and the authoritarian control of the state by Lima- and north coast–based elites, the second other against which Arequipeños imagined their community was the Altiplano of southern highland Peru, the *"Mancha India"* lying so uncomfortably close, yet upon which turn-of-the-century Arequipeños, like their colonial and preconquest forebears, had come so clearly to depend—especially with the wool trade.

With their "peripheral wisdom" (Fernandez 2000), local cultural entrepreneurs thus came to see the Arequipeño social space as a distinct place where race and class tensions had been harmoniously worked out over long centuries. Like the locals who inhabited the picantería, rural smallholders in the campiña were key symbols of this "reality." In so remaking the valley's heterogeneous peasantry and drawing a picture of matronly picanteras, there is also a sense that these urban entrepreneurs were trying to remind the emerging proletarians in the city about "proper" behavior (cf. Comaroff and Comaroff 1992).

The twin forces of labor unrest on the coast and indigenous uprisings in the highlands, then, framed the social space within which middle-sector intellectuals experimented with a discourse of mestizaje. Arequipa's cultural entrepreneurs tried in various ways and diverse media to make sense of the ongoing heterogeneity of postwar Peruvian society, and in so doing they imagined their mestizo community as lying between the two racially and now spatially polarized poles of Peruvian identity.

The exploration of Arequipeño identity as pivoting fundamentally on the realities of racial mixing emerged in the late nineteenth and early twentieth centuries with writers such as Nieves y Bustamante, Polar, and Mostajo, with artists, and with musicians, and it reached its apogee toward the mid-twentieth century with writers as well placed as Bustamante y Rivero, Bustamante de la Fuente, and Peralta. At around this period many writers of greater and lesser stature and of various political persuasions joined in examining Arequipeño traits as the country worried about its identity and future. Despite Arequipeños' occupational diversity and whether individual people traced their origin to elite or humble families, Arequipa at the turn of the century was said by these writers to be characterized by a broad, peculiarly egalitarian mass of small-scale entrepreneurs and valley property holders, as even Belaúnde ([1960] 1967) had noted. So there was a real sense, objectively, of a social space already in place upon which urban middle sectors could plausibly draw to make sense of their and the nation's position.

The advanced development of print media facilitated the standardization of this knowledge and these representations and played a huge role in spreading these quite inclusive ideas about Arequipeño identity. As in Europe, mass literacy was crucial in fostering regional identity in Arequipa. As discussed above, focusing on literacy draws our attention to the central importance of two key educational institutions—the (secondary) Colegio de la Independencia and the Universidad Nacional de San Agustín, with their colonial Spanish and Catholic antecedents. Both not only developed literacy broadly among the urban population of Arequipa across classes but also served as the main institutions where this sense of regional community was inculcated and reproduced in successive generations of Arequipeños.

In the Arequipa case, it is not a coincidence that Jorge Polar—arguably the key person who launched the development of this Arequipeño tradition—himself shuttled between "political" and "cultural" terrain over a long career. He traced his ancestry directly to key political actors in the mid-nineteenth century, trained at both the key educational institutions that incubated regionalist sentiment, then served as rector of one of them (UNSA) for twenty years (1896–1908 and 1916–1924), interrupted by a first period of service as deputy of Cailloma province affiliated with the decentralist/independent party, as well as two years (1904–1906) as minister of justice, instruction, education, and welfare in the Pardo regime.

Once established as "real" and "authentic," Arequipa's mestizo "essence" was then read back onto its history by middle-sector intellectuals as a way of coping with the rapidly changing realities of the period. In tune with growing European and North American progressivist, positivist, evolutionist discourse, Arequipeño writers' chief concern was to show that their regionalism was authentic, that it rested on an objective social reality—a traditional, place-bound, mestizo peasantry—and that it could therefore serve as a model for true national identity. Belaúnde, principally, had argued that what had been worked out in Arequipa over so many generations—the regional reality of an essential mestizaje—was in fact a template for an achievable overall national identity. Anchoring this in Arequipa was a direct challenge on geographic, historical, and political grounds to Mariátegui's insistence on the inherent racial opposition between coast and mountains (see N. Miller 1999, 159, 161).

Arequipa's cultural entrepreneurs tried in various ways and in different media to make sense of the ongoing heterogeneity of postwar Peruvian society, and in so doing they imagined their mestizo community as lying between the two racially and now spatially polarized poles of Peruvian identity. So, in this context, mestizaje worked to establish both difference and sameness, which in Arequipa's case seemed "natural" because of its intermediate position between coast and highlands.

While the correspondence between dominant/subordinate as culture/nature (see Ortner [1974] 2004) is of course simplistic, such structuralist models can provide useful insights (Graeber 2015, 76–80). Arequipeños experienced a double opposition: more natural than Lima (grounded, of the earth), but more cultured than serranos (civilized, of the city). Imagining Arequipa to be on the "nature" end of the dichotomy in relation to Lima, Arequipeños found themselves in a constant struggle against Lima to promote their more "authentic" social categories, definitions, and identities. Therefore, cultural markers were more overt; like all minorities, Arequipeños were more actively and explicitly involved in constructing a self—especially focusing on linguistic particularities—than was the linguistically unmarked (and therefore hegemonic) majority. A key concern of cultural entrepreneurs in this "Mostajo" phase was defining the category and establishing its symbols. This is how Mariano Melgar's themes of noble suffering resonated with and were folded into this new iteration of Arequipeños' more generalized sense of frustration and subordination in relation to national elites ruling from Lima. The subordinate depends on the dominant other in order to establish or affirm its unity or sameness—a sublimation of the symbolic violence the state projects onto peripheral peoples and regions.

Yet Arequipeño unity against Lima was entangled with its relations with highland indigenous people—a second other against whom Arequipeños identified. Now, as the dominating agent in this relationship, Arequipeños didn't so much have to name themselves as to mark the other (the reciprocal of their relationship with Lima). Hence the symbolic violence toward Indians inherent in this ambiguous mestizo discourse. This discourse was fundamentally about distinguishing Arequipeños in a national field dominated by Lima, but at the same time it cast Arequipeños in the conservative, "white"-city, non- (or even anti-) indigenous mode for which they are mostly known, predicated on distinguishing themselves from those highland indigenous peoples. Here, then, is the cultural logic animating images such as the one by Vinatea (fig. 4.3) or the ones by Núñez Ureta in figs. 4.5a and 4.5b, where one always sees the prominence of *both* the city (*ciudad blanca*, colonial mansions, churches of *sillar*, etc.) *and* the countryside (Misti, volcanoes generally, bucolic countryside, peasant farmers, local cuisine, etc.).

Because of the need to mark regional distinctiveness from Lima, these urban cultural entrepreneurs ruralized and browned this anti-Lima imagery during this "Mostajo" phase of regional identity by anchoring it in the most telluric, place-bound symbols available in the region. In essence, then, every Arequipeño is like "mestizo" plebeians who heroically fought against the center and is now like rural smallholders who toil honestly for their daily bread. In this urban middle-sector response to the "national problem," regional mestizo discourse was not authentically indigenous. This is the cultural basis for Arequipeños' elevation of their mestizo "essence"—a mestizaje that was a browning of Spanish identity, far from some authentic hybridity. A "mestizo" discourse functioned well in this in-between situation, since though it involved a "browning" of regional identity it was really code for "white enough"—at once serving to distinguish Arequipeños from both Lima *and* the Altiplano (and from all the meanings thereby implied).

Given the cultural ambiguity of this mestizo discourse, resting fundamentally on politically conservative foundations, it comes as little surprise, for example, to learn that Germán Leguía y Martínez—cousin of President Leguía who went on to become his authoritarian minister of interior—was led to argue that Arequipa's mestizaje, drawn from many racial tendencies, had been present virtually since the conquest:

> Different from other colonizers who, to establish their power, coldly, calculatedly, without scruple, annihilated the autochthonous element, the Spanish invader, after the fierce fight in which he certainly showed wicked, blind fury, frequently changed his affection and tied his destiny with the destiny and the affections of the local woman, not just taking her as a transitory companion, but as a stable and legitimate wife.
>
> And in this crossing began the seed of a new race, creole or native to this place, in which was amalgamated the hidden sweetness, deep apathy and sad self-awareness of the quechua [*sic*]; the burning, dreamy, yet clear judgment [*sindéresis*] of the arab [*sic*]; the strong tenacity and audacious turbulence of the iberian [*sic*]; the bloody energy

and rude geniality of the visigoth [*sic*]. (Leguía y Martínez [1913] 1996, 611–612)

All these processes point toward middle-sector intellectuals as the main cultural entrepreneurs advancing ideas about regionalism during this period. They found themselves increasingly hemmed in, caught between looming problems on the coast and in the sierra and increasingly dominated by the authoritarian state as bureaucratic field. Despite the state's dominance, nothing seemed to be under way to address mounting problems—hence the appeal of the anti-Limeño Valdivian tradition. In inventing the mestizo tradition, they were projecting their own sense of fragmentation and change in the quickening society of early twentieth-century Peru onto an imagined, local, authentic folk, anchored in a place, and then drawing symbolic power from that back into debates in the national field. In a world of flux, uncertainty, and even danger, sturdy entrepreneurial Arequipeño everymen and everywomen represented welcome solidity and stability indeed. It is important to note that all this was possible because it was taking place in a continuing urban social space hardly changed from the early nineteenth century.

In defining Arequipeño traditionalism against these two others, then, traditionalist discourse in this period also acted to blur class distinctions within regional society, exporting disorder, so to speak, even as race was foregrounded by a mestizo discourse that surreptitiously reproduced the neocolonial social order. This double opposition, symbolized by the rural mestizo smallholder, gave Arequipeño mestizaje its vigor and "reality." Hence the curious mix among Arequipeños of political conservatism, populism, racism, and individualist entrepreneurial spirit. Arequipeños' cross-class regional identity, then, results from both material and cultural processes.

Mestizaje has tended to be understood as an ideology that appears to be inclusive, in that everyone is eligible to be "mestizo," but that in practice masks difference, as it tends to privilege "whiteness." The social effect of this mestizo discourse was to shift the category of *criollo* to cover mixed-race descendants. It's sort of the reverse of what happened with "white" in the United States, where even a drop of African blood made one "black." In Arequipa, even a drop of Spanish blood made one "white"—though such an ancestry was labeled "mestizo" or "*criollo*" (see Telles and Flores 2013).

The mestizo is of course typically understood as the product of the

Spanish thesis and the Indian antithesis. But to apply this to Arequipa required discovering the "indigenous" in Arequipa itself, which meant anchoring the "real" Arequipeño essence in a rural place—the campiña. People of the nearby sierra of Arequipa (e.g., Cailloma, the punas of the Salinas and Cañaguas areas, etc.) were certainly "indigenous"—they spoke Quechua, herded camelids, dressed in ponchos, went barefoot or wore sandals—but they were too much so. Whatever their own self-perception, they were not regarded as of "noble" Inka stock.

So the urge to essentialize Arequipeños' mestizo identity required elevating the most telluric of qualities about campiña smallholders. "Real" Arequipeños were those illiterate but honest, hard workers of the campiña who worked and ate and played hard, whose music and food were "authentic," unlike that of either corrupt Limeños or lazy Indians.

These cultural entrepreneurs' construction of a mestizo plebeian everyman was a twofold process. In the first place, it borrowed directly from the *loncco/ccala* distinction already made by campiña residents. But secondarily, it was reinforced by the incorporation of the *loncco* imagery into the urban middle-class effort—a form of symbolic violence through its imposition on *all* campiña smallholders, not just on the illiterate, poor, subsistence farmers and day laborers (albeit with misunderstanding of the term *loncco*, as we have seen).

It is important to note, however, that all the verbal and visual imagery developed during this period was still highly selective. While proud smallholders were prominent, the working poor of the countryside were typically left out, though Vinatea and, especially, Núñez included more character types in their paintings than the British romantics did in their paintings of their own countryside (Barrell 1980). As I noted in the preface, this was Williams's (1973) crucial point: all this writing and painting about country life is a very selective, arms-length urban imagining of the countryside, quite far from people's lived reality—though in Arequipa it is one marked by much less social distance than seems typically to be the case.

My informants' insistence on being called *agricultores*, then, is as much a resistance to this imposition of indigenous traits—this *symbolic violence*—as it is an opposition to serranos. Hence Don Aurelio's castigation of me: I had failed to recognize both the crucial emic distinction in the countryside between *agricultores* and *campesinos*, and their standing as fellow citizens of regional society. As we learned, the city was always in a tight social, economic, and cultural symbiosis with the campiña. For example, unlike people in cities in the north, indigenous artisans ornamented key public buildings with representations of crops and even of the sun and moon. Catholic processions in Arequipa were (and are) interjected with rural imagery, such as the entry of *ccapo* on the city's anniversary (see Basadre [1929] 1947, 108).

The signifier (e.g., Gibson or other poets) takes the place of the signified (the many and weak),

> . . . the spokesman . . . of the group he is supposed to express, not least because his distinction, his "outstandingness," his visibility constitute the essential part, if not the essence, of this power, which, being entirely set within the logic of knowledge and acknowledgment, is fundamentally a symbolic power; but also because the representative, the sign, the emblem, may be, and create, the whole reality of groups which receive effective social existence only in and through representation. (Bourdieu 1986, 252)

Since the countryside is seen as less changed, it can much better serve as a repository of traditional culture. The campiña is a place that is and can only be, finally, unique. Dwellers in this rural area are seen as anchored in this place, an alter ego for increasingly mobile urbanites, and best poised to carry forward the theme of honor and striving to be an honorable citizen.

> Tradition was viewed as a kind of repertoire of the customs and habits, ceremonies and trades being endangered by industrialization, a repertoire looked upon by folklorists and ethnographers as valuable and as needing to be perpetuated and rescued for posterity. (Hofer 1984, 133)

The primary impetus, then, was to construct an image of plebeian, folk Arequipa as authentic, in reaction to the haughty dismissal of non-modern ways of being as superstitious or backward. This is of great interest, as both Polar and Mostajo were positivists celebrating folk Arequipeños as symbolic of a possible, specifically Peruvian way of being *modern*. Despite their modernist efforts, however, this folk tradition is not really subject to the verification or measurement required for a truly "scientific" description (see Mullen 2000).

Though this "folklorization" process (Mendoza 2000, 48) has roots back to the late-colonial period (e.g., Echevarría [1804] 1958), the process peaked during the 1890–1970 period as a local variant of the *indigenismo* sweeping the Andes and Mexico during this time. As I have documented, urban middle-class intellectuals were the main authors of this invented tradition. Unlike in Cuzco, however, locals had access to education in the cities and there were strong social ties between city and countryside—key differences that shaped the emergence of Arequipeño regionalist sentiment in its modern iteration.[9]

In what one might say constitutes part of the prehistory of identity politics (cf. Hale 1997; Brubaker and Cooper 2000), primarily middle sectors of Arequipeño society invented a mestizo discourse in the early decades of the twentieth century—precisely because of its ambiguity, or multivocality, I argue—to make sense of a politically, economically, and culturally volatile period. Early twentieth-century Arequipeño mestizo discourse attempted to address the national question by camouflaging the Indian question in an apparently inclusive "mestizo" identity. But since Arequipeños fashioned their sense of themselves in opposition to two cultural poles in the national field, theirs constitutes an unusual case of a discursive *browning* of regional identity—even as it was fundamentally not inclusive of the Altiplano indigenous population, despite the long shared history at a popular level. Urban intellectuals' class position militated against their grasp of the overall unity of the central Andean space—not just historically, but also what it might have been politically, in consonance with an ecological reality that pre-Hispanic state formulations understood.

An additional local particularity is that as second city, Arequipa had a more generally literate population and literary tradition, so that its regionalism was heralded in a way that no other regionalism in Peru has been. The relative autonomy and ubiquity of print media by the early nineteenth century, so prominent in Arequipa, granted cultural entrepreneurs—writers, artists, musicians—a certain social space for the production and circulation of novel ideas. This in turn was dependent on the presence of a literate public—usually urban—with appropriate cultural capital to understand (consume) the images being circulated. Hence, in conclusion, the pivotal role of key educational institutions—most notably the Colegio de la Independencia and the affiliated Universidad Nacional de San Agustín—in reproducing regionalist identity. As a result, a narrative of how one part of Peruvian society dealt with the shifting political and economic realities of the later nineteenth century was both produced and "captured" in print more than occurred in other regions of the country.

Yet while the immediate audience for this invented tradition occupied local social space—fellow writers, painters, and musicians appealing to a literate urban middle class experimenting with modern ways of being—the field within which this cultural production circulated failed when projected onto the national field, where the coast/highlands polarity was sharp and allowed no in-between social space like the one that occurred regionally in Arequipa. Almost every one of these cultural entrepreneurs journeyed to Lima to practice their craft. In the process, these entrepreneurs created a space for more "authentic" practitioners to operate; El Torito (charango player Angel Múñoz Alpaca) or Los Dávalos could make a career out of interpreting and writing *criollo* music *away from Arequipa* because of the space forged by these cultural entrepreneurs.

This 1890–1970 "Mostajo" period of experimentation—what Ballón Lozada calls the "golden age of Arequipeño letters"—offers us a fascinating look at one way a discourse of mestizaje played out. The idea of mestizaje is usefully ambiguous, since it "allows for racialized discourse to oscillate from cultural absolutism to cultural relativism, from the means to a homogeneous and naturalized national cultural identity to the site of a heterogeneous postcolonial one" (Martínez-Echazábal 1998, 23). Arequipeño cultural entrepreneurs never overcame the contradictions inherent in such an ambivalent discourse, particularly since "mestizo" was a gloss not only for a classless non-Limeño/non-elite subjectivity but also a non-Indian one.

The hegemony of these symbolic forms in regional social space, which I have described as "Arequipeño regional culture," resulted from the ability of these cultural entrepreneurs to more effectively mobilize social and especially cultural (linguistic, literary, artistic) capitals to exercise symbolic power in a social space largely abandoned by regional elites (see Bourdieu 1991). That the invention of Arequipeño traditionalism was largely a project of individuals from unorganized middle sectors is also shown by contrasting Cayma and Yanahuara, on the one hand, with Paucarpata and Sabandía, on the other. In the latter rural districts, lying to the south of the city, various elite families (wool merchants mostly—e.g., Ricketts, Stafford) maintained rural retreats, mostly in the decades before and especially after the war with Chile (Polar [1891] 1958, 71–72; Belaúnde [1960] 1967). Admiring the peasant life around them, these *ccalas*, as locals came to call them, idealized the lifeways of the local peasants. Thus, although encounter and even interaction similar to that of Cayma and Yanahuara also occurred here, there were no middle sectors in Sabandía and Paucarpata. It was the picantería in Yanahuara or Cayma, a view of the city from Antiquilla (fig. 4.3) that predominated. We learned that *ccala* families as late as the 1930s would hire groups of musicians from town to play *yaravíes* and other music at fiestas in their old country homes, but these musical groups were not local; rather, they were itinerant and mostly urban in origin.

Finally, to relocate these cultural processes in social space, because this imaginary was not reproduced in actual ritual—it circulated and was consumed by being read about rather than performed—this "literary regionalism" focusing on the "mestizo" character of Arequipa was not organically tied to popular sentiment or practice. And without the bureaucratic machinery of the state to reproduce these ideas via school curricula or other means, sites for performing or contesting such identity were more fluid, and the imposed categories were weaker—hence the importance of the picantería as the key arena in which plebeian and scholar, farmer and worker, meet and celebrate their cultural citizenship.

For more liberal writers (e.g., Mostajo), this discourse took a more democratic-socialist form, emphasizing the role, heritage, and wisdom of urban artisans and plebeians as well as of smallholders in Cayma and Yanahuara, where Mostajo lived. More conservative writers (e.g., Belaúnde) took a more moralistic approach, emphasizing the principles that Arequipeños shared (or used to share) that could serve the nation. Other writers, some from elite backgrounds (e.g., Gibson), romanticized the speech and lives of everyday, rural citizens, but from a comfortable distance. All these perspectives rested on the shared understanding of the region's marked populism, the idea that, whether as *montoneros* or in a rearguard civilian role, these smallholders and urban plebeians had indeed joined the fight against Limeño-based caudillos or Chileans in the nineteenth century and that their heroism had been exemplary and inspiring.

The failure of *lo arequipeño* to serve as a template for national identity resulted from the mismatch between the cultural unity forged in Arequipa, expressed in the cultural production of regional intellectuals, artists, writers, and others (and founded on deeper regional cultural unity at a popular level, as I have shown), and the lack of corresponding political integration at the regional level where such cultural ideas could be politicized and promoted via the symbolic power of state actors in the bureaucratic field. Because these ideas found no political traction, these voices were marginalized at the national level even as they strengthened at the regional level as "culture"—hence the secessionist undercurrent in the rhetoric of "the Independent Republic." Intellectuals in Peru (or elsewhere in Latin America) never had the institutional basis to mount an independent critique of the state (N. Miller 1999), and in this light the

1950 attack by Odría on the Colegio de la Independencia—that cradle of regionalist thought—was aimed directly at extinguishing regional intellectual production that could threaten central state control.

The temporary, abortive effort to drag regionalism from cultural back onto political terrain in the events of the 1930s (the Arequipa-based coup against Leguía and then the resistance against Sánchez Cerro) illustrated the degree to which regionalist identity was a product of urban intellectuals and not of the urban plebeian and rural masses they described and idealized. While the middle sectors waxed nostalgic about an already-disappearing simpler way of life, symbolized by rural smallholders, the valley farmers themselves were leveraging their ties to the city and new-found wealth from dairying.

4. REPRODUCING REGIONAL IDENTITY IN THE ABSENCE OF STATE MACHINERY

Literary elements, like those examined in chapter 4 and analyzed above, are consumed and are therefore less enduring overall, so they wither— selected out, so to speak, rusting away in museums and libraries unless picked up again and reinvigorated via new cultural entrepreneurs. Given this, I want to conclude this penultimate section with a brief examination of two ways this subnational identity has been reproduced in the absence of the levers available to those who control the state machinery: First, we will look at who is schooled where and who controls the curriculum in these educational institutions. Second (in the next section), we will discuss how both *peleas* and pilgrimage constitute the main sites for the actually ritualized reproduction of collective identity.

Central state control over education is a key arena in which those who control the state exercise power, and a centralized, national curriculum was already emerging in nineteenth-century Peru. Efforts to create a national, standardized educational system and curriculum began in the 1850s with Castilla (Basadre 1962, 1311), emphasizing practical arts and spiritual training at the elementary level and preprofessional liberal arts training for those who could afford to continue into high school. By midcentury secondary students in the first four (of six) years of schooling were to cover not just classic subjects like grammar, rhetoric, mathematics, and science but also "Geografia del Peru . . . [and] Historia del Peru," complemented by similar studies in the last two-year cycle (Basadre 1962, 2089). School textbooks on the history of Peru had begun to appear by the 1870s (Basadre 1962, 2096). Movement was already underway by the 1920s toward a centralized educational system and curriculum, which undermined the relative autonomy and social reproductive power of the Colegio de la Independencia and UNSA.

Of course, critical to the reproductive function of schooling is actual instruction. Regional identity in the middle "mestizo" period was anchored both in the Colegio de la Independencia and UNSA as well as being "underground" in such basic institutions as church and family. It bears repeating that virtually all the cultural entrepreneurs examined above studied and/or taught at the Colegio de la Independencia and/or the Universidad Nacional de San Agustín. The outsized influence on the construction of "the Independent Republic of Arequipa" of Jorge Polar, for example, was due to his direct engagement with these institutions over many decades.

Here is where actual school personnel—teachers—make a big difference, for they can cooperate with, interpret, or resist the state's impulse to control curriculum and instruction (vom Hau 2009). One small example is teachers' instructional use of *láminas*, in Arequipa produced by the Arequipa-based Mario Cuzzi publisher and available in all local bookstores selling school supplies. *Láminas* are one-page mini posters about various facets of regional and national history, geography, and many other topics; for example, one recounts the "Fundación española e incaica" that repeats the (erroneous) standard story of "Ari-quepay" of Mayta Cápac (see chapter 4) and then goes on to list the names of Pizarro's contingent who founded Arequipa. The one big story of heroic statesmen and regional pride is spread and reproduced among new generations in such ways.

The end of classic Arequipa, that golden age of regional letters, was the end of a period of literary experiment in European ideas and trends invading Peru during the 1920s, partly romantic, tied to the Colegio de la Independencia and UNSA. Arequipa's growth after World War II; its slowly changing demographics and class structure, with the beginnings of working-class mobilization; and the centralization and national standardization of the curriculum under Odría spelled the end of this institutional site of reproduction of *lo arequipeño*.

In sum, this *browning* of regional identity developed into a broadly meaningful cultural category shared across social classes (signaling Arequipeños' marked lack of class consciousness) in response to at least three factors: first, its resonance with ongoing popular desire for inclusion in regional society; second, the surprisingly strong indigenous roots and popular understandings of place, anchored in pilgrimage; and third, as a way of solving the obdurate problems blocking resolution of the national question in regional terms, with Arequipeños' sense of being in between the racialized poles of highlands (Indian) and coast (white).

The somewhat politicized social space within which this cultural production took place had collapsed by the early 1930s in the binary politics of an advancing wave of left agitation (APRA or PCP) and the conservative and/or reactionary response and finally repression by a militarized state. The inability of cultural entrepreneurs during the "Mostajo" apogee to break into the national field with these symbolic forms—whether from voluntary emigration, silencing, or forced exile—doomed regionalist sentiment to strictly cultural terrain, which had finally dissipated by the 1970s in a wave of nostalgia as the central state consolidated control over national culture in a variety of ways, especially via several generations of citizens weaned on centrally controlled school curricula. The exhaustion of this narrative undermined the cross-class unity of regional culture, which helps us understand the distinction Baltazar Caravedo Molinari (1978) made between the cross-class unity of the 1950 uprising and the splintered, more overtly class-based nature of actors' participation in the 1955 (and later) uprisings.

C. Conversion of Capitals: Emergence of a Dairying Elite and Bull-on-Bull Fighting

Arequipa's regional identity is now reproduced less through schooling than through everyday Arequipeños' ongoing participation in Candelaria pilgrimage—the Virgen de Chapi pilgrimages—and in dairymen's practice of bull-on-bull fighting, unique to Arequipa. These are the only two arenas where Arequipa's traditionalist narrative is *produced* and *reproduced* through familiar social processes of congregating believers and adherents. The earlier "mestizo" phase of the regionalist tradition involved *consumption* of the cultural capital created by artists and writers—early twentieth-century cultural entrepreneurs, some with political ties or aims, many already looking back and lamenting the erosion of Arequipeños' mid-nineteenth-century fighting spirit.

However heterogeneous campiña smallholders may have previously been, their long and direct exposure to the vicissitudes of supplying local markets, unprotected by any traditional rights or duties, let alone by communal organizations, led them to be fundamentally conservative in their political and economic orientation. Affected by the ups and downs of the market for their products, they were less buffered from wider political and economic forces. It was therefore in the direct material interests of urban artisans as well as of rural smallholders to be engaged with the wider politics of nation building, since they were so directly affected by them. This is evidenced by urban plebeians' participation in a long series of rebellions, from the 1780 poster rebellion; through the 1834 uprising, the 1854–1856 civil war, and the 1950 and 1955 uprisings; to the protests against the Velasco regime's 1970s agrarian (and other) reforms, against the sale of the regional electric utility in 2002, and, most recently, against mining in the Tambo valley, in 2010 and subsequently.

Although the degree of engagement by rural smallholders with these popular uprisings is hard to determine, local farmers shared regional pride in this heroic past, even though they did not generally share urban intellectuals' folkloric view of themselves. Romantics' reification of an Arequipeño folk was at the center of the construction of a regional tradition extolling "the Independent Republic of Arequipa." The imposition of this "structure" on rural and/or plebeian members of regional society entailed an unintended symbolic violence: a largely well meaning, we may say, if uninformed and finally insidious attempt to render Arequipeño society in categories of folk authenticity and something else left unspecified—a crypto class politics that although neither realized or materialized, was imagined.

Again, as with the urban plebeians described by Chambers (1999), farmers' primary concern has always been to similarly distinguish themselves from mere *cholos*. An unanticipated consequence of urban intellectuals' romantic description of rural life, aimed at audiences in a national field, was the establishment of a rural other against which, however sympathetically, an anxious urban middle class could measure its progress and sophistication. While initially a more elite phenomenon, delighting in rural pleasures (in Tingo or Sabandía) became a sort of incipient, middle-class "tourism" that wound up objectifying country folk. Don Aurelio's comment both recognized and voiced concern about this unwarranted supposition or assumption that plebeian or rural Arequipa was a bounded cultural group of some sort—as if all countryside dwellers were part of an undifferentiated mass of rural workers (fig. 6.2). Again, their pushback argued in effect that they are not country bumpkins or landless workers; they are ordinary, property-owning, honorable members of regional society.

It quickly became apparent in my main interviewing period how very important it was to most of my informants that I recognize them as full members of the imagined community of Arequipa. In approaching any particular one of my randomly selected households for an interview, for

FIGURE 6.2

*Threshing team near Arequipa, 1920. From https://plus.google.com/photos
/113518930836788618970/albums/5498831386660455265/5514417377867248546
?banner=pwa&pid=5514417377867248546&oid=113518930836788618970;
site discontinued. Accessed 23 July 2013.*

example, I was typically received as *ingeniero*—a high-status honorific accorded me as a gringo. After a number of initial fumbling attempts to talk about the real reasons I was knocking at their door, asking politely if I could query them about their ownership and use of land and cattle, I quickly learned to present myself as an *ingeniero* in a setting of conversation with people who considered themselves proper landowners. In interviews across the campiña I would find myself constrained to present myself and conduct the interview formally, whether seated in the parlor of a relatively prosperous home in Tiabaya, with plastic-covered furniture obviously little used except for such rare occasions, or similarly ceremoniously seated at a table in a one-room house with a dirt floor and small windows at the opposite, uppermost end of the valley, in Canchamayo (upper Chiguata). In both extremes the home itself was presented as a site of consumption, aping urban styles—and not centrally a site of workaday production, which was typically out back.

In other words, whether in a more remote, somewhat poorer district like Chiguata or in a somewhat more prosperous district like Sabandía (with its dairying emphasis) or Tiabaya (with its emphasis on onion and garlic production), it was rare that I was not properly received in ways clearly indicating their sense that our interaction was one involving relative social equals (despite my being the epitome of a gringo, a tall white male), symbolized by sitting in their parlor or its equivalent, by their universal literacy, and by the formalities during our interaction. As an interview progressed—taking down detailed information about their agricultural and animal-husbandry practices on each of the parcels they owned or managed (I usually took far more of their time than they had anticipated)—it was clear that, almost to a person, they were making sure that I was aware that they were competent, knowledgeable managers of their productive property and not unschooled, illiterate campesinos.

Since we interacted warmly in ensuing months, Aurelio's admonishment of me—coupled with the nature of my interaction with 117 other campiña farmers—seemed much less a comment on my odd gringo snoopiness than an emphatic declaration of where smallholders like him stand. This disposition of relative social equality finds its major expression in the very public performance of bullfighting and *paso* horse riding, for example by his nephew Federico.

So on the face of it, the rise of rural symbols in Arequipeño traditionalism, albeit shifting to focus on bulls and horses, appears to continue the traditionalist iteration just examined. But I argue that while we are dealing with similar cultural materials—anchored in the lifeways (real or purported) of campiña farmers—in fact there had been a fundamental shift in the social location of the production and performance of this identity.

Farmers' status anxiety really emerged about midcentury, an era in the countryside marked by two trends new to the region: the beginning of a rapid increase in *serrano* (highlander, read "Indian") immigration to Arequipa, which swamped the more intimate social space within which earlier cultural entrepreneurs had worked, and the parallel development of regional dairying stimulated by the entrance of industrial milk production. Cultural production of plebeian or rural traits was rapidly appropriated from urban intellectuals by the rising class of self-made, proud, independent *agricultores*. The defunct Sociedad Agricola de Arequipa (founded 1916) was reorganized in 1945 and in August a year later held the first Feria Exposición Ganadera in the Colegio de la Independencia.

So while urban intellectuals grew nostalgic, prominent valley smallholders were converting cash earned selling milk to Leche Gloria into cultural capital, invested in bulls and horses, to distinguish themselves as honorable citizens from the rural working poor. Gone was the almost-proletarian imagery to be found, for example, in much of the 1920s and 1930s poetry of Guillermo Mercado or in the 1950 murals of Teodoro Núñez in the Hotel Libertador in Arequipa (figs. 4.5a and 4.5b). Gone was the emphasis on mestizaje, which had faded as the field within which this imagery was produced and consumed shifted from the national to the regional. Regional understanding of the campiña became less romanticized, inflected by this view-from-afar (e.g., Gibson's poetry above), and much more anchored directly in the *practice* of valley farming, particularly in the very public *performances* of bullfighting and horsemanship.

Now the production of rural symbolism in regional culture is much more in the hands of rural dwellers themselves, growing out of their actual practice, especially that of an emerging subset of prosperous dairymen in their practice of *peleas* and of raising and displaying *paso* horses. Smallholders' ability to express this disposition through public performance did not come about until they gained sufficient economic capital to be converted into status competition with bulls and horses and all the practices surrounding their care and display. This began to really take form in the 1940s when Leche Gloria built its milk plant and created a regional market for milk. Thus, the most surprising finding of my decades of work in rural Arequipa: *the reification of "traditional" Arequipa by smallholders themselves came about largely via their relationship with the insertion of multinational capital (industrial milk production) into the regional economy.*

Given traditionalist writers' silence about *peleas*, the rise to prominence of this local form of bullfighting points to the successful effort by campiña smallholders to get their own voice into regional play.[10] Upwardly mobile smallholders who aspired to validate their citizenship in regional society attempted to move in Arequipeño social circles, especially those with links to prominent local families, and leveraged dairy wealth into cultural capital that, in its display, opened new doors of opportunity. It was members of this emerging elite who filled the space left by the decline of local aristocratic families (Belaúnde 1987).[11] Though no official list of winning bulls exists to help date this emergence, Céspedes Carpio (2010, 66) has constructed a list that begins in 1918.

However objectified campiña smallholders were by this urban-based mestizo and folklorization discourse, their own aspirations and peasant conservatism coincided with it in major outlines. Claudio Lomnitz-Adler's (1992) concept of "intimate cultures" helps us understand regionally specific cultures through a class lens. At the heart of campiña culture is a strong sense of cultural citizenship as *arequipeños netos* ("real Arequipeños")—both drawing from a legacy of popular engagement with regional politics and society and basking in the honor bestowed by evocative representations (however skewed) of them by earlier cultural entrepreneurs, competing for legitimate position in the imagined community.

Peleas quickly became the heart of this identity. When the opportunity for increased income via dairying presented itself, campiña smallholders responded vigorously, changing cultivation practices in the 1940s toward producing forage and herding milk cattle. Agricultural census data clearly show valley agriculturists shifting from cultivation of a more characteristic suite of Andean food crops to alfalfa and dairy cattle.

The majority of prosperous campiña farmers tied into dairying benefited enormously from the cash flow and wealth creation stemming from involvement with Gloria, despite Gloria's monopsony and despite periodic price controls enacted by the central government. Cattle merchants, like those from Sabandía whom I described in chapter 5, were especially well positioned to convert capitals in this manner, since they were already well versed in the many details and the art of animal husbandry and had something of a reputation as wheeler-dealers. I quickly learned how much there is to know when I was invited to try my hand at milking and plowing.

With new wealth generated by the Leche Gloria plant from the early 1940s, a set of elite landowners emerged in the campiña, validating and consolidating their position by converting dairy profits into symbolic power in the form of fine bulls and the bullfighting performance. Given general scarcity of arable land for sale, investing new income into land itself was not an option for most (though my landlady's father—a prosperous local cattle merchant—had purchased land in the Moquegua valley).

While there has been a fundamental shift in the primary locus of milk production—from the campiña putting-out system of independent households to the somewhat larger farms with rectangular fields out in the new irrigation projects—*peleas* are nevertheless primarily a performance in the traditional campiña. The larger publics gathered almost every weekend for *peleas* are primarily urban plebeians; neither bull owners nor these publics would pack up and make the hour-long trip out to the irrigation projects. In this way, "traditional" campiña districts like Sabandía, Characato, and others are reproduced through practice centered on the performance of bullfighting.

It is this *performance* of bull-on-bull fighting, then, that both epitomizes this spirit and captures what is most different about this current iteration of regional identity from those that preceded it. In bullfighting, rural citizens are not just represented; they perform. And audiences are part of the overall performance. Through the ritual performance, enacted somewhere in the valley virtually every weekend, everyday Arequi-peños collectively reproduce their sense of themselves.

Bullfighting quickly came to constitute a metaphor for this sense of competition and of striving to bring order out of the inchoate feelings of regional pride (Fernandez 1986). And as the notion of modern citizen-ship developed—where honor became linked to patriotism (Chambers 1999, 185)—participation in peleas came to validate cultural citizenship in the regional community. In a hardly-unfamiliar process, Peruvian flags fly and the (ponderous) national anthem is sung to open *peleas*. Here again there is conflation with gender, as masculine "citizens" are required for modern nation-states (note leaders in relation to *montone-ros* in the Pampeña Arequipeña, described below).

Years later, as I was launching this book project, I ran into Federico at a juice stand near the local city market. He recounted all the family de-mands on his time and how much it was costing to stay in the horse-and-bull honor game. He said he was going to sell his horses, since they had become too expensive—too much upkeep and overhead. He said he felt like he was becoming like his own father, the head of the family (Manuel had died in the 1980s), as he was the oldest brother and had never mar-ried. He remembered his father advising him not to get involved in these social circuits, presumably for just these reasons. Cares were mounting: he was going to have to sell two topos in Yumina Chico to raise some money for family members. I was struck with how cattle could move from being draft animals to fighting bulls freighted with symbolic sig-nificance to animals sold for slaughter (Appadurai 1986; Kopytoff 1986).

So here was Federico confiding in me his anxiety about keeping up the huge investment of time and money not only in horses but also in the care, feeding, training, and hauling around of the fighting bulls him-self. On top of time and expense devoted to the direct care and manage-ment of the animals, there was also the cost in time and money of partic-ipation in the activities and social events of ACPATPA (for bulls) and the Asociación Regional del Sur de Criadores y Propietarios del Caballo Pe-ruano de Paso (Southern Regional Association of Breeders and Owners of Peruvian Paso Horses; ARSCPCPP). Yet he recently told me he sim-ply was in love with bulls; he has now sold all the dairy cows, but he still has seven *toros* and he still participates in *peleas*. He spoke endearingly about the temperament of his favorite of all, Rommel, though the bull fought but twice; for a small fee, Federico allows tourists on their way by his stall to visit the old mill, some from as far away as Africa, to sit on this huge but gentle animal, generating quite an income.

I couldn't help but note to myself that Federico's lamenting whether he could keep all this up was coupled with his surprising lack of investment in improving his milking stall. I thought back to his shirtpocket accounting. It made me realize that while there is direct, substantial material investment in fighting bulls, it is finally all about a way of life, which comes to be symbolized by fighting bulls and *paso* horses—a fine example of substantive rationality.

While such a masculinized honor/shame system has counterparts in many parts of the world, of course, what is missing from the campiña system is a corresponding protection of "our" women in various parts of public space. This suggests that though bullfighting is performance anchored in a long-standing rural culture of smallholder concern about recognition of their honorable citizenship, the honor system is not so ancestral as to have centrally involved women's virtue in relation to family honor, corroborating my claims that the tradition is quite recent and that smallholders are, in fact, relatively integrated into regional society. Again, Aurelio's admonition suggested that while status anxiety is just under the surface, there is not a feeling of existential threat to their way of life.

Inculcation of this gendered habitus stems from the doxic, taken-for-grantedness of the high esteem accorded adept managers of prize bulls or horses. Boys learn early on how to manage large animals, with all the pride that that entails, and in the case of wealthier families even to ride *paso* horses. Much of the day-to-day work of herding dairy cattle is left to boys, as much for such cultural as for energetic reasons (see Flannery, Marcus, and Reynolds 2009). Young men are the primary attendees at *peleas de toros*, and they throng onto the *cancha* when winners are announced.

Such a dramatic spectacle would surely have found a prominent place in the traditionalist recounting of Arequipa's attributes. In an echo of colonial social distinctions, patrician Arequipeños like V. A. Belaúnde never mentioned *peleas de toros*. Members of the declining aristocracy, nostalgic for the village (*aldeana*) Arequipa of old, would not have been caught dead at so plebeian an event as a *pelea*. And even so astute and middle class an observer as Mostajo did not write about *peleas* (or if he did it was certainly not prominent; his voluminous output was scattered in many short-lived journals and has not all been collected and published; see Ballón Lozada 2000). Mostajo's silence on the matter is yet another confirmation that the tradition was largely invented in the mid-twentieth century.

If *peleas* are hardly mentioned in the traditionalist discourse, from whence, then, do they spring? What is their social origin? The *peleas* tradition is directly tied to the ongoing quest for honor in regional social space by a rural smallholder status group, recently empowered by industrial dairying. It emerges in the mid-twentieth century when local smallholders, now rapidly converting into dairymen, found themselves for the first time with a cash flow sufficient to start acquiring the accoutrements of respectable living. Construction and sale of concrete homes and sales of cars, trucks, televisions, and other domestic consumer goods grew sharply from the 1950s on, an Arequipeño echo of the global postwar economic boom. Mining had begun at Cerro Verde by 1940 (though the mine we know did not open until 1976), fueling the regional economy.

Investing in cattle made sense on economic grounds. Raising and selling cattle especially made sense in more remote areas, where transport of crops to market was prohibitive. West-slope valleys had a long tradition of raising beef cattle, and as we learned from Federico López's story, there was active cattle buying from relatively remote communities, such as in the Majes/Colca, Siguas, Tambo, and other valleys.

Investing in cattle also made cultural sense. Eager to be recognized as honorable citizens, it was an obvious step to link cattle with competitive display of symbols of courage and hard work. Cattle being movable capital (and of course "capital" derives from the Latin for "heads" of cattle), unlike cultivated crops, everyone who could used wealth generated in the wool or cattle trade or from wine estates on the coast to buy land in the valley. Raising fighting bulls came to symbolize a seigneurial way of life as much as a business (Bourdieu 1986).

Peruvian *paso* horse breeding is also a big deal among elite dairymen in Arequipa. But how did this north-coast style become part of Arequipeño identity? Apart from emulating emerging national status symbols, it may well be directly linked with the person of General Pedro Diez Canseco, so prominent in the political life of the country in the 1860s and 1870s. Much respected both nationally and locally, after retiring to Arequipa from a splendid military career he would ride his *paso* horse back and forth from his house on Calle San Francisco in central Arequipa to his fields toward Tiabaya (Belaúnde 1987, 126–127). The strong linkage between valorizing Hispanic roots and love of the traditional countryside is made evident in V. A. Belaúnde's memorializing of both him (his maternal grandfather) and his maternal uncle Jesús Diez Canseco (1967, 130–131).

One's social class position—determined by property ownership, symbolized by animals—lay at the heart of this status group's code of honorable behavior. All the symbols of "proper" Arequipeño behavior and taste unite the emerging agricultural elite with regional consumption styles and distinguish Arequipeños from highland Indians. While the practical aspects of estate management were evident in the advertisements in *La Campiña* of the 1920s—for the latest developments in agricultural technology and inputs like fertilizer—the magazine was most notable for its advertisements for all the latest imported fashions. These goods and styles not only had been consumed by the country-estate-dwelling commercial elites, aspiring to patrician status (linked to Spanish notions of landowning privilege), but now were also purchased by the newer *agricultores* emerging from rural smallholders themselves—people like Federico (who wanted US cowboy hats) and others that I knew in Sabandía.

Of course, concern with status is also tied to disparagement of recent immigrants from Puno and Cuzco as "dirty Indians"—a widely shared attitude among my campiña farmer informants. There was a nearly constant refrain in my interviewing that Arequipeños needed to live a more ordered life, that there was great need for more municipal control of the mass of serrano immigrants on the street, urinating on the corners of the cathedral and other public monuments and spaces.

Interestingly enough, plebeians' understanding of themselves as (modern) citizens of regional society is much more aligned with the state's notion of citizenship. This is anchored in their ownership of property and is the basis for their marked political conservatism. It is in this sense that the emergence of *peleas de toros* is a characteristic of propertied (rural, cattle-owning) *citizens* (read "male" and "white")—an assertion of their rightful place in regional society characterized in very Spanish concerns, since the colonial period, with social position and honor. The Rodríguez Banda case best exemplifies this point, particularly in its evocation of traditionalist imagery and values (Fundación José Rodríguez Banda 1993).

Though we know *peleas* are a quite recent invention, then, the tradition is faithful to the culture of today even as it is made to represent the past. *Peleas* quench people's insatiable search for authenticity, the ongoing performance being intended to be like the thing of the past that it is meant to re-create. For consumers of authentic experience, individuals feel themselves proud to be in touch both with a "real" world and with their "real" selves (Handler and Saxton 1988, 243). But who is authorized to perform this, when there is no central authority to certify authenticity? Hence the social effect of campiña farmers' symbolic power, resulting from their conversion of income from intensified dairying into cultural capital whose source and nature are fundamentally misrecognized (Bourdieu 1986). Bullfighting performances are contained events with a narrative encounter of equal partners; audiences consume the coherent experience of bullfighting performances that pleasingly contrast with the often incoherent quality of their everyday lives in the Independent Republic of Arequipa.

NOTES

PREFACE

1. I began work on sustainable forestry issues, both in Peru away from militarized areas (with Brazil nut harvesters in Madre de Dios on a 1989 Fulbright Scholarship) and in the US Pacific Northwest, where I am from and now live. I worked from 1990 to 2002 with harvesters of wild edible mushrooms and floral greenery nontimber forest products.

CHAPTER 1

1. It should be noted, though, that the main plaza has palm trees, suggesting coastal affiliation, as do the main plazas in Sabandía, Tiabaya, Characato, and other campiña villages.

2. Much of this back-and-forth discourse about Arequipa as a second city can be found on the web; see, e.g., "Arequipa segunda ciudad??? Patrimonio cultural??," *ForosPerú*, http://www.forosperu.net/showthread.php?s=afc669bc5014cfef61314fa40 34bbc43&t=49144.

3. Also, since my fieldwork in the valley of Arequipa so clearly involved Spanish-speaking, self-consciously mestizo smallholders, I then and since have often felt that my interests were rather marginal to the mainstream of Andean anthropology and archaeology that is so focused on non- or pre-Hispanic cultural elements or patterns. With their focus on cultural continuities (see Appadurai 2013, 285), that anthropologists had largely missed the emergence of Sendero Luminoso was more than telling. Missing in so much of this work was the on-the-ground agency and practices of everyday people.

4. The phrase *ni chicha ni limonada* is usually translated as "not easily categorized," as in "neither fish nor fowl." "Chicha" is apparently of Kuna origin (*chichab* = "maize"). In the Andes, while primarily associated with maize, whether fermented or not, the word can be used to refer to almost any homemade drink. The phrase is widespread in South and Central America and the Caribbean but not in Mexico,

suggesting that it spread along colonial trade routes from Panama through the Andes. "Ni chicha ni limonada" was the title of a 1970 song by Chilean folksinger Victor Jara and of a 2009 collection of short stories by Guatemalan-born David Unger. Other meanings include "not recognizable," "not worth anything," and "nothing left to drink," either alcoholic or not (*limonada* referring to any nonalcoholic drink).

5. In many respects, my present effort picks up where John Wibel (1975) left off and Alberto Flores Galindo (1977) didn't go—examining popular engagement with the urban-centered construction of regional culture, in relation to the development of a regional oligarchy in Arequipa.

CHAPTER 2

1. The mood at Chapi during the midnight Mass and the procession next day was quite solemn, however, in contrast to the festive atmosphere prevailing at other Candelaria shrines, especially at Copacabana in Bolivia. Whether immigrant Puneños will merge their Candelaria worship with that of Chapi remains to be seen. There may be slowly growing participation by recently immigrated Puneños in Chapi pilgrimage, though from the casual observation of two Arequipa colleagues, the increase seems mostly to be in itinerant merchants.

2. Note how earthquakes cause a break in ingrained habitus, reminding us that even the earth is unstable and, more importantly, in a Durkheimian sense, that we are part of larger systems.

3. José Antonio Chávez Chávez (1993, 103–104) argued that the Inka had officially banned the name "Putina" on account of its 1454 eruption and devastation, and since so many locals had fled this eruption, the Spanish never learned this name from those who remained. But it seems highly unlikely that locals could have forgotten the name of so important a mountain.

Misti is a widespread term used by Quechua-speaking locals in southern highland Peru to refer to generally unwanted, town-dwelling outsiders (e.g., Allen 2002, 9–15). Mostajo (1934, in Ballón 1999, 142–143) noted that Aymara speakers in Huancané used *miste* to refer to something half-good, so he speculated that the name was a local (Altiplano-based?) reference to the mountain being just "half-indigenous," suggesting a sort of mestizaje. An Englishman, Samuel Curson, was apparently the first to use *Misti* (as *Misté*) in print, in 1824 (unsigned review of Samuel Curson, "Narrative of an Ascent to the Peak of Misté [*sic*]," by Samuel Curson, *North American Review* 19: 266. https://books.google.com/books?id=ZIAFAAAAQAAJ&pg =PA266&lpg=PA266&dq=Curson+Arequipa+Peru&source=bl&ots=dsRjNjCRYQ &sig=nJABc9boJwSovX8I2Ly563MQraQ&hl=en&sa=X&ved=0ahUKEwj4hvmAr -XQAhUEnZQKHePtDQ4Q6AEIJTAC#v=onepage&q=Curson%20Arequipa %20Peru&f=false. (cf. Bustinza Menéndez and Huamán Asillo 2002). Also, like Bishop Ventura Travada y Córdoba and later Francisco Mostajo, Arequipeños' particular interest in this mountain was probably enhanced by Christian trinitarian understandings, particularly of Calvary, that added emphasis to the central place occupied by Misti.

4. Putina—"the mountain that growls" (Bustinza Menéndez and Huamán Asillo 2002, 45)—was the Pukina name for the volcano, and like its Aymara name Anuqara ("dog"), it referred to the posture the mountain presented from the Altiplano side as it sat looking at the sun setting in the ocean. In central Andean cosmology, dogs were understood to guide the soul safely in the afterlife, and death was associated with the western ocean. Since either name—Anuqara or Putina—was associated with death cults, they were probably banished by the Spanish on religious grounds very early on (cf. Bustinza Menéndez and Huamán Asillo 2002, 44–45). Regardless of its name(s), *visitador* (inspector) Cristóbal de Albórnoz noted in 1568 that all the Indians of La Chimba, Characato, and Chiguata worshiped the volcano as a *pacarisca* (*huaca principal*, "main holy site") (Julien 2002; Echeverría [1804] 1958). (Putina is also the name of a village on the eastern shore of Lake Titicaca not far from the Bolivian border.)

5. In the Colca valley, unirrigated quasi terraces at higher, wetter (but colder) elevations (ca. 3,700 meters) appear to be very old (2400 BCE or older), while lower-elevation irrigated bench terracing (in use to the present) appears later, by at least 500–600 CE. "The shift of terrace cultivation downslope, with irrigation added, can be related both to changing climatic conditions and to increasing population pressure which necessitated dependable production in a region of undependable precipitation." Rather than leading to collapse, however, climate stress seems to have stimulated the development of more efficient, more productive agriculture at lower, somewhat warmer elevations (Denevan 2001, 199–200).

6. For example, the primary agricultural lands of Cabanaconde, the premiere maize-producing village situated at the lower end of the Colca valley, lie between 3,000 and 3,350 meters above sea level (Gelles 2000).

7. Given the relative marginality of much of the Arequipa basin for maize cultivation, the very localized Inka investment in nicely faced terracing in the Paucarpata and Sabandía areas points to their primary role in support of Putina worship by *panaqa* officials in Yumina.

8. Such west-slope place-names as "Atiquipa" (coastal *loma* [fog-nourished bluffs] in northern Arequipa) and even "Iquipi," "Arica," and "Iquique" may well share etymological origins with "Arequipa" (Julio A. Bustinza Menéndez, pers. comm., 4 July 2015). A general overview of the region can be found on Google Earth: https://www.google.com/maps/@-17.9276845,-72.4188349,462677a,35y,25.75t/data=!3m1!1e3.

9. That the Pukina-speaking Colla ethnic group switched to Quechua under Inka influence nicely accounts for both the clear linguistic boundary between Quechua and Aymara right at the northern end of the lake and the Inka name for this quarter of their empire: Collasuyu, in apparent gratitude for their decisive political support.

10. The Chili is the only river of note between Majes-Colca, with its oddly oriented watershed, and the Tambo, which drains from the *puna*. The entire right/

north bank of the Rio Chili was called La Chimba, meaning "the other side" (from the Spanish city, but perhaps also "the other side" across the river from Collasuyu (see Mostajo in Ballón Lozada 1999). The Inka state had relocated Challapas, Chillques, and several small *mitmaq* groups to La Chimba, already well settled by a mix of Quechua speakers and Aymara or Pukina speakers, including people from Yanahuara and Chumbivilcas (now Cuzco Department), Collaguas from the upper Colca valley, and Lampas, Cabanillas, and Collas from Chucuito (Galdos Rodríguez 1990b, 191–213; Julien 2002; cf. Málaga Núñez-Zeballos 1997, 62). The annual Feast of the Cross at Cancahuani hill near Characato may derive from resettled Chumbivilcanos' practice of pilgrimage to the shrine (*huaca*) of Cancahuani near Ccapacmarcay north of Santo Tomás. Mostajo ([1924] 1956) noted that Lari were resettled in what is now the *pago* (hamlet) of La Tomilla in Cayma, suggesting that at least in this sector, the Inka did enlarge the total cultivated area of the valley beyond what they found.

11. Guaman Poma de Ayala ([1615/1616] 1987, 108) stated that the eleventh Inka, Huayna Cápac, ordered all but a few of the *huacas* of the kingdom destroyed; included in those saved were those of Putina and Coropuna. In a later chapter, under "Idolos y Huacas de los Conde Suyos," Guaman Poma focuses on the mountain "Coropona Urco," that is, Coropuna mountain (*cerro*, with a sense of maleness) and on Mama Cocha, that is, the Pacific Ocean, mentioning only the great quantity of local *huacas* too numerous to name (Guaman Poma de Ayala [1615/1616] 1987, 274–275). A bit later Guaman Poma lists the major idols and *huacas* of Conde Suyos to which the Inka sacrificed: Coro Pona (that is, Coropuna) and Putina (that is, Misti). The fact that Guaman Poma indicates Putina lying in Condesuyos contradicts Julien's assertion that the Rio Chili constituted the boundary between Kuntisuyu and Collasuyu.

12. Labor was probably easier to extract from the local population, since abundant water there and in nearby Characato allowed for less strict labor scheduling (planting, harvest) (cf. D'Altroy 1994, 190) Also, there may be a connection between the strong cultural tradition of *chicha* consumption among valley farmers and the Inka stimulation of maize cultivation in Yumina, Paucarpata, and especially Characato ("place where maize is traded").

13. Testifying to the legacy of Altiplano ties, in Yumina a special bagre (catfish) dish is prepared (two ways, fried or boiled); Yumina is the only place in the campiña where this is done. Bagre are found in the springs in the area. There may be a connection between bagre consumption and worship of snakes, as Pukina mythology about the Copacabana-area islands connects snakes and fish (Bouysse-Cassagne 2010, 297). I took a special interest in and spent a lot of time in Yumina, having lived for over a year near the main road down below in Sabandía, its district capital. Sabandía, an elongated town along the road from Arequipa to Characato, does not descend from a *curacazgo* (local polity); rather, it started growing in the late eighteenth century (Galdos Rodríguez 1990a, 200) and continued to grow in the nineteenth century, when newly emerging English merchants, such as William Stafford

and Guillermo Ricketts, built country homes there. Though the event may well be a later, even postcolonial, addition, every 15 August young men bring burros laden with *ccapo* down from the lower slopes of Pichu Pichu into the Yumina plaza at dusk, following the dirt track alongside the canal from the spring to the church, celebrating the Virgen de la Asunta, Yumina's (and Arequipa's) patron saint. It is intriguing that not only does the small church in Yumina face due east, toward the rising sun and the highest point on Pichu Pichu, but it also fronts directly on a little plaza on the other side of which is a large concrete-walled pond. One wonders whether the half-kilometer canal linking the spring farther east with this pool is not Inka in origin, and whether the plaza was the very location of important ritual. My speculation does not correspond to the initial description of a now-protected archaeological site there, however (Cardona Rosas 2002, 106).

14. While labor mobilization had begun through the imposition of *mitmaq* populations in La Chimba, it may well be that there simply wasn't sufficient time for the Inka state to establish other key processes of labor (e.g., taking of women as *aclla* [royal concubines], for which there appears to be no record for Arequipa) and land mobilization (La Lonte 1994) or symbolic reorganization. Mobilization of land for state purposes appears to have been limited, perhaps just to Yumina and Paucarpata, as noted. It seems the Colca valley, with its higher and more predictable rainfall, was one of the main foci of Inka attention on "the other side of the mountains" after all.

15. *Chullpas* are also found farther north (e.g., in Chuquibamba). *Chullpa* burials were characteristic of the northern, western, upper Urkosuyu (versus Umasuyu) half of the Altiplano cosmological division, supporting the idea that Churajón was a settlement linked to Colla, Lupaqa, or some other northern Altiplano people. They may have been refaced with fancy stonework during Inka times, as happened in Titicaca proper.

16. The huge discrepancy between terracing of this magnitude and material remains of a central administration capable of building and administering it remains something of a mystery. Perhaps Churajón experienced an influx of settlers or Pukina refugees (perhaps ritual elites; see Bouysse-Cassagne 2010) from the Altiplano escaping the collapse of Tiyawanaku, as happened in the upper Moquegua valley (B. D. Owen's 2005 "Distant Colonies and Explosive Collapse," cited in Malpass, n.d.) and probably elsewhere in the periphery of the Tiyawanaku interaction sphere. This could account both for the closer (ethnic?) ties with Moquegua and the Tambo valley and with the Altiplano and for the seeming lack of integration of Churajón with other villages in the Arequipa basin.

17. The historical geography of "Colesuyo" has been treated in Rostworowski de Diez Canseco 1988, 263; Espinoza de la Borda 2003; Galdos Rodríguez 1985, 1990b; and Málaga Medina 1975. Mostajo thought that Garcilaso was the source of the error conflating Collasuyu with Collisuyo/Colesuyo. In any case, Moquegua and Tacna were both eventually elevated to departmental status in the confusing political geography preceding the War of the Pacific, as we will see.

18. The cacique of Puquina maintained control, interdigitated with that of other caciques all along the major villages of this zone, over land and labor from the Arequipa valley proper across and over to the Tambo drainage and to the coast (Málaga Medina 1975, 77). A Pocsi-based *curacazgo* maintained vertical trade relations with colonists on the coast at Chule, near present-day Mejía (Galdos Rodríguez 2000, 190); as late as 1814 a legal dispute arose over the continued right of Pocsinos to harvest guano from the islands of Cocotea and Yñañe off the mouth of the Tambo River and to pasture llamas on the nearby *lomas* (ibid.; Julien 1985). Part of the tribute paid by Pocsinos was hot peppers (*ají*) and coca, both products of lower-elevation production zones. Like the Pukina-speaking enclaves of Capachica and Coata near Puno (Bouysse-Cassagne 2010, 294), Pocsinos were noted textile producers, paying tribute in kind with textiles until the Toledan reforms and then, after that, paying with money derived from the sale of textiles (Galdos Rodriguez 2000, 196). *Mitmaq* ties with Altiplano caciques are evident not only in these early *repartimiento* and *encomienda* documents, but also in the toponymy of the southern Arequipa and upper Moquegua, which is replete with names linking the area to the Altiplano (e.g., Puquina and a second Coata, near Carumas, among many other examples). These altitudinal relations were strong, and they continue, as, for example, in the ongoing ties camelid herders in the Lake Salinas region maintain with various midaltitude hamlets through the upper Tambo: barter exchange of alpaca rope and bags, as well as of *sesina* (dry lamb meat) and *charqui* (jerky), by Salinas-area herders for crops produced in the *suni* (potatoes, other tubers, barley), *kichwa* (maize, some fruits), and *yunga* (fruits) ecozones in Puquina, southern campiña, and middle Tambo continued at least into the late twentieth century (Love 1988).

19. While I focus on pilgrimage, there are a number of other continuing ideas syncretized into modern practice in Arequipa. On All Saints Day (1 November), for example, *bizcochos* (pastries) of babies are made and eaten—a rather widespread Andean practice of remembering the dead by eating bread babies.

20. While in English we speak of the Virgin at the Feast of Candlemas, in Spanish she is the Virgen de la Candelaria.

21. The number of days in December and January went unchanged by the Gregorian calendrical reforms of 1582.

22. La Candelaria is the patron saint of the Canary Islands; veneration of her there seems closely linked to pre-Castilian Guanche veneration of a sun goddess Chaxiraxi, stemming from her apparition to locals on a beach on Tenerife, from where she was transferred to a cave. Observation of Groundhog Day in the United States stems from similar syncretic practices from various parts of Europe, fusing this day with pre-Christian beliefs about animals predicting the boundary between winter and spring.

23. While sources vary on whether Lari in Cayma refers to Aymara-speakers tied to Lari in the Colca (Collaguas) (most likely) or to Quechua-speaking *mitimaes* populations relocated from Lares; Cuzco legend associates her with this Lari-Lari cemetery (Mostajo [1924] 1956).

24. Challapampa (sacred plain) in Cerro Colorado district of Arequipa is very near the church in Cayma. There may be ancient ties with the community at the very northern, most sacred spot on the Island of the Sun in Lake Titicaca.

25. In the sixteenth century Holy Roman Emperor Charles V of Spain is reported to have honored the Virgin of Characato with a donation of a golden shawl embroidered with gold thread (Quiroz Paz Soldán and Málaga Medina 1985). But since he abdicated in 1556 and died in 1558, this does not fit with the dates from Vargas Ugarte. This royal donation may have been made by his son, Philip II of Spain, in his father's name, then connected with her prominence during that first 1582 earthquake.

26. See Allen 2002, 231, on *majeño* dance: "A misti dance favored by Paucartambo hacendados during the early twentieth century. Sonqueños adopted the dance after the expropriation of haciendas in the 1970s. In 1975 they simply identified majeño—with his comically brutal white face and elegant riding clothes—as a hacendado." Urban migrants connect with their rural roots as they perform traditional dances, a process of "inclusive otherness" (de la Cadena 2000, 286).

27. It is increasingly apparent that such large-scale, even continental, trade linkages characterized the political economy of preconquest central-highland South America and adjacent Amazonia. Trade linkages of the Inka state with coastal Ecuador (and probably to Panama and even Central America) are well known but underappreciated, while trade links east into southern Amazonia are apparent in the Middle Horizon and Tiyawanaku (Hornborg 2014).

28. Candelaria worship in the Colca valley was superseded by a series of Franciscan evangelizing efforts and temple building in the eighteenth century. To the long list of places where devotion to the Virgen de la Candelaria thrives we can add Mejía (perhaps with ties to the early port of Chule), the upper reaches of Arica, and even Cocharcas (Cuzco) and Ayacucho (Hall 2004). The extent of Candelaria worship south of Copacabana is unclear; in Argentina the Virgen de la Candelaria is the patron saint of Humahuaca, directly on the colonial trade route, but not of Jujuy, Salta, or Tucumán. Settlements in the Department of Arequipa not in the Candelaria galaxy all lie well to the north, such as Chuquibamba (whose patron saint is Mary of the Immaculate Conception), Colca (as described), and throughout Condesuyos Province, as well as Cotahuasi—all major areas of Cuzqueño (and earlier Wari) rather than Altiplano influence. The Virgen del Buen Paso is the patron saint of Caravelí, though there is a place called La Candelaria in the District of Uraca, in the Province of Castilla. The Virgen de la Candelaria in Puno was recognized in November 2014 as "patrimonio mundial inmaterial" (immaterial world heritage) ("Álvarez: Distinción a la Candelaria incrementará el turismo en Puno," *RPP*, 27 November 2014, http://www.rpp.com.pe/2014-11-27-alvarez-distincion-a-la-candelaria-incrementara-el-turismo-en-puno-noticia_745820.html).

It is not clear the extent to which Puneño immigrants are starting to participate in Chapi pilgrimage, as noted, though a separate celebration of the Candelaria of Puno has been going on for at least a decade. Since La Candelaria is the patron saint of Puno, there are very interesting issues about cultural, religious, and regional identities at stake. My thanks to Alejandro Málaga Núñez-Zeballos for sharing his pioneering research into the distribution of Candelaria worship.

29. The map at https://urpfau20151tv8grup007.files.wordpress.com/2015/04/mapa-topografico-ciudad-arequipa.jpg shows the rough paths of the four roads out of Arequipa. The main colonial-era roads were the ones shown heading most in the cardinal directions (e.g., the road heading southeast forks; the old road is the one heading more directly south, not the one heading southeast).

30. A Candelaria sits above the images of Christ at the Chiguata procession.

31. That Churajón escaped Guaman Poma's notice may be additional evidence that the site was a Pukina ethnic enclave. Interestingly, there are indications that pilgrimage to the ruined site of Churajón continued after this disaster (Máximo Neira Avendaño, pers. comm., 20 July 1997).

32. Miguel Zárate has argued that there were three images placed by the friars in each of the *chullpas* at Churajón (Máximo Neira Avendaño, pers. comm., 20 July 1997), which were shifted down to Chapi.

33. Much of this history is presented in in the YouTube video *Presencia de María Santísima en la evangelización de América Latina: La Sma. Virgen de Chapi* (http://www.youtube.com/watch?v=yRnj-Ni3RX4), where there is also one of the surprisingly rare photos of Pope John Paul II crowning the Virgen de Chapi (at 17:00). Similar stories about dedication to a specific place are told about most Marian apparitions; Mary seems to want to stay in a lot of places (that being devotees' point)—not only as Candelarias, as in Characato, Cayma, Charcani, Chapi, and Copacabana, but also in many other sites throughout Latin America, such as Loja (Ecuador), Guadalupe (Mexico), Luján (Argentina), and in Europe, e.g., Lourdes (France) and elsewhere.

34. Though more study is needed, Chapi devotion supplanting Characato devotion seems to be as much a result of top-down policy by Church authorities as of bottom-up preference of devotees. (It also has been the result of the destruction at Characato from the 1958–1960 earthquakes, as noted.)

35. President Alan García visited Chapi on 7 December 1985, decorated La Mamita with La Gran Cruz de la Orden del Sol del Perú and prayed to her on his knees. In May 2011, near the end of his second presidency, García claimed that Osama bin Laden had actually been miraculously taken out by the late Pope John Paul II with the help of the Virgin Mary, since the deceased pope was beatified on the very day bin Laden was killed.

CHAPTER 3

1. It is also worth noting, in this context, that the lower reaches of the Tambo valley—home to important sugar estates like Chucarapi and Pampa Blanca (both

belonging to the Lira family)—were kept in Arequipa Department when Moquegua was created in 1839.

2. Examination of the current ethno-politics surrounding Evo Morales, as president of Bolivia, and his movement's irredentist claims on southern Peru are well beyond the scope of this book. There are important links between these efforts and Peru's recent president Ollanta Humala who, though moving in a strongly neoliberal direction, maintained ties with an ethno-nationalist movement (Movimiento Etnocacerista) evoking the peasant-based resistance of Andrés Cáceres, Peruvian hero of the War of the Pacific.

3. The 1784 incorporation of Chiloé, to the south of the Captaincy of Chile, by the Viceroyalty of Peru to resist English piracy, along with the similar but brief attempt in 1805 to incorporate Paposo on what was then the north side of Chile, can be usefully compared to Lima's attempt to retain more direct control of Arequipa. In fact, Chiloé was governed from 1804 to 1812 by Alvarez y Jiménez, the former intendent of Arequipa (from 1785–1796) who in 1784 had ordered an expedition to the top of Misti (Marchena F. 2005, 68). Even with such aspirations for relative autonomy, both Arequipa and Chiloé were relatively royalist strongholds, tied to the growing European-centered geopolitics of trade.

4. This shows, by the way, how early an at least partly literate urban population had developed in the city—important as an audience for print media over the ensuing century, as we shall see. Local elites' involvement in this uprising was spurred by the insinuation of racial impurity, important since the rumor was that taxation was going to be extended to mixed-race subjects (Chambers 2003, 44).

5. From north to south, the first four partidos were:

1. Condesuyos de Arequipa, which became the Province of Condesuyos, with its capital Chuquibamba, on 21 June 1825. During the Peru-Bolivia Confederation the upper and lower parts of the Cotahuasi valley were separated from Condesuyos and joined to create the Province of La Unión (the name celebrating the Peru-Bolivia Confederation), with its capital at Cotahuasi. Castilla, with its capital Aplao, was formed from Condesuyos on 21 March 1854, named in honor of then president Ramón Castilla.

2. Camaná, with its capital Camaná, which included not only the lower part of the Majes/Colca river, as now, but also the coastal parts of Condesuyos: Acarí, Yauca, Atiquipa, Caravelí, Atico, and Molleguaca. These latter parts, briefly known as the Corregimiento de Atiquipa o de la Costa (with a probable Atiquipa-Arequipa etymological tie) in the late 1500s (Espinoza de la Borda 2003, 191), were combined into the Province of Caravelí, which was elevated to provincial status on 22 February 1935 (Galdos Rodríguez 1990a, 244), with its capital Caravelí.

3. The Province of Arequipa, which included not only the city (with La Chimba), its capital, but also (having long since incorporated Characato)

the campiña and valleys of Vítor and Siguas and the coast. When the intent to build the railroad became established, the coastal portion was elevated to provincial status as Islay on 18 December 1862, with its capital Mollendo.

4. Caylloma, which was first the Corregimiento de Collaguas (1565), which became the partido, then the Province of Caylloma, continuing to include the ethnically distinct peoples of Cabanaconde and Collaguas. The capital was moved to Chivay from Cailloma in 1932. District reorganization in 1999 extended the province southwest onto the plains of Majes, since Colca water had been diverted for irrigation there, allowing for the growth of population centers.

Continuing from north to south, the southern three partidos of the intendancy included:

5. Colesuyo, which was originally a lower-elevation colony of Chucuito/Lupaqa. Briefly organized by the Spanish into the Corregimiento of Chucuito (as described in chapter 2), this region was separated in 1590 as the Corregimiento de Ubinas or Colesuyu, becoming the Partido de Colesuyo in the late eighteenth century. A province of Arequipa at independence, Colesuyo (later Moquegua) and its sister provinces to the south were swept up in the border disputes emerging in the 1830s.

6. The Partido of Arica, whose capital was Arica and which contained Tacna. The Partido of Arica formed a province of Arequipa until the border disputes heated up in the 1830s.

7. Tarapacá, whose capital was Iquique and which was a province of Arequipa after independence. Tarapacá was the home or birthplace of three presidents of Peru: Ramón Castilla, Guillermo Billinghurst, and Remigio Morales Bermúdez (among other early Republican notables). Tarapacá had been separated from Colesuyo early in the colonial period (Espinoza de la Borda 2003).

6. The relative demographic decline in the south was due in some measure to death among highlanders from epidemics in the late 1850s (Gootenberg 1991b, 131).

7. Juan Manuel Polar, the father of Jorge Polar (discussed in chapter 4), was active in this movement and again in the 1867 uprising.

8. Indeed, the UNSA played a similar role—inculcating love of *patria chica*—at the regional level to the one the University of Chile performed at the national level there (see N. Miller 1999, 77), the latter, of course, tied to the modernizing Chilean state.

9. Production of the famed liqueur Anís Nájar, for example, was started in 1854 by Pedro Múñoz-Nájar, a Spaniard who had migrated to Arequipa and married a woman from Miraflores, where the first factory was built. Their descendant Alberto

Múñoz-Nájar headed the Chamber of Commerce in 1999 and is a leader in the continuing effort to liberalize trade, labor, and other policies.

CHAPTER 4

1. There are undoubtedly fairly direct links between Arequipeño intellectuals' increasing emphasis on mestizaje and the 1910 Mexican revolution (with José Vasconcelos's proclamation of the mestizo as "the cosmic race").

2. The role of Catholic intellectuals in Arequipeño regionalism—including deeper analysis of V. A. Belaúnde's work in this regard—is a topic remaining to be documented.

3. While this conversation in Peru came earlier than in Mexico, by the 1920s mestizaje became enshrined as state ideology in Mexico—but not in Peru (N. Miller 1999, 138).

4. In 1880 Nieves organized a group of women to aid the combatants in the War of the Pacific. In 1921, on the centennial of national independence (and presumably with Leguía's authoritarian regime in mind), Nieves was awarded a gold medal by the Colegio de Abogados for her novel *Jorge, el hijo del pueblo*.

5. This "scientific" treatment of racial possibilities is echoed by Guinassi Morán (1908), among others, and remarkably prefigures the work of Argentine sociologist Mario Bunge. A false polarity developed between those who "equated miscegenation with barbarism and degeneration; [while] adherents of the latter prescribed cross-racial breeding as the antidote to barbarism and the means to creating modern Latin American nation-states. Closer examination of these supposedly antithetical positions, however, reveals them to be differently nuanced variations of essentially the same ideology, one philosophically and politically grounded in European liberalism and positivism, whose role it was to 'improve' the human race through 'better breeding' and to support and encourage Western racial and cultural supremacy" (Martínez-Echazábal 1998, 30).

6. On a personal note, I found my worn (but unmarked) copy of Polar's book and a companion volume of key writings (Bermejo 1958) in a bookstore in lower Manhattan in 1977. I have often wondered if these had belonged to Nicolás Sánchez-Albórnoz, who was on the New York University faculty in the mid-1970s.

7. As a provincial, left-center, populist organic intellectual, Mostajo is usefully compared with Nazario Chávez Aliaga in Cajamarca (cf. Taylor 2000).

8. In our era he might well have been a zine mogul and had a Twitter following.

9. In 2001 I was privileged to view a large slice of the Vargas brothers' *fototeca* (photo collection) thanks to their granddaughter Roxana Chirinos. (Much of this is now available on the web.) Of humble social origins, the Vargas brothers nevertheless focused on new, avant-garde styles and ideas rather than on the quotidian rhythms and everyday lives of people around them. They nurtured local talent, such

as Jorge Vinatea Reynoso and Martín Chambi, though in terms of subject matter the contrast with Chambi could not be more stark. They experimented with the novelty of electric lighting as it played in the streets and buildings of nocturnal Arequipa city. It is telling that in the Vargas brothers' oeuvre there is little attention paid to everyday practices of the common folk of the city, let alone the campiña. Rather, the brothers focused on staged scenes exploiting the artistic possibilities of the new medium. Oriented to the modernist outlook that photography afforded, this was hardly *paisajista* (a genre focused on the countryside). The Vargas brothers represent that portion of the middle sectors in Arequipa of the 1920s fascinated by modernism and by the possibilities for opening up what they considered the overly conservative, stultifying cultural climate of Arequipa (McElroy 1985, xvii ff.).

In regard to the history of photography in Arequipa, figs. 4.2, 5.2, and 6.2 are photographs taken about 1920 by an unknown photographer as part of a series to be made into postcards. The links shown have now been taken down, and I am unable to retrieve them. Fully documenting this set of images would be a valuable project.

10. Given the particularly intense and in some ways archetypal experience of city-country relations in industrializing Britain of the nineteenth century, it may be that a special emphasis on valorizing and rescuing Arequipeño traditions came via input from Gibson's exposure to British romantic poets. I an unaware of an analysis of Gibson's production in relation to English romanticism. Gibson left for Lima in the late 1910s, where he was a close associate of Abraham Valdelomar and the Grupo Colónida. He worked at the National Library under González Prada for a while before leaving for Europe. He scarcely returned to Peru after 1925, though his daughter later founded *Caretas* magazine. He dedicated several of his 1928 sonnets to Mostajo and did some work on *Arequipeñismos* (speech localisms) in poetry dedicated to most of the people I examine in this section (Coloma Porcari 2005).

11. Interestingly, the names of Vinatea's paintings are not standardized; many Wikipedia entries, for example, say that the painting shown in fig. 4.3 is titled *El Poeta Loncco*.

12. A recent documentary on the centenary of his birth wonderfully explores Núñez Ureta's long and productive life: the YouTube video *Sucedió en El Perú: Teodoro Núñez Ureta*, seven parts, including a revelatory 1988 interview (http://www .youtube.com/watch?v=GT1PARNxgs0&list=PLAMJrgnKWX_-7XBHSTGQfdC ThzwpfhZZo). While I have included images of the wonderful representations of campiña and city in two murals at the Hotel de Turistas, they can be better seen in part three of this documentary, from 08:51–09:38.

13. El Torito was related to the family of caciques of Cayma, the Alpaca; Don Matias Alpaca y Guascar was cacique of Cayma in 1822 (Zegarra Meneses 1973, 78).

14. Time has not permitted an investigation of Manuel J. Bustamante de la Fuente, a lawyer and key regionalist who not only played a central role in the decentralist coup of 1930 that brought down Leguía, but also went on to a distinguished career that enabled the formation of a foundation that has been central to the publication of diverse writings chronicling the Arequipeño tradition (e.g., Neira Aven-

daño et al. 1990; Rivera Martínez 1996). He successfully leveraged his control of the local brewery to sponsor many cultural-revival initiatives.

15. Machinery I saw in the old Huayco wool textile mill, for example, was dated from 1935—during the height of import substitution industrialization.

CHAPTER 5

1. The Comunidad Campesina de Chiguata (CCC) is one of the very few Velasco-era agrarian-reform actions taken in the valley of Arequipa—a takeover of the Hacienda Santa Maria there. I talked with a member of the leadership group but it was clear they had never functioned well, and by the mid-1980s the estate had been parceled out to the former *comuneros*. I learned that there was tension over water for cultivation in Chiguata because the CCC was taking too much for its eucalyptus plantings. Its history—indeed, a history of the agrarian reform in Arequipa—remains to be written.

2. Interestingly, had regional elites been more centrally dependent on campiña agriculture rather than on commerce or, for some, wines produced in lower-elevation valleys, with the traditionalist discourse I have been describing, one could imagine a situation where the distinctive qualities of local products might well have been extolled—as happened in France with wine and cheese, for example, in the constructed senses of *terroir* (see Matthews 2015).

3. Unlike Cajamarca peasants, Arequipeño smallholders had relatively less experience migrating to the coast for work (which had led to APRA radicalization in the north [Taylor 2000]).

4. The term is not apparently used in other parts of Peru, but a cognate *longo* is used as a derogatory term for certain highland Indians in the Otavalo region of Ecuador (F. Salomon, pers. comm., 15 August 2005). While we would surmise that *lonccos* were indigenous leaders recognized by the colonial state in some fashion, as I argue, current usage erroneously glosses the term with "mestizo" smallholder (*chacarero*). A curious, recent example of pushback against the Arequipeño-as-mestizo tradition has it that there was no biological and little cultural or linguistic mixing of the local indigenous inhabitants with Spanish rural dwellers (see the Wikipedia entry "Loncco," http://es.wikipedia.org/wiki/Loncco). Rather, so this unsubstantiated but intriguing argument goes, the localisms found in the speech of old-timers in the campiña—the *lonccos*—this group claims, are descended from archaic Spanish.

There is more to the *loncco* story than this, and more than has been written to date (a thorough study of the matter is warranted). In Chile the term is used by the Mapuche for local leaders (male heads of patrilineal descent groups) who deal with the state (Mariella Bacigalupo, pers. comm., 18 July 2015), recognized in Republican Chile as a way of dealing with Mapuche demands for political autonomy. This points to the possibility that the Inka state used the term to identify local leaders of ethnically distinct peoples they were administering, suggesting that the Inka state recognized a greater degree of ethnic distinctiveness in the populations they encountered in Arequipa (Puquina?). It may well be that *loncco* referred to prominent local *kurakas* (state-recognized indigenous leaders) in certain dealings with urban Spaniards, particularly in the Corregimiento of Characato y Vítor (see chapter 6).

5. I quote Antero Peralta Vásquez extensively in this section, not only because of his colorful writing but also because he epitomizes the common emphases about picanterías about which many have written.

6. There are suggestive linkages here between literary regionalists, tied to modernism, and the church, tied to Marian maternal imagery. One wonders about links between this praise of motherly picanteras with broader popular Candelaria devotion, since Mary is so tightly identified as the nurturing mother of the imagined community. A displaced Mary figure perhaps? Within the court cases analyzed by Chambers (1999) lie early hints of this connection, such as pressures on women to sacrifice for the larger good, a Marian inspiration for female self-abnegation and for sacrificing for others, including for the family's self-esteem (see below in this chapter re male honor contests via bull fighting).

In addition, part of this feminized countryside imagery had to do with larger trends in the feminization of the church (the rise of Marian worship in recent decades) and of piety, due to the withdrawal of the church from active state functions and relationships with the emergence of the modern secular state. Discussion of either of these points is obviously well beyond the present study.

7. I don't suspect that the location—fabled Pampa de Miraflores—is important in this context. That is, I don't suspect that there is some indigenous substrate. Rather, this is where the first bullring (for the better-known *corrida de toros*, with matador) was built (in the mid-1700s), and the bull owners probably decided to use that.

CHAPTER 6

1. We are somewhat late in joining this conversation, however, "the study of nationalism ha[ving] truly become a topic within anthropology only during the 1980s and 1990s" (Eriksen 1993, 98).

2. Attempts at revising Peruvian history to retroactively inject a mestizo essence came in 1971, when, on the sesquicentenary of independence from Spain, the Velasco government commissioned a whole effort to promote the 1780s rebellion of Túpac Amaru as launching a half-century of struggle against Spain, which united all classes and ethnicities in a common cause, to establish a mestizo national identity (Fisher 1979).

3. Some recent writers have even gone so far as to claim that the old *tambos* of La Chimba were the original arenas for mestizaje (Medina 1998).

4. Again, when exactly this occurred will remain unclear until someone carries

out a careful search of archival materials to construct a social history of campiña villages (something obviously well beyond the scope of this project). Given my focus in this monograph on the currently understood regional culture of Arequipa, it has not been possible to explore in any depth important questions about when colonial status distinctions and the system of dual indigenous/Spanish political authorities in the valley changed. It is nevertheless safe to assume these changes.

5. A woman I met on the steps of the main cathedral in April 1997 belonged to what was apparently a nonsanctioned *cofradía* (religious lay organization) of support for Chapi. Seeing me talking with her at some length, a local guard escorted her away. She had related that though church authorities had brought the Virgen de Chapi into the center of town on various occasions, she really "never wanted to go."

6. It may be that Mary's association with the 1582 earthquake and subsequent removal to a small chapel away from the cemetery by 1604 represent non-Collaguas locals' appropriation of her into more clearly regional, somewhat culturally distinct understandings centering on tectonic forces and water.

7. Characato locals claim that the moniker comes from their reputation as hard workers. When workers in the *salitre* mines in Chile were organized by nationality, they asked one group where they were from; rather than saying Arequipa, they said Characato, and thereby Chileans picked up and used the name.

8. The role of Chapi priest Pablo Retamozo Málaga in fostering Chapi worship after the 1868 earthquake, and the degree of his sympathies for everyday rural Arequipeños, remains to be examined by historians. He was central to the martyrs of Quequeña incident in 1883.

9. But mestizaje does also in practice incorporate some recognition of difference (Wade 2005)—for example, being "mestizo" on the "indigenous" side, as de la Cadena discovered in Cuzco (de la Cadena 2000). Mestizaje in both senses is operating in Arequipa, where "whiteness" lies behind claims of the region's "mestizo" identity, yet where both approaches implicitly understood mestizaje as a lived process rather than a fixed, timeless identity (Wade 2005) that included plebeian concerns. Such a construction of a subordinate other placed Arequipeños from outside the immediate metropolitan area or valley of Arequipa (e.g., Colca, Cotahuasi, Majes) in a culturally ambiguous situation—a topic needing study. Increasing racializing of indigenous identity in the southern highlands was nevertheless predicated on Indian labor in the Altiplano, and Hispanized elites there sought to be "modern" through "white" patterns of consumption and education (Jacobsen 1993, 333)—seemingly a reverse polarity with what was going on in Arequipa.

10. Arequipa bullfighting constitutes an excellent example, therefore, of the temporally shallow nature of "tradition" (Hobsbawn and Ranger 1983) narratives that serve the interests of some groups at the expense of others.

11. A social history of elite Arequipeño families with active management or other interests in valley agriculture of the late nineteenth to late twentieth centuries, including those tied to the wool-trade decline of the early 1920s and the 1930s depression, would be a valuable contribution.

BIBLIOGRAPHY

Abu Lughod, Lila. 1991. "Writing against Culture." In *Recapturing Anthropology: Working in the Present,* edited by Richard G. Fox, 137–162. Santa Fe, NM: SAR Press.

Acevedo, Juan. 1981. *¡Hola Cuy!* Lima: Ital-Peru.

Allen, Catherine J. 2002. *The Hold Life Has: Coca and Cultural Identity in an Andean Community.* 2nd ed. Washington, DC: Smithsonian Institution Press.

Alvarez-Calderón, Annalyda. 2013. "Indigenous Leaders and Peruvian National Policy Making in Puno, 1900–30." Paper delivered at the annual meeting of the American Historical Association, New Orleans, January 2013.

Anderson, Benedict. 1991. *Imagined Communities: Reflections on the Origin and Spread of Nationalism.* Rev. and extended ed. London: Verso.

Appadurai, Arjun. 1986. "Introduction: Commodities and the Politics of Value." In *The Social Life of Things: Commodities in Cultural Perspective,* edited by Arjun Appadurai, 3–63. Cambridge: Cambridge University Press.

———. 2013. "In My Father's Nation: Reflections on Biography, Memory, Family." In *The Future as Cultural Fact: Essays on the Global Condition,* 101–111. New York: Verso.

Applebaum, Nancy. 1999. "Whitening the Region: Caucano Mediation and 'Antioqueño Colonization' in Nineteenth-Century Colombia." *Hispanic American Historical Review* 79, no. 4: 631–667.

———. 2003. *Muddied Waters: Race, Religion, and Local History in Colombia, 1846–1948.* Durham, NC: Duke University Press.

Arce Espinoza, Mario Rommel. 2003. "Historia Menuda: 'Arequipa' de Jorge Polar." Arequipa: *Arequipa al Dia,* 4 February 2003.

———. 2009. "Las chicherías y picanterías de Arequipa." http://www.forosperu.net /temas/tradiciones-arequipenas.239383/. Accessed 10 February 2015.

———. 2016. *Avatares de un Libro Subversivo en Arequipa.* Arequipa: Universidad Católica Santa Maria.

Arequipa: Homenaje en su IV centenario. 1940. Lima: Tipografia Peruana.

Armaza, Emilio. 1960. "Percy Gibson." *Caretas,* no. 205, September 1960, 26–30.

Balda, Ann, and Jorge Latorre. 2014. "Max T. Vargas y la moda internacional en el contexto de la fotografía arequipeña." *Revista de Comunicación* 8: 7–37.

Ballón Landa, Alberto. (1908) 1958. "Estudios de sociología Arequipeña: Discurso preliminar." In *Prosistas e historiadores*, edited by Vladimiro Bermejo, 81–123. Primer Festival del Libro Arequipeño. Lima: Librería-Editorial Mejía Baca.

Ballón Lozada, Hector. 1987. *Las ideas Socio-Políticas en Arequipa, 1540–1900*. Arequipa: PubliUNSA.

———. 1992. *Cien años de vida política de Arequipa: 1890–1990*. Arequipa: UNSA.

———. 1996. *Deán Juan Gualberto Valdivia: Vida y obras*. Arequipa: Universidad Nacional de San Agustín.

———. 1999. *Mostajo y el folklore arequipeño*. Arequipa: Ediciones Jhader.

———. 2000. *Mostajo y la historia de Arequipa*. Arequipa: Edit. UNSA.

Barrell, John. 1980. *The Dark Side of the Landscape: The Rural Poor in English Painting, 1730–1840*. Cambridge: Cambridge University Press.

Barriga, Fr. Victor M. 1951. *Los terremotos en Arequipa*. Arequipa: La Colmena.

———. 1952. "Memorias para la historia de Arequipa: Relaciones de la visita al Partido de Arequipa por el Gobernador-Intendente don Antonio Álvarez y Jiménez." Vol. 4. Arequipa: Edit. La Colmena.

Basadre, Jorge. (1929) 1947. *La multitud, la ciudad, y el campo en la historia del Perú*. Lima: Edit. Huascarán.

———. 1962. *Historia de la República del Perú*. 5th ed. 6 vols. Lima: Talleres Gráficos Villanueva.

———. 1968. *Historia de la República del Perú*. 6th ed. 17 vols. Lima: Talleres Gráficos Villanueva.

———. 1977. "Reconsideraciones sobre el problema histórico de la Confederación Perú-Boliviana." *Revista de Historia de América*, no. 83: 93–119. http://hapi.ucla.edu/journal/detail/403. Accessed 14 August 2013.

———. (1931, 1978) 1992. *Perú, problema y posibilidad: Y otros ensayos*. Caracas, Venezuela: Biblioteca Ayacucho.

Basso, Keith. 1996. *Wisdom Sits in Places: Landscape and Language among the Western Apache*. Albuquerque: University of New Mexico Press.

Bastien, Joseph. 1978. *Mountain of the Condor: Metaphor and Ritual in an Andean Ayllu*. Prospect Heights, IL: Waveland Press.

Bauer, Brian S., and Charles Stanish. 2001. *Ritual and Pilgrimage in the Ancient Andes: The Islands of the Sun and the Moon*. Austin: University of Texas Press.

Bedregal La Vera, Jorge. 2008. *La Ruta del loncco: Raices del hombre arequipeño*. Arequipa: El Taller.

Belaúnde, Víctor Andrés. (1915) 1963. "La cuestión social en Arequipa." In *Meditaciones peruanas*, 116–127. Lima: Talleres Graficos.

———. 1918. "Sobre el regionalismo." Letter to the editor, *El Heraldo de Arequipa*, 18 June.

———. (1960) 1967. *Arequipa de mi infancia*. In *Meditaciones peruanas*, 8–251. Lima: Ediciones de Ediventas S.A. Lumen.

———. 1987. *Meditaciones peruanas*. Lima: Edición de la Comisión Nacional del Centenario.

Bermejo, Vladimiro, ed. 1958. *Prosistas e historiadores*. Primer Festival del Libro Arequipeño. Lima: Librería-Editorial Mejía Baca.

Bernedo Málaga, Leonidas. 1949. *La cultura puquina o prehistoria de la provincia de Arequipa*. Lima: Dirección de Educación y Artística y Extensión Cultural.

Bonilla, Heraclio. 1973. *Islay y la economía del sur peruano en el siglo XIX*. Lima: Instituto de Estudios Peruanos.

———. 1974. *Guano y burguesía*. Lima: Instituto de Estudios Peruanos.

———. 1980. *Un siglo a la deriva: Ensayos sobre el Perú, Bolivia y la guerra*. Lima: Instituto de Estudios Peruanos.

Bonilla, Heraclio, and Karen Spalding. 1972. "La Independencia en el Perú: Las palabras y los hechos." In *La independencia en el Peru*, 15–64. Lima: Instituto de Estudios Peruanos.

Bourdieu, Pierre. 1986. "The Forms of Capital." In *Handbook of Theory and Research for the Sociology of Education*, edited by John G. Richardson, 241–258. New York: Greenwood Press.

———. 1989. "Social Space and Symbolic Power." *Sociological Theory* 7, no. 1: 14–25.

———. 1991. "Identity and Representation: Elements for a Critical Reflection on the Idea of Region." In *Language and Symbolic Power*. Cambridge, MA: Harvard University Press.

———. 1994. "Rethinking the State: Genesis and Structure of the Bureaucratic Field." *Sociological Theory* 12, no. 1: 1–18.

Bouysse-Cassagne, Thérèse. 1986. "Urco and Uma: Aymara Concepts of Space." In *Anthropological History of Andean Polities*, edited by John V. Murra, Nathan Wachtel, and Jacques Revel, 201–227. Cambridge: Cambridge University Press.

———. 2010. "Apuntes para la historia de los puquinahablantes." *Boletín de Arqueología PUCP*, no. 14: 283–307.

Bronner, Fred. 1977. "Peruvian Encomenderos in 1630: Elite Circulation and Consolidation." *Hispanic American Historical Review* 57, no. 4: 633–659.

Brown, Kendall Walker. 1986. *Bourbons and Brandy: Imperial Reform in Eighteenth-Century Arequipa*. Albuquerque: University of New Mexico Press.

Brubaker, Rogers. 1996. *Nationalism Reframed: Nationhood and the National Question in the New Europe*. Cambridge: Cambridge University Press.

Brubaker, Rogers, and Frederick Cooper. 2000. "Beyond 'Identity.'" *Theory and Society* 29, no. 1: 1–47.

Brush, Stephen. 1977. *Mountain, Field, and Family*. Philadelphia: University of Pennsylvania Press.

Burga, Manuel, and Alberto Flores Galindo. 1981. *Apogeo y crisis de la República aristocrática*. Lima: Rikchay Peru.

———. 2001. "Lo andino hoy en el Perú." *Quehacer* (DESCO: Centro de Estudios y Promoción del Desarrollo), no. 128: 64–68.

Burga, Manuel, and Wilson Reátegui. 1981. *Lanas y capital mercantil en el sur: La Casa Ricketts, 1895–1935*. Lima: Instituto de Estudios Peruanos.

Bustamante de la Fuente, Manuel J. 1971. *La Monja Gutiérrez y la Arequipa de ayer y de hoy*. Lima: Gráfica Morsom.

Bustamante y Rivero, José Luis. (1947) 1996. "Arequipa." In *Imágen y leyenda de Arequipa: Antología 1540–1990*, edited by Edgardo Rivera Martínez, 613–631. Lima: Fundación Manuel J. Bustamante de la Fuente.

———. 1958. "Arequipa y su destino histórico." In *Prosistas e historiadores*, edited by Vladimiro Bermejo, 144–146. Primer Festival del Libro Arequipeño. Lima: Librería-Editorial Mejía Baca.

Bustinza Menéndez, Julio A., and Luis Daniel Huamán Asillo. 2002. "El topónimo original del volcán Misti." *Historia* 5: 41–51.

Cabrera Valdez, Ladislao. (1924) 1958. "Los primeros españoles en Arequipa." In *Prosistas e historiadores*, edited by Vladimiro Bermejo, 19–26. Primer Festival del Libro Arequipeño. Lima: Librería-Editorial Mejía Baca.

Cañedo-Argüelles, Teresa. 1993. "La organización del poder indígena en el Colesuyo (siglo XVI)." *Revista Complutense de Historia de America* 19: 21–51.

Caravedo Molinari, Baltazar. 1978. *Desarrollo desigual y lucha política en el Perú 1948–1956: La burguesía arequipeña y el estado peruano*. Lima: Instituto de Estudios Peruanos.

Cardona Rosas, Augusto. 2002. *Arqueología de Arequipa: De sus albores a los Incas*. Arequipa: Centro de Investigaciones Arqueológicas de Arequipa and Sociedad Minera Cerro Verde, S.A.A.

———. n.d. "Los Caminos Tradicionales de Arequipa." Arequipa: Centro de Investigaciones Arqueológicos de Arequipa. http://www.angelfire.com/pe/CIARQ/caminos.html.

Cardona Rosas, Augusto, and Karen Wise. n.d. *Arequipa: Doce mil años de arte y cultura*. Arequipa: Sociedad Minera Cerro Verde S.A.A.

Carpio Muñoz, Juan Guillermo. 1976. *El yaraví arequipeño: Un estudio histórico-social y un cancionero*. Arequipa: By the author.

———. 1981–1983. *Texao: Arequipa y Mostajo*. 4 vols. Arequipa: By the author.

———. 1984. *Arequipa en la guerra con Chile*. Arequipa: Mutual Arequipa.

———. 1990. "La inserción de Arequipa en el desarrollo mundial del capitalismo (1867–1919)." In *Historia general de Arequipa*, edited by Máximo Neira Avendaño et al., 489–578. Arequipa: Fundación Manuel J. Bustamante de la Fuente.

———. 1999. *Diccionario de arequipeñismos*. 3 vols. Arequipa: Industria Gráfica Regentus.

Centeno, Miguel Angel, and Fernando López-Alves, eds. 2001. *The Other Mirror: Grand Theory through the Lens of Latin America*. Princeton: Princeton University Press.

Cerrón-Palomino, Rodolfo. 2010. "Contactos y desplazamientos linguísticos en los Andes centro-sureños: El puquina, el aimara y el quechua." *Boletín de Arqueología PUCP*, no. 14: 255–282.

Céspedes Carpio, Miguel Angel. 2010. *Las peleas de toros en Arequipa*. Arequipa: By the author.

Chambers, Sarah. 1999. *From Subjects to Citizens: Honor, Culture, and Politics in Arequipa, Peru, 1780–1854*. University Park: Pennsylvania State University Press.

———. 2003. "Little Middle Ground: The Instability of a Mestizo Identity in the Andes, Eighteenth and Nineteenth Centuries." In *Race and Nation in Modern Latin America*, edited by Nancy P. Appelbaum, Anne S. Macpherson, and Karin Alejandra, 32–55. Durham: University of North Carolina Press.

Chavarría, Jesús. 1968. "A Communication on University Reform (in Forum)." *Latin American Research Review* 3, no. 3: 192–195.

———. 1970. "The Intellectuals and the Crisis of Modern Peruvian Nationalism: 1870–1919." *Hispanic American Historical Review* 50, no. 2: 257–278.

Chávez Chávez, José Antonio. 1993. *La erupción del Volcán Misti*. Arequipa: Impr. ZENIT.

Chávez O'Brien, Eleana. 1987. *El mercado laboral en la ciudad de Arequipa*. Lima: Fundación Manuel J. Bustamante de la Fuente.

Clifford, James. 1986. "Introduction: Partial Truths." In *Writing Culture: The Poetics and Politics of Ethnography*, edited by James Clifford, 1–26. Berkeley: University of California Press.

Coaguila, Jaime F. 2008. "Jueces, abogados y escribanos: Recetario para una construcción relacional de la identidad arequipeña." *Revista de Antropología Social* (Universidad Complutense de Madrid) 17: 351–376.

Cohen, Abner. (1974) 1996. "The Lesson of Ethnicity." In *Theories of Ethnicity: A Classical Reader*, edited by Werner Sollors, 370–384. New York: New York University Press.

Collin Delavaud, Claude. 1968. *Les régions côtières du Pérou septentrional: Occupation du sol, aménagement régional*. Lima: Institut français d'études andines.

Collins, Randall. 1994. *Four Sociological Traditions*. New York: Oxford University Press.

Coloma Porcari, César. 2005. "La culinaria tradicional arequipeña en la pluma de Percy Gibson Moller." *Sillar de Arequipa*. https://sites.google.com/site/sillardearequipa/la-culinaria-tradicional-arequipena-en-la-pluma-de-percy-gibson-moller. Accessed 12 February 2017. Originally published in *Caretas*, no. 1887, 18 August, 42–44.

Colque Valladares, Víctor. 1976. *Dinámica del movimiento sindical en Arequipa 1900–1968*. Estudios Sindicales, no. 4. Lima: Taller de Estudios Urbano Industriales, Programa Académico de Ciencias Sociales, Pontificia Universidad Católica.

Comaroff, John, and Jean Comaroff. 1992. *Ethnography and the Historical Imagination*. Boulder, CO: Westview Press.

Compañía Cervecera del Sur. 2002. *Francisco Mostajo: Antología de su obra*. 6 vols. Arequipa: Edit. Industria Gráfica Regentus S. R. Ltda.

Condori, Víctor. 2008. *Arequipa y la independencia del Peru: 1821–1824*. http://

naufragoaqp.blogspot.com/2008/02/arequipa-y-la-independencia-del-per.html. Accessed 22 January 2013.

Cornejo Polar, Jorge. 1998. "La poesía en Arequipa en el siglo XX." In *Estudios de literatura peruana*, 239–261. Lima: Universidad de Lima, Fondo de Desarrollo Editorial.

Cornejo Velásquez, Hernán. 2006. "El simbolismo de la comida arequipeña." *Investigaciones Sociales* 10, no. 17: 41–65. http://revistasinvestigacion.unmsm.edu.pe /index.php/sociales/article/view/7047/6236. Accessed 21 July 2016.

Cotler, Julio. 1978. *Clases, estado y nación en el Perú*. Lima: Instituto de Estudios Peruanos.

D'Altroy, Terence N. 1994. "Public and Private Economy in the Inka Empire." In *The Economic Anthropology of the State*, edited by Elizabeth M. Brumfield, 169–221. Monographs in Economic Anthropology, no. 11. Lanham, MD: University Press of America.

Davies, Keith A. 1984. *Landowners in Colonial Peru*. Austin: University of Texas Press.

de la Cadena, Marisol. 2000. *Indigenous Mestizos: The Politics of Race and Culture in Cuzco, Peru, 1919–1991*. Durham, NC: Duke University Press.

Delanty, Gerard, and Krishan Kumar. 2006. Introduction to *The Sage Handbook of Nations and Nationalism*, edited by Gerard Delanty and Krishan Kumar, 1–4. London: Sage.

Denevan, William M. 2001. *Cultivated Landscapes of Native Amazonia and the Andes*. New York: Oxford University Press.

Deustua, José, and José Luis Rénique. 1984. *Intelectuales, indigenismo y decentralismo en el Perú, 1897–1931*. Debates Andinos, no. 4. Cusco: Centro de Estudios Rurales Andinos "Bartolomé de las Casas."

Domingues, José Mauricio. 2006. "Nationalism in South and Central America." In *The Sage Handbook of Nations and Nationalism*, edited by Gerard Delanty and Krishan Kumar, 541–554. London: Sage.

Donkin, R. A. 1979. *Agricultural Terracing in the Aboriginal New World*. Viking Fund Publications in Anthropology, no. 56. Tucson: University of Arizona Press.

Echeverría, Francisco Javier de. (1804) 1958. "Descripción de la ciudad de Arequipa, su población y agricultura." In *Prosistas e historiadores*, edited by Vladimiro Bermejo, 5–15. Primer Festival del Libro Arequipeño. Lima: Librería-Editorial Mejía Baca.

Eley, Geoff, and Ronald Grigor Suny. 1996. "Introduction: From the Moment of Social History to the Work of Cultural Representation." In *Becoming National: A Reader*, edited by Geoff Eley and Ronald Grigor Suny, 3–37. New York: Oxford University Press.

El Santuario de Chapi Chico. n.d.

Eriksen, Thomas Hylland. 1993. *Ethnicity and Nationalism: Anthropological Perspectives*. London: Pluto Press.

Espinosa, Juan. (1839) 1996. "Cartas a Mauricio Rugendas." In *Imágen y leyenda de Arequipa: Antología 1540–1990*, edited by Edgardo Rivera Martínez, 294. Lima: Fundación Manuel J. Bustamante de la Fuente.

Espinoza de la Borda, Álvaro M. 2003. "Los corregimientos de Arequipa y la fragmentación del Kuntisuyu." *Historia* (Universidad Nacional de San Agustín, Arequipa, Perú) 6: 177–192.

Fernandez, James W. 1986. *Persuasions and Performances: The Play of Tropes in Culture*. Bloomington: Indiana University Press.

———. 2000. "Peripheral Wisdom." In *Signifying Identities: Anthropological Perspectives on Boundaries and Contested Identities*, edited by Anthony P. Cohen, 117–144. London: Routledge.

Fisher, John. 1979. "Royalism, Regionalism, and Rebellion in Colonial Peru, 1808–1815." *Hispanic American Historical Review* 59, no. 2: 232–257.

———. 1987. "Imperialism, Centralism, and Regionalism in Peru, 1776–1845." In *Region and Class in Modern Peruvian History*, edited by Rory Miller, 21–34. Liverpool, England: Institute of Latin American Studies.

———. 2003. *Bourbon Peru: 1750–1824*. Liverpool, England: Liverpool University Press.

Flannery, Kent V., Joyce Marcus, and Robert Reynolds. 1989. *Flocks of the Wamani: A Study of Llama Herders on the Punas of Ayacucho, Peru*. Walnut Creek, CA: Left Coast Press.

Flores Galindo, Alberto. 1977. *Arequipa y el sur andino: Ensayo de historia regional (siglos XVIII–XX)*. Lima: Edit. Horizonte.

———. 2010. *In Search of an Inca: Identity and Utopia in the Andes*. Edited and translated by Carlos Aguirre, Charles F. Walker, and Willie Hiatt. New York: Cambridge University Press.

Flores Galindo, Alberto, Orlando Plaza, and Teresa Oré. 1978. "Oligarquía y capital comercial en el sur peruano." *Debates en Sociología* 3: 53–75.

Fundación José Rodríguez Banda. 1993. *Nuestra leche: GLORIA y el desarrollo ganadero del Sur*. Arequipa: Universidad Nacional San Agustín and Cuzzi and Cia.

Galdos Rodríguez, Guillermo. 1985. *Kuntisuyu: Lo que encontraron los españoles*. Arequipa: Chávez Editores and Fundación Manuel J. Bustamante de la Fuente.

———. 1987. *Comunidades prehispánicas de Arequipa*. Arequipa: Fundación Manuel J. Bustamante de la Fuente.

———. 1990a. "Administración colonial." In *Historia general de Arequipa*, edited by Máximo Neira Avendaño et al., 235–264. Arequipa: Fundación Manuel J. Bustamante de la Fuente.

———. 1990b. "Naciones ancestrales y la conquista Incaica." In *Historia general de Arequipa*, edited by Máximo Neira Avendaño et al., 185–213. Arequipa: Fundación Manuel J. Bustamante de la Fuente.

———. 2000. *El puquina y lo puquina*. Arequipa: Facultad de Ciencias Histórico Sociales, Universidad Nacional de San Agustín.

Gelles, Paul. 2000. *Water and Power in Highland Peru: The Cultural Politics of Irrigation and Development.* New Brunswick, NJ: Rutgers University Press.

Gellner, Ernest. 1983. *Nations and Nationalism.* Oxford: Blackwell.

Gibson, Percy. 1916. *Jornada heróica: Trompetería en tono mayor al 2 de mayo.* Arequipa: Imprenta de los hermanos Santiago y Mario Quiróz.

Giddens, Anthony. 1990. *The Consequences of Modernity.* Palo Alto, CA: Stanford University Press.

Goldstein, Paul. 2009. "Diasporas within the Ancient State: Tiwanaku as Ayllus in Motion." In *Andean Civilization: A Tribute to Michael E. Moseley*, edited by Joyce Marcus and Patrick Ryan Williams, 277–302. Cotsen Institute of Archaeology Monograph, no. 63. Los Angeles: Cotsen Institute of Archaeology, University of California.

Gómez G., Rodolfo A. 1977. *Padre e hijo: Narraciones arequipeñas.* Arequipa: Impr. Edit. El Sol.

Gómez Rodríguez, Juan, and Thomas Love. 1978. "La migración rural en Arequipa." Paper presented at Symposium on Internal Migration in Peru, AMIDEP, Arequipa, Peru, December.

González, Mike. 2007. "José Carlos Mariátegui: Latin America's Forgotten Marxist." *International Socialism: A Quarterly Journal of Socialist Theory*, no. 115. http://www.isj.org.uk/index.php4?id=336&issue=115. Accessed 15 June 2013.

Gootenberg, Paul. 1991a. "North-South: Trade Policy, Regionalism, and Caudillismo in Post-Independence Peru." *Journal of Latin American Studies* 23, no. 2: 273–308.

———. 1991b. "Population and Ethnicity in Early Republican Peru: Some Revisions." *Latin American Research Review* 26, no. 3: 109–157.

———. 2004. "Between a Rock and a Softer Place: Reflections on Some Recent Economic History of Latin America." *Latin American Research Review* 39, no. 2: 239–257.

Graeber, David. 2015. *The Utopia of Rules: On Technology, Stupidity, and the Secret Joys of Bureaucracy.* New York: Melville House.

Guaman Poma de Ayala, Felipe. (1615/1616) 1987. *El primer nueva corónica y buen gobierno.* Copenhagen: Det Kongelige Bibliotek. http://www.kb.dk/permalink/2006/poma/info/en/frontpage.htm. Accessed 17 December 2012.

Guinassi Morán, Luis. 1908. *Ensayos de sociología peruana.* Lima: Tipografía Quiróz.

Gutiérrez, Ramón. 1997. "La Iglesia de Cayma: Una obra excepcional de la arquitectura Arequipeña." *Revista Archivo Arzobispal de Arequipa*, no. 4: 39–60.

Gutiérrez Paucar, Javier. 1990. *Del estado centralista al estado regionalizado.* Lima: CONCYTEC.

Hale, Charles. 1997. "Cultural Politics of Identity in Latin America." *Annual Review of Anthropology* 26: 567–590.

Hall, Linda B. 2004. *Mary, Mother and Warrior: The Virgin in Spain and the Americas.* Austin: University of Texas Press.

Hammel, Eugene. 1969. *Power in Ica: The Structural History of a Peruvian Community*. Boston: Little, Brown.

Handler, Richard, and William Saxton. 1988. "Dyssimulation: Reflexivity, Narrative, and the Quest for Authenticity in 'Living History.'" *Cultural Anthropology* 3, no. 3: 242–260.

Heggarty, Paul, and David G. Beresford-Jones. 2010. "Archaeology, Language, and the Andean Past: Principles, Methods, and the New 'State of the Art.'" *Boletín de Arqueología PUCP*, no. 14: 29–60.

Hobsbawm, Eric J. 1992. *Nations and Nationalism since 1780: Programme, Myth, Reality*. 2nd ed. Cambridge: Cambridge University Press.

Hobsbawm, Eric J., and Terence Ranger, eds. 1983. *The Invention of Tradition*. Cambridge: Cambridge University Press.

Hofer, Tamás. 1984. "The Perception of Tradition in European Ethnology." *Journal of Folklore Research* 21, nos. 2–3: 133–147.

Hornborg, Alf. 2014. "Political Economy, Ethnogenesis, and Language Dispersals in the Prehispanic Andes: A World System Perspective." *American Anthropologist* 116, no. 4: 810–823.

Hudson, Rex A., ed. 1993. *Peru: A Country Study*. Washington, DC: Federal Research Division, Library of Congress.

Hunt, Shane. 1973. "Growth and Guano in Nineteenth Century Peru." Research Program in Economic Development, no. 34. Princeton: Woodrow Wilson School.

Isbell, William H. 2010. "La arqueología wari y la dispersión del quechua." *Boletín de Arqueología PUCP*, no. 14: 199–220.

Isbell, William H., and Helaine Silverman, eds. 2006. *Andean Archaeology III: North and South*. New York: Springer.

Itzigsohn, José, and Matthias vom Hau. 2006. "Unfinished Imagined Communities: States, Social Movements, and Nationalism in Latin America." *Theory and Society* 35, no. 2: 193–212.

Jacobsen, Nils. 1993. *Mirages of Transition: The Peruvian Altiplano, 1780–1930*. Berkeley: University of California Press.

Jacobsen, Nils, and Cristóbal Aljovín de Losada, eds. 2005. *Political Cultures in the Andes, 1750–1950*. Durham, NC: Duke University Press.

Jansen, Robert. 2009. "Populist Mobilization: Peru in Historical and Comparative Perspective." PhD diss., UCLA.

Jennings, Justin. 2010. *Beyond Wari Walls: Regional Perspectives on Middle Horizon Peru*. Albuquerque: University of New Mexico Press.

Jennings, Justin, and Willy Yépez Alvarez. 2008. "The Inka Conquest and Consolidation of the Cotahuasi Valley of Southern Peru." *Ñawpa Pacha: Journal of Andean Archaeology*, no. 29: 119–152.

Julien, Catherine J. 1983. *Hatunqolla: A View of Inka Rule from the Lake Titicaca Region*. Berkeley: University of California Press.

———. 1985. "Guano and Resource Control in Sixteenth Century Arequipa." In

Ecology and Civilization: An Interdisciplinary Perspective on Andean Ecological Complementarity, edited by Masuda Shozo, Shimada Izumi, and Morris Craig, 185–231. Papers from Wenner-Gren Foundation for Anthropological Research Symposium No. 91. Tokyo: University of Tokyo Press.

————. 1991. *Condesuyo: The Political Division of Territory under Inka and Spanish Rule*. Bonner Amerkanistische Studien, no. 19. Bonn: Seminar für Völkerkunde.

————. 2002. "Las *huacas pacariscas de Arequipa y el Volcán Misti.*" *Historia* 5: 9–40.

Kaerger, Karl. (1899) 1979. *Condiciones agrarias en la sierra surperuana.* Lima: Instituto de Estudios Peruanos.

Kaiser, Robert J. 2002. "Homeland Making and the Territorialization of National Identity." In *Ethnonationalism in the Contemporary World: Walker Connor and the Study of Nationalism*, edited by Daniele Conversi, 229–247. London: Routledge.

Klaiber, Jeffrey L. 1975. "The Popular Universities and the Origins of Aprismo, 1921–1924." *Hispanic American Historical Review* 55, no. 4: 693–715.

Klarén, Peter Flindell. 2000. *Peru: Society and Nationhood in the Andes.* New York: Oxford University Press.

Knight, Alan. 2005. "Is Political Culture Good to Think?" In *Political Cultures in the Andes, 1750–1950*, edited by Nils Jacobsen and Cristóbal Aljovín de Losada, 25–57. Durham, NC: Duke University Press.

Kopytoff, Igor. 1986. "The Cultural Biography of Things: Commoditization as Process." In *The Social Life of Things: Commodities in Cultural Perspective*, edited by Arjun Appadurai, 64–91. Cambridge: Cambridge University Press.

Kristal, Efrain. 1987. *The Andes Viewed from the City: Literary and Political Discourse on the Indian in Peru 1848–1930.* New York: Peter Lang.

Kroneberg, Clemens, and Andreas Wimmer. 2012. "Struggling over the Boundaries of Belonging: A Formal Model of Nation Building, Ethnic Closure, and Populism." *American Journal of Sociology* 118, no. 1: 176–230.

La Lonte, Darrell E. 1994. "An Andean World-System: Production Transformations under the Inka Empire." In *The Economic Anthropology of the State*, edited by Elizabeth M. Brumfield, 16–41. Monographs in Economic Anthropology, no. 11. Lanham, MD: University Press of America.

La Sierra ("Organo de la Juventud Renovadora Andina" of Lima), 3, no. 27: 19–21.

Larson, Brooke. 1998. *Cochabamba, 1550–1900: Colonialism and Agrarian Transformation in Bolivia.* Durham, NC: Duke University Press.

————. 2004. *Trials of Nation Making: Liberalism, Race, and Ethnicity in the Andes, 1810–1910.* Cambridge: Cambridge University Press.

Lazo Carpio, Juan. 1996. *Menelik.* Arequipa: Gamma, Taller de Publicidad y Comunicación Integral.

Leguía y Martínez, Germán. (1913) 1996. "Los Fundadores y el Modo de Ser Arequipeño." In *Imágen y leyenda de Arequipa: Antología 1540–1990*, edited by Edgardo Rivera Martínez, 611–612. Lima: Fundación Manuel J. Bustamante de la Fuente.

Lévesque, Rodrigue. 2008. *Railways of Peru*. Vol. 2. Gatineau, Quebec: By the author.

Lomnitz-Adler, Claudio. 1992. *Exits from the Labyrinth: Culture and Ideology in the Mexican National Space*. Berkeley: University of California Press.

Long, Norman, and Bryan R. Roberts, eds. 1979. *Peasant Cooperation and Capitalist Expansion in Central Peru*. Austin: University of Texas Press.

Love, Thomas. 1983. "Economic Articulations and Underdevelopment in Southern Peru." PhD diss., University of California, Davis.

———. 1988. "Andean Interzonal Bartering: Why Does It Persist in a Cash-Market Economy?" *Michigan Discussions in Anthropology* 8: 87–101.

———. 1989. "Limitations to the Articulation of Modes of Production: The Southwestern Peru Region." In *State, Capital, and Rural Society: Anthropological Perspectives on Political Economy in Mexico and the Andes*, edited by Benjamin S. Orlove, Michael Foley, and Thomas Love, 147–179. Boulder, CO: Westview Press.

———. 2005. "Pequeños Propietarios de la Campiña y los Usos Políticos del Lugar y el Mestizaje." In *Yuyayninchis: Revista de la Escuela Profesional de Antropología*, edited by F. Palacios, 1:115–136. Arequipa: Universidad Nacional de San Agustín.

Lozada Stanbury, Jorge. 1988. *Las regiones del sur del Perú*. Lima: Edit. Monterrico.

Maccormack, Sabine. 1991. *Religion in the Andes: Vision and Imagination in Early Colonial Peru*. Princeton: Princeton University Press.

Málaga Medina, Alejandro. 1975. "Los corregimientos de Arequipa: Siglo XVI." *Historia* 1: 47–85.

———. 1990. "Organización eclesiástica de Arequipa." In *Historia general de Arequipa*, edited by Máximo Neira Avendaño et al., 275–307. Arequipa: Fundación Manuel J. Bustamante de la Fuente.

Málaga Núñez-Zeballos, Alejandro. 1997. "La Santísima Virgen Candelaria del Santuario de San Miguel Arcángel de Cayma." *Revista Archivo Arzobispal de Arequipa*, no. 4: 61–78.

———. 2002. "El enojo de los dioses: Terremotos y erupciones en Arequipa del siglo XVI." In *El hombre y los Andes: Homenaje a Franklin Pease G. Y.*, edited by Javier Flores Espinoza and Rafael Varon Gabai, vol. 2, 905–913. Lima: Fondo Editorial, Pontificia Universidad Católica del Peru.

———. 2011. *La Virgen de Arequipa: Historia de la milogrosa Virgen de Chapi*. Arequipa: Universidad Católica de Santa Maria.

Mallon, Florencia E. 1983. *The Defense of Community in Peru's Central Highlands: Peasant Struggle and Capitalist Transition, 1860–1940*. Princeton: Princeton University Press.

———. 1995. *Peasant and Nation: The Making of Postcolonial Mexico and Peru*. Berkeley: University of California Press.

Malpass, Michael A. n.d. "Ancient People of the Andes." Published as *Ancient People of the Andes*. Ithaca, NY: Cornell University Press, 2016.

Manrique, Nelson. 1986. *Colonialismo y pobreza campesina: Caylloma y el Valle del Colca siglos XVI–XX*. Lima: DESCO (Centro de Estudios y Promoción del Desarrollo).

————. 1999. *La piel y la pluma: Escritos sobre literatura, etnicidad y racismo*. Lima: SUR Casa de Estudios del Socialismo.

Marchand, Marianne H., Morten Boas, and Timothy M Shaw. 1999. "The Political Economy of New Regionalisms." *Third World Quarterly* 20, no. 5: 897–910.

Marchena F., Juan. 2005. "'Su Majestad quiere Saber.' Información oficial y reformismo borbónico: El mundo andina bajo la mirada de la ilustración." *Procesos: Revista Ecuatoriana de Historia*, no. 22: 45–83.

Mariátegui, José Carlos. (1928) 1971. *Seven Interpretive Essays on Peruvian Reality*. Translation by Marjory Urquidi. Austin: University of Texas Press.

Marsilli, Maria N. 2005. "'I Heard It through the Grapevine': Analysis of an Anti-Secularization Initiative in the Sixteenth-Century Arequipan Countryside, 1584–1600." *Americas* 61, no. 4: 647–672.

Martínez-Echazábal, Lourdes. 1998. "Mestizaje and the Discourse of National/Cultural Identity in Latin America, 1845–1959." *Latin American Perspectives* 25, no. 3: 21–42.

Matthews, Mark. 2015. *Terroir and Other Myths of Winegrowing*. Oakland: University of California Press.

McElroy, Keith. 1985. *Early Peruvian Photography: A Critical Case Study*. Ann Arbor: UMI Research Press.

Medina, E. 1998. "Reconstruyendo la historia de Arequipa." *El Pueblo*, 13 July 1998, 4.

Melillo, Edward D. 2012. "The First Green Revolution: Debt Peonage and the Making of the Nitrogen Fertilizer Trade, 1840–1930." *American Historical Review* 117, no. 4: 1028–1060.

Mendoza, Zoila. 2000. *Shaping Society through Dance: Mestizo Ritual Performance in the Peruvian Andes*. Chicago: University of Chicago Press.

Miller, Nicola. 1999. *In the Shadow of the State: Intellectuals and the Quest for National Identity in Twentieth-Century Spanish America*. New York: Verso.

Miller, Rory. 1987. "Introduction: Some Reflections on Foreign Research and Peruvian History." In *Region and Class in Modern Peruvian History*, edited by Rory Miller, 7–20. Liverpool, England: Institute of Latin American Studies.

Miró Quesada Sosa, Aurelio. 1998. *Historia y leyenda de Mariano Melgar (1790–1815)*. Lima: Fondo Editorial Universidad Nacional Mayor de San Marcos.

Mitchell, William P. 1985. "On Terracing in the Andes." *Current Anthropology* 26, no. 2: 288–289.

Montoya, Rodrigo. 1980. *Capitalismo y no capitalismo en el Perú: Un estudio histórico de su articulación en un eje regional*. Lima: Mosca Azul Editores.

Morrison, Allen. 2004. "The Tramways of Arequipa, Peru: An Illustrated History." http://www.tramz.com/pe/aq/aqoo.html. Accessed 23 June 2013.

Mostajo, Francisco. (1924) 1956. *San Gil de Cayma: Leyenda Folklórica Arequipeña*. Arequipa: La Colmena.

————. (1925) 1958. "Aportes para la historia de Arequipa." In *Prosistas e historiado-*

res, edited by Vladimiro Bermejo, 54–70. Primer Festival del Libro Arequipeño. Lima: Librería-Editorial Mejía Baca.

———. 1928. "Opinion Suelta." *Chirapu*, no. 3.

Mostajo Chávez, Julio. 1942. *El problema agrario en la Provincia de Arequipa.* Arequipa: Tésis Bachillerato, Derecho, UNSA.

Motta Zamalloa, Edmundo. 1979. *Ethos y Sociedad Agraria: Análisis del "Astero de Plata."* Arequipa: Tésis Bachiller Antropologia, UNSA.

———. 1985. *El agua, la serpiente y la Candelaria de Arequipa.* Lima: Univ. Nacional Mayor de San Marcos, Seminario de Historia Rural Andina.

Mullen, Patrick B. 2000. "Belief and the American Folk." *Journal of American Folklore* 113, no. 448: 119–143.

Murra, John. 1975. "Un reino Aymara en 1567." In *Formaciones económicas y políticas del mundo andino*, 193–223. Lima: Instituto de Estudios Peruanos.

Murra, John V., Nathan Wachtel, and Jacques Revel, eds. 1986. *Anthropological History of Andean Polities.* Cambridge: Cambridge University Press.

Neira Avendaño, Máximo. 1990. "Arequipa Prehispánica." In *Historia general de Arequipa*, edited by Máximo Neira Avendaño et al., 5–184. Arequipa: Fundación Manuel J. Bustamante de la Fuente.

Neira Avendaño, Máximo, Guillermos Galdos Rodríguez, Alejandro Málaga Medina, Eusebio Quiroz Paz Soldán, and Juan Guillermo Carpio Muñoz, eds. 1990. *Historia general de Arequipa.* Arequipa: Fundación Manuel J. Bustamante de la Fuente.

Nieves y Bustamante, Maria. (1892) 1958. *Jorge, el hijo del pueblo.* Arequipa: Talleres Juan Gutenberg.

Nugent, David. 1997. *Modernity at the Edge of Empire: State, Individual, and Nation in the Northern Peruvian Andes, 1885–1935.* Stanford: Stanford University Press.

Núñez, Lautaro. 1986. "The Evolution of a Valley: Population and Resources of Tarapacá over a Millennium." In *Anthropological History of Andean Polities*, edited by John V. Murra, Nathan Wachtel, and Jacques Revel, 23–34. Cambridge: Cambridge University Press.

Núñez Pinto, Miguel Urbano. n.d. "Antología de Poesía 'Loncca' Arequipeña."

Ødegaard, Cecilie Vindal. 2010. *Mobility, Markets, and Indigenous Socialities: Contemporary Migration in the Peruvian Andes.* London: Ashgate.

ONERN (República del Perú, Presidencia de la República, Oficina Nacional de Evaluación de Recursos Naturales). 1974. *Inventario, Evaluación y Use Racional de los Recursos Naturales de la Costa: Cuencas de los Ríos Quilca y Tambo.* 3 Vols. Lima: Impresa ONERN.

Orlove, Benjamin S. 1977. *Alpacas, Sheep, and Men: The Wool Export Economy and Regional Society in Southern Peru.* New York: Academic Press.

———. 1993. "Putting Race in Its Place: Order in Colonial and Postcolonial Peruvian Geography." *Social Research* 60: 301–336.

————. 1998. "Down to Earth: Race and Substance in the Andes." *Bulletin of Latin American Research* 17, no. 2: 207–222.

Orlove, Benjamin S., ed. 1997. *The Allure of the Foreign: Imported Goods in Postcolonial Latin America.* Ann Arbor: University of Michigan Press.

Orlove, Benjamin S., and Ella Schmidt. 1995. "Swallowing Their Pride: Indigenous and Industrial Beer in Peru and Bolivia." *Theory and Society* 24, no. 2: 271–298.

Ortner, Sherry B. (1974) 2004. "Is Female to Male as Nature Is to Culture?" In *Anthropological Theory: An Introductory History*, 3rd ed., edited by R. Jon McGee and Richard L. Warms, 371–384. Boston: McGraw-Hill.

Oviedo, Carlos. 1992. *Genio y figura de los arequipeños.* Lima: Vicepresidencia de Relaciones Institucionales de Southern Peru Copper Corporation a través de la Dirección de Proyección Insitucional.

Pacheco Vélez, César. 1967. "Estudio preliminar." In *Trayectoria y destino: Memorias*, by V. A. Belaúnde, vol. 1, vii–lxvi. Lima: Ediciones de Ediventas S.A.

————. 1978. "Decentralismo y regionalismo en el pensamiento de Víctor Andrés Belaúnde." *Mercurio Peruano* 494–495: 26–44.

Painter, Michael. 1991. "Re-creating Peasant Economy in Southern Peru." In *Golden Ages, Dark Ages: Imagining the Past in Anthropology and History*, edited by Jay O'Brien and William Roseberry, 81–106. Berkeley: University of California Press.

Peralta Vásquez, Antero. 1977. *La faz oculta de Arequipa.* Arequipa: Cooperativa Editorial Universitaria;

Pike, Fredrick B. 1967a. "Church and State in Peru and Chile since 1840: A Study in Contrasts." *American Historical Review* 73, no. 1: 30–50.

————. 1967b. "Heresy, Real and Alleged, in Peru: An Aspect of the Conservative-Liberal Struggle, 1830–1875." *Hispanic American Historical Review* 47, no. 1: 50–74.

Polar, Jorge. (1891) 1958. *Arequipa: Descripción y estudio social.* Lima: Editorial Lumen.

Pons Muzzo, Gustavo. 1961. *Las fronteras del Peru: Estudio histórico.* Lima: Iberia. http://www.scielo.org.co/scielo.php?pid=S0121-16172009000300008&script=sci _arttext; site discontinued. Accessed 10 October 2012.

Poole, Deborah. 1982. "Los Santuarios religiosos en la economía regional andina." *Allpanchis* 19: 75–116.

————. 1997. *Vision, Race, and Modernity: A Visual Economy of the Andean Image World.* Princeton: Princeton University Press.

Quijano, Aníbal. 1967. *La emergencia del grupo cholo y sus implicaciones en la sociedad peruana.* Lima: Instituto de Estudios Peruanos.

Quiróz, Alfonso W. 2008. *Corrupt Circles: A History of Unbound Graft in Peru.* Washington, DC: Woodrow Wilson Center Press.

Quiroz Paz Soldán, Eusebio. 1990. "Arequipa: Una autonomía regional 1825–1866." In *Historia general de Arequipa*, edited by Máximo Neira Avendaño et al., 419–488. Arequipa: Fundación Manuel J. Bustamante de la Fuente.

————. 1991. *Vision histórica de Arequipa: 1540–1990.* Arequipa: PubliUNSA.

Quiroz Paz Soldán, Eusebio, and Alejandro Málaga Medina. 1985. *Historia del santuario de Chapi en Arequipa*. Arequipa: PubliUNSA.

Rénique, José L. 1979. "Los decentralistas arequipeños en las crisis del año 30." *Allpanchis Phuturinqa* 12, no. 13: 51–78.

Rey, Pierre Philippe. (1969) 1976. *Las alianzas de clases*. Mexico: Siglo Veintiuno Edit.

Ricketts Rey de Castro, Patricio. 1990. *Arequipa*. 2nd ed. Lima: Ediciones Taller.

Rivera Martínez, Edgardo, ed. 1996. *Imágen y leyenda de Arequipa: Antología 1540–1990*. Lima: Fundación Manuel J. Bustamante de la Fuente.

Rocha, Álvaro. n.d. "El indiscreto encanto de las picanterías arequipeñas." *Rumbos de sol y piedra*, 29 February 2016, at http://larepublica.pe/turismo/gastronomia /738261-el-indiscreto-encanto-de-las-picanterias-arequipenas.

Rodríguez, César Atahualpa. (1930) 1958. "Ciudad de Piedra." In *Prosistas e historiadores*, edited by Vladimiro Bermejo, 123–131. Primer Festival del Libro Arequipeño. Lima: Librería-Editorial Mejía Baca.

Romero, Emilio. 1929. *Tres ciudades del Perú*. Lima: Impr. Torres Aguirre.

Roseberry, William. 1989. "Anthropology, History, and Modes of Production." In *State, Capital, and Rural Society: Anthropological Perspectives on Political Economy in Mexico and the Andes*, edited by Benjamin S. Orlove, Michael Foley, and Thomas Love, 9–37. Boulder, CO: Westview Press.

———. 1995. "Latin American Peasant Studies in a 'Postcolonial' Era." *Journal of Latin American Anthropology* 1, no. 1: 150–177.

Rostworowski de Diez Canseco, Maria. 1988. *Historia del Tahuantinsuyu*. Lima: Instituto de Estudios Peruanos.

Sahlins, Peter. 1989. *Boundaries: The Making of France and Spain in the Pyrenees*. Berkeley: University of California Press.

Saignes, Thierry. 1985. *Caciques, Tribute, and Migration in the Southern Andes: Indian Society and the 17th Century Colonial Order (Audiencia de Charcas)*. Translation from the Spanish by Paul Garner. Translation amplified and revised by Tristán Platt. London: University of London Institute of Latin American Studies.

Salles-Reese, Veronica. 1997. *From Viracocha to the Virgin of Copacabana: Representation of the Sacred at Lake Titicaca*. Austin: University of Texas Press.

Sallnow, Michael. 1987. *Pilgrims of the Andes: Regional Cults in Cuzco*. Washington, DC: Smithsonian Institution Press.

Santos Mendoza, Arturo. 1996. *Arequipa: Rebelde y revolucionaria*. Arequipa: By the author.

Scott, James. 1998. *Seeing Like a State: How Certain Schemes to Improve the Human Condition Have Failed*. New Haven: Yale University Press.

Siebert, Lee, Tom Simkin, and Paul Kimberly. 2010. *Volcanoes of the World*. 3rd ed. Washington, DC: Smithsonian Institution; Berkeley: University of California Press.

Sillar, Bill. 2012. "Accounting for the Spread of Quechua and Aymara between

Cuzco and Lake Titicaca." In *Archaeology and Language in the Andes: A Cross-Disciplinary Exploration of Prehistory*, edited by Paul Heggarty and David Beresford-Jones, 295–319. Oxford: Oxford University Press.

Skuban, William E. 2007. *Lines in the Sand: Nationalism and Identity on the Peruvian-Chilean Frontier*. Albuquerque: University of New Mexico Press.

Soto Rivera, Roy. 2005. *Antero Peralta en la historia de Arequipa*. Arequipa: By the author.

St. John, Ronald Bruce. 1994. *The Bolivia-Chile-Peru Dispute in the Atacama Desert*. Boundary and Territory Briefing, vol. 1, no. 6. Durham, UK: International Boundaries Research Unit, University of Durham.

Stanish, Charles. 2003. *Ancient Titicaca: The Evolution of Complex Society in Southern Peru and Northern Bolivia*. Berkeley: University of California Press.

Starn, Orin. 1994. "Rethinking the Politics of Anthropology: The Case of the Andes." *Current Anthropology* 35, no. 1: 13–38.

Stavig, Ward. 1999. *The World of Túpac Amaru: Conflict, Community, and Identity in Colonial Peru*. Lincoln: University of Nebraska Press.

Stern, Steve. 1993. *Peru's Indian Peoples and the Challenge of Spanish Conquest: Huamanga to 1640*. 2nd ed. Madison: University of Wisconsin Press.

Szykulski, Józef, et al. 2000. *Investigaciones arqueológicas en Churajón, Departamento de Arequipa—Perú: Informe de los trabajos de 1998/1999*. Arequipa: Universidad Católica "Santa Maria" de Arequipa.

Tacca Quispe, Lorenzo W. 2010. "La serpiente en los Andes prehispánicos: Imágenes en el valle de Arequipa." *Historia* 9: 15–19.

Tamayo Herrera, José. 1988. *Regionalización: ¿Mito o realidad? E identidad nacional: ¿Utopía o esperanza?*. Lima: Centro de Estudios País y Región.

Tambiah, Stanley. 1996. *Leveling Crowds: Ethnonationalist Conflicts and Collective Violence in South Asia*. Berkeley: University of California Press.

Taylor, Lewis. 2000. "The Origins of APRA in Cajamarca, 1928–1935." *Bulletin of Latin American Research* 19, no. 4: 437–459.

Telles, Edward, and René Flores. 2013. "Not Just Color: Whiteness, Nation, and Status in Latin America." *Hispanic American Historical Review* 93, no. 3: 411–449.

Thorp, Rosemary, and Geoffrey Bertram. 1978. *Peru 1890–1977: Growth and Policy in an Open Economy*. New York: Columbia University Press.

Thurner, Mark. 1997. *From Two Republics to One Divided: Contradictions of Postcolonial Nationmaking in Andean Peru*. Durham, NC: Duke University Press.

———. 2004. Review of *Beyond Imagined Communities: Reading and Writing the Nation in Nineteenth-Century Latin America*, edited by Sara Castro-Klarén and John Charles Chasteen. *American Historical Review* 109, no. 5: 1606–1608.

———. 2008. "Jorge Basadre's 'Peruvian History of Peru'; or, The Poetic Aporia of Historicism." *Hispanic American Historical Review* 88, no. 2: 247–283.

Ticona, Christian, and Arlen Palomino. 2013. "Fiesta de Virgen de Chapi para todo el Perú: La declaran Patrimonio de la Nación." *LaRepublica.pe*, 2 May 2013.

http://www.larepublica.pe/02-05-2013/fiesta-de-virgen-de-chapi-para-todo-el -peru-la-declaran-patrimonio-de-la-nacion.

Travada y Córdoba, Ventura. (1752) 1996. "Descripción de la ciudad de Arequipa." In *Imágen y leyenda de Arequipa: Antología 1540–1990*, edited by Edgardo Rivera Martínez, 107–118. Lima: Fundación Manuel J. Bustamante de la Fuente.

Tristán, Flora. (1838) 1971. *Peregrinaciones de una paria*. Lima: Moncloa Campodonico Edit.

"Una visita a don Francisco Mostajo." 1927. *La Sierra* ("Organo de la Juventud Renovadora Andina" of Lima), 3, no. 27: 19–21.

Valdivia Rodríguez, Angel Eduardo. 1989. *Evocaciones de un cholo arequipeño: Homenaje al 450 aniversario de la fundación española de Arequipa, 1540–1990*. Lima: Offaber.

van Buren, Mary. 1996. "Rethinking the Vertical Archipelago: Ethnicity, Exchange, and History in the South Central Andes." *American Anthropologist* 98, no. 2: 338–351.

Vargas Ugarte, Rubén. 1956. *Historia del Perú: Virreinato (siglo xviii) 1700–1790*. Lima.

Velasquez C., Luis. 1976. *El ccarozzo, el chogñi i yo: Relato costumbrista de Arequipa*. Lima: By the author.

Verosub, K. L., and J. Lippman. 2008. "Global Impacts of the 1600 Eruption of Peru's Huaynaputina Volcano." *Eos, Transactions American Geophysical Union* 89, no. 15: 141–142.

Villacorta Paredes, Juan. 1971. *Pintores peruanos de la República*. Lima: Talleres Gráficos de Editorial Universo S.A.

vom Hau, Matthias. 2009. "Unpacking the School: Textbooks, Teachers, and the Construction of Nationhood in Mexico, Argentina, and Peru." *Latin American Research Review* 44, no. 3: 127–154.

Wade, Peter. 2005. "Rethinking 'Mestizaje': Ideology and Lived Experience." *Journal of Latin American Studies* 37, no. 2: 239–257.

Walker, Charles. 1989. Review of *The Andes Viewed from the City: Literary and Political Discourse on the Indian in Peru, 1848–1930*, by Efrain Kristal. *Revista Andina* 7, no. 2: 587–589.

———. 1999. *Smoldering Ashes: Cuzco and the Creation of Republican Peru, 1780–1840*. Durham, NC: Duke University Press.

Warleigh-Lack, Alex. 2006. "Towards a Conceptual Framework for Regionalisation: Bridging 'New Regionalism' and 'Integration Theory.'" *Review of International Political Economy* 13, no. 5 (December): 750–771.

Weismantel, Mary. 2001. *Cholas and pishtacos: Stories of Race and Sex in the Andes*. Chicago: University of Chicago Press.

Wibel, John F. 1975. "The Evolution of a Regional Community within Spanish Empire and Peruvian Nation: Arequipa, 1780–1845." PhD diss., Stanford University.

Wiener, Charles. (1880) 1996. "Arequipa." In *Imágen y leyenda de Arequipa: Antología 1540–1990*, edited by Edgardo Rivera Martínez, 358–359. Lima: Fundación Manuel J. Bustamante de la Fuente.

Williams, Raymond. 1973. *The Country and the City.* New York: Oxford University Press.

———. 1977. *Marxism and Literature.* New York: Oxford University Press.

———. 1985. *Keywords.* New York: Oxford University Press.

Wilson, Patricia A., and Carol Wise. 1986. "The Regional Implications of Public Investment in Peru, 1968–1983." *Latin American Research Review* 21, no. 2: 93–116.

Winterhalder, Bruce. 1994. "The Ecological Basis of Water Management in the Central Andes: Rainfall and Temperature in Southern Peru." In *Irrigation at High Altitudes: The Social Organization of Water Control Systems in the Andes*, edited by William P. Mitchell and David Guillet, 21–67. Society for Latin American Anthropology Publication, no. 12. Arlington, VA: Society for Latin American Anthropology and American Anthropological Association.

Wolf, Eric. 1983. *Europe and the People without History.* Berkeley: University of California Press.

Zeballos Barrios, Carlos O. 1978. *Souvenir de Arequipa.* Arequipa: Cuzzi Impr.

Zegarra Meneses, Guillermo. 1973. *Arequipa, en el paso de la colonia a la República: Visita de Bolívar.* 2nd ed. Arequipa: Edit. Cuzzi Cia.

Zevallos Vera, Manuel. 1965. *Arequipa: Espíritu y materia. Estampas folklóricas.* Arequipa: Taller de la Univ. Nacional de San Agustín.

INDEX

agency, xii, 226, 277

agrarian reform, xv, 184, 289

agriculture, xii, xv, xxi, 6, 9, 17–18, 26–27, 34, 38, 56, 73, 75, 78–80, 83, 92, 98, 115–116, 130–131, 136, 146, 160, 183–186, 190, 202, 205–206, 209, 211, 214, 220, 231, 238, 247–248, 268, 270, 274, 279, 289, 291. *See also* crops

Altiplano, 1, 2, 5, 9, 13, 15–16, 19, 22–23, 27, 30–39, 43, 45–46, 48–50, 52–53, 55–56, 64, 71–72, 74, 76, 84–85, 88–89, 91, 89, 101–102, 112, 115, 121, 127, 147, 149, 159–160, 162, 188, 215, 219, 231, 238–241, 246–247, 250–251, 253, 256, 260, 278–283, 291

archaeology, xix, 32, 182, 215, 277. *See also* Early Horizon; Late Horizon; Late Intermediate; Middle Horizon

Arequipa city: literary tradition of, xiii, xvi–xvii, xix, 12–13, 70, 92, 118–120, 122, 124, 127, 130, 135, 138, 141, 144–145, 150–153, 159, 164, 180–181, 185, 192, 195–196, 198–201, 230, 252, 260–264, 290; re other Peruvian and Andean cities, 2–3; as second city, xi, 1–4, 260, 277; UNESCO recognition of, xi; as white city, xi, 151, 221, 255

Arequipa region

—cross-class nature of, 8–10, 11, 13, 15, 50, 72, 78, 86, 92, 94, 98, 119, 121, 127, 133, 135, 149, 172–174, 219, 221–222, 232, 244–245, 248–249, 257, 261, 265

—historiography of, 4

—rivers of (*see also* Colca; Tambo; Majes); Acarí, 31, 42, 177, 285; Ocoña, 32–33, 42, 53, 177; Siguas, 35, 40, 43, 53, 216, 273, 286

—settlements outside campiña in: Aplao, 177, 285; Atiquipa, 42, 279, 285; Camaná, 40, 42, 44, 85, 177, 285; Chuquibamba, 42–43, 177, 281, 283, 285; Cotahuasi, xi, 32, 35, 37, 113, 124, 177, 283, 285; La Joya, 53, 184, 209, 213; Orqopampa, 41; Pampacolca, 43, 82, 203; San Juan de Siguas, 184; Santa Isabel de Siguas, 184; Santa Rita de Siguas, 184; Viraco, 43, 203, 212; Vítor, 9, 40, 42–43, 53, 73, 184, 286; Yauca, 177, 285. *See also* campiña; class (social); *Collaguas*; corregimiento; identity: regional (*mistianidad*)

Arequipa valley/basin. *See* campiña

Argentina, 1–2, 41, 81–82, 90, 116, 160–161, 211, 283–284; Buenos Aires, 2, 46, 76, 78, 82, 160, 201; Humahuaca, 52, 283; Jujuy, 49, 283; Salta, 49, 283; Tucumán, 49, 51, 283

Arica, 42–44, 52, 74, 77, 82, 85, 87–88, 101–102, 104–105, 108–110, 112, 118, 128–129, 131, 135, 241, 279, 283, 286